D1663452

Artificial Intelligence

Springer
Berlin
Heidelberg
New York
Barcelona
Budapest
Hong Kong
London
Milan
Paris
Santa Clara
Singapore
Tokyo

John Debenham

Knowledge Engineering

Unifying Knowledge Base and Database Design

With 288 Figures

 Springer

John Debenham
Professor of Computer Science
University of Technology, Sydney
School of Computing Sciences
PO Box 123
Broadway NSW 2007
Australia
E-mail: debenham@socs.uts.edu.au

ISBN 3-540-63765-6 Springer-Verlag Berlin Heidelberg New York

Library of Congress Cataloging-in-Publication Data

Debenham, John K.
    Knowledge engineering : unifying knowledge base and database
design / John Debenham.
        p.   cm. -- (Artificial intelligence)
    Includes bibliographical references and index.
    ISBN 3-540-63765-6 (hardcover : alk. paper)
    1. Knowledge acquisition (Expert systems) 2. Database design.
I. Title. II. Series: Artificial intelligence (Berlin, Germany)
QA76.76.E95D42 1998
006.3'32--dc21   98-9721
                                                              CIP

© Springer-Verlag Berlin Heidelberg 1998
Printed in Germany

The use of general descriptive names, trademarks, etc. in this publication does not imply, even in the absence of a specific statement, that such names are exempt from the relevant protective laws and regulations and therefore free for general use.

Cover design: Künkel + Lopka Werbeagentur, Heidelberg
Typesetting: Camera-ready by author
SPIN: 10652875   45/3142 – 5 4 3 2 1 0 – Printed on acid-free paper

Preface

This monograph describes a methodology for the design of knowledge-based systems. A knowledge-based system contains knowledge as well as information and data. The information and data in such a system can be modelled and implemented as a database. The knowledge in such a system can be implemented either in a programming language or in an expert systems shell. This methodology has two distinguishing features. First, it is "unified". A unified methodology represents the data, information and knowledge in a homogeneous manner, as well as the relationships between them. Second, the methodology builds a maintenance mechanism into the design. In knowledge engineering terms, the representation used by this methodology to model knowledge bases applies equally to databases. In database terms, the representation used by this methodology to model databases applies equally to the database rules.

The unified methodology unifies the design of the "knowledge base component" and the "database component". "Unification" is achieved in five senses. First, during the design process four models are constructed. These four models all represent the data, information and knowledge "things" in a unified way. Second, the form of representation used for the data, information and knowledge things in one model meshes with the representation used in the following model. Third, the overall structure of these four models is unified. The structure of the requirements model determines the structure of the conceptual model, the structure of the conceptual model determines that of the functional model, and the structure of the functional model determines that of the internal model. Fourth, constraints are used in a unified way, and so constraints for knowledge are included. Fifth, the term "normalisation" is used in a far more general sense that the normalisation of databases. In the unified methodology there is one principle of normalisation which may be applied to normalise data, information and knowledge. This principle is a non-trivial generalisation of the conventional normalisation of databases.

The unified methodology builds a maintenance mechanism into the design. The methodology is based on the belief that an analysis of maintenance is best achieved in a unified representation. The majority of design methodologies, including KADS, treat the "rule base" component separately from the "database" component, and do not consider maintenance analytically. If these two components are represented and treated separately then the interrelationship between the things in them cannot be represented and manipulated within the resulting models. There are two issues in maintenance: first, the issue of how to *engineer* a model so that it is inherently easy to maintain, and second, given a model, the issue of how to *control* the maintenance of that model. The unified methodology addresses the first issue.

This monograph is intended for specialists who are interested in building maintainable knowledge-based systems. It should be of interest both to professional system builders and to researchers into design methodologies. The unified methodology has a theoretical basis expressed in the λ-calculus. The unified methodology is also presented informally using a schema notation. The λ-calculus representation is used to develop the foundations of the methodology. The schema notation is used when the methodology is applied. The unified methodology is presented as a complete, integrated package. The methodology has four design steps: requirements specification, system analysis, system function and system layout. Each of these four steps generates one of the four models. Each step consists of a sequence of design tasks. The practitioner may choose to experiment with the entire methodology, or may choose to extract sections of the methodology and to blend those sections with other approaches to design and maintenance.

The work reported has its origins in 1982 when a joint research project commenced with Mike McGrath of Telecom Australia. In that project the substantial Telecom Telephone Accounting System for the Sydney region was constructed as a deductive database using logic programming. That database consisted of some 250 megabytes of "information" and a substantial and complex set of rules or "knowledge". That deductive database is believed to be the first large, commercial database implemented in logic. This design exercise involved a large number of design decisions. Those design decisions were made on a more or less *ad hoc* basis. Following that project, from 1984 to 1988 research concentrated on assembling a set of systematic techniques for addressing those design decisions. This set of techniques is referred to here as the "non-unified" methodology. During 1989 to 1993 that non-unified methodology was developed further in a collaborative research project between the University of Technology, Sydney and the CSIRO Division of Information Technology. An experimental Computer Assisted Knowledge Engineering (CAKE) tool was constructed to support that collaborative research project. An experimental version of this tool was trialed in a commercial environment in 1993. The results of those trials led to the exploration of the value of a unified approach to design. During the period 1994 to 1997 work has concentrated on the development of a complete unified methodology. That unified methodology is described here.

This book is illustrated with examples expressed in logic programming. Logic programming is chosen because it is simple and widely understood, but it is *not* being promoted here as a practical language for implementing expert, knowledge-based systems or deductive database systems. The unified methodology is independent of logic programming. The general principles illustrated in those examples may be expressed in any other general purpose knowledge language.

This monograph is not intended to be a complete account of knowledge-based systems design. The reader is assumed:

- To be familiar with expert systems to the level of the standard introductory texts such as [Waterman, 1985].
- To have had some experience constructing knowledge-based systems.
- To be familiar with database systems to the level of the standard introductory texts such as [Date, 1995].
- To understand the practical issues involved in designing and maintaining a database system.

However, this monograph does not give a complete account of knowledge-based systems design. For example, "plausible inference", "machine learning" and "data mining" are not mentioned. So the book is not an introductory text. With the exception of the first two chapters, the material presented is not generally available elsewhere.

Chapter 1 describes the foundations on which the work is developed. Chapter 2 describes a "non-unified" design methodology for knowledge-based systems in which conventional database design techniques are employed to perform much of the design work. Chapters 3 and 4 describe the unified approach to knowledge representation, Chap. 5 the schema notation used when the unified methodology is applied, and Chap. 6 the normalisation of the unified representation.

The four steps of the unified methodology for the design knowledge-based systems are described in Chaps. 7–10 respectively. These four steps are:

- Step 1 is *requirements specification*. In this step a *requirements model* is constructed which specifies *what* the system should be able to do. This step is described in Chap. 7.
- Step 2 is *system analysis*. During system analysis a *conceptual model* is constructed. The conceptual model is a complete representation of the knowledge required by the system. It specifies *how* the system will do what it is required to do, and contains a "coupling map" which represents a structure used to support maintenance. The conceptual model employs a unified form of knowledge representation, and inherits the specification of *what* the system should be able to do by links from the requirements model. This step is described in Chap. 8.
- Step 3 is *system function*. During system function a *functional model* is constructed which is "functional" in the sense that it shows how the knowledge in the conceptual model may be employed to deliver the functionality specified in the requirements model. This step is described in Chap. 9.

- Step 4 is *system layout*. During system layout an *internal model* is derived which serves as a complete system specification. This step is described in Chap. 10.

Maintenance is considered in Chap. 11, and a case study is presented in Chap. 12.

Three conventions are used. First, new terms, where they are defined, are written in italics and a reference to each definition is given in the index at the end of this monograph. Italics are also used for emphasis. The context should indicate whether a phrase in italics is being defined or is being emphasised. Second, if a term is used in the general text before it has been defined then the first appearance of that term is shown within double quotation marks. So if a term appears within double quotation marks in the general text then the reader is called upon to provide an intuitive meaning of that term until the term is defined. This monograph uses many terms in an unconventional sense. For example, the terms "data", "information" and "knowledge" are used in an idiosyncratic sense. The definitions of all technical terms used are referenced in the index. Third, single quotation marks are used to delineate formal strings.

I would like to thank all those who have assisted in the development of this monograph. I thank the University of Technology, Sydney, for their generous study leave provisions during which the greater part of the writing was done. I thank my colleague Dr Andrew Blair for his many suggestions. I thank the CSIRO's Division of Information Technology at North Ryde, Sydney, for welcoming me to their laboratory. I thank the chief of that Division, Professor John O'Callaghan, and the head of that Laboratory, Dr Craig Lindley, for their hospitality. I thank the CSIRO-Macquarie University Joint Centre for Advanced Systems Engineering for welcoming me to their laboratory, and I thank the Director of that Centre, Professor Ray Offen. I thank Springer-Verlag for their assistance in publishing this book; in particular, I thank Dr Hans Wössner, Andrew Ross and Gabriele Fischer.

University of Technology, Sydney   *John K. Debenham*

December 1997

Table of contents

1 Fundamentals

1.1 Introduction

The subject of this monograph is *Knowledge Engineering*, the design and maintenance of knowledge-based systems. *Design* is a process that begins with an analysis of requirements and ends with a complete system specification. Given a change in circumstances, *maintenance* is the business of modifying the system specification to reflect those changes and of specifying the alterations required to an implementation of the system to reflect those modifications. A knowledge-based system contains knowledge as well as information and data. The information and data in such a system can be modelled and implemented as a database. A *knowledge engineering methodology* addresses the design and maintenance of the knowledge as well as of the information and data. A *unified* knowledge engineering methodology treats the data, information and knowledge in a homogeneous manner. This monograph describes a unified methodology beginning in Chap. 3.

This chapter reviews the fundamental formalisms and concepts on which the following chapters depend. Section 1.2 reviews the use of logic as a knowledge language and the use of the λ-calculus. The reader who is familiar with Horn clause logic and the λ-calculus may wish to read this section quickly. Section 1.3 discusses the meaning of the basic terms "data", "information" and "knowledge" [Stonier, 1986]. These terms are defined in a rather idiosyncratic sense and are used throughout this text. An understanding of the meaning of these terms is fundamental to understanding much of what follows. Section 1.4 defines the term "knowledge-based system". This definition does not vary substantially from the sense in which this term is commonly used.

1.2 Formalisms

Two formalisms are used extensively throughout this monograph. They are:

- logic, and
- λ-calculus.

This section contains an introductory review of:

- logic as a knowledge language,
- logic as a programming language,
- logic as a database language, and
- λ-calculus.

The review is not intended to be a self-contained tutorial. It is intended to provide a concise "check list" of both the required features of the formalisms used and the way these formalisms are employed.

1.2.1 Logic as a knowledge language

Logic is chosen to illustrate this text principally because the notation of logic is widely understood. Logic is not being promoted here as a practical formalism for use either in the design of knowledge-based systems or in the implementation of knowledge-based systems. Logic is a simple formalism and is widely understood. Logic is also a sufficiently powerful formalism to illustrate the examples discussed here. This text could have been illustrated using any general purpose knowledge language.

Any formalism that admits a "declarative semantics" and can be interpreted both as a programming language and as a database language is a *knowledge language*. Logic admits a declarative semantics and can be interpreted both as a programming language [Clocksin & Mellish, 1994] [Covington et al., 1997] [Hogger, 1984] and as a database language [Chakravarthy et al., 1982] [Dahl, 1982]. So logic is a knowledge language [Bowen & Kowalski, 1982] [Kowalski, 1982].

In logic, *terms* are either *constants* or *variables*, or are constructs built from constants, variables and *functions*. The natural data structures in logic are "lists" and "trees". Lists and trees may be constructed by using special dyadic "list" and triadic "tree" functions respectively. A *predicate*, or strictly an *n-adic predicate*, has the form:

$$P : \times^n T \rightarrow \{ \text{TRUE, FALSE} \}$$

where T is the set of terms. Any ordered set of n arguments is a *tuple*, or strictly an *n-tuple*. A *constant tuple* is a tuple that contains no variables. If $\underline{x}$ is a tuple such that:

$$P(\underline{x}) = TRUE$$

then the tuple $\underline{x}$ is said to *satisfy* the predicate P. If a predicate can reasonably be stored as a table it is a *relation*. This notion of a relation is intended to be consistent with the notion of a "relation" as used in relational database (that is a "flat file"). The above phrase "can reasonably be stored as a table" means that a relation has only a finite number of tuples that satisfy it, and that this finite number cannot be too large. The definition of a relation is subjective. In a given application some predicates will also be relations. The distinction between predicates and relations is only of interest when deciding which predicates should be stored and which should be deduced. This distinction is considered in detail in Chap. 10.

A fundamental statement form in first-order predicate logic is the *clause* or *Horn clause*. A clause is a sentence with the special form:

$$(\forall ..)...(\forall ..) A \leftarrow (B \wedge C \wedge D \wedge ....)$$

in which all variables are universally quantified and A, B, C and D are predicates. A clause is often written in shorthand form as:

$$A \leftarrow B, C, D, ...$$

This sentence is to be read "A is true if B and C and D and .... are true". The '←' symbol means "is implied by" and the commas mean "and". In a clause there may be at most one predicate to the left of the ← symbol. This single predicate is the *head*. There may be any number of predicates to the right of the ← symbol. Together these predicates are the *body*. No "nots" and no "ors" are permitted. Predicates that occur in the body of a clause and that are not also the head predicate of that clause are the *body predicates* of that clause. So if the head predicate of a clause makes a recursive appearance in the body of that clause then it is *not* a body predicate of that clause.

A collection of clauses, all of which have the same head predicate, is a *clause group*, or simply a *group*. The following collection of clauses is a group:

person/ancestor(x, y) ← person/father(x, y)
person/ancestor(x, y) ← person/mother(x, y)
person/ancestor(x, y) ← person/ancestor(x, z), person/father(z, y)
person/ancestor(x, y) ← person/ancestor(x, z), person/mother(z, y)

The unique head predicate of each clause in a clause group is the *head predicate* of that group. For example, person/ancestor is the head predicate of the group shown above. Those predicates that are body predicates in *any* of the clauses in a clause group are together the *body predicates* of that group. person/ancestor is the head predicate of the group, so despite the fact that it also appears on the right of the ← symbol it is *not* a body predicate in that group. The group shown above enables information about the head predicate, namely person/ancestor, to be deduced from the body predicates, namely person/father and person/mother. The following *dependency notation* is used for groups:

person/ancestor ⇐ person/father, person/mother

in which the single head predicate of the group is written to the left of the '⇐' symbol and the group's body predicates are written to the right of the '⇐' symbol. A group is a *categorical group* if it contains sufficient clauses to enable *all* the tuples that satisfy the head predicate to be deduced from the tuples that satisfy the body predicates. Within an intuitive interpretation of the predicates involved, the group given above, with head predicate person/ancestor, is a categorical group.

Any given group is expressed in terms of a set of predicates, and represents a rule that enables the information in the "head" predicate to be deduced from the information in the "body" predicates. A second group may be expressed in terms of the same set of predicates as the first group and may have as its head predicate one of the body predicates in the first group. Given a set of predicates, the set of all groups that enable each of those predicates to be derived from the other is a *cluster*. Consider the chunk of expertise "the sale price of spare parts is the cost price marked up by a universal mark-up rate". The wisdom in this chunk of expertise may be represented by the three single clause clause-groups:

part/sale-price(x, y) ← part/cost-price(x, z), is-the[mark-up](w),
   y = z × w   [A]
part/cost-price(x, z) ← part/sale-price(x, y), is-the[mark-up](w),
   y = z × w   [B]
is-the[mark-up](w) ← part/cost-price(x, z), part/sale-price(x, y),
   y = z × w   [C]

The functional structure of these three single clause clause-groups can be represented more succinctly using the notation for clause-groups:

part/sale-price ⇐ part/cost-price, mark-up   [A']
part/cost-price ⇐ part/sale-price, mark-up   [B']
mark-up ⇐ part/cost-price, part/sale-price   [C']

These three clause-groups taken together represent all of the wisdom contained in the original, single chunk of expertise. These three clause-groups together represent *all* valid logical implications between the three constituent predicates. These three groups are a *cluster*. This cluster can be represented using the following notation for clusters:

[part/sale-price, part/cost-price, mark-up]   [D]

This cluster consists of all valid groups that may be expressed in terms of the three predicates part/sale-price, part/cost-price and mark-up. So clusters may be used to represent rules. A cluster consists of a set of groups. Each group consists of a set of clauses. Each clause is expressed in terms of a set of predicates.

A *goal statement* is a clause with a special predicate "Ans" as its head predicate [Green, 1969]. For example:

Ans(x) ← part/sale-price(1234, x)

is a goal statement that reads "x is the answer if x is the sale price of part number 1234". A goal statement with no body predicates is a *solution*.

The *resolution principle* is a formal method of logical deduction. See [Robinson, 1965] [Chang & Lee, 1973] or any book on logic programming. Given two clauses that can be "unified", the resolution principle may be applied to them to derive a new clause. Applying resolution to the above goal statement suppose that it is possible to derive the clause:

Ans($12) ←

then this clause is a solution. The example above can be interpreted as a computer program that executes the command "*calculate* the sale price of part 1234". This is an example of *pure logic programming*, or simply *logic programming*. The adjective "pure" indicates the absence of additional programming features that are required to enhance logic's capability as a practical programming language. In Sect. 1.2.2 two types of additional programming features are discussed. The first feature is the provision of specific computational features such as procedures to perform simple arithmetic. The second feature is the provision of control facilities such as find one answer only or find all possible answers [Kowalski, 1979a].

The above example can also be interpreted as a database that executes the command "*retrieve* the sale price of part 1234". This is an example of *pure logic database*, or simply *logic database*. The adjective "pure" indicates the absence of additional database features that are required to enhance logic's capability as a practical database language. In Sect. 1.2.3 two types of additional database features are discussed. The first feature is the provision of specific computational features such as procedures to perform store and retrieve operations. The second feature is the provision of control facilities such as "find all but without repetition".

When the resolution principle is applied to two given clauses this may result in the derivation of a third clause. If the resolution principle is to be used to derive a solution from a set of clauses and a goal statement then a strategy is required. This strategy determines the order in which the resolvents are to be constructed. Such a strategy is a *search strategy*. An *admissible* search strategy has the property that if a problem has a solution, then the search strategy will find that solution eventually. Horn clauses together with resolution and any admissible search strategy are *Horn clause logic*, or simply *clausal logic* [Kowalski, 1991].

1.2.2 Logic as a programming language

Pure Horn clause logic may be extended to a practical programming language by introducing a set of additional computational procedures and by providing additional control facilities [Walker, 1987].

In order to perform arithmetic in pure logic, it would be necessary to represent all the rules of addition, subtraction, multiplication and division in logic as well as defining what numbers are within the logic! This would be absurd if clausal logic is to be executed on a computer that can perform arithmetic operations directly, efficiently and quickly. The arithmetic facilities of the machine, and other basic, low-level operations, may be made available to clausal logic using *inbuilt predicates*. The programmer may treat an inbuilt predicate as though all true facts about it are stored [Van Emden, 1977]. Consider the predicate plus(x , y , z), that is taken to mean "x + y = z", the programmer may proceed as though:

plus(1 , 1 , 2) , plus(2 , 3 , 5) and so on

are all stored. Likewise, times(x , y , z) meaning "x × y = z", and less-than(x , y) that means "x < y", may be provided as inbuilt functions for arithmetic multiplication and inequality. One feature of inbuilt predicates is that they may be provided without compromising the declarative semantics of clausal logic.

Using inbuilt predicates clauses such as:

item/sell(x , y) ← item/cost(x , z), is-the[mark-up](w), times(z , w , y)

can be executed efficiently.

The inbuilt predicates "plus" and "times" are rather clumsy as a practical notation so the conventional arithmetic notation is used in subsequent examples. A clause such as:

P(x, z) ← Q(x, y), x × (y + 1) = z

may be translated by a language complier into a form such as:

P(x, z) ← Q(x, y), plus(y, 1, w), times(x, w, z)

so that it can use the inbuilt predicates.

The "is-a" predicate, and its restriction the "is-the" predicate, are inbuilt predicates. Suppose that it is required to find a single, valid item number. This can be achieved by the goal statement:

Ans(x) ← item/cost(x, y)

The presence of the variable "y" makes this form a little messy. Instead, an *is-a predicate* that has the form:

is-a[<descriptor>](x)

may be used. The goal statement:

Ans(x) ← is-a[item](x)

will achieve the same result as the previous goal statement. On occasions, the descriptor in "is-a[<descriptor>](x)" will only apply to one label. The descriptor "today's-date" is presumably associated with only one label. To draw attention to this fact, a special restriction of the "is-a predicate", namely the *is-the predicate*, may be used. The goal statement:

Ans(x) ← is-the[today's-date](x)

retrieves today's date. The "is-a" and "is-the" inbuilt predicates are useful.

When a logic program is executed with an admissible search strategy the special answer predicate, "Ans", finds the "first" answer and then the computation will halt [Clark & McCabe, 1982]. Here the "first" means the first answer located by the particular admissible search strategy used. The Ans predicate is sometimes referred to as the *find-one predicate*. The goal statement:

Ans(x, y) ← item/cost(x, y)

that reads "for any x and y, x and y are the answer if item number x costs y" might return the solution:

Ans(#1234, 12) ←

Most implementations of logic programming provide some form of *find-all predicate* that enables *all* correct solutions to be calculated. The predicate:

tuple/find-all-list((x), y)

may be used to activate "find-all" searches. In this predicate, "(x)" is a tuple that is usually present in at least one of the body predicates "to the left of" this predicate in the body of a clause, and "y" is a logic programming list that is usually present in the head predicate or in at least one of the predicates "to the right of" this predicate in the body of a clause. This predicate operates as follows. When control is passed to this predicate the value of the tuple (x) is added to the list y, the predicate then "fails" and the search "backtracks" to look for the next tuple (x) *until* the search for new tuples (x) is unsuccessful. The search strategy finally halts when an exhaustive search of the search space has been completed. By this stage, the list y contains at least one version of every tuple (x) that satisfies all of the predicates to the left of the tuple/find-all-list predicate. For example, the goal statement:

Ans(z) ← item/cost(x, y), tuple/find-all-list((x, y), z)

reads "find a list consisting of all x and y such that item number x costs y". Most implementations of logic programming contain special predicates that achieve the same result as the tuple/find-all-list predicate but possibly in a different way.

The ability to perform for-all searches efficiently has consequences for the effective mechanisation of negation. The logical equivalence:

$$(\forall x) \sim P(x) \leftrightarrow \sim (\exists x)P(x)$$

shows that the problem of showing "that it is not the case that there exists an x such that P(x) is true" is equivalent to the problem of showing "that for all x it is not the case that P(x) is true".

Whenever a new predicate is introduced in logic programming it should be accompanied by a statement of what that predicate "means". The reason for this is more than expository. Given the meaning of each predicate in a first-order sentence it is not only possible but usually easy to demonstrate the validity of that sentence. The validity of each sentence in a logic program may be checked individually. When all sentences in a logic program have been shown individually to be valid, the program is partially correct [Vanthiehen et al., 1996] [Zhang & Nguyen, 1994]. There is no need for loop invariants and the like to show that logic programs are partially correct [Gries, 1981].

A key property of logic as a programming language is that it admits a *declarative semantics*. That is, the statements in logic programs may be interpreted as statements of fact, in addition to the conventional *imperative semantics* in which a logic program is interpreted as a sequence of commands. The imperative semantics is determined by the particular control strategy used. Languages that admit a declarative semantics are also referred to as being *non-imperative*. A programming language that admits a declarative semantics cannot contain any purely imperative statement forms. The assignment statement found in conventional programming languages is purely imperative as its operation can only be explained in terms of *how* it works. So there can be no assignment statement, or analogue of the assignment statement, in logic programming.

Logic programming admits trivial correctness proofs, is non-deterministic and is non-goal dependent. Other properties include the following:

- It is very *high level* in that the programs are often "very close" to their description in natural language.
- It is a very *simple* language with one statement form.
- It is a very *powerful* language in that complex programs can be written quickly and accurately with few statements.
- There is no distinction between program and data.
- There is no distinction between input and output of predicate arguments. Furthermore, partially completed data structures containing both labels and variables can be passed by unification from one clause to another.
- It is not necessary or even correct to think of a logic variable as the name for a machine storage location.
- The imperative semantics for logic programs is "totally defined" in the sense that, unlike conventional programming languages, it is comparatively simple to explain *exactly* how a logic program will behave. A consequence of this is that it is impossible for a syntactically correct program to perform an illegal or undefined operation, such as the "array subscript out of bounds" error and the like that plague many students while learning to use conventional programming languages.

Logic programming is based on positive Horn clause logic. If it is required to introduce negation, then negation is introduced either by the specification of a "negative" predicate or by an extension to the control mechanism [Kowalski, 1979b].

Negation may be introduced through the specification of "negative" predicates by the programmer. If P and Q are two predicates with the property that P is true if, and only if, Q is not true, then P is the *negative predicate* of Q, and vice versa. Consider the "item/cost" predicate introduced above, its negative predicate can be specified by:

not[item/cost](x,y) ← x ≠ 1234, x ≠ 2468, x ≠ 3579
not[item/cost](x,y) ← x ≠ 1234, x ≠ 2468, y ≠ 8
not[item/cost](x,y) ← x ≠ 1234, y ≠ 25, x ≠ 3579
not[item/cost](x,y) ← x ≠ 1234, y ≠ 25, y ≠ 8
not[item/cost](x,y) ← y ≠ 12, x ≠ 2468, x ≠ 3579
not[item/cost](x,y) ← y ≠ 12, x ≠ 2468, y ≠ 8
not[item/cost](x,y) ← y ≠ 12, y ≠ 25, x ≠ 3579
not[item/cost](x,y) ← y ≠ 12, y ≠ 25, y ≠ 8

where the string "not[item/cost]" is a predicate name. The clause:

not[item/cost](#6, 18) ←

is "true". After all, it is true to say that "it is not the case that item number 6 costs $18". The reason for this may be that there is no such thing as item number 6, or that there is no such thing as an item that costs $18. The definition of the predicate not[item/cost] is considerably more involved than the definition of the predicate item/cost. For predicates with a large number of tuples it is often not practical to construct the definition of the corresponding negative predicate.

A way of introducing negation through an extension to the control mechanism is based on the "*negation as failure*" principle. Using this principle a statement is assumed to be "false" if an attempt to prove it to be "true" fails. See [Clark, 1978]. If the goal statement:

Ans ← item/cost(#4321 , 16)

cannot be resolved with any of the given clauses then the negation as failure principle "assumes" that "it is not the case that item number 4321 costs \$16". The reason for this *might* be that there is no item with item number 4321. For the negation as failure principle to work the attempt to derive a solution from the goal statement must fail. There are a number of sufficient conditions for failure that lie beyond the scope of this discussion. See for example [Lloyd, 1984]. As a more subtle example, suppose that it is required to demonstrate that "no invoice could cost \$19". One way of doing this is to attempt to find an invoice that *does* cost \$19 using the goal statement:

Ans(x) ← invoice(x , 19)

An attempt to derive a solution from this goal statement will not fail if such an attempt computed the cost of every possible invoice. This attempt would continue to compute forever and would not reach a conclusion.

1.2.3 Logic as a database language

Pure Horn clause logic may be extended to a database language by providing additional database features and by providing additional control facilities such as those required to answer complex queries.

For the purpose of this discussion, the system architecture is a logic knowledge base that has access to a relational database (DB). This access may supported by six second-order predicates that provide the additional database features. These six second-order predicates that can support access to an auxiliary relational database are:

FIND <tuple> IN(<name>) RES (<boolean variable>)
ADD <tuple> TO(<name>) RES (<boolean variable>)
REPLACE <tuple1> WITH <tuple2> IN(<name>) RES (<boolean variable>)
DELETE <tuple> FROM(<name>) RES (<boolean variable>)
CLEAR(<name>) RES (<boolean variable>)
LOAD <tuple-list> INTO(<name>) RES (<boolean variable>)

where <name> is the name of a relation that is stored in the auxiliary relational database. When executed, these six predicates operate as follows. FIND will set <boolean variable> to 'true' if <tuple> is a constant tuple that is in the value set of the relation named <name> otherwise <boolean variable> will be set to 'false'. ADD will set <boolean variable> to 'true' if <tuple> has been added successfully to the value set of the relation named <name> otherwise <boolean variable> will be set to 'false'. REPLACE will set <boolean variable> to 'true' if <tuple1> and <tuple2> are both constant tuples and if <tuple1> has been successfully replaced with <tuple2> in the value set of the relation named <name> otherwise <boolean variable> will be set to 'false'. DELETE will set <boolean variable> to 'true' if <tuple> is a constant tuple that has been successfully deleted from the value set of the relation named <name> otherwise <boolean variable> will be set to 'false'. CLEAR will set <boolean variable> to 'true' if there is a relation named <name> and all of the tuples in its value set have been deleted. LOAD will set <boolean variable> to 'true' if <tuple-list> is list of constant tuples that has been successfully loaded into the value set of the relation named <name> otherwise <boolean variable> will be set to 'false'.

Other additional database predicates include the "BEFORE" predicate where:

BEFORE(<event1>, <event2>)

will be 'true' if <event1> occurs before <event2>, and is 'false' otherwise.

If the logic knowledge base is permitted to interact with the database without restriction then anomalies can occur. Consider the goal statement:

Ans(x) ← REPLACE (x, 8) WITH(x, 9) IN(item/cost) RES(ok),
    x < 1 999

that reads "x is the answer if x is the number of an item that cost $8 and that has been increased to $9 and x < 1 999". This goal will fail if the number of the only item that costs $8 is #3579, because 3 579 is not less than 1 999. In the process of the calculation, the leftmost predicate in the goal may have been satisfied, that is, the cost of item number 3579 may have been increased from $8 to $9. This is undesirable as a failed goal statement should have no effect on the system. Changes should only be made to stored information by the particular instantiation of a goal statement that succeeded in returning a solution. Suppose that the goal statement:

Ans(x) ← REPLACE (x, 8) WITH(x, 9) IN(item/cost) RES(ok),
    x > 3 500

succeeds and returns the solution "Ans(3579) ←", as a result the cost of item number #3579 would have been increased from $8 to $9. Consider the goal statement:

Ans(x) ← FIND (x, 12) IN(item/cost) RES(ok1),
    ADD (x, 13) TO(item/cost) RES(ok2),
    P(x)

where P(x) is any predicate. Suppose that the first domain of the item/cost relation has been identified as the "key". That is, the item/cost relation is constrained
to hold at most one cost price for each item number. Then, after resolving the
leftmost predicate in its body the goal statement becomes:

Ans(#1234) ← ADD (1234, 13) TO(item/cost) RES(ok2), P(1234)

This statement is a consequence of the fact that item number 1234 costs $12, and
this statement attempts to assert that item number 1234 costs $13. This goal
should fail and the calculation should backtrack. This behaviour may be enforced
by "locking" the record:

item/cost(1234, 12)

in the database. A *locked record* cannot be altered until it is "unlocked". In this
example the record in the relation item/cost:

item/cost(1234, 12)

would be locked when the above resolution is performed. This would prevent the
relation from holding an entry for the cost of item number 1234 other than $12.
This record will then remain locked until *either* the goal is satisfied *or* the strategy
backtracks to the point of the above resolution and looks, perhaps unsuccessfully,
for another matching tuple.
    A database may be designed to accommodate a variety of major requirements.
Suppose that a major requirement is to retrieve the list of items with a given cost,
and suppose that within the database there is a structure to facilitate this. This
structure can be made available to the logic using the special predicate:

cost/item-list(x , y)

If this special predicate is instantiated with x set to some constant value then "y"
will be set to the list of all item numbers of items costing the given value of x.
This inbuilt predicate should be identified at design time. In the relation
'item/cost' the functional dependency is from 'item' to 'cost'. The 'cost/item-list'
predicate provides the inverse of this dependency and is an *inverse predicate*. In an
intuitive sense the predicate "cost/item-list" is the "inverse" of the predicate
"item/cost". This inverse predicate should *not* be treated as an "ordinary" predicate.
It may only operate efficiently with the first argument as "input" and the second
argument as "output". This predicate may only be capable of finding efficiently
the list of all item numbers with a given price. The goal statement:

Ans(x) ← cost/item-list(3, x)

will find the list of all item numbers of items that cost $3. Inverse predicates are useful. If the 'cost/item-list' predicate is mechanised efficiently then the goal statements:

- to show that there are only three items that cost $17;
- there is no item costing $19;

can be satisfied efficiently.

The systems designer has three choices for the implementation of an inverse predicate. First, if the inverse predicate is a relation, then its value set may be stored as a relation in the ordinary way. Second, an inverse predicate may be defined in terms of its "original" predicate using the tuple/find-all-list predicate. For example:

cost/item-list(x, y) ← item/cost(z, x), tuple/find-all-list((z), y)

Third, an inverse predicate may be defined in terms of the other predicates in the system, some of which may themselves be inverse predicates. The notion of inverse predicates gives the system designer the option of considering and catering for, at the system design stage, possibly expensive for-all searches.

Logic is a "universal" database language in the sense that data description, data manipulation, transaction specification and integrity checking can all be represented in one formalism, namely logic, that also provides the essential syntax of a wide variety of powerful languages for the user interface. In addition to the properties cited above, the properties of logic as a programming language translate directly into properties of logic as a database language. Within a logic database implementation, logic may also be used as a powerful programming language for performing complex calculations on or with the data.

Positive Horn clause logic provides the foundation for logic database. The problems with introducing negation into logic programming apply to logic database as well. In addition, a logic database may have substantial real relations stored in the relational database. Executing goal statements in a logic database can generate expensive searches. Consider an attempt to establish that there is *no* item in the item/cost relation with the two properties that it costs $3 and that its item number is a multiple of seventeen:

Ans ← item/cost(x , 3), times(z , 17 , x)

This could initiate an expensive search of the whole of the item/cost relation. One way of reducing the cost of searches such as this within the logic itself, is to use inverse predicates such as the cost/item-list predicate referred to above.

1.2.4 λ-calculus

From Chap. 3 onwards a variant of the λ-calculus and a variant of the typed λ-calculus is used. The λ-calculus is used to define "recognising" functions. A λ-calculus expression of the form:

λ<variable list>•[<function>]•

when applied to a list of arguments that matches the list <variable list>:

λ<variable list>•[<function>]•<argument list>

is defined to be the value of the <function> in which the variables in the <function> that occur also in the <variable list> have been replaced with the corresponding arguments in the <argument list>. In the examples considered here, the <function> is a first-order logic expression. A first-order logic expression containing n variables is a function from the n'th cartesian product of the domain of discourse to the set {true, false}. The expression:

λxy•[costs(x, y) ∧ is-a[x:part-number] ∧ is-a[y:dollar-amount]]•

has value 'true' if it is applied to a pair containing both a valid part number and its corresponding cost in dollars.

The typed λ-calculus expressions are "two level" expressions that are used to generate recognising functions of the type described above. These expressions contain a "typed variable list" that consists of a list of "typed variables". A *typed variable* is a pair of the form "<variable> : <type>". Types are discussed in detail in Chap. 3. For the purpose of this discussion '**X**' is a type that denotes "any type". Typed λ-calculus expressions have the form:

λ<typed variable list>•λ<variable list>•[<predicate>]••

This typed expression may be applied to a list of "item names" of a type that match the type of the variables in the <typed variable list>. Items are defined in Chap. 3. Each item is associated with a recognising function expressed in the λ-calculus as illustrated above. Suppose that P is the name of an item then S_P denotes the λ-calculus recognising function associated with P. Item names are customarily written in italics. If a typed λ-calculus expression is applied to an argument list that consists of a list of item names that match the types of the variables in its outer variable list:

λ<typed variable list>•λ<variable list>•[<predicate>]••<argument list>

then the value of this expression is defined to be the recognising function obtained by replacing each typed variable with the corresponding item name in the argument list. If the expression:

$$\lambda P:\mathbf{X}^1 Q:\mathbf{X}^1 \bullet \lambda xy \bullet [S_P(x) \wedge S_Q(y) \wedge costs(x,y)] \bullet\bullet$$

is applied to the two item names '*part*' and '*cost*' then it has value:

$$\lambda xy \bullet [S_{part}(x) \wedge S_{cost}(y) \wedge costs(x,y)] \bullet\bullet$$

Further, if:

$$S_{part} = \lambda x \bullet [\ is\text{-}a[x:part\text{-}number]\ ] \bullet$$
$$S_{cost} = \lambda x \bullet [\ is\text{-}a[x:dollar\text{-}amount]\ ] \bullet$$

then:

$$\lambda P:\mathbf{X}^1 Q:\mathbf{X}^1 \bullet \lambda xy \bullet [S_P(x) \wedge S_Q(y) \wedge costs(x,y)] \bullet\bullet (part,\ cost) =$$
$$\lambda xy \bullet [\ costs(x,\ y) \wedge is\text{-}a[x:part\text{-}number] \wedge\ is\text{-}a[y:dollar\text{-}amount]\ ] \bullet$$

This expression is the recognising function considered above.

1.3 Data, information and knowledge

The fundamental terms "data", "information and "knowledge" are used here in a unique, idiosyncratic sense. Given an application, a *data thing* is a fundamental, indivisible thing in that application. Data things can be represented naturally by populations and labels. The associations between the things in an application are of two distinct types. If an association *can* be described by a succinct, computable rule it is an *explicit association*. If an association can *not* be described by a succinct, computable rule it is an *implicit association*. An *information thing* is an implicit association between data things. A *knowledge thing* is an explicit association between data things or information things. Associations are often "functional" in the sense that they represent a function *from* one set of things *to* another thing. Such an association is a *functional association*. If an information thing is functional then it can be represented by a relation with a key. If a knowledge thing is functional then it can be represented by a clause group. A *rule* is a *functional* "explicit" association *from* a set of information things or data things called the *body to* a single data or information thing called the *head*. So a rule is knowledge.

1.3.1 Associations

In relational database a structural feature of many relations is the "functional dependency" *from* the key domains *to* the non-key domains. In a relation, domain A is *functionally dependent* on the set of domains {B} if for each tuple in the relation to each value in the set of domains {B} there corresponds precisely one value in domain A, at any given time. Suppose that in a large organisation the branch name and department name are sufficient to determine the manager of that department within that branch:

branch/department/manager(branch-no., dept-no., manager-name)

The identification of the first two domains of this relation as the "key" means that if the branch number and department number are known then the corresponding manager's name is determined uniquely. The third domain of this relation is functionally dependent on a compound key consisting of both branch and department taken together. A relation can represent a functional dependency between data things. This function does not have a succinct definition. The only way that this function can be specified is by listing all tuples (consisting of: branch number, department number and manager's name) that satisfy it.

Consider the rule "To convert from degrees Fahrenheit to degrees Celsius, subtract 32 and divide by 1.8". This rule is in functional form. It is a function *from* degrees Fahrenheit *to* degrees Celsius. This function is also between two data things that are "degrees Fahrenheit" and "degrees Celsius". It differs from the relation previously discussed in one way. This function is:

$$f : (\deg F) \rightarrow (\deg C)$$

and it can be described by the succinct, computable rule:

$$f(x) = (x - 32) \div 1.8$$

Both of the above examples concern functions between data things. The first association *cannot* be defined succinctly in the sense that a succinct, computable definition that will work "for all time" cannot be constructed. The first association is an *implicit functional association*. The second association *can* be defined succinctly by a computable rule that works "for all time". The second association is an *explicit functional association*. The word "association" rather than "dependency" is used to acknowledge that the context of this discussion is more general than functional dependencies in relations.

The previous "degrees" example concerned a functional association between two data things. Functional associations between information things are also of interest. Consider the two relations:

item/sale-price(<u>item-number</u>, dollar-amount)
item/cost-price(<u>item-number</u>, dollar-amount)

where item/sale-price(x, y) means "x is the number of an item whose selling price is \$y", and item/cost-price(x, y) means "x is the number of an item whose cost price is \$y". Consider the rule, "selling price is 1.25 times buying price" that might be represented by the clause:

item/sale-price(x , y) ← item/cost-price(x, z), y = 1.25 × z

this rule is also in functional form. It represents a function *from* the relation item/cost-price *to* the relation item/sale-price. The nature of this function is explicit. This function is succinct and computable. It enables the information associated with the relation item/sale-price to be deduced from the information associated with the relation item/cost-price. This association is an explicit functional association between information things.

The previous discussion has developed the context in which the meaning of the terms "data", "information" and "knowledge" can be expressed. In an application:

- *data* is the set of fundamental, indivisible things.
- *information* is the set of implicit associations between the data things.
- *knowledge* is the set of explicit associations between the information things and/or the data things.

These three definitions make no reference to implicit associations between information things. This may appear to be an omission. Implicit associations between information things are also implicit associations between data things.

The distinction between implicit and explicit associations is hard to draw. Consider the relation shown in Fig. 1.1 for which the general rule "that if a ≤ 4 then b = 2 × a" always holds. The first three tuples of this relation are instances of this general rule, and the remaining tuples represent exceptions to this general rule. This association can also be represented in clausal logic as:

R(x, y) ← ≤(x, 4), y = 2 × x
R(5, 6) ←
R(8, 3) ←
R(9, 4) ←

This association is "part implicit" and "part explicit". This apparent dilemma is unlikely to occur in practical applications. Associations tend to be principally implicit or principally explicit. If an association has both a substantial implicit part and a substantial explicit part then the association should be decomposed into two, or more, sub-associations each of which is either implicit or explicit.

Information and knowledge things are associations between other things. In a trivial sense, a thing associates with itself. If an information or knowledge thing

a	b
1	2
3	6
4	8
5	6
8	3
9	4

Fig. 1.1   Part implicit, part explicit association

is a trivial association between two or more other things then that thing is *tautological*. The representation of a tautological thing is also called tautological. The implicit association between "employee" and "employee" is tautological if its meaning is given by "employee/employee(x, y) means that x is an employee, y is an employee and x and y are the same". The relation "employee/employee" is *not* tautological if its meaning is given by "employee/employee(x, y) means that x is an employee, y is an employee and x understudies the duties of y". Consider the explicit association between "part/cost-price" and "part/cost-price" defined by:

part/cost-price(x, y) ← part/cost-price(x, y)

This association is tautological.

1.3.2 Data things

The *data things* in an application are the fundamental, indivisible things. For example, in a university student management system:

- a particular student number could be a fundamental, indivisible thing, so this fundamental, indivisible thing *is a physical thing* in that it exists in the application;
- the concept of "student number" could be a fundamental, indivisible thing, so this fundamental, indivisible thing is *not* a non-physical thing but it *is* associated with a set of physical things (the set of student numbers), and
- the concept of "student" could be a fundamental, indivisible thing, so this fundamental, indivisible thing is *not* a non-physical thing and it is *not* associated with a set of physical things.

These three examples illustrate three different types of data things. The way in which a data thing is represented depends on its "nature". The *nature* of a data thing is either:

part
part-number
1234
2468
3579
8642
7531

Fig. 1.2 A thing-population, identifying name-population and labels

1) a physical thing,
2) a non-physical thing that is associated with a set of physical things, or
3) a non-physical thing that is *not* associated with a set of physical things.

If a data thing *is* a physical thing then it may be represented by a *label*. If a data thing is *not* a physical thing then it may be represented by a *population*. If a population is naturally associated with a set of labels it is a *name-population*. If a population is not a name-population then it is a *thing-population*. For each thing-population a particular corresponding name-population is identified. This particular corresponding name-population is the *identifying population*. At any particular time, a thing-population, together with its identifying name-population, are associated with a particular set of labels. Figure 1.2 shows the thing-population "part", the name-population "part-number" and an associated set of five labels.

The representation of a data thing should be linked back to the thing that it represents by a statement of the meaning of that representation. The thing-population, name population and labels illustrated in Fig. 1.2 are all formal strings, but they represent real data things. This linkage from the formal representation to the things in the application is achieved by specifying the "meaning" of that representation. That is, a specification of which real things are represented as a 'part'. This specification can be expressed as "a 'part' is.....".

A data thing can be composed of two or more component data things. If a physical department in a large organisation is uniquely identified by both the branch number in which that department is situated and the department number within that branch then the *compound population* "branch_department" can be used to represent physical departments.

The only structure in data of interest here is the "type hierarchy". If, as a general rule, all labels associated with the thing-population A are also associated with the thing-population B, then the thing-population A is a *sub-type* of the thing-population B. The collection of all sub-type relationships is the *type hierarchy*. The type hierarchy has a lattice structure in general.

1.3.3 Information things

An *information thing* in an application is an implicit association between data things. In a retail application:

- a particular part number could be associated with a particular dollar amount, and so this association is between physical things;
- the concept of "part" could be associated with the concept of "cost", and so this association is between two non-physical things that are *not* naturally associated with a set of physical things; and
- the concept of "part number" could be associated with the concept of "dollar amount", and so this association is between two non-physical things that *are* each naturally associated with a set of physical things.

These three examples illustrate three different types of information things. The way in which an information thing is represented depends on its "nature". The *nature* of an information thing is either:

1) an association between physical things,
2) an association between non-physical things that are *not* naturally associated with a set of physical things, or
3) an association between non-physical things that *are* each naturally associated with a set of physical things.

An information thing may be represented:

- in case 1 by a *tuple*;
- in case 2 by a set of thing-populations that are a *relation*; and
- in case 3 by a set of name-populations that are *domains*.

At any particular time each relation, together with its corresponding set of domains, is associated with a particular set of tuples (see Fig. 1.3).

The representation of an information thing should be linked back to the thing that it represents by a statement of the meaning of that representation. The relation, domains and tuples illustrated in Fig. 1.3 are all formal strings, but they represent real information things. This linkage from the formal representation to the application is achieved by specifying the "meaning" of that representation. That is, a specification of the meaning of the implicit association. This specification can be expressed as "the tuple (x, y) satisfies the relation part/cost-price if x is a number of a part and y is its cost in dollars".

1.3.4 Knowledge things

A *knowledge* thing in an application is an explicit association between information and/or data things. In a retail application:

part/cost-price

part-number	dollar-amount
1234	1.23
2468	2.34
3579	3.45
8642	4.56
7531	5.67
1470	6.78

Fig. 1.3 A relation, its domains and set of tuples

- the sale price of a particular part number could be associated with the cost price of that part number and a mark-up rate, and so this association *is* between physical things;
- the concepts of "part/sale-price", "part/cost-price" and "mark-up" could be associated with each other, and so this association is between non-physical things that are *not* naturally associated with a set of physical things; and
- the concepts of "part-number/dollar-amount", "part-number/dollar-amount" and "factor" could be associated with each other, and so this association is between non-physical things that *are* naturally associated with a set of physical things.

These three examples illustrate three different types of knowledge things. The way in which a knowledge thing is represented depends on its "nature" [Van De Velde, 1993]. The *nature* of a knowledge thing is either:

1) an association between physical things,
2) an association between non-physical things that are *not* naturally associated with a set of physical things, or
3) an association between non-physical things that *are* naturally associated with a set of physical things.

A knowledge thing may be represented:

- in case 1 by a set of *instances* (such a set of instances may be infinite);
- in case 2 by a set of thing-populations and relations that are a *cluster*; and
- in case 3 by a set of name-populations and domains that are *fields*.

At any particular time each cluster, together with its corresponding set of fields, are associated with a particular set of instances (see Fig. 1.4).

The representation of a knowledge thing should be linked back to the thing that it represents by a statement of the meaning of that representation. The cluster, fields and instances illustrated in Fig. 1.4 are all formal strings, but they represent real knowledge things. This linkage from the formal representation to the application can be achieved by specifying the "meaning" of the representation. That is, a specification of the meaning of the explicit association. As the association is

[part/sale-price, part/cost-price, mark-up]

part-number	dollar-amount	part-number	dollar-amount	factor
1234	1.48	1234	1.23	1.2
2468	2.81	2468	2.34	
3579	4.14	3579	3.45	
8642	5.47	8642	4.56	
7531	6.80	7531	5.67	
1470	8.14	1470	6.78	

Fig. 1.4 A cluster, its fields and set of instances

explicit its specification can be expressed as a succinct computable rule. This succinct computable rule can be represented as a set of logic clauses. Consider the clauses:

part/sale-price(x, y) ← part/cost-price(x, z), is-the[mark-up](w),
  $y = z \times w$
part/cost-price(x, z) ← part/sale-price(x, y), is-the[mark-up](w),
  $y = z \times w$
is-the[mark-up](w) ← part/cost-price(x, z), part/sale-price(x, y),
  $y = z \times w$

The role of clausal logic in the representation of an application is as a formalism for expressing the meaning of the knowledge things in that application.

1.4 Knowledge-based systems

In this section the meaning of "knowledge-based systems" is discussed in terms of the nature of the application, and in terms of the way in which the system is designed, implemented and maintained.

It is unsatisfactory to distinguish between those systems that are "knowledge-based" and those systems that are "not knowledge-based" on the basis of the way that a system is implemented. Consider a system that represents an application containing a substantial amount of real knowledge, in which that knowledge has been carefully modelled and that has been implemented in the BASIC language. Also, consider a system that represents an application containing little real knowledge as such, in which the design, if any, uses a formalism that can not represent declarative knowledge conveniently, and that has been implemented in a sophisticated knowledge processing language. In the sense in which the term "knowledge-based" is used here, the first is considered to be such a system and the second is not [Klein & Methlie, 1995].

The definition of a knowledge-based system given below refers to both the nature of the application and to the way in which the system is designed, implemented and maintained [Brightman & Harris, 1994]. A *knowledge-based system* is a system that represents an application containing a significant amount of real knowledge, and has been designed, implemented and possibly maintained with due regard for the structure of the data, information and knowledge [Durkin, 1994]. The definition requires that the system should represent a "significant amount of real knowledge". This requirement is sufficiently precise for the purpose here. The concept of "real knowledge" is defined in Sect. 1.3. A "significant amount" means that the application boundary of the system should identify an area of the application that is appropriately dealt with using knowledge-based systems deign techniques. The definition of a knowledge-based system requires that the design, implementation and maintenance should be conducted in a certain manner. This is discussed in Sects. 1.4.1–1.4.3.

The term "expert systems" is used here to refer to prototype knowledge-based systems [Benchimol et al., 1987]. An *expert system* is a system in which the knowledge and is deliberately represented "as it is", possibly in the same form that it was extracted from an expert [Waterman, 1985]. In an expert system the represented knowledge should endeavour to solve problems in the same way as the expert knowledge source solved them.

Knowledge-based systems and expert systems are different:

- Expert systems perform in the manner of a particular trained expert. A knowledge-based system is not constrained in this way. In a knowledge-based system the represented knowledge should be "modular" in the sense that it can easily be placed alongside knowledge extracted from another source.
- Expert systems do not necessarily interact with corporate databases. In general, knowledge-based systems belong on the corporate system platform and should be integrated with all principal, corporate resources.
- Expert systems usually perform tasks that are "contained". A knowledge-based system should be based on carefully modelled and engineered knowledge that should enable it to expand across boundaries between previously separated tasks.

The term "expert systems" is often associated with the knowledge of a particular expert and has something of a pioneering flavour whereas the term "knowledge-based systems" has more of a systems architectural flavour.

1.4.1 Design

The definition of a knowledge-based system refers to a system that "is *designed* with due regard for the structure of the data, information and knowledge". The term "is designed" is taken here to refer to the "design methodology" used [Addis, 1985] [Martin, 1988]. A *design methodology* is a method that given an application produces a design for a computer system for that application and is sufficiently prescriptive for it to be useful in a teamwork situation. A design methodology is usually expressed so that it is independent of any particular computer language or computer platform [Luger & Stubblefield, 1989].

If an application contains a "significant amount of real knowledge" then that application contains a significant amount of real, explicit associations between real information and/or data things. These explicit associations may have a functional structure. A design technique is said *"to have given due regard for the structure of those explicit associations"* if the raw structure of the explicit associations is faithfully represented and is preserved as much as possible during the design process. Consider the piece of raw expertise "the sale price of spare parts is the cost price marked up by a universal mark-up rate". This chunk of expertise can be represented as the cluster:

[part/sale-price, part/cost-price, mark-up]

This cluster contains three functional interpretations denoted in the group notation:

part/sale-price $\Leftarrow$ part/cost-price, mark-up
part/cost-price $\Leftarrow$ part/sale-price, mark-up
mark-up $\Leftarrow$ part/cost-price, part/sale-price

Each of these three groups can be implemented as a single clause:

part/sale-price(x, y) $\leftarrow$ part/cost-price(x, z), is-the[mark-up](w),
$\quad$ y = z × w
part/cost-price(x, z) $\leftarrow$ part/sale-price(x, y), is-the[mark-up](w),
$\quad$ y = z × w
is-the[mark-up](w) $\leftarrow$ part/cost-price(x, z), part/sale-price(x, y),
$\quad$ y = z × w

Alternatively, each of these three groups can be implemented as a number of programs expressed in an imperative language. The design technique used is said *"to have faithfully represented the raw structure of an explicit association"* if all of the functional interpretations of that explicit association have been represented. The design technique used is said *"to have preserved the raw structure of the explicit associations"* if as the design process proceeds the explicit associations are not decomposed into component functional associations until it is necessary to do so. In the above example this means that the design technique should preserve the raw expertise in some form that is equivalent to a cluster until it is necessary to break that form down into three groups. Then the three groups should be persevered until it is necessary to break those individual groups down into procedures and so on.

1.4.2 Implementation

The definition of a knowledge-based system refers to a system that "is *implemented* with due regard for the structure of the data, information and knowledge". An implementation is said *"to have given due regard for the structure of the explicit associations present in the knowledge"* if the raw structure of the explicit associations is preserved as much as possible by the implementation. This does not necessary mean that the explicit associations should be implemented in some declarative knowledge processing language. This does mean that if an association such as:

part/sale-price(x, y) ← part/cost-price(x, z), is-the[mark-up](w),
$\quad$ y = z × w

as implemented as a set of procedures in an imperative language then the interrelationships between the members of that set of procedures should be acknowledged in the system documentation.

For completeness a review is given of the different ways in which a system might be implemented. This review provides a taxonomy of various ways in which any system, including a knowledge-based system, might be implemented. In the implementation of most computer systems there is a distinction between "program" and "data". The taxonomy of computer system implementations is based on:

- the way that the real knowledge is stored;
- the way that the real information is stored;
- the way that the real data is stored;
- the amount of the system (representations of knowledge, information and data) that is designed specifically to accommodate updates; and
- the amount of the system (representations of knowledge, information and data) that represents specifically queries that the system is designed to respond to.

The represented knowledge, information and data, that is designed specifically to accommodate updates is the *update scope*. The represented knowledge, information and data, that represents specifically queries that the system is designed to respond to is the *query scope*. Beyond the queries and updates that the system is designed to support there are more substantial "maintenance operations" that are usually be performed by skilled personnel. The nature of maintenance operations is not considered in this section.

An implementation in which all of the knowledge is encoded in a conventional, imperative programming language, the information is either stored explicitly in simple storage technology or implicitly in a conventional programming language, the data is stored in simple storage technology, the query scope is information and data, and the update scope is data, is a *data processing implementation* as shown in Fig. 1.5.

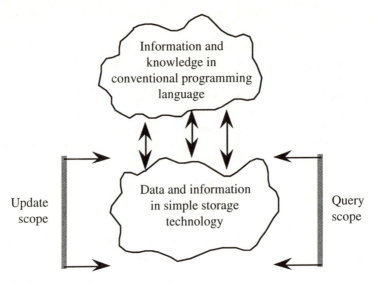

Fig. 1.5   Data processing implementation

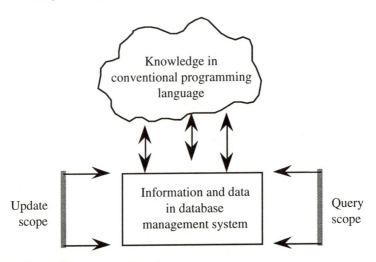

Fig. 1.6   Database implementation

An implementation in which the knowledge is encoded in a conventional programming language, that employs a database management system for information and data storage, in which the query scope is information and data, and the update scope is information and data, is an *information-based implementation*, or *database implementation* as shown in Fig. 1.6.

An implementation in which the knowledge, information and data is encoded in an expert systems shell, that is not integrated with corporate systems but that may have access only to corporate database systems, is an *expert systems implementation* as shown in Fig. 1.7 [Van Weelderen & Sol, 1993].

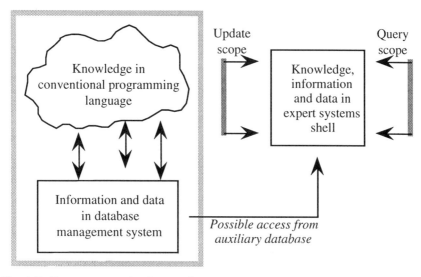

Fig. 1.7   Expert systems implementation

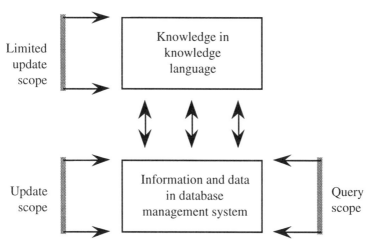

Fig. 1.8   Deductive database implementation

An implementation in which the knowledge is encoded in a knowledge language, that employs a database management system for information and data storage, in which the query scope is information and data, and the update scope is information and data and possibly limited knowledge, is a *deductive database implementation* as shown in Fig. 1.8 [Minker, 1988].

An implementation in which the knowledge is encoded in a knowledge language, that employs a database management system for information and data storage, in which the query scope is knowledge, information and data, and the

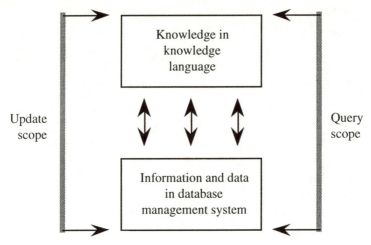

Fig. 1.9 Knowledge-based implementation

update scope is knowledge, information and data, is a *knowledge-based implementation*, as shown in Fig. 1.9 [Napheys & Herkimer, 1988].

A knowledge-based implementation is more than a conventional database system where the host programming language has been replaced by a knowledge language [Widom & Finkelstein, 1990]. In general, a knowledge-based implementation supports queries and updates that interact with the full extent of the knowledge component as well as with the information and data components. A knowledge-based implementation may be expected to *explain how* it has derived a piece of information. A deductive database implementation is not necessarily be expected to do this [Lee & Compton, 1995].

1.4.3 Maintenance

The definition of a knowledge-based system refers to a system that "is *maintained* with due regard for the structure of the data, information and knowledge". Two aspects of maintenance are identified. The first aspect is the recognition by the maintenance procedure of the relationship between real knowledge things and their implementation. The second aspect is the recognition by the maintenance procedure of the interrelationships between the representations of the knowledge things [Van Harmelen & Balder, 1992].

The first aspect of maintenance is the recognition by the maintenance procedure of the relationship between real knowledge things and their implementation. Consider again the piece of raw expertise "the sale price of spare parts is the cost price marked up by a universal mark-up rate". This chunk of expertise can be represented as the cluster:

[part/sale-price, part/cost-price, mark-up]

This cluster contains three functional interpretations denoted in the group notation as:

part/sale-price $\Leftarrow$ part/cost-price, mark-up
part/cost-price $\Leftarrow$ part/sale-price, mark-up
mark-up $\Leftarrow$ part/cost-price, part/sale-price

Each of these three groups can be implemented as a single clause:

part/sale-price(x, y) $\leftarrow$ part/cost-price(x, z), is-the[mark-up](w),
    $y = z \times w$
part/cost-price(x, z) $\leftarrow$ part/sale-price(x, y), is-the[mark-up](w),
    $y = z \times w$
is-the[mark-up](w) $\leftarrow$ part/cost-price(x, z), part/sale-price(x, y),
    $y = z \times w$

Each of these three clauses can be implemented as at least two imperative programs. The first clause can be implemented as an imperative program that calculates the sale price of any given part, it can also be implemented as an imperative program that calculates the part number that has any given sale price. So the raw expertise represented by this cluster can find its way into at least six different imperative programs. If this piece of expertise should change subsequently due to changing circumstances in the application then the system may require maintenance. This maintenance task may impact six or more imperative programs. A key issue in managing maintenance is locating these six or more procedures in the implementation that may require modification. So the maintenance procedure must be able to recognise the relationship between the raw expertise and the implementation of that expertise.

The second aspect of maintenance is the recognition by the maintenance procedure of the interrelationships between the representations of knowledge things. Consider the raw expertise "the profit on a part is the product of the cost price of the part and the mark-up factor of the part less 1". This may be represented as the clause:

part/profit(x, y) $\leftarrow$ part/cost-price(x, w),
    part/mark-up-factor(x, u), $y = w \times (u - 1)$ [A]

Consider also the raw expertise "the tax payable on a part is 10% of the product of the cost-price of the part and the mark-up factor of the part". This may be represented as the clause:

part/tax(x, y) $\leftarrow$ part/cost-price(x, w),
    part/mark-up-factor(x, u), $y = (w \times u) \times 0.1$ [B]

Both [A] and [B] have buried within them the sub-rule "the selling price of a part is the cost price of that part multiplied by the mark-up factor of the part". This sub-rule may be represented as the clause:

part/sale-price(x, y) ← part/cost-price(x, z),
    part/mark-up-factor(x, w), y = (z × w)   [C]

If the expertise represented in clause [C] changes then both clause [A] and clause [B] will have to be modified. Clauses [A] and [B] share sub-rule [C]. If clause [C] had not been explicitly identified then clauses [A] and [B] would share an unstated sub-rule. If the expertise in that unstated sub-rule changes then both clause [A] and clause [B] will have to be modified. So the maintenance procedure must be able to recognise the interrelationships between the representations of the knowledge things.

Clauses [A] and [B] can be re-expressed so that they do not share a sub-rule. If [A] is expressed as "the profit on a part is the sale price of the part less the cost price of the part" then this may be represented as the clause:

part/profit(x, y) ← part/sale-price(x, z),
    part/cost-price(x, w), y = z − w   [D]

If [B] is expressed as "the tax payable on a part is 10% of the sale price of that part" then this may be represented as the clause:

part/tax(x, y) ← part/sale-price(x, z), y = z × 0.1   [E]

Clauses [D] and [C] together imply clause [A] and clauses [E] and [C] together imply clause [B]. [D] and [E] do *not* share a sub-rule.

1.5 Summary

- Clausal logic, and its extensions to both a programming language and a database language, are used to illustrate this text.
- A variant of the λ-calculus, and a variant of the typed λ-calculus, are used to define "recognising" functions in this text.
- Data is the set of fundamental, indivisible things in an application. Data may be represented by labels, thing-populations and name-populations.
- Information is set of the implicit associations between data things in an application. Information may be represented by relations, domains and tuples.
- Knowledge is the set of explicit associations between information things and/or data things in an application. Knowledge may be represented by clusters, fields and instances.
- Clausal logic is a formalism that may be used to express the meaning of knowledge things.
- A knowledge-based system is a system that represents an application containing a significant amount of real knowledge, and is designed, implemented and possibly maintained with due regard for the structure of the data, information and knowledge.
- The maintenance of knowledge-based systems is concerned with two issues: first, the recognition by the maintenance procedure of the relationship between real knowledge things and their implementation, and second, the recognition by the maintenance procedure of the interrelationships between the representations of knowledge things.

2 Non-unified design

2.1 Introduction

This chapter presents the basic approach taken by many traditional methodologies for the design of knowledge-based systems. Traditional methodologies that take this approach are called "non-unified" design methodologies. This presentation of the basic traditional approach is intended to enable a comparison to be made between those traditional design methodologies and the methodology presented in subsequent chapters here. The methodology presented in subsequent chapters is a "unified design" methodology. The role of this chapter is to place that methodology in perspective with respect to the basic approach used in traditional design practice [Le Roux, 1994].

Section 2.2 describes what is meant by a "non-unified" design methodology: such a methodology employs a "non-unified" representation. Section 2.3 describes a particular non-unified representation. In such a representation the data, information and knowledge things are represented in different ways. If a real thing is to be represented in such a representation then that thing must be classified as data, information or knowledge. The business of "classification" is discussed in Sect. 2.4. The business of representing a thing, after it has been classified, is discussed in Sect. 2.5. The particular non-unified representation described does not represent all that is necessary for it to be a complete specification of the required knowledge-based system. In Sect. 2.6 two design steps are described that develop that non-unified representation into a complete specification.

2.2 Non-unified methodology

The data, information and knowledge things in an application are related to each other in a hierarchic structure [Mittra, 1998]. Any design methodology that represents these things will also represent this hierarchic structure. In the representation of this hierarchic structure, the representation of the data things determines the vocabulary in terms of which the information things must be represented, and the representation of the data and the information things determines the vocabulary in terms of which the knowledge things must be represented.

A *unified design methodology* is a methodology that represents the data, information and knowledge things in a homogeneous manner, and that represents the hierarchic relationships between them in a homogeneous manner. The knowledge representation employed by a unified design methodology should not distinguish between data, information and knowledge. A key disadvantage in using a unified methodology is that well known modelling tools, such as ER modelling for database systems [Chen, 1976], can not be used. That is, if a unified methodology is to be used then new techniques will have to be learnt to model even the basic things in a conventional database application. The remainder of this chapter is concerned with the basic approach taken by many traditional, non-unified methodologies for designing knowledge-based systems [Blair et al., 1995] [Gonzalez & Dankel, 1993].

A *non-unified design methodology* is a methodology that does not represent data, information and knowledge in a homogeneous manner. For example, a methodology that uses ER or BR modelling to construct a representation of the data and information, and that uses some other modelling tool to construct a representation of the knowledge is a non-unified methodology [Debenham, 1989]. An advantage in using a non-unified methodology is that well known data and information analysis techniques can be applied to identify and model the data and the information. Identification and representation of the data and information things determines the vocabulary in terms of which the knowledge must then be represented. If ER modelling [Chen, 1976] is used to model the data and information things then the set of relations identified can be interpreted as a set of logic predicates in terms of which the knowledge things are represented. The value in such an approach is that well known methods can be employed to perform a substantial amount of the work involved in building a model of a knowledge-based system [Miles & Huberman, 1997].

Any practical design methodology should address system maintenance [Buckner & Shah, 1991]. Most design methodologies construct some form of "conceptual model" [Blum, 1994]. The conceptual model is a complete representation of the knowledge required by the system. It specifies *how* the system will do what it is required to do. It is not a complete system specification. It does not contain a representation of the system requirements. One approach to maintenance is to introduce "coupling relationships" into the conceptual model. A *coupling relationship* links two things in the conceptual model if a modification to one of those things could, in general, require that the other thing should be checked for correctness, and possibly modified, so that the consistency and correctness of the conceptual model is preserved. Coupling relationships may be employed by both unified and non-unified design methodologies.

2.3 Non-unified representation

A non-unified design methodology employs a *non-unified representation*. In a non-unified representation, data, information and knowledge things are not represented in a homogeneous manner. An approach to non-unified representation is described that employs BR modelling [Nijssen & Halpin, 1989] [Verheijen & Van Bekkum, 1982] to represent the data and information things, and a hybrid model to represent the knowledge things. In this approach, the hierarchic structure of data, information and knowledge is exploited. That is, the relationships that are identified by BR modelling are interpreted as predicates. Then the knowledge things are represented in terms of these predicates alone. In this way BR modelling makes a substantial contribution to the analysis of the knowledge. Using conventional jargon, BR modelling determines the procedure names in terms of which the knowledge things are represented. ER (or entity-relationship) modelling is more widely used than BR modelling. The choice of BR modelling here to illustrate a non-unified representation is arbitrary. That is, ER modelling "works just as well as" BR for this purpose.

A non-unified methodology uses a non-unified representation to construct the conceptual model of an application. The conceptual model described here consists of two separate parts. One part is a model of the data and information things. The other part is a model of the knowledge things. The model of the data and information things is constructed using BR modelling and that of the knowledge things using a hybrid model.

BR and ER modelling were originally designed for use in database systems. When designing a database system, BR analysis is employed to construct a BR model using a set of well defined diagrammatic constructs. By contrast the rules in a database system are often dealt with informally by practitioners. The BR model together with the informal representation of the database rules are developed by practitioners into a complete system specification. The BR model can be implemented in a database management system, and the database rules can be implemented in a host programming language [Campbell & Halpin, 1994]. This process is illustrated in Fig. 2.1 which does not attempt to show the system requirements.

In the non-unified design methodology described here BR modelling and a hybrid approach to knowledge modelling is used to construct a non-unified representation of a knowledge-based system. BR modelling is used to construct a model of the data and the information things in the application. As a by-product this model identifies the predicates in terms of which the knowledge is then represented. Using a hybrid approach to knowledge modelling, a model of the knowledge things is then be constructed in terms of these predicates. This knowledge model also uses a set of well defined diagrammatic constructs. When built, these two models together constitute the conceptual model. The conceptual model is then developed into a complete system specification. This system specification is then used to implement the knowledge-based system in an architecture consisting

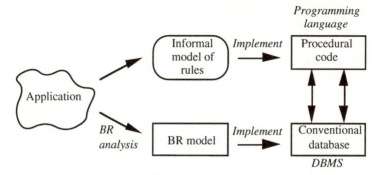

Fig. 2.1   Conventional database design

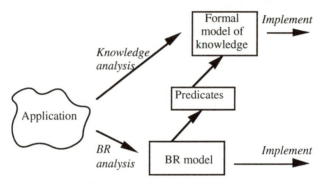

Fig. 2.2   Non-unified methodology for knowledge-based systems

of a conventional database system together with either an expert systems shell or a conventional host programming language [Harris-Jones et al., 1992]. The language used to implement the system does not concern us here. This design process is illustrated in Fig. 2.2.

2.3.1 Data and information representation

Data things are represented by populations and labels. Information things are represented by relations, domains and tuples [Reddy et al., 1993] [Tsichritzis & Lochovsky, 1982]. In this section the discipline of BR analysis is applied to construct a model of the data things and information things in a given application.

A *data thing* is a fundamental, indivisible thing in the application. Populations represent data things that are *not* physical things. Populations are sometimes associated with a particular "sets of labels". The population "spare part number" is associated with a particular set of labels (that is the set of spare part numbers). If a population is associated with a particular set of labels then it is a *name-population*. The population "spare part" that refers to the abstract thing "spare part" is *not* associated with a particular set of labels. If a population is *not* associated with a particular set of labels then is a *thing-population*. The notation

Fig. 2.3   Representation of thing-population

Fig. 2.4   The identifying population

of Binary Relationship (BR) modelling [Nijssen and Halpin, 1989] is described in outline only.   In BR modelling a name-population is a "LOT" (Lexical Object Type), and a thing-population is a "NOLOT" (NOn-Lexical Object Type).

A thing-population (or NOLOT) is represented by an oval shape.   The diagram in Fig. 2.3 might represent the thing-population "spare part".

A thing-population may be associated with a number of different name-populations.   The thing-population "spare part" may be associated with the two name-populations "spare part name" and "spare part number".   A particular name-population is identified for each thing-population.   This particular name-population has the property that each label in this name-population uniquely identifies each thing in the thing-population.   This particular name-population is the *identifying population*.   For the thing-population "spare part" the name-population could be "spare part number" whose labels might be the set of numbers from 1 000 to 4 999.   The identifying population is shown in parentheses beneath the thing-population name inside the oval shape.   See Fig. 2.4.

The only structure in data that is relevant to this discussion is the "type hierarchy".   If, as a general rule, all labels associated with population A are also associated with population B, then population A is a *sub-type* of population B.   Alternatively, a *sub-type relationship* is said to exist from population A to population B.   The collection of all sub-type relationships is the *type hierarchy*.   The type hierarchy has a lattice structure in general.   The type hierarchy is represented on a BR diagram by denoting that population "A" is a sub-type of population "B" as shown in Fig. 2.5.   In established approaches to data analysis it is common for the sub-type relationship to be restricted to being between thing-populations only.   This restriction is adopted here.

If the set of labels associated with a given population is the set-theoretic cartesian product of the sets of labels associated with two or more other populations then that given population is a *compound population*.   If the labels associated with the population "spare-part_model" are the cartesian products of the labels associated with the populations "spare-part" and "model" then the population "spare-part_model" is a compound population.

An *information thing* is an implicit association between two or more data things in the application.   As an information thing is an *implicit* association it has, by definition, no succinct description.   If an information thing is an association between data things that *are* physical things then it may be represented by a

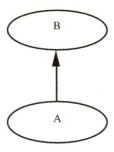

Fig. 2.5 Sub-type relationship

tuple. If an information thing is an association between data things that are *not* physical things and that are *not* naturally associated with a set of labels then that information thing may be represented by a *relation*. If an information thing is an association between data things that are *not* physical things and that *are* naturally associated with a set of labels then that information thing may be represented by a set of *domains*. This set is a *domain set*. At any particular time each relation, together with its corresponding domain set, are associated with a particular set of tuples. This particular set of tuples is the *value set* of that relation. See Fig. 2.6. The set of tuples associated with a relation will usually change in time but the meaning of that relation should remain constant. In general, a relation has constraints associated with it. The set of tuples associated with that relation should satisfy these constraints.

BR analysis is a methodology for constructing a representation of the data things and information things in an application. Suppose that BR analysis is applied to the fact "spare parts have a cost". Suppose that this fact is interpreted as an implicit association between the thing-population "spare part" and the thing-population "cost". Suppose that the identifying name-population "part number" is chosen for the thing-population "spare part". Suppose that the labels in the population "part number" are any number between 1 000 and 4 999. Suppose that the identifying name-population "dollars" is chosen for the thing-population "cost". Using the BR modelling notation this fact can be represented using the notation shown in Fig. 2.7. That notation can be read from left to right as "spare parts have a cost", or from right to left as "the cost of a spare part". There is a double arrow over the "have a" box. That double arrow denotes that "spare part determines cost". The reverse is not necessarily true because in this example the cost is unlikely to determine the spare part. The double arrow denotes an information functional dependency *from* the population "spare part" *to* the population "cost". That is, the information thing represented in Fig. 2.7 contains an implicit *functional association*. There is a black dot drawn on the line between "spare part" and the "have a" box. That black dot denotes that *all* spare parts are involved in this functional association. That is, the black dot denotes that *all* spare parts have a cost.

The sub-type relationships between thing-populations are shown on a BR diagram. If "car part" is a sub-type of "spare part" then this fact is added to the

part/cost-price	
part-number	dollar-amount
1234	1.23
2468	2.34
3579	3.45
8642	4.56
7531	5.67
1470	6.78

Fig. 2.6 A relation, its domains and its set of tuples or value set

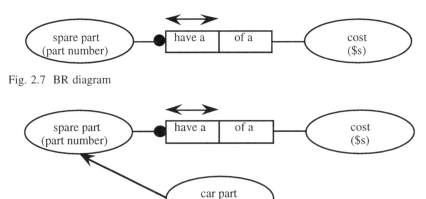

Fig. 2.7 BR diagram

Fig. 2.8 BR diagram with sub-type relationship

diagram shown in Fig. 2.7 to give the diagram shown in Fig. 2.8. The thing-population "car part" is not shown with an identifying name-population in Fig. 2.8. It is presumed that "car part" inherits its identifying name-population from the thing-population "spare part", namely "part number".

The non-unified design methodology illustrated in Fig. 2.2 shows BR analysis as the first step in the construction of a conceptual model. The role of BR analysis in the construction of the conceptual model for a knowledge-based systems application is illustrated with three chunks of expertise.

The first chunk of expertise is "the selling price of a spare part is the cost price of that spare part marked up by the mark-up rate for that spare part". Applying BR analysis to extract a representation of the data and information things in this chunk suppose that the BR diagram shown in Fig. 2.9 is derived. That BR diagram contains a representation of four data things and three information things.

The second chunk of expertise is "the selling price of a spare part is the cost price of that spare part marked up by a universal mark-up rate". In this second chunk the association between the populations "spare part" and "mark-up rate" is explicit. That association is described by the rule that "all spare parts are subject to the same universal mark-up rate". A BR diagram only shows implicit associations. The association between the populations "spare part" and "mark-up rate" is

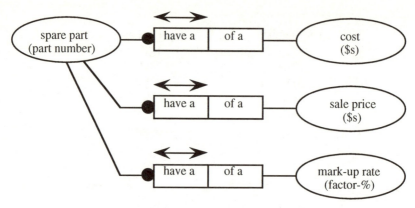

Fig. 2.9 BR diagram for first chunk of expertise

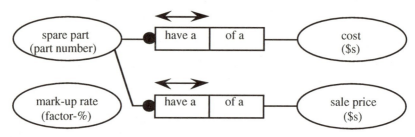

Fig. 2.10 BR diagram for second chunk of expertise

not shown on the BR diagram. The BR diagram for this second chunk of expertise is shown in Fig. 2.10.

The third chunk of expertise is "the selling price for spare parts costing less than $20 is the cost price marked up by 30 percent, and the selling price for spare parts costing $20 or more is the cost price marked up by 25 percent". In this third chunk the association between the populations "spare part" and "mark-up rate" is explicit. That association is described by the rule that "all cost prices less than $20 are associated with a mark-up rate of 30%, and all costs prices of $20 or more are associated with a mark-up rate of 25%". The BR diagram for this third chunk is as shown for the second chunk in Fig. 2.10.

2.3.2 Knowledge representation

Knowledge things may be represented by clusters, fields and instances. The set of instances associated with a cluster at any particular time is the *value set* of that cluster. A hybrid approach to modelling knowledge is used here as part of the non-unified representation for knowledge-based systems applications.

A *knowledge* thing is an explicit association between two or more data and/or information things. If a knowledge thing is an association between things that are physical things then it may be represented by a set of *instances*. If a knowledge thing is an association between things that are *not* physical things and that are *not*

[part/sale-price, part/cost-price, mark-up]

part/sale-price		part/cost-price		mark-up rate
part-number	$-amount	part-number	$-amount	factor-%
1234	1.48	1234	1.23	1.2
2468	2.81	2468	2.34	
3579	4.14	3579	3.45	
8642	5.47	8642	4.56	
7531	6.80	7531	5.67	
1470	8.14	1470	6.78	

Fig. 2.11 A cluster, its fields and instances

naturally associated with a set of labels then that knowledge thing may be represented by a set of thing-populations and relations that are a *cluster*. If a knowledge thing is an association between things that are *not* physical things and that *are* naturally associated with a set of labels then that knowledge thing may be represented by a set of name-populations and domains. These name populations and domains are *fields*. This set of name-populations and domains is a *field set*. At any particular time each cluster, together with its corresponding field set, are associated with a particular set of instances. Consider again the second chunk of expertise in Sect. 2.3.1 above "the selling price of a spare part is the cost price of that spare part marked up by a universal mark-up rate". Suppose that the product of the BR analysis of this chunk is as shown in Fig. 2.10. The cluster, fields and instances that represent this chunk could be as shown in Fig. 2.11. The set of instances associated with a cluster will usually change in time but the meaning of that cluster may well remain constant. In general, a cluster has constraints associated with it. The set of instances associated with a cluster should satisfy these constraints.

Knowledge analysis is shown in Fig. 2.2 as a design step of the non-unified methodology. During knowledge analysis a hybrid model of the knowledge is constructed. This hybrid model, together with its associated BR model, constitute the conceptual model. As shown in Fig. 2.2 the non-unified method for constructing the conceptual model has three main steps:

- apply BR analysis to build a BR model of the data and information;
- extract a set of predicates from the BR model, and
- build a model of the knowledge expressed in terms of that set of predicates.

To introduce the notation for the hybrid knowledge model, consider again the second chunk of expertise in Sect. 2.3.1 above "the selling price of a spare part is the cost price of that spare part marked up by a universal mark-up rate". The result of applying BR analysis to this chunk is shown in Fig. 2.10. The diagram in Fig. 2.10 contains a representation of four data things and two information things. Six predicates are extracted from that BR model:

is-a[x:spare-part] that means "x is a valid spare part number"
is-a[x:mark-up-rate] that means "x is the universal mark-up rate"
is-a[x:cost] that means "x is a valid cost price"
is-a[x:sale-price] that means "x is a valid sale price"
part/sale-price(x, y) that means "y is the sale price identified with part x"
part/cost-price(x, y) that means "y is the cost price identified with part x"

A fundamental principle of non-unified design is that the knowledge things *must* be represented in terms of these six predicates only. If this is not possible then one reason may be that the BR model is incomplete. The hybrid knowledge model uses two distinct notations. These two distinct notations are "cluster diagrams" and "dependency diagrams".

Cluster diagrams are used to represent knowledge. A chunk of knowledge is an explicit association. Suppose that BR analysis has been applied to a given chunk and that a set of predicates has been extracted from that BR model. The *cluster diagram* for that chunk is an undirected graph containing a node for each of these predicates, together with an additional node to which all the other nodes are joined by an arc. The arc from a "predicate" node to the additional node is drawn thickly if the chunk of knowledge enables the entire value set of that predicate node to be derived from the value sets of the other predicate nodes. The cluster diagram for the above example is shown in Fig. 2.12. On that cluster diagram the arc to the "mark-up-rate" node is not a thick one because the mark-up rate can not be derived correctly due to the possibility of rounding errors introduced by dividing sale prices by cost prices. The cluster diagram gives a succinct view of what the chunk of knowledge is.

Dependency diagrams are used to represent rules. The dependency diagram notation is more detailed than the cluster diagram notation. A dependency diagram represents a rule, or "if-then", structure. A given chunk of knowledge may have a number of valid if-then interpretations. The chunk of knowledge illustrated on the cluster diagram in Fig. 2.12 has two valid if-then interpretations. Using logic programming these two if-then interpretations can be expressed as:

part/sale-price(x, y) ← part/cost-price(x , z), is-a[w:mark-up-rate],
$\quad$ y = z × w   [A]

part/cost-price(x, y) ← part/sale-price(x , z), is-a[w:mark-up-rate],
$\quad$ z = y × w   [B]

Each of these two if-then interpretations may be represented using a dependency diagram.

A *rule* is a *functional* "explicit" association *from* a set of information things or data things called the *body to* a single data or information thing called the *head*. A rule is a chunk of knowledge that contains one functional explicit association. Suppose that BR analysis has been applied to a given rule and that a set of predicates has been extracted from that BR model. One of these predicates will repre-

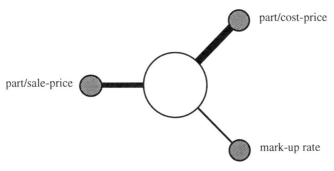

Fig. 2.12 Cluster diagram for second chunk of expertise

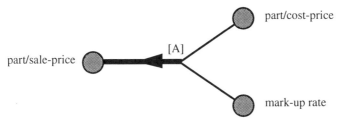

Fig. 2.13 Dependency diagram for rule [A]

sent the head of that rule. This predicate is the *head predicate*. A *dependency diagram* for a rule named [G] with head predicate P is a directed tree. In this directed tree there is a node labelled [G]. There is a directed arc from this node labelled [G] to a node labelled P. There is a node for each body predicate. These nodes are labelled with a body predicate name. There is an arc between each node labelled with a body predicate and the node labelled [G]. For rule [A] above the dependency diagram is shown in Fig. 2.13. Likewise a dependency diagram can be constructed for rule [B]. Further these two dependency diagrams can be shown on one *combined diagram* in which each predicate is shown as one node. The combined diagram for rules [A] and [B] is shown in Fig. 2.14. The combined diagram for a chunk of knowledge presents a more detailed view of the structure of that chunk than the corresponding cluster diagram.

The dependency diagram notation also identifies "incomplete rules" and "non-unique rules. A rule is an *incomplete rule* if it does not contain sufficient expertise to enable the complete value set of the head predicate to be derived from the body predicates. Incomplete rules are identified in the dependency diagram notation by a "flash" on the arc to the head predicate node as shown in Fig. 2.15. A rule is a *non-unique rule* if it enables a member of the value set of its head predicate to be derived in two or more different ways. Non-unique rules are a maintenance hazard. Non-unique rules are identified in the dependency diagram notation by a "bar" on the arc to the head predicate node as shown in Fig. 2.16.

Consider the chunk of expertise "the selling price for spare parts with a part number less than 9 999 is the product of the cost of the spare part and the mark-up-factor, where the mark-up-factor is determined by the type of the spare part".

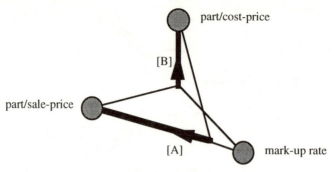

Fig. 2.14 Combined diagram for rules [A] and [B]

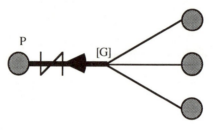

Fig. 2.15 Diagram for an incomplete rule [G]

Suppose that a BR analysis of this example identifies a number of predicates including:

part/cost-price(x, y)
part/sale-price(x, y)
part/part-type(x, y)
part-type/mark-up-factor(x, y)

Without presenting unnecessary detail these predicates are assumed to have their "obvious" intuitive meaning. One interpretation of this chunk expressed in logic programming in terms of these predicates is:

part/sale-price(x, y) ← part/cost-price(x, z),
    x < 9 999,   part/part-type(x, v),
    part-type/mark-up-factor(v, w),   y = (z × w)   [C]

that is an incomplete clause group. The group:

part/sale-price(x, y) ← part/cost-price(x , z),
   z = 20 , y = z × 1.25
part/sale-price(x, y) ← part/cost-price(x , z),
   z < 20 , y = z × 1.3
part/sale-price(x, y) ← part/cost-price(x , z),
   z ≥ 20 , y = z × 1.25   [D]

is not a unique group.

The goal of conceptual modelling is to build a model of an application that is, in some sense, a "good" model. One criterion for "good" modelling is that the model should support maintenance effectively. Raw expertise may be in a form that contains hidden maintenance hazards. Consider the chunk of raw expertise [E1] "the profit on a part is the product of the cost price of that part and the mark-up factor of that part less 1". Consider also the chunk of raw expertise [E2] "the tax payable on a part is 10% of the product of the cost price of that part and the mark-up factor of that part". Both [E1] and [E2] have buried within them the sub-rule [E3] "the selling price of a part is the cost price of that part multiplied by the mark-up factor of that part". If the expertise represented in rule [E3] changes then both rule [E1] and rule [E2] should be modified. If rule [E3] has not been explic-itly identified then rules [E1] and [E2] "share an unstated sub-rule between them" and consequently constitute a hidden maintenance hazard. A method for constructing a "good" conceptual model should include techniques for identifying and removing hazards of this form.

To illustrate how the conceptual model may be modified to remove mainte-nance hazards consider the chunks [E1], [E2] and [E3]. Suppose that a BR analy-sis of this example identifies a number of predicates including:

part/profit(x, y)
part/cost-price(x, y)
part/sale-price(x, y)
part/mark-up-factor(x, y)
part/tax-payable(x, y)
is-a[x:tax-rate]

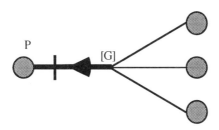

Fig. 2.16 Diagram for non-unique rule [G]

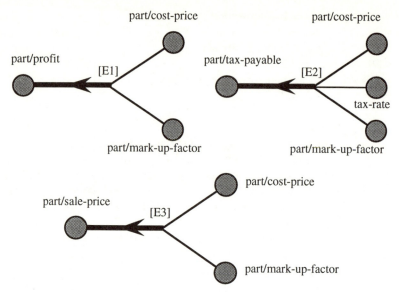

Fig. 2.17 Dependency diagrams for interpretations of [E1], [E2] and [E3]

Without presenting unnecessary detail these predicates are assumed to have their "obvious" intuitive meaning. Each of the three rules [E1], [E2] and [E3] contain at least one if-then interpretation. Expressed in terms of these predicates the dependency diagrams for three chosen if-then interpretations of [E1], [E2] and [E3] are shown in Fig. 2.17. Expressed in terms of these predicates in logic programming, these chosen if-then interpretations of [E1], [E2] and [E3] are:

part/profit(x, y) ← part/cost-price(x, w),
    part/mark-up-factor(x, u), $y = w \times (u - 1)$ [E1]

part/tax-payable(x, y) ← part/cost-price(x, z), part/mark-up-factor(x, w),
    is-a[v:tax-rate], $y = (z \times w) \times v$ [E2]

part/sale-price(x, y) ← part/cost-price(x, z),
    part/mark-up-factor(x, w), $y = (z \times w)$ [E3]

The clue to simplifying rules [E1] and [E2] comes from the observation that the set of body predicates in [E3] is a subset of the sets of body predicates in both [E1] and [E2]. Hence rule [E3] may be buried inside both rule [E1] and rule [E2]. Rules [E1] and [E2] can be expressed so that they are independent of rule [E3] hence generating rules [F1] and [F2] respectively. Rule [F1] is "the profit on a part is the difference between the sale price and the cost price of that part". Rule [F2] is "the tax payable on a part is the product of the sale price of that part and the tax rate". Expressed in terms of the above predicates the dependency diagrams

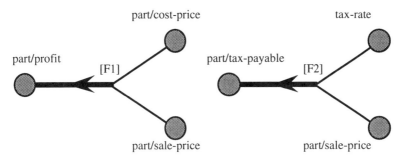

Fig. 2.18 Dependency diagrams for rules [F1] and [F2]

for rules [F1] and [F2] are shown in Fig. 2.18. Expressed in terms of these predicates in logic programming, rules [F1] and [F2] are:

part/profit(x, y) ← part/sale-price(x, z), part/cost-price(x, w),
    y = z − w   [F1]

part/tax-payable(x, y) ← part/sale-price(x, z), is-a[v:tax-rate],
    y = z × v   [F2]

The above example illustrates the use of a method for removing one form of maintenance hazard from a conceptual model. Using that method the "poor" representation is logically implied by the "improved" representation. Using the resolution principle [E1] may be deduced from [F1] and [E3], and [E2] may be deduced from [F2] and [E3]. In general there is no logical implication from a "poor" representation to an "improved" representation. Continual reference to the knowledge source is required to develop an improved representation in this way. This form of improvement is a potentially expensive process. The improved representation developed above was considered because the set of body predicates in one rule is a subset of the sets of body predicates in another rule. The set of body predicates in [E1] is a subset of the set of body predicates in [E2], but that there is no intuitively satisfactory simplification of [E2] using the expertise in [E1]. This form of conceptual model improvement is not discussed further here. This form of conceptual model improvement is considered in detail in the context of unified design in Chap. 6.

2.4 Classification

Classification is the business of deciding whether a real thing in a given application is to be treated as a data thing, information thing or knowledge thing. *Representation* is the business of representing in the conceptual model a real thing in the application that has been classified. In Sect. 2.3 a non-unified approach to conceptual modelling is described. That conceptual model consists of two separate parts. One part is a model of the data and information things, and the other part is a model of the knowledge things. Given a real thing in an application, there is usually a considerable variety of ways in which it can be classified [Tansley & Hayball, 1993]. There is often no *a priori* correct classification of a thing as data, information or knowledge. This observation has substantial implications for the maintenance of knowledge systems. It is necessary for the designer of a system to convey to those responsible for maintenance how the real things in the application have been classified in that system. The business of classification is illustrated by analysing the sample fact "the interest rate on savings accounts is 5 percent" in six different ways.

Analysis 1

Suppose that "the interest rate on savings accounts" is taken as a fundamental, indivisible thing. Then the sample fact would be classified as data. It can be represented by associating the label "5" with a population named:

interest-rate-on-savings-accounts

In Analysis 1, the sample fact is classified as a data thing, and is represented as a label that is associated with a population. In this example, the constraint that "this population can have at most one label associated with it at any one time" can be introduced.

Analysis 2

Suppose that "interest-rate" and "account-type" are taken as fundamental, indivisible things, and so they are data things. Furthermore, suppose that the sample fact is taken as an implicit functional association between these two data things. The sample fact is classified as information. It can be represented by associating the tuple ('savings', '5') with other similar tuples in a relation:

account-type/interest-rate(account-description , rate)

In Analysis 2 the sample fact is classified as an information thing, and is represented as a tuple that is grouped with other, similar tuples in a relation. As the above relation has its first argument as its key, this constraint ensures that there can be at most one tuple in the relation that represents the interest rate on savings accounts.

Analysis 3

Suppose that, as in Analysis 2, "interest-rate" and "account-type" are taken as fundamental, indivisible things and so, in addition, is "account number". Three data things are identified. Furthermore, suppose that two different implicit functional associations are identified between these three populations. These two implicit functional associations are represented by the two relations:

account/interest-rate(<u>account-number</u> , rate)
account/account-type(<u>account-number</u> , account-description)

These two associations are information things. Furthermore, suppose that the sample fact is taken as an explicit functional association between these two information things. The sample fact would then be classified as a knowledge thing. It can be represented by associating the clause:

account/interest-rate(x , '5') ← account/account-type(x , 'savings')

with other similar clauses in a clause group. In Analysis 3, the sample fact is classified as a knowledge thing, and is represented as a clause that is grouped with other, similar clauses in a group. A knowledge constraint may be attached to this clause group that specifies that there can be at most one clause referring to each account type.

Analysis 4
Suppose that "account-number", "account-type", "mean-balance" and "interest-payable" are taken as fundamental indivisible things and so they are data things. Furthermore, suppose that three different implicit functional associations, in the sample fact, are identified between these data things. These three implicit functional associations are represented by the three relations:

account/account-type(<u>account-number</u> , account-description)
account/mean-balance(<u>account-number</u> , mean-balance)
account/interest(<u>account-number</u> , interest)

These three associations are information things. Furthermore, suppose that the sample fact is taken as an explicit functional association between these three information things. The sample fact would then be classified as a knowledge thing. The sample fact can be represented by associating the clause:

account/interest(x , y) ← account/account-type(x , 'savings'),
    account/mean-balance(x , z), y = z × (5/100)

with other similar clauses in a clause group. In Analysis 4 the sample fact is classified as a knowledge thing, and is represented as a clause that is grouped with other, similar clauses in a group. A knowledge constraint may be attached to this group as in Analysis 3.

Analysis 5
Suppose that the same populations and the same relations are identified as in
Analysis 4. Instead of using these to represent the sample fact as a clause, these
relations are used to store the information implied by the sample fact for every
savings account in the application. Suppose that account number 1234 happens
to be a savings account with mean balance $200, then this instance of the sample
fact can be represented by associating the three tuples with the relations:

account/account-type('1234', 'savings')
account/mean-balance('1234', '200')
account/interest('1234', '5')

These three tuples would be grouped with similar tuples for all other savings
accounts in the application. In Analysis 5, that uses the same populations and
relations as Analysis 4, the sample fact is stored implicitly as a set of tuples. In
addition, the sample fact can also be stored as an information integrity constraint
to ensure that the stored information is consistent. The first argument is the key
in each of these three relations. This ensures that each account number identifies
an account that has a unique account type.

Analysis 6
Suppose that accounts are identified by their "account-no.", and that each account
has an "interest-rate". Suppose that an implicit functional association is identified
between these two things and defines the relation:

account/interest-rate(account-number , rate)

Suppose that the only savings accounts in the application have account numbers
1234, 2468 and 3579, then the sample fact may be represented as:

account/interest-rate('1234' , '5')
account/interest-rate('2468' , '5')
account/interest-rate('3579' , '5')

In Analysis 6 the single, sample fact is represented as a *set of tuples*.

The sample fact "the interest rate on savings accounts is 5 percent" has been
classified accurately in six different ways. This example illustrates that the
distinction between the knowledge, the information and the data in an application
must be related to the analysis technique used and the way in which it is applied.
Any effective maintenance strategy relies on a specification of how each real thing
has been classified. Alternatively, it is incorrect to identify:

- that which *can* be represented by labels as "data";
- that which *can* be represented by tuples as "information", and
- that which *can* be represented by clauses as "knowledge".

as has been illustrated by the example above.

2.5 Representation

Given a real thing in an application that has already been classified, *representation* is the business of representing that thing in the conceptual model [Fensel & Van Harmelen, 1994]. Classification is discussed in Sect. 2.4. The basis for classifying the things in an application is summarised in Fig. 2.19. Having classified a real thing that thing can be represented using the concepts shown in Fig. 2.20. The business of representing a real thing may require further analysis of the nature of that thing [Schreiber et al., 1993]. If a knowledge thing is to be represented then the valid if-then interpretations of that thing must first be correctly identified. Representation is concerned substantially with that further analysis of the things that are to be represented [Schefe, 1982].

Raw expertise can sometimes be represented in an "if-then" form such as logic programming. In general, a knowledge thing is not necessarily stated in an "if-then" form. Consider "the selling price of a part is the purchase price of that part multiplied by the mark-up rate for that part". Suppose that this thing has been classified as knowledge, that BR analysis has been applied, and that a number of predicates have been identified including:

part/sell-price(x, y)
part/buy-price(x, y)
part/mark-up(x, y)

The wisdom in this thing can be represented as the cluster shown in Fig. 2.21.

The cluster shown in Fig. 2.21 does not show any functional associations. That cluster does not indicate which "if-then" interpretations of the thing are valid. The given thing could imply any or all of the following three different "if-then" interpretations:

if a part's buying price is known **and** a part's mark-up rate is known, **then** the
part's selling price is the buying price multiplied by the mark-up rate.
if a part's selling price is known **and** a part's mark-up rate is known, **then** the
part's buying price is the selling price divided by the mark-up rate.

and:

Data	fundamental, indivisible things
Information	implicit associations between data things
Knowledge	explicit associations between data and/or information things

Fig. 2.19 Classification of things

	Represented as:		
	if a physical thing	if not a physical thing	
		but associated with a set of physical things	and not associated with a set of physical things
Data	label	name-population	thing-population
Information	tuple	domain set	relation
Knowledge	instance	field set	cluster

Fig. 2.20 Representation of things

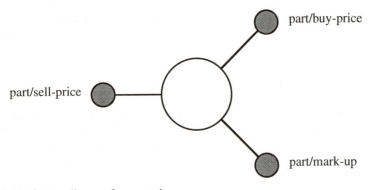

part/buy-price

part/sell-price

part/mark-up

Fig. 2.21 Cluster diagram for example

if a part's selling price is known **and** a part's buying price is known, **then** the mark-up rate is the quotient of the selling price and the buying price.

These three if-then interpretations of the given thing can be represented in logic programming as three single clause clause-groups:

part/sell-price(x, y) ← part/buy-price(x, z), part/mark-up(x, w),
$$y = z \times w$$
[A]

part/buy-price(x, z) ← part/sell-price(x, y), part/mark-up(x, w),
$$y = z \times w$$
[B]

part/mark-up(x, w) ← part/buy-price(x, z), part/sell-price(x, y),
$$y = z \times w$$
[C]

The essence of these three single clause clause-groups can be represented more succinctly using the "dependency" notation introduced in Sect. 1.2.1:

part/sell-price ⇐ part/buy-price, part/mark-up   [A]

part/buy-price ⇐ part/sell-price, part/mark-up   [B]

part/mark-up ⇐ part/buy-price, part/sell-price   [C]

This notation means that the head predicate may be derived from the body predicates using the corresponding clause-groups. This "dependency" notation represents the functional dependencies shown on the dependency diagram.

The representation of a knowledge thing requires further analysis of that thing. This further analysis is concerned with determining which of the possible "if-then" interpretations of that thing are valid. This may involve repeated reference to the knowledge source. Representation is a potentially costly, but necessary, part of the business of constructing the conceptual model.

2.6 Specification

The *specification* of a system contains all the detail required to enable a programmer to construct an implementation of that system. The conceptual model does not contain either a representation of the particular tasks that the system is expected to perform, or details of how the system should be implemented. The conceptual model is not a complete system specification. The system specification is developed from the conceptual model, first by adding in a representation of the particular tasks that the system is expected to perform, and second by adding in details of how the system should be implemented [Jullien et al., 1992]. When the representation of the particular tasks that the system is expected to perform are added to the conceptual model, the augmented conceptual model is the *functional model*. When the details of how the system should be implemented are added to the functional model, the augmented functional model is the *internal model*.

2.6.1 Functional model

The *functional model* shows how the expertise in the conceptual model may be employed to perform the particular tasks that the system is expected to perform [Nwana et al., 1991]. The functional model is developed from the conceptual model. The knowledge in a conceptual model may be represented as a collection of clusters. On this collection of clusters the predicates that can accommodate the "in flow" of information from system updates are identified by "inward" flowing

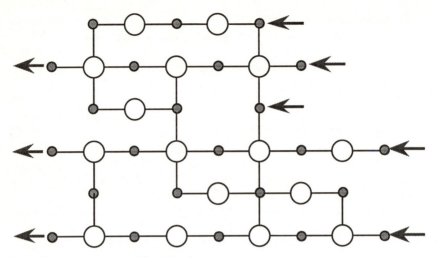

Fig. 2.22 Conceptual model with tasks shown

arrows, and the predicates that can service the "out flow" of information through system queries are identified by "outward" flowing arrows. The functional model is then defined to be the "best" set of dependency diagram that can be extracted from the conceptual model so as to enable the "query predicates" to be derived from the "update predicates". In Chap. 9 it is shown that the problem of extracting the "best" set of such dependency diagrams is NP-complete under a wide interpretation of what is "best". The process of deriving the functional model is not dealt with here. That process is dealt with in detail in the context of unified design in Chap. 9. A pictorial representation of this process is shown in Figs. 2.22–2.23. Figure 2.22 shows the updates and queries added to a conceptual model. Figure 2.23 shows a subset of the conceptual model shown in Fig. 2.22. That subset can service both the updates and the queries.

2.6.2 Internal model

The *internal model* shows how the functional model should be implemented. The internal model shows those predicates that should be stored in the physical model and those predicates that should be deduced when required. To develop the functional model shown in Fig. 2.23 into an internal model the predicates that are to be stored must be identified. One possible solution is shown in Fig. 2.24 in which those predicates that are to be stored are denoted as square nodes.

Ideally the internal model should be that implementation of the functional model that optimises performance in some sense. In Chap. 10 it is shown that the problem of deciding how to implement the functional model so as to optimise performance is NP-complete under a wide interpretation of what is "performance". The business of deriving the internal model is not considered further here. It is dealt with in detail in the context of unified design in Chap. 10.

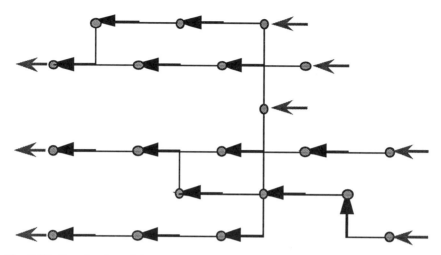

Fig. 2.23 Functional model

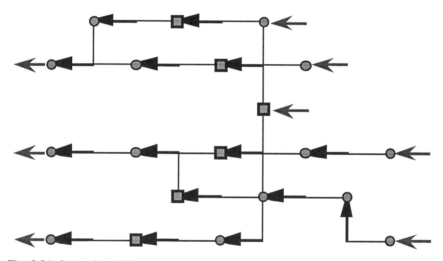

Fig. 2.24 Internal model

2.7 Summary

- Any design methodology for knowledge-based systems can exploit the hierarchic structure of data, information and knowledge.
- BR analysis and a hybrid approach to knowledge analysis can form the basis of a non-unified design methodology for knowledge-based systems.
- Knowledge may be modelled using cluster diagrams and dependency diagrams.
- The goal of conceptual modelling is to build a model of the application that is, in some sense, a "good" model.
- Knowledge analysis should attempt to remove maintenance hazards from the conceptual model.
- There is no *a priori* correct classification of a thing as data, information or knowledge.
- The identification of all valid functional associations within a thing is a potentially costly, but necessary, part of the business of knowledge representation.
- The functional model shows how the expertise in the conceptual model may be employed to perform the particular tasks that the system is expected to perform.
- The internal model shows how the functional model should be implemented.

3 Items

3.1 Introduction

A non-unified design methodology for knowledge-based systems was outlined in Chap. 2. That methodology employs a non-unified representation for the conceptual model. That conceptual model consists of two separate parts: a model of the data and information things, and a model of the knowledge things. The model of the data and information things was constructed using a BR model, and the model of the knowledge things using a hybrid model. In that non-unified design methodology, data, information and knowledge things are represented and treated differently from each other.

This chapter describes a unified representation for conceptual modelling. In this unified representation data things, information things and knowledge things are all represented in the same way as "items". This representation provides the foundation for conceptual modelling in a *unified design methodology* which is a methodology that uses a "unified representation" throughout the design process. In a *unified representation* the data, information and knowledge things are all represented in a homogeneous manner. The hierarchic relationships between the data, information and knowledge things are also represented in a homogeneous manner. A unified representation does not distinguish between data, information and knowledge in any way.

Section 3.2 introduces the concepts on which the notion of an "item" relies. Each item contains a representation of the "meaning" of that item and two powerful classes of constraints on that item. Items are defined formally in Sect. 3.3. Sections 3.4–3.6 consider respectively data items, information items and knowledge items. An algebra of items, including a single rule of composition for items, is given in Sect. 3.7. This single rule of composition enables data, information and knowledge items to be joined with one another regardless of their type. In Sect. 3.8 the use of items to represent an entire system is discussed.

Items are a unified representation. In Sect. 2.2 coupling relationships are introduced into the conceptual model as a representation of the maintenance structure of that model. Items are not powerful enough to support a complete analysis of system maintenance in terms of the coupling relationships. "Objects" are introduced in Chap. 4 as "item building operators". Objects are also a unified representation. They support a complete analysis of maintenance in terms of the coupling relationships. Items and objects together provide the foundation of a unified approach to conceptual modelling for knowledge-based systems. Practical notations for both items and objects are given in Chap. 5.   In Chap. 6 "normalisation" is discussed. Normalisation is a process that reduces the complexity of the coupling relationships and that may be applied to all or part of the conceptual model. Normalisation of the conceptual model should increase the ease with which that model may be subsequently maintained. A complete unified design methodology is described in Chaps. 7–10. Chapter 11 addresses maintenance, and a case study is discussed in Chap. 12.

3.2 Unified representation

In Chap. 2 a non-unified representation for conceptual modelling is discussed. In that representation classical information analysis are used to represent the "database component". Then the relations identified during this information analysis are used as the predicates in terms of which the "knowledge base component" is represented [Schmidt & Brodie, 1982]. Classical information analysis is employed to identify the vocabulary in terms of which the knowledge is expressed. In that non-unified representation the data and information is treated differently from the knowledge [Brodie et al., 1984]. The use of a non-unified methodology requires that the user treat knowledge differently from data and information that hence encourages "non-unified thinking".

Systems may be constructed without using any rigorous design methodology. In a "methodology-free" approach to design, the internal model is constructed directly using "common sense". A "methodology-free" approach also tends to encourages "non-unified thinking". Consider the sample fact "the sale price of parts is the cost price marked up by a universal mark-up factor". A "methodology-free" approach to designing a system that includes this fact could lead to the identification of the relationship between "parts" and their "cost". This relationship can be represented by the relation shown in Fig. 3.1. The knowledge in the fact can be represented by the single clause group:

part/sale-price(x, y) ← part/cost-price(x, z), is-a[mark-up](w), y = z × w

This clause and the relation shown in Fig. 3.1 do *not* share any similar structure.

The use of a unified representation for conceptual modelling requires a shift away from the "non-unified thinking" that is encouraged by the use of either a non-unified methodology or a "methodology-free" approach.

part/cost-price

part-number	dollar-amount
1234	1.23
2468	2.34
3579	3.45
8642	4.56
7531	5.67
1470	6.78

Fig. 3.1 Relation 'part/cost-price'

A unified representation is described here. In this representation the data, information and knowledge things are all represented and treated in the same way. This unified representation is expressed in terms of "items" introduced in detail in Sect. 3.3. This section introduces the concepts on which the notion of an item is built, and which make it a unified representation.

In non-unified design methodologies, information is treated quiet differently from knowledge. Information is modelled using some technique and may be implemented as relations. There is a fundamental similarity between information and knowledge in that they both represent associations [Gottinger & Weimann, 1995]. Information things are implicit associations, and knowledge things are explicit associations. This observation is the starting point for the development of the unified representation. A unified representation for conceptual modelling does not necessarily lead to a complete integration of the way in which all things are represented and treated during the whole design process. By using "items" all things may be represented and treated in the same way during conceptual modelling and during the whole design process.

The shift in thinking away from "non-unified thinking" does not necessary mean that the general spirit of traditional analysis techniques has to be abandoned. In the unified methodology described here the general spirit of traditional information analysis techniques, such as ER modelling, is retained. This unified methodology represents a new discipline with attendant costs for education. The retention of the general spirit of traditional techniques is intended to reduce the cost of using this unified methodology when compared with one that abandoned completely the general spirit of traditional information analysis.

In Sect. 3.3, the structure of items is described. Part of an item's structure is its "semantics". An item's semantics is an expression that specifies the meaning of that item. The approach taken to the specification of item semantics contains the essence of the unified representation. The significance of the approach taken to the specification of item semantics in the unified methodology may be appreciated by considering first the way in which "meaning" is specified for the representation of the data, information and knowledge things in the non-unified conceptual model described in Sect. 2.3.

First, consider the specification of the meaning of the representation of data things in the non-unified conceptual model. A data thing is represented in the

part			car-part	
part-number	← ← ← ← ←		car-part-number	
1234	sub-type		2468	
2468			7531	
3579			1470	
8642				
7531				
1470				

Fig. 3.2 Thing-population 'part' and sub-type 'car-part'

non-unified conceptual model as either a thing-population, name population or label. Each thing-population is associated with an identifying name-population. Each name-population is associated with a set of labels. Consider the "spare parts" things in a warehouse application. These spare parts can be modelled by the thing-population "part". The thing-population "part" could be associated with the identifying name-population "part-number" that in turn is associated with a set of labels. See Fig. 3.2. The meaning of "part" is specified by giving the meaning of the predicate:

is-a[x:part-number] that means "x is a valid part number"

Further, the thing-population "part" could have a sub-type "car-part" as illustrated in Fig. 3.2.

Second, consider the specification of the meaning of the representation of information things in the non-unified conceptual model. An information thing is represented in the non-unified conceptual model as either a relation, a domain set or a tuple. This representation may be expressed in terms of an ER or BR model. Each relation is associated with a particular domain set. Each domain set is associated with a set of tuples. Consider the "spare parts have a sale price" information thing in a warehouse application. This thing can be modelled by representing the association between "part" and "sale-price". The relation "part/sale-price" could be associated with the domain set "{part-number, dollar-amount}", that in turn is associated with a set of tuples. See Fig. 3.3. The meaning of "part/sale-price" is specified by giving the meaning of the predicate:

part/sale-price(x, y) that means "y is the sale price identified with part x"

The meaning of this relation is specified in a similar way to the meaning of the thing-population "part" considered above.

Third, consider the specification of the meaning of the representation of knowledge things in the non-unified conceptual model. A knowledge thing is represented in the non-unified conceptual model as either a cluster, field set or an instance. This representation may be expressed in terms of the hybrid model described in Sect. 2.3. Each cluster is associated with a particular field set. Each

part/sale-price

part-number	dollar-amount
1234	1.48
2468	2.81
3579	4.14
8642	5.47
7531	6.80
1470	8.14

Fig. 3.3 Relation 'part/sale-price'

field set is associated with a set of instances. Consider the "The selling price of a spare-part is its purchase price multiplied by a universal mark-up factor" knowledge thing in a warehouse application. This thing can be modelled by representing the association between "part/sale-price", "part/cost-price" and "mark-up" as a cluster:

[part/sale-price, part/cost-price, mark-up]   [1]

This cluster could be associated with the field set "{part-number/dollar-amount, part-number/dollar-amount, factor-%}". This field set is associated with a set of instances. See Fig. 3.4. The meaning of [1] may be specified by the clauses:

part/sale-price(x, y) ← part/cost-price(x, z), is-a[mark-up](w), y = z × w
part/cost-price(x, z) ← part/sale-price(x, y), is-a[mark-up](w), y = z × w
is-a[mark-up](w) ← part/cost-price(x, z), part/sale-price(x, y), y = z × w

The meaning of cluster [1] is specified by clauses. This illustrates how the meaning of the representation of knowledge things is specified in a completely different way to the specification of the meaning of the representation of both information things and data things [Blair, 1994a].

The clue to unifying the specification of the meaning of the representation of data, information and knowledge things is found in the tables shown in Fig. 3.2, Fig. 3.3 and Fig. 3.4. The *contents* of these tables may change in time, even if the *meaning* of the respective data, information and knowledge things remains unchanged. The idea is to specify "meaning" by giving a function that *recognises* the rows in these tables at any time. The contents of such a table is called the "value set" in Sect. 3.3. The following function recognises the value set of the cluster "[part/sale-price, part/cost-price, mark-up]":

(v, w, x, y, z) ∈ Value set of [part/sale-price, part/cost-price, mark-up]
if and only if   (v, w) ∈ Value set of part/sale-price
    ∧   (x, y) ∈ Value set of part/cost-price
    ∧   (z) ∈ Value set of mark-up
    ∧   ((v = x) → (w = y × z))

[part/sale-price, part/cost-price, mark-up]

part/sale-price		part/cost-price		mark-up
part-number	dollar-amount	part-number	dollar-amount	factor-%
1234	1.48	1234	1.23	1.2
2468	2.81	2468	2.34	1.2
3579	4.14	3579	3.45	1.2
8642	5.47	8642	4.56	1.2
7531	6.80	7531	5.67	1.2
1470	8.14	1470	6.78	1.2

Fig. 3.4 Cluster [part/sale-price, part/cost-price, mark-up]

This example is simple because the structure of the knowledge is simple. In this example the knowledge is not even recursive. This example does not show how the definition of a value set can be extended to apply to complex, recursive knowledge things.

The definition of a value set can be extended to apply to complex, recursive knowledge things. Consider the "If two persons have the same address then they are cohabitants" knowledge thing. This thing can be represented by the cluster:

[person/cohabitant, person/address]   [2]

The meaning of cluster [2] may be defined by the single clause:

person/cohabitant(x, y) ← person/address(x, z), person/address(y, z), x ≠ y

A first attempt at constructing the value set of cluster [2] could be as shown in Fig. 3.5. From the table shown in Fig. 3.4 it is easy to construct a recognising function for the rows. For the table shown in Fig. 3.5 it is *not* so easy to construct such a recognising function. A function may be specified that recognises the value set of cluster [2] displayed in a different way. Consider the function:

(u, v, w, x, y, z) ∈ Value set of [person/cohabitant, person/address]
if and only if
       (u, v) ∈ Value set of person/cohabitant
∧   (w, x) ∈ Value set of person/address
∧   (y, z) ∈ Value set of person/address
∧   (((u = w) ∧ (v = y) ∧ (u ≠ v)) ∧ (x = z))

This function recognises the instances in the table shown in Fig. 3.6. Hence if the table shown in Fig. 3.6 is considered to be the value set of cluster [2] then the value set of cluster [2] has a simple recognising function. The tuple (Joan, 7)

[person/cohabitant, person/address]

person/cohabitant		person/address	
name	name	name	house number
Peter	Jane	Peter	12
Peter	Ray	Mary	14
Jane	Peter	Joan	7
Jane	Ray	John	9
Ray	Peter	Mark	8
Ray	Jane	Anne	14
Mary	Anne	Jane	12
Anne	Mary	Ray	12
John	Drew	Drew	9
Drew	John	Diane	8
Mark	Diane		
Diane	Mark		

Fig. 3.5   Labels related to [person/cohabitant, person/address]

does not occur in the person/address component in Fig. 3.6. The reason for this is that "Joan" is not a cohabitant of another person. The value set of cluster [2] is defined using a double occurrence of the component predicate person/address. The value sets of complex recursive clusters may be defined in this way by introducing multiple occurrences of component predicates [Ioannidis & Wong, 1988].

The specification of the value set of knowledge things is illustrated with another example. Consider the "Workers are supervised by the managers of the departments in which they work, department managers are supervised by the General Manager" knowledge thing. This thing can be represented by the cluster:

[employee/supervisor, employee/department, person/job]   [3]

The meaning of one of the functional dependencies within cluster [3] may be specified by the clause group:

employee/supervisor(x, y) ← person/job(x, 'manager'),
        person/job(y, 'general manager')
employee/supervisor(x, y) ← person/job(x, 'worker'),
        employee/department(x, z),
        person/job(y, 'manager'), employee/department(y, z)

A first attempt at constructing the value set of cluster [3] could be as shown in Fig. 3.7. For the table shown in Fig. 3.7 it is *not* easy to construct a recognising function for the value set. A function may be specified that recognises the value set of cluster [3] displayed in a different way. Once again this is achieved

[person/cohabitant, person/address]

person/cohabitant		person/address		person/address	
name	name	name	house num	name	house num
Peter	Jane	Peter	12	Jane	12
Jane	Peter	Jane	12	Peter	12
Peter	Ray	Peter	12	Ray	12
Ray	Peter	Ray	12	Peter	12
Jane	Ray	Jane	12	Ray	12
Ray	Jane	Ray	12	Jane	12
Mary	Anne	Mary	14	Anne	14
Anne	Mary	Anne	14	Mary	14
John	Drew	John	9	Drew	9
Drew	John	Drew	9	John	9
Mark	Diane	Mark	8	Diane	8
Diane	Mark	Diane	8	Mark	8

Fig. 3.6   Value set of [person/cohabitant, person/address]

by introducing multiple occurrences of the component predicates. Consider the function:

$(q, r, s, t, u, v, w, x, y, z) \in$ Value set of
    [employee/supervisor, employee/department, person/job]
if and only if
        $(q, r) \in$ Value set of employee/supervisor
$\land$ $(s, t) \in$ Value set of person/job
$\land$ $(u, v) \in$ Value set of person/job
$\land$ $(w, x) \in$ Value set of employee/department
$\land$ $(y, z) \in$ Value set of employee/department
$\land$ $((q = s) \land (t = $ 'manager'$) \land (v = $ 'gen mngr'$) \land$
           $(w,x,y,z$ <u>are</u> $\perp) \to (r = u))$
$\lor$ $((q = s) \land (q = w) \land (r = y) \land (x = z) \land$
           $(t = $ 'worker'$) \land (v = $ 'manager'$) \to (r = u))$

This function recognises the instances in the table shown in Fig. 3.8. So if the table shown in Fig. 3.8 is considered to be the value set of cluster [3] then the value set of cluster [3] has a simple recognising function. In this value set the set of tuples associated with both person/job and employee/department are incomplete as they have tuples missing. In the first three rows the values of the tuples in employee/department are the "null value". A *null value*, written $\perp$, means that that value of a tuple in a particular component is irrelevant to the value set as a whole.   The tuples in the second occurrence of both person/job and employee/department are repetitive. In Sect. 3.3 items are defined formally. This definition includes a specification of item semantics. The specification of an

[employee/supervisor, employee/department, person/job]

employee/supervisor		employee/department		person/job	
person-name	person-name	person-name	dept-name	person-name	job-descrip
Peter	Jane	Peter	'dispatch'	Jane	'gen mngr'
Ray	Peter	Ray	'dispatch'	Peter	'manager'
Paul	Peter	Paul	'dispatch'	Ray	'worker'
Richard	Peter	Richard	'dispatch'	Paul	'worker'
Janet	Jane	Janet	'packing'	Richard	'worker'
Anne	Janet	Anne	'packing'	Janet	'manager'
Mary	Janet	Mary	'packing'	Anne	'worker'
Drew	Janet	Drew	'packing'	Mary	'worker'
John	Janet	John	'packing'	Drew	'worker'
Diane	Jane	Diane	'office'	John	'worker'
Mark	Diane	Mark	'office'	Diane	'manager'
				Mark	'worker'

Fig. 3.7 Labels for [employee/supervisor, employee/department, person/job]

item's semantics is based on the idea of recognising the contents of that item's value set. The examples above demonstrate that this involves value sets that contain multiple occurrences of the cluster's components, value sets that are incomplete and repetitive, and value sets that may contain the null value $\perp$.

In Sect. 3.3 the structure of items is described. Items provide the foundation of a unified approach to conceptual modelling used by the unified design methodology. This unified design methodology is based on the belief that the data, information and knowledge things should all be modelled in a completely homogeneous way, and should all be treated in a completely homogeneous way during the design process. The work reported here is based on the belief that this unified design methodology is preferable to any non-unified methodology such as the particular non-unified methodology described in Chap. 2. This belief is despite the fact that the system may be eventually implemented as:

• a relational data base component, and
• a knowledge base component.

The thesis here is that a unified treatment of the design process is justified despite the fact that the design may be implemented as a "non-unified implementation".

[employee/supervisor, employee/department,					
employee/supervisor		person/job		person/job	
person-name	person-name	person-name	job-descrip	person-name	job-descrip
Peter	Jane	Peter	'manager'	Jane	'gen mngr'
Janet	Jane	Janet	'manager'	Jane	'gen mngr'
Diane	Jane	Diane	'manager'	Jane	'gen mngr'
Ray	Peter	Ray	'worker'	Peter	'manager'
Paul	Peter	Paul	'worker'	Peter	'manager'
Richard	Peter	Richard	'worker'	Peter	'manager'
Anne	Janet	Anne	'worker'	Janet	'manager'
Mary	Janet	Mary	'worker'	Janet	'manager'
Drew	Janet	Drew	'worker'	Janet	'manager'
John	Janet	John	'worker'	Janet	'manager'
Mark	Diane	Mark	'worker'	Diane	'manager'

Fig. 3.8   Value set of [employee/supervisor, employee/department, person/job]

3.3 Item structure

In this section items are described. The language of the λ-calculus is used to describe the notions on which the unified representation is based. Two useful functions are introduced. Given a set of labels P, the function ":" is defined to mean:

$$x:P \begin{cases} = x & \textit{if } x \text{ is in P} \\ \text{is 'undefined'} & \textit{otherwise} \end{cases}$$

The ":" function is used frequently in situations where A is a name-population and x is a label name. For example, #1234:part-number has value #1234 if 1234 is a valid part number. Another function, namely the "is-a" function is closely related to the ":" function. Given an expression E, the "is-a" function is defined to mean:

$$\text{is-a[Ex]} \begin{cases} = \textbf{T} & \textit{if } Ex = x \\ = \textbf{F} & \textit{otherwise} \end{cases}$$

If $E = \lambda x \bullet x:P \bullet$ then $Ex = x:P$ and the definition of "is-a" becomes:

person/job]

employee/department		employee/department	
person-name	dept-name	person-name	dept-name
$\perp$	$\perp$	$\perp$	$\perp$
$\perp$	$\perp$	$\perp$	$\perp$
$\perp$	$\perp$	$\perp$	$\perp$
Ray	'dispatch'	Peter	'dispatch'
Paul	'dispatch'	Peter	'dispatch'
Richard	'dispatch'	Peter	'dispatch'
Anne	'packing'	Janet	'packing'
Mary	'packing'	Janet	'packing'
Drew	'packing'	Janet	'packing'
John	'packing'	Janet	'packing'
Mark	'office'	Diane	'office'

where the two 'person/job' columns correspond to (s, t) and (u, v) in the function

$$\text{is-a}[x{:}P] \begin{cases} = \mathbf{T} & \textit{if } x \text{ is in } P \\ = \mathbf{F} & \textit{otherwise} \end{cases}$$

The first type of predicate is an n-argument, first-order predicate that is "essentially" an m-argument predicate where $m \leq n$. Given an n-argument predicate E, E is *essentially* an m argument predicate if m is the least integer such that there exists an m-argument predicate F with:

$$(\forall x_1)...(\forall x_n)[\ E(x_1,...,x_n) \leftrightarrow F(y_1,...,y_m)\ ]$$

where $(\forall i)(\exists j)(y_i = x_j)$. If the predicate $P(x,y,z)$ means "$y < z$" then P is essentially a two-argument predicate.

The second type of predicate is "separable" predicates. Given a predicate J of the form:

$$J(y_1^1,...,y_{m_1}^1,y_1^2,...,y_{m_2}^2,...........,y_1^n,...,y_{m_n}^n)$$

Define the set $\{Y_1, Y_2,..., Y_n\}$ by $Y_i = \{y_1^i,...,y_{m_i}^i\}$. If J can be written in the form:

$$J_1 \wedge J_2 \wedge ... \wedge J_m$$

where each J_i is a predicate in terms of the set of variables X_i with:

$X_i \subset Y_1 \cup Y_2 \cup ... \cup Y_n$, and

for each X_i ($\exists j$) such that X_i does *not* contain any of the variables in Y_j

then predicate J is *separable* into the partition $\{X_1, X_2,..., X_m\}$. Given the predicate $J(y_1^1, y_2^1, y_1^2, y_2^2, y_1^3, y_2^3)$ that means:

$$(y_2^2 = y_1^1 + y_2^1) \wedge (y_2^3 > y_1^3)$$

J is separable into the partition $\{ \{y_1^1, y_2^1, y_1^2, y_2^2\}, \{y_1^3, y_2^3\} \}$ by:

$$J_1(y_1^1, y_2^1, y_1^2, y_2^2) \wedge J_2(y_1^3, y_2^3)$$

where $J_1(y_1^1, y_2^1, y_1^2, y_2^2)$ means $(y_2^2 = y_1^1 + y_2^1)$ and $J_2(y_1^3, y_2^3)$ means $(y_2^3 > y_1^3)$

The notion of an "item" is first introduced informally. "Items" are named triples, and consist of four parts:

- a unique name
- item semantics,
- item value constraints and
- item set constraints.

The item *name* is a unique letter string that, by convention, is written in italic script. The item *semantics* is an expression that defines the meaning of that item by recognising the contents of that item's "value set". Recognising functions are described informally in Sect. 3.2. The item value constraints is an expression that is satisfied by the members of that item's value set. The item set constraints is an expression constructed from the primitives "Card", "Uni" and "Can" that represents structural constraints on that item's value set. An item with name A, item semantics S_A, item value constraints V_A and item set constraints C_A is written as the named triple $A(S_A, V_A, C_A)$, or as the name A.

Formally, given a unique name A, an n-tuple $(m_1, m_2,..., m_n)$,

$$M = \sum_{i=1}^{n} m_i , \text{ such that:}$$

- S_A is an M-argument λ-calculus expression of the form:

$$\lambda y_1^1 ... y_{m_1}^1 ... y_{m_n}^n \bullet [S_{A_1}(y_1^1,...,y_{m_1}^1)$$
$$\wedge \ S_{A_2}(y_1^2,...,y_{m_2}^2) \wedge \ .... \wedge \ S_{A_n}(y_1^n,...,y_{m_n}^n)$$
$$\wedge \ J(y_1^1...y_{m_1}^1...y_{m_n}^n)] \bullet$$

where $\{A_1,...,A_n\}$ is an ordered set of not necessarily distinct item names, each item whose name is in this set is called a *component* of item A, and J is not a separable predicate;

- V_A is an M-argument λ-calculus expression of the form:

$$\lambda y_1^1 ... y_{m_1}^1 ... y_{m_n}^n \bullet [V_{A_1}(y_1^1,...,y_{m_1}^1)$$
$$\wedge \ V_{A_2}(y_1^2,...,y_{m_2}^2) \wedge \ .... \wedge \ V_{A_n}(y_1^n,...,y_{m_n}^n)$$
$$\wedge \ K(y_1^1...y_{m_1}^1...y_{m_n}^n)] \bullet$$

where $\{A_1,...,A_n\}$ are the names of the components of item A, K is essentially an m-argument predicate where $\min(M,2) \leq m \leq M$;

- and expression C_A is an expression of the form:

$$C_{A_1} \wedge C_{A_2} \wedge ... \wedge C_{A_n} \wedge (L)_A$$

where C_{A_i} is the set constraints of the component whose name is A_i and L is a logical combination of:

- Card lies in some numerical range;
- $Uni(A_i)$ for some i, $1 \leq i \leq n$; and
- $Can(A_i, X)$ for some i, $1 \leq i \leq n$, where X is a non-empty subset of $\{A_1,...,A_n\} - \{A_i\}$;

subscripted with the name of the item A,

then the named triple:

$$A[S_A, V_A, C_A]$$

is an n-adic *item* with *item name* A, S_A is the *item semantics* of A, V_A is the *item value constraints* of A and C_A is the *item set constraints* of A.

The item semantics S_A defines the meaning of item A. If item A represents an association then S_A defines that association. If S_A describes an implicit association then A is an *information item*, if S_A describes an explicit association then A

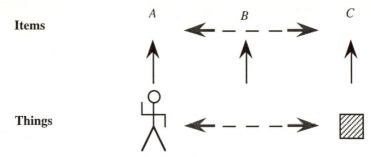

Fig. 3.9 The complete model assumption

is a *knowledge item*, and if S_A describes no association at all then A is a *data item*. If S_A represents an association between two or more things then the items that represent those two or more things are components of A.

The *Complete Model Assumption* states that *if* the conceptual model contains an item that represents an association between two or more things *then* there exist items in the conceptual model that represent those two or more things. The complete model assumption is illustrated in Fig. 3.9. In Fig. 3.9 item B represents an association between two things. This association could be between a person and their address. In this example, item A represents "person" and item C represents "address". Items A and C are components of item B. The complete model assumption requires that *if* item B is in the conceptual model of an application *then* items A and C are in that model as well.

The item semantics of an item is a recognising function for the value set of that item. Some examples of item semantics are discussed. The semantics of the data item named "*part*" could be:

$\lambda x \bullet [\text{is-a}[x:\text{part-number}]] \bullet$

This expression recognises the labels related to the name-population "part-number". The semantics of the information item named "*part/cost-price*" could be:

$\lambda xy \bullet [\text{ is-a}[x:\text{part-number}] \wedge \text{is-a}[y:\text{dollar-amount}] \wedge \text{costs}(x, y)] \bullet$

that may be written more conveniently as:

$\lambda xy \bullet [\text{ costs}(x:\text{part-number}, y:\text{dollar-amount})] \bullet$

This expression recognises the tuples of the relation "part/cost-price" that has domains "part-number" and "dollar amount". The semantics of the knowledge item named "*[part/sale-price, part/cost-price, mark-up]*" could be:

$\lambda x_1 x_2 y_1 y_2 z \bullet [$ sells-for$(x_1$:part-number, x_2:dollar-amount$)$

$\quad \wedge$ costs$(y_1$:part-number, y_2:dollar-amount$)$

$\quad \wedge$ is-a$[z$:mark-up-factor$]$

$\quad \wedge ((x_1 = y_1) \rightarrow (x_2 = z \times y_2))] \bullet$

This expression recognises the instances of the cluster [part/sale-price, part/cost-price, mark-up] as described in Sect. 3.2. This cluster represents a knowledge thing that associates the relations "part/cost-price" and "part/sale-price" with the population "mark-up". In Chap. 2 the meaning of this knowledge thing is defined using three single-clause clause-groups.

The "value set" of an item is the set of labels that are recognised by the item semantics of that item. Given any particular item, its value set may change in time. Given an item A the *value set* of A at time τ is denoted by $\gamma^\tau(A)$. Consider the item:

$$A[S_A, V_A, C_A]$$

the condition that an element belongs to the value set of A at time τ is S_A as applied at time τ. For a data item, if $S_A = \lambda x \bullet [$is-a$[x$:P$]] \bullet$ then the condition that a label belongs to the value set of A at time τ is:

$$\lambda x \bullet [\text{is-a}[x{:}P]] \bullet = \lambda x \bullet [x{:}P = x] \bullet$$

Associated with a data item there are those labels that "belong to" that item's name-population at the time that the evaluation is performed. Consider the n-adic information item:

$$A[S_A, V_A, C_A] =$$
$$A[\lambda x_1 x_2 ... x_n \bullet [R(x_1{:}P_1, x_2{:}P_2, ..., x_n{:}P_n)] \bullet, V_A, C_A]$$

the condition that a tuple belongs to the value set of A at time τ is:

$$S_A = \lambda x_1 x_2 ... x_n \bullet [R(x_1{:}P_1, x_2{:}P_2, ..., x_n{:}P_n)] \bullet$$

Associated with an information item there are the tuples that "belong to" that item's relation at the time that the evaluation is performed. This relation has domains $(P_1, P_2,..., P_n)$.

Consider the value sets of knowledge items. Consider the knowledge item *[part/sale-price, part/cost-price, mark-up]* whose semantics is given above. The value set of this item is shown in Fig. 3.10. The components of this item are *part/sale-price, part/cost-price* and *mark-up*. These components each occur once in the value set. In Sect. 3.2 it is shown that not all knowledge items have a value

[part/sale-price, part/cost-price, mark-up]

part/sale-price		part/cost-price		mark-up
part-number	dollar-amount	part-number	dollar-amount	factor
1234	1.48	1234	1.23	1.2
2468	2.81	2468	2.34	1.2
3579	4.14	3579	3.45	1.2
8642	5.47	8642	4.56	1.2
7531	6.80	7531	5.67	1.2
1470	8.14	1470	6.78	1.2

Fig. 3.10 Labels in the value set of a knowledge item

set in which each component of that item occurs once. Consider the knowledge thing whose meaning is defined by the recursive clause group:

$$P(w,x) \leftarrow P(y,z), \ P(u,v), \ Q(w,y,u), \ R(x,z,v), \ x > 5$$
$$P(w,x) \leftarrow Q(w,x,x), \ x \leq 5$$

The semantics of any item that represents this knowledge thing will employ multiple occurrences of the component P. The value set of any such item will not be represented by a table that contains one occurrence of each of its components P, Q and R. The value sets of some knowledge items may be expressed in terms of one occurrence of each item component and some may not.

Suppose that a knowledge item A has n distinct components:

$$A_1[\ S_1, \ V_1, \ C_1 \ ]$$
$$A_2[\ S_2, \ V_2, \ C_2 \ ]$$
$$\ldots \ldots \ldots \ldots \ldots$$
$$A_n[\ S_n, \ V_n, \ C_n \ ]$$

where the i'th component A_i is an m_i-adic item. Item A is said to have *elementary semantics* if its semantics S_A:

$$\lambda y_1^1 \ldots y_{m_1}^1 \ldots y_{m_n}^n \bullet [S_{A_1}(y_1^1,\ldots,y_{m_1}^1)$$
$$\wedge \ S_{A_2}(y_1^2,\ldots,y_{m_2}^2) \wedge \ldots\ldots \wedge \ S_{A_n}(y_1^n,\ldots,y_{m_n}^n)$$
$$\wedge \ J(y_1^1 \ldots y_{m_1}^1 \ldots y_{m_n}^n)] \bullet$$

has the property that each component occurs once and only once in S_A. If the knowledge item:

[part/sale-price, part/cost-price, mark-up]

has semantics:

$$\lambda x_1 x_2 y_1 y_2 z \bullet [\text{ sells-for}(x_1\text{:part-number, } x_2\text{:dollar-amount})$$
$$\wedge \text{ costs}(y_1\text{:part-number,} y_2\text{:dollar-amount})$$
$$\wedge \text{ is-a}[z\text{:mark-up-factor}])$$
$$\wedge ((x_1 = y_1) \rightarrow (x_2 = z \times y_2))] \bullet$$

then this knowledge item has elementary semantics. This knowledge item has elementary semantics because each component occurs once only in its item semantics. The three components of this knowledge item are the two information items and the data item:

part/cost-price[$\lambda xy \bullet [\text{costs}(x\text{:part-number, } y\text{:dollar-amount})] \bullet$, V_1, C_1]
part/sale-price[$\lambda xy \bullet [\text{sells-for}(x\text{:part-number, } y\text{:dollar-amount})] \bullet$, V_2, C_2]
mark-up[$\lambda x \bullet [x\text{:mark-up-factor}] \bullet$, V_3, C_3]

This knowledge item's semantics can be written as:

$$\lambda x_1 x_2 y_1 y_2 z \bullet [S_{part/sale-price}(x_1, x_2) \wedge S_{part/cost-price}(y_1, y_2)$$
$$\wedge S_{mark-up}(z) \wedge ((x_1 = y_1) \rightarrow (x_2 = z \times y_2))] \bullet$$

In general the components of a data item are other data items, the components of an information item are data items, and the components of a knowledge item are either data items or information items. All data and information items can be defined as items with elementary semantics. Hence the components of any data, information or knowledge item is assumed to be an item with elementary semantics.

Given two items A and B, where the semantics of both of these items are expressed in terms of n variables. If π is permutation such that:

$$(\forall x_1 x_2 ... x_n)[S_A(x_1, x_2, ..., x_n) \leftarrow S_B(\pi(x_1, x_2, ..., x_n))]$$

then item B is a *sub-item* of item A. If item B is a sub-item of item A then at any time τ the (possibly permuted) value set of item B will be a subset of the value set of item A. That is:

$$(\forall \tau) [\pi(\gamma^\tau(B)) \subset \gamma^\tau(A)]$$

This notion of a "sub-item" is a generalisation of the traditional notion of a "sub-type" in conventional data analysis. If data item A is a sub-item of data item B then A is a *sub-type* of B. For consistency, the terms sub-type and sub-item are used interchangeably for data items.

Given a knowledge item whose item semantics is:

$$\lambda x_1 x_2 y_1 y_2 z \bullet [\ S_{part/sale-price}(x_1, x_2) \wedge S_{part/cost-price}(y_1, y_2)$$
$$\wedge\ S_{mark-up}(z) \wedge (((x_1 \leq 1\,999) \wedge (x_1 = y_1)) \rightarrow (x_2 = z \times y_2))\ ]\bullet$$

This knowledge item is a sub-item of the item *[part/sale-price, part/cost-price, mark-up]* discussed above.

The item *value constraints* of item *A* is an expression that constrains the values that may belong to that item's value set. The value constraints of an item are expressed in terms of the value constraints of that item's component items. In the data item *part* considered above, the constraint that "part-numbers must be greater than 1 000 and less than 9 999" can be expressed as:

$$\lambda x \bullet [\ 1\,000 < x < 9\,999\ ]\bullet$$

In the information item *part/cost-price* considered above, the constraint that "for things whose identifier lies between 1 000 and 1 999 the cost of that thing lies between 0 and 300 units" can be expressed as:

$$\lambda xy \bullet [\ V_{part}(x) \wedge V_{cost-price}(y) \wedge$$
$$((1000 < x < 1\,999) \rightarrow (0 < y \leq 300))\ ]\bullet$$

This expression may be expanded to:

$$\lambda xy \bullet [\ (1\,000 < x < 9\,999) \wedge (0 < y) \wedge$$
$$((1\,000 < x < 1\,999) \rightarrow (0 < y \leq 300))\ ]\bullet$$

In the knowledge item *[part/sale-price, part/cost-price, mark-up]* considered above, the constraint that "labels in the second domain associated with the first argument are greater than the corresponding labels associated with the second domain of the second argument" can be expressed as:

$$\lambda x_1 x_2 y_1 y_2 z \bullet [\ V_{part/sale-price}(x_1, x_2) \wedge V_{part/cost-price}(y_1, y_2) \wedge$$
$$V_{mark-up}(z) \wedge ((\ x_1 = y_1\ ) \rightarrow (\ x_2 > y_2\ ))]\bullet$$

This expression may be expanded to:

$$\lambda x_1 x_2 y_1 y_2 z \bullet [\ (1\,000 < x_1 < 9\,999) \wedge (1 < x_2) \wedge$$
$$(1\,000 < y_1 < 9\,999) \wedge (0 < y_2) \wedge$$
$$((y_1 < 1\,999) \rightarrow (y_2 \leq 300)) \wedge (0 < z < 3) \wedge$$
$$((\ x_1 = y_1\ ) \rightarrow (\ x_2 > y_2\ ))\ ]\bullet$$

Examples of item value constraints for data, information and knowledge items are given above.

The item *set constraints* of item A is an expression that represents structural constraints on that item. In this presentation, an item's set constraints consists of a logical combination of the three primitives "Card", "Uni" and "Can" only. Other primitives may be introduced but are not described here. The terms in the item set constraints are subscripted with the name of the component to which that constraint applies. Suppose that component B is an item that in turn has components $\{D_1, D_2,..., D_n\}$. If these three primitives are subscripted with the item name B then the meaning of these three primitives is:

- Card means "the number of labels in the value set of component B". The item set constraints may contain an arithmetic expression involving "Card".
- Uni(D_i) means that component named D_i is a "universal component". A *universal component* is a component with the property that in the value set of B every permissible member of the value set of its component D_i must occur.
- Can(D_i, X) where X is a non-empty subset of:

$$\{D_1, D_2,..., D_n\} - \{D_i\}$$

means that the set of components X is a "candidate" for the component D_i.

Given a component, a *candidate* is minimal sets of (other) components such that in the value set of B the members of the value sets of X functionally determine the members of the value set of D_i.

The constraints "Uni" and "Comp" introduced above may be expressed in first-order logic. Uni(D_i) may be expressed as:

$$(\forall y_1^i ... y_{m_i}^i)[S_{D_i}(y_1^i,...,y_{m_i}^i) \rightarrow$$
$$[(\exists y_1^1,...,y_{m_1}^1)...(Ey_1^i,...,y_{m_i}^i)...(\exists y_1^n,...,y_{m_n}^n)$$
$$S_A(y_1^1,...,y_{m_1}^1,...,y_{m_n}^n)]]$$

where:

$$(\exists y_1^1,...,y_{m_1}^1)...(Ey_1^i,...,y_{m_i}^i)...(\exists y_1^n,...,y_{m_n}^n)$$

denotes the string $(\exists y_1^1,...,y_{m_1}^1)...(\exists y_1^n,...,y_{m_n}^n)$ *excluding* $(\exists y_1^i,...,y_{m_i}^i)$. The constraint Can($D_i$, X) may be expressed as:

$$(\forall x_1^1 \ldots x_{m_1}^1 \ldots x_{m_n}^n)(\forall y_1^1 \ldots y_{m_1}^1 \ldots y_{m_n}^n)[$$
$$[\ S_A(x_1^1,\ldots,x_{m_1}^1,\ldots,x_{m_n}^n) \wedge S_A(y_1^1,\ldots,y_{m_1}^1,\ldots,y_{m_n}^n)$$
$$\wedge\ (\bigwedge_{j\in F} \bigwedge_{k=1}^{m_j} x_k^j = y_k^j\ )\ ] \rightarrow \bigwedge_{k=1}^{m_i} x_k^i = y_k^i\ ]$$

where F is such that $X = \{\ D_j : j\in F\ \}$. The item set constraints of an item are structural constraints on the value set of that item. In the data item *part* considered above, the constraint that "there are no more than 100 part numbers" can be expressed as:

$(\text{Card} \leq 100)_{part}$

In the information item *part/cost-price* considered above, the constraint that in its value set "all labels associated with the first argument must be in this association, and any label associated with the second argument corresponds to at most one label associated with the first argument" can be expressed as:

$C_{part} \wedge C_{cost\text{-}price} \wedge (\text{Uni}(part) \wedge \text{Can}(cost\text{-}price, \{part\}))_{part/cost\text{-}price}$

Given expressions for C_{part} and $C_{cost\text{-}price}$ this may be expanded to:

$(\text{Card} \leq 100)_{part} \wedge (\text{Uni}(part) \wedge \text{Can}(cost\text{-}price, \{part\}))_{part/cost\text{-}price}$

In the knowledge item *[part/cost-price, part/sale-price, mark-up]* considered above, the constraint on the value set that "all tuples associated with the first and second argument must be in this relationship, and a set of arguments for each pair of components is sufficient to determine the arguments of the third" can be expressed as:

$C_{part/sale\text{-}price} \wedge C_{part/cost\text{-}price} \wedge C_{mark\text{-}up} \wedge$
$(\text{Uni}(part/sale\text{-}price) \wedge \text{Uni}(part/cost\text{-}price)$
    $\wedge \text{Can}(part/sale\text{-}price, \{part/cost\text{-}price, mark\text{-}up\})$
    $\wedge \text{Can}(part/cost\text{-}price, \{part/sale\text{-}price, mark\text{-}up\})$
    $\wedge \text{Can}(mark\text{-}up, \{part/sale\text{-}price, part/cost\text{-}price\})$
    $)_{[part/sale\text{-}price, part/cost\text{-}price, mark\text{-}up]}$

Given expressions for the set constraints of the components this may be expanded to:

(Uni(*part*) ∧ Can(*sale-price*, {*part*}))*part/sale-price* ∧
  (Uni(*part*) ∧ Can(*cost-price*, {*part*}))*part/cost-price* ∧
  (Card ≤ 100)*part* ∧
(Uni(*part/sale-price*) ∧ Uni(*part/cost-price*)
  ∧ Can(*part/sale-price*, {*part/cost-price*, *mark-up*})
  ∧ Can(*part/cost-price*, {*part/sale-price*, *mark-up*})
  ∧ Can(*mark-up*, {*part/sale-price*, *part/cost-price*})
)*[part/sale-price, part/cost-price, mark-up]*

The above examples illustrate the construction of item set constraints for data items, information items and knowledge items.

There are a number of different senses in which two items can be considered to be "equal". Two of these senses of "item equality" are described now. Given two items $A[\ S_A,\ V_A,\ C_A\ ]$ and $B[\ S_B,\ V_B,\ C_B\ ]$ A and B are *identical*, written $A \equiv B$, if S_A, S_B, V_A and V_B are all n argument λ-calculus expressions such that:

$$(\forall x_1 x_2 ... x_n)[S_A(x_1,x_2,...,x_n) \leftrightarrow S_B(x_1,x_2,...,x_n)]$$
$$(\forall x_1 x_2 ... x_n)[V_A(x_1,x_2,...,x_n) \leftrightarrow V_B(x_1,x_2,...,x_n)]$$
$$C_A \leftrightarrow C_B$$

A and B are *equal*, written $A = B$, if S_A and S_B are both n argument λ-calculus expressions such that:

$$(\forall x_1 x_2 ... x_n)[S_A(x_1,x_2,...,x_n) \leftrightarrow S_B(x_1,x_2,...,x_n)]$$

If two items are either identical or equal then they will not necessarily have the same name.

The basic structure of data items, information items and knowledge items is the same. Items provide the basis for a unified representation for the conceptual model of knowledge-based systems.

3.4 Data items

The "universal data item" is a representation of the universal data thing whose value set is the universe of discourse. The *universal data item* is a data item with item name U and is defined by:

$U[\ \lambda x \bullet x : U \bullet,\ \lambda x \bullet \mathbf{T} \bullet,\ \emptyset\ ]$

where "U" is the "universe of discourse" and **T** is the constant "true" expression. U is a data item whose item semantics is $\lambda x \bullet x : U \bullet$. Every label in the universe of discourse U is in the value set of U. The universal data item U has no item value constraints and has no item set constraints.

The "null data item" is a representation of the null data thing whose value set is always empty. The *null data item* is a data item with item name Λ and is defined by:

$$\Lambda[\ \lambda x \bullet x : \Lambda \bullet,\ \lambda x \bullet \mathbf{T} \bullet,\ \emptyset\ ]$$

where "Λ" is the "null universe" and **T** is the constant "true" expression. Λ is an item whose item semantics is $\lambda x \bullet x : \Lambda \bullet$. The value set of Λ is the empty set. The null data item Λ has no item value constraints and no item set constraints.

In general an item:

$$A[\ S_A,\ V_A,\ C_A]$$

is a data item if its semantics S_A does not represent an association.

The *semantics* of a data item is an expression that recognises the set of labels in the value set of that item at any time. The value set of a data item is a representation of the set of labels that are associated with the identifying name-population of the thing-population that implements that data item. The semantics of the data item *part* is the λ-calculus expression:

$$\lambda x \bullet [\text{is-a}[x : \text{part-number}]] \bullet$$

The semantics of the data item *"part"* is a λ-calculus expression that recognises valid part numbers. The set of valid part numbers could at present be the set of labels shown in Fig. 3.2.

The *data constraints* of a data item consist of the "value constraints" and the "set constraints". The *value constraints* of a data item are constraints on the values of the individual labels that are in the value set of that data item. A value constraint is represented by a λ-calculus expression that should be "true" when applied to any label in the value set. For example,

$$\lambda x \bullet [1\,000 < x < 9\,999)\ ] \bullet$$

could be a value constraint on the *"part"* data item whose value set is as shown in Fig. 3.2.

The *set constraints* of a data item are constraints on the whole value set of that item. The requirement "there are no more than 100 different parts" can be represented as:

$$(\text{Card} \leq 100)_{part}$$

and could be a set constraint on the data item named *part*.

The item *part* could be:

part[λx•[is-a[x:part-number]]•, λx•[(1 000 < x < 9 999)]•, (Card $\leq$ 100)$_{part}$]

Consider also the item:

boat-part[λx•[is-a[x:part-number] $\wedge$ x $\leq$ 999]•,
    λx•[(1 000 < x < 9 999)]•, (Card $\leq$ 100)$_{part}$]

The data item *boat-part* is a sub-item, or sub-type, of the data item *part* because:

$\gamma^\tau(boat\text{-}part) \subset \gamma^\tau(part)$

More examples of data items are:

price[λx•[is-a[x:dollar-amount]]•, λx•[0 $\leq$ x]•, $\emptyset$]
cost-price[λx•[is-a[x:dollar-amount]]•, λx•[0 < x]•, $\emptyset$]
sale-price[λx•[is-a[x:dollar-amount]]•, λx•[0 < x]•, $\emptyset$]
tax[λx•[is-a[x:dollar-amount]]•, λx•[0 $\leq$ x]•, $\emptyset$]
mark-up[λx•[is-a[x:mark-up-factor]]•, λx•[0 < x < 3]•, $\emptyset$]
machine[λx•[is-a[x:machine-name]]•, λx•[x = AB $\vee$ x = CD]•,
    (Card $\geq$ 2)$_{machine}$]
type[λx•[is-a[x:type-description]]•, λx•[x = lathe $\vee$ x = press]•,
    (Card $\geq$ 2)$_{type}$]
employee[λx•[is-a[x:employee-id]]•, λx•[100 < x $\leq$ 499]•,
    (Card $\geq$ 10)$_{employee}$]
MD[λx•[is-a[x:MD-id]]•, λx•[100 < x $\leq$ 499]•, (Card = 1)$_{MD}$]

where *MD* stands for "Managing Director".

A *compound data item* is a data item that may be constructed from a set of *component data items* in the following way. Given a set of n (component) data items:

$A_1[S_1, V_1, C_1]$
$A_2[S_2, V_2, C_2]$
. . . .
$A_n[S_n, V_n, C_n]$

where each A_i is an m_i-adic component data item, and $M = \sum\limits_{i=1}^{n} m_i$. Then the

item with item name:

part_machine
part-number_machine-number
1234_AB
2468_AB
3579_AB
1234_CD
2468_CD
3579_CD

part
part-number
1234
2468
3579

machine
machine-number
AB
CD

Fig. 3.11 A compound data item and its component data items

$(A_1\_A_2\_\cdots\_A_n)$

item semantics the M-argument expression:

$$\lambda y_1^1 \dots y_{m_1}^1 \dots y_{m_n}^n \bullet [S_{A_1}(y_1^1,\dots,y_{m_1}^1)$$
$$\wedge\ S_{A_2}(y_1^2,\dots,y_{m_2}^2)\ \wedge\ \dots\dots\dots\ \wedge\ S_{A_n}(y_1^n,\dots,y_{m_n}^n)]\bullet$$

and item value constraints:

$$\lambda y_1^1 \dots y_{m_1}^1 \dots y_{m_n}^n \bullet [V_{A_1}(y_1^1,\dots,y_{m_1}^1)$$
$$\wedge\ V_{A_2}(y_1^2,\dots,y_{m_2}^2)\ \wedge\ \dots\dots\dots\ \wedge\ V_{A_n}(y_1^n,\dots,y_{m_n}^n)]\bullet$$

and item set constraints:

$$C_{A_1} \wedge C_{A_2} \wedge \dots \wedge C_{A_n} \wedge$$
$$(\text{Uni}(A_1) \wedge \dots \wedge \text{Uni}(A_n))_A$$

is a compound data item. Consider the compound data item:

part_machine[$\lambda xy \bullet$[is-a[x:part-number] $\wedge$ is-a[y:machine-name]]$\bullet$,
    $\lambda xy \bullet$[$(1\,000 < x < 9\,999) \wedge (y = AB \vee y = CD)$]$\bullet$,
    $(\text{Uni}(part) \wedge \text{Uni}(machine))_{part\_machine} \wedge$
        $(\text{Card} \leq 100)_{part} \wedge (\text{Card} \geq 2)_{machine}$)]

The value set of this compound data item is shown in Fig. 3.11 together with the value sets of its two component data items. If a data item is not a compound data item then it is a *simple data item*.

    At any particular time, the value set of a compound data item is the Cartesian product of the value sets of its component data items taken in sequence. The labels in the value set of a compound data item are customarily denoted by a sequence of component label names each separated by an underscore. See Fig. 3.11. In that example the compound data item "*part_machine*" has the two component data items, namely "*part*" and "*machine*". The compound name-population "part-number_machine-number" has two component name-populations, namely "part-number" and "machine-number". The compound labels in the value set of *part_machine* are the Cartesian product of pairs of labels from the value sets of the two items *part* and *machine*.

3.5 Information items

An item:

$$A[\ S_A,\ V_A,\ C_A\ ]$$

is an information item if its semantics, S_A, represents an implicit association.

The *semantics* of an information item is a λ-calculus expression that recognises the members of the value set of that information item at any time. As information items represent *implicit* associations the semantics of information items cannot therefore be defined succinctly as a computable expression in some formal language. The semantics of an information item is a λ-calculus expression that includes a predicate that recognises the implicit association. The meaning of that predicate is defined informally. That predicate will be "true" when its arguments are tuples that are in the value set of that information item. The members of the value set of an information item will, in general, change in time, but the "meaning" of the information item may well remain constant. If the information item "*part/cost-price*" has components "*part*" and "*cost-price*" then the semantics of this information item could be the expression:

$$\lambda xy \bullet [\ S_{part}(x) \wedge S_{cost\text{-}price}(y) \wedge costs(x,\ y)\ ] \bullet$$

or:

$$\lambda xy \bullet [\ costs(x\text{:part-number},\ y\text{:dollar-amount})\ ] \bullet$$

where the predicate "costs(x, y)" means "x costs y". The predicate "costs" may have value "true" for the set of tuples shown in Fig. 3.12.

The *information constraints* of an information item consist of the "value constraints" and the "set constraints". The *value constraints* are constraints on the values of the members of the value set of that information item. A value constraint may be specified by defining a predicate that is "true" for all the members of the value set. For example:

part/sale-price	
part	sale-price
part-number	dollar-amount
1234	1.72
2468	3.74
3579	3.28
8642	6.38
7531	9.07
1470	9.49

Fig. 3.12 An information item, its components and value set

$$\lambda xy\bullet[\ V_{part}(x) \wedge V_{cost\text{-}price}(y) \wedge ((x < 1\,999) \to (y \le 300))\ ]\bullet$$

or:

$$\lambda xy\bullet[\ (1\,000 < x < 9\,999) \wedge (0 < y) \wedge ((x < 1\,999) \to (y \le 300))\ ]\bullet$$

could be a value constraint in the "*part/cost-price*" information item. An information item inherits the value constraints of its component data items. In the
expression above the sub-expression:

$$\lambda xy\bullet[\ (1\,000 < x < 9\,999) \wedge (0 < y)\ ]\bullet$$

is inherited from that item's components.

The *set constraints* are structural constraints on the value set of the information
item. The following are set constraints:

- the identification of the "universal components". A *universal component* is a
  component with which every permissible value must be associated. For
  example, every valid part-number might be required to be a member of the
  value set of the *part* component shown in Fig. 3.12 and *part* is a universal
  component of *part/cost-price*.
- the identification of the set of "candidates" for each component. Given a
  component, a *candidate* is minimal sets of (other) components such that the
  labels associated with those (other) candidate components functionally determine the labels associated with the given component. For example, consider
  the item *part/cost-price* shown in Fig. 3.12. The component *part* has no
  candidates and the component *cost-price* has one candidate set that contains the
  single component {*part*}.

The set constraints of the item *part/cost-price* could be:

$$C_{part} \wedge C_{cost\text{-}price} \wedge (Uni(part) \wedge Can(cost\text{-}price, \{part\}))_{part/cost\text{-}price}$$

or:

$(\text{Card} \le 100)_{part} \wedge (\text{Uni}(part) \wedge \text{Can}(\textit{cost-price}, \{part\}))_{part/cost-price}$

The item set constraints inherit the set constraints of the component items.
The information item *part/cost-price* could be:

part/cost-price[$\lambda xy \bullet$[$S_{part}(x) \wedge S_{cost-price}(y) \wedge \text{costs}(x, y)$]•,
    $\lambda xy \bullet$[$V_{part}(x) \wedge V_{cost-price}(y) \wedge ((x < 1\,999) \to (y \le 300))$]•,
    $C_{part} \wedge C_{cost-price} \wedge$
            $(\text{Uni}(part) \wedge \text{Can}(\textit{cost-price}, \{part\})_{part/cost-price}$]

or:

part/cost-price[$\lambda xy \bullet$[costs(x:part-number, y:dollar-amount)]•,
    $\lambda xy \bullet$[$(1\,000 < x < 9\,999) \wedge (0 < y) \wedge ((x < 1\,999) \to (y \le 300))$]•,
    $(\text{Uni}(part) \wedge \text{Can}(\textit{cost-price}, \{part\}))_{part/cost-price} \wedge (\text{Card} \le 100)_{part}$]

The *inverse of an item* can be useful when constructing a conceptual model.
The inverse of the item *part/cost-price* is the *cost-price/part-list* item. The value
set of the *cost-price/part-list* item contains the list of all part numbers corresponding to a given cost price. The inverse of the *part/cost-price* item could be:

cost-price/part-list[$\lambda xy \bullet$[list-costs(x:dollar-amount, y:part-number-list)]•,
    $\lambda xy \bullet$[**T**]•,
    $(\text{Can}(\textit{part-list}, \{\textit{cost-price}\}))_{cost-price/part-list}$]

A "sub-item" is defined in Sect. 3.3. Given two items *A* and *B*, where the
semantics of both of these items are expressed in terms of n variables, if π is
permutation such that:

$$(\forall x_1 x_2 ... x_n)[S_A(x_1,x_2,...,x_n) \leftarrow S_B(\pi(x_1,x_2,...,x_n))]$$

then item *B* is a *sub-item* of item *A*. In Sect. 3.4 an example of a sub-item
relationship between data items is given. Consider the two information items:

employee/department[$\lambda x_1 x_2 \bullet$[works-in(x_1:person-id, x_2:dept-desc)]•,
    $\lambda x_1 x_2 \bullet$[$(1 < x_1 < 100)$]•,
    $(\text{Uni}(employee) \wedge \text{Can}(department, \{employee\}))_{/employee/department}$
        $\wedge (\text{Card} \le 50)_{employee}$]

manager/department[$\lambda x_1 x_2$•[manages(x_1:person-id, x_2:dept-desc)]•,
$\lambda x_1 x_2$•[$(1 < x_1 < 100)$]•,
(Uni(*manager*) $\wedge$ Can(*department*, {*manager*}))/*manager/department*
$\wedge$ (Card ≤ 10)*manager*]

If each manager of a department "works in" that department then:

$$(\forall x_1 x_2)[S_{employee/department}(x_1,x_2) \leftarrow S_{manager/department}(x_1,x_2)]$$

and the *manager/department* item is a sub-item of *employee/department*.
Other information items are:

part/sale-price[λxy•[sells-for(x:part-number, y:dollar-amount)]•,
λxy•[$(1\,000 < x < 9\,999)$]•,
(Uni(*part*) $\wedge$ Can(*sale-price*, {*part*}))*part/sale-price* $\wedge$
(Card ≤ 100)*part*]
machine/type[λxy•[has-type(x:machine-name, y:type-description)]•,
λxy•[$(x = AB \vee x = CD)$ $\wedge$ $(y = lathe \vee y = press)$]•,
(Uni(*machine*) $\wedge$ Can(*type*, {*machine*}))*machine/type* $\wedge$
(Card ≥ 2)*machine* $\wedge$ (Card $= 2$)*type*]
person/cohabitant[$\lambda x_1 x_2$•[lives-with(x_1:person-id, x_2:person-id)]•,
$\lambda x_1 x_2$•[$((1 < x_1 < 1\,000) \wedge (1 < x_2 < 1\,000)$]•,
(Card ≤ 500)*person*]
person/address[$\lambda x_1 x_2$•[has-address(x_1:person-id, x_2:address-desc)]•,
$\lambda x_1 x_2$•[$(1 < x_1 < 1\,000)$]•,
(Uni(*person*) $\wedge$ Can(*address*, {*person*}))*person/address* $\wedge$
(Card ≤ 500)*person*]
employee/responsible-to[
$\lambda x_1 x_2$•[is-responsible-to(x_1:employee-id, x_2:employee-id)]•,
$\lambda x_1 x_2$•[$((1 < x_1 < 1\,000) \wedge (1 < x_2 < 1\,000)$]•,
(Can(*responsible-to*, {*employee*}))*employee/responsible-to* $\wedge$
(Card ≤ 500)*employee*]
employee/supervisor[$\lambda x_1 x_2$•[has-supervisor(x_1:employee-id,
x_2:employee-id)]•,
$\lambda x_1 x_2$•[$((1 < x_1 < 1\,000) \wedge (1 < x_2 < 1\,000)$]•,
(Can(*supervisor*, {*employee*}))*employee/supervisor* $\wedge$
(Card ≤ 500)*employee*]

3.6 Knowledge items

An item:

$$A[\ S_A,\ V_A,\ C_A\ ]$$

is a knowledge item if its semantics, S_A, represents an explicit association.

The *semantics* of a knowledge item is a λ-calculus expression that recognises the members of the value set of that knowledge item at any time. As knowledge items represent *explicit* associations the semantics of knowledge items can usually be defined succinctly as a computable expression in some formal language. In general, the members of the value set of a knowledge item will change in time, but the "meaning" of the knowledge item may remain constant. The expression:

$$\lambda w_1 w_2 x_1 x_2 y_1 y_2 z_1 z_2 \bullet [\ S_{part/sale\text{-}price}(w_1, w_2) \wedge S_{part/cost\text{-}price}(x_1, x_2) \wedge$$
$$S_{part/type}(y_1, y_2) \wedge S_{type/mark\text{-}up}(z_1, z_2) \wedge$$
$$(((\ w_1 = x_1 = y_1\ ) \wedge (\ y_2 = z_1\ )) \rightarrow (x_2 = z_2 \times y_2))\ ]\bullet$$

or:

$$\lambda w_1 w_2 x_1 x_2 y_1 y_2 z_1 z_2 \bullet [\ \text{sells-for}(w_1:\text{part-number}, w_2:\text{dollar-amount})$$
$$\wedge\ \text{costs}(x_1:\text{part-number}, x_2:\text{dollar-amount})$$
$$\wedge\ \text{has-type}(y_1:\text{part-number}, y_2:\text{type-description})$$
$$\wedge\ \text{factor-of}(z_1:\text{type-description}, z_2:\text{mark-up-factor}) \wedge$$
$$(((\ w_1 = x_1 = y_1\ ) \wedge (\ y_2 = z_1\ )) \rightarrow (w_2 = z_2 \times x_2))\ ]\bullet$$

could be the semantics of the item that represents the cluster:

[part/sale-price, part/cost-price, part/type, type/mark-up]

and whose value set could be as shown in Fig. 3.13.

The *knowledge constraints* of a knowledge item consist of the "value constraints" and the "set constraints". The *value constraints* are constraints on the members of the value set of that knowledge item. A value constraint may be specified by defining an expression that is "true" for all the members of the value set. For example,

$$\lambda w_1 w_2 x_1 x_2 y_1 y_2 z_1 z_2 \bullet [\ V_{part/sale\text{-}price}(w_1, w_2) \wedge V_{part/cost\text{-}price}(x_1, x_2) \wedge$$
$$V_{part/type}(y_1, y_2) \wedge V_{type/mark\text{-}up}(z_1, z_2) \wedge$$
$$(\ w_1 = x_1\ ) \rightarrow (\ w_2 > x_2\ )]\bullet$$

[part/sale-price, part/cost-price, part/type, type/mark-up]

part/sale-price		part/cost-price		part/type		type/mark-up	
part-number	dollar-amount	part-number	dollar-amount	part-number	type-descrip	type-descrip	mark-up-factor
1234	1.72	1234	1.23	1234	car	car	1.4
2468	3.74	2468	2.34	2468	bike	bike	1.6
3579	3.28	3579	3.45	3579	car	car	1.4
8642	6.38	8642	4.56	8642	car	car	1.4
7531	9.07	7531	5.67	7531	bike	bike	1.6
1470	9.49	1470	6.78	1470	car	car	1.4

Fig. 3.13 A knowledge item, its components and value set

or:

$$\lambda w_1 w_2 x_1 x_2 y_1 y_2 z_1 z_2 \bullet [\ (1\,000 < w_1 < 9\,999) \wedge (1 < w_2) \wedge$$
$$(1\,000 < x_1 < 9\,999) \wedge (0 < x_2) \wedge$$
$$((x_1 < 1\,999) \rightarrow (x_2 \leq 300)) \wedge$$
$$(1\,000 < y_1 < 9\,999) \wedge (y_2 = \text{lathe} \vee y_2 = \text{press}) \wedge$$
$$(z_1 = \text{lathe} \vee z_1 = \text{press}) \wedge (0 < z_2 < 3) \wedge$$
$$(w_1 = x_1) \rightarrow (w_2 > x_2)\ ] \bullet$$

could be a value constraint on the knowledge item *[part/sale-price, part/cost-price, part/type, type/mark-up]*.

The *set constraints* of an item are structural constraints on the whole value set of that item. Given the knowledge item:

[part/sale-price, part/cost-price, part/type, type/mark-up]

the notation Uni(*part/cost-price*) means that *part/cost-price* is a universal component, and

Can(*part/sale-price*, {*part/cost-price, part/type, type/mark-up*})

means that the set of components {*part/cost-price, part/type, type/mark-up*} is a candidate for the component "*part/sale-price*".

The following is a knowledge item:

[part/sale-price, part/cost-price, part/type, type/mark-up][
$\lambda w_1 w_2 x_1 x_2 y_1 y_2 z_1 z_2 \bullet [$ $S_{part/sale-price}(w_1, w_2) \wedge$
    $S_{part/cost-price}(x_1, x_2) \wedge S_{part/type}(y_1, y_2) \wedge$
    $S_{type/mark-up}(z_1, z_2) \wedge$
    $((w_1 = x_1 = y_1) \wedge (y_2 = z_1)) \rightarrow (x_2 = z_2 \times y_2))]\bullet,$
$\lambda w_1 w_2 x_1 x_2 y_1 y_2 z_1 z_2 \bullet [$ $V_{part/sale-price}(w_1, w_2) \wedge$
    $V_{part/cost-price}(x_1, x_2) \wedge$
    $V_{part/type}(y_1, y_2) \wedge V_{type/mark-up}(z_1, z_2) \wedge$
    $(w_1 = x_1) \rightarrow (w_2 > x_2)]\bullet,$
(Uni(*part/sale-price*) $\wedge$ Uni(*part/cost-price*) $\wedge$
Can(*part/sale-price*, {*part/cost-price, part/type, type/mark-up-factor*}) $\wedge$
Can(*part/cost-price*, {*part/sale-price, part/type, type/mark-up-factor*})

)*[part/sale-price, part/cost-price, part/type, type/mark-up-factor]* $\wedge$
$C_{part/sale-price} \wedge C_{part/cost-price} \wedge C_{part/type} \wedge$
$C_{type/mark-up-factor}$]

or:

[part/sale-price, part/cost-price, part/type, type/mark-up][
$\lambda w_1 w_2 x_1 x_2 y_1 y_2 z_1 z_2 \bullet [$ sells-for(w_1:part-number, w_2:dollar-amount)
    $\wedge$ costs(x_1:part-number, x_2:dollar-amount)
    $\wedge$ has-type(y_1:part-number, y_2:type-description)
    $\wedge$ factor-of(z_1:type-description, z_2:mark-up-factor)
    $\wedge ((w_1 = x_1 = y_1) \wedge (y_2 = z_1)) \rightarrow (w_2 = z_2 \times x_2))]\bullet,$
$\lambda w_1 w_2 x_1 x_2 y_1 y_2 z_1 z_2 \bullet [$ $(1\,000 < w_1 < 9\,999) \wedge (1 < w_2) \wedge$
    $(1\,000 < x_1 < 9\,999) \wedge (0 < x_2) \wedge$
    $((x_1 < 1\,999) \rightarrow (x_2 \leq 300)) \wedge$
    $(1\,000 < y_1 < 9\,999) \wedge (y_2 = \text{lathe} \vee y_2 = \text{press}) \wedge$
    $(z_1 = \text{lathe} \vee z_1 = \text{press}) \wedge (0 < z_2 < 3) \wedge$
    $(w_1 = x_1) \rightarrow (w_2 > x_2)]\bullet,$
(Uni(*part/sale-price*) $\wedge$ Uni(*part/cost-price*) $\wedge$
Can(*part/sale-price*,
    {*part/cost-price, part/type, type/mark-up-factor*}) $\wedge$
Can(*part/cost-price*,
    {*part/sale-price, part/type, type/mark-up-factor*})
)*[part/sale-price, part/cost-price, part/type,*
        type/mark-up-factor]
    $\wedge$

$(\text{Uni}(part) \wedge \text{Can}(sale\text{-}price, \{part\}))_{part/sale\text{-}price} \wedge$
　　$(\text{Card} \leq 100)_{part} \wedge$
$(\text{Uni}(part) \wedge \text{Can}(cost\text{-}price, \{part\}))_{part/cost\text{-}price} \wedge$
　　$(\text{Card} \leq 100)_{part} \wedge$
$(\text{Uni}(part) \wedge \text{Can}(type, \{part\}))_{part/type} \wedge$
　　$(\text{Card} \leq 100)_{part} \wedge (\text{Card} \geq 2)_{type} \wedge$
$(\text{Uni}(type) \wedge \text{Can}(mark\text{-}up\text{-}factor, \{type\}))_{type/mark\text{-}up\text{-}factor}$
　　$\wedge \ (\text{Card} \geq 2)_{type} \ ]$

The components and value set of this knowledge item are shown in Fig. 3.13.

The explicit association between "cost-price" and "sale-price" in an application where the sale price is the cost price marked up by a universal mark-up factor is a knowledge thing. This knowledge thing can be represented by the knowledge item:

$[part/sale\text{-}price, part/cost\text{-}price, mark\text{-}up][$
　$\lambda x_1 x_2 y_1 y_2 z \bullet [\ sells\text{-}for(x_1:part\text{-}number, x_2:dollar\text{-}amount)$

　　　$\wedge \ costs(y_1:part\text{-}number, y_2:dollar\text{-}amount)$

　　　$\wedge \ is\text{-}a[z:mark\text{-}up\text{-}factor]$

　　　$\wedge \ ((\ x_1 = y_1 \ ) \rightarrow (x_2 = z \times y_2)) \ ]\bullet,$
　$\lambda x_1 x_2 y_1 y_2 z \bullet [\ (1\,000 < x_1 < 9\,999) \wedge (1 < x_2) \wedge$
　　　$(1\,000 < y_1 < 9\,999) \wedge (0 < y_2) \wedge$
　　　$((y_1 < 1\,999) \rightarrow (y_2 \leq 300)) \wedge (0 < z < 3) \wedge$
　　　$((\ x_1 = y_1 \ ) \rightarrow (\ x_2 > y_2 \ )) \ ]\bullet,$
　$(\text{Uni}(part/sale\text{-}price) \wedge \text{Uni}(part/cost\text{-}price)$
　　　$\wedge \text{Can}(part/sale\text{-}price, \{part/cost\text{-}price, mark\text{-}up\})$
　　　$\wedge \text{Can}(part/cost\text{-}price, \{part/sale\text{-}price, mark\text{-}up\})$
　　　$\wedge \text{Can}(mark\text{-}up, \{part/sale\text{-}price, part/cost\text{-}price\})$
　　$)_{[part/sale\text{-}price, part/cost\text{-}price, mark\text{-}up]}$
　　　$\wedge \ (\text{Uni}(part) \wedge \text{Can}(sale\text{-}price, \{part\}))_{part/sale\text{-}price} \wedge$
　　　$(\text{Uni}(part) \wedge \text{Can}(cost\text{-}price, \{part\}))_{part/cost\text{-}price} \wedge$
　　　$(\text{Card} \leq 100)_{part} \ ]$

The value set of this knowledge item is shown in Fig. 3.10. The following knowledge item represents an association between the two information items *person/cohabitant* and *person/address*. These two information items are discussed in Sect. 3.5. This knowledge item represents the knowledge thing "if two different people cohabit then they have the same address".

[person/cohabitant, person/address][

$\lambda x_1 x_2 y_1 y_2 z_1 z_2 \bullet$[lives-with($x_1$:person-id, x_2:person-id)

   $\wedge$ has-address(y_1:person-id, y_2:address-desc)

   $\wedge$ has-address(z_1:person-id, z_2:address-desc)

   $\wedge$ (($x_1 = y_1$) $\wedge$ ($x_2 = z_1$) $\wedge$ ($x_1 \neq x_2$) $\wedge$ ($y_2 = z_2$))]$\bullet$,

$\lambda x_1 x_2 y_1 y_2 z_1 z_2 \bullet$[($1 < x_1 < 1\,000$) $\wedge$ ($1 < x_2 < 1\,000$) $\wedge$

   ($1 < y_1 < 1\,000$) $\wedge$ ($1 < z_1 < 1\,000$)]$\bullet$,

(Uni(*person/cohabitant*)

   $\wedge$ Can(*person/cohabitant*, {*person/address*})

)*[person/cohabitant, person/address]*

   $\wedge$ (Uni(*person*)

     $\wedge$ Can(*address*, {*person*}))$_{person/address}$

   $\wedge$ (Card $\leq$ 500)$_{person}$]

The following knowledge item represents an association between the data item *MD* and the two information items *person/responsible-to* and *person/supervisor*. These two information items are discussed in Sect. 3.5. The data item *MD* is discussed in Sect. 3.4. The knowledge item that follows represents the knowledge thing "if a person is supervised by the Managing Director then that person is responsible to the Managing Director, otherwise a person is responsible the same person whom their supervisor is responsible to". This rule is recursive.

[employee/responsible-to, employee/supervisor, MD][

$\lambda w_1 w_2 x_1 x_2 y_1 y_2 z \bullet$[responsible-to($w_1$:employee-id, w_2:employee-id)

   $\wedge$ has-supervisor(x_1:employee-id, x_2:employee-id)

   $\wedge$ responsible-to(y_1:employee-id, y_2:employee-id)

   $\wedge$ is-a[z:MD-id]

   $\wedge$ (((($w_1 = x_1$) $\wedge$ ($x_2 = z$) $\wedge$ (y_1, y_2 <u>are</u> $\perp$))

     $\rightarrow$ ($w_2 = z$))

    $\vee$ ((($w_1 = x_1$) $\wedge$ ($x_2 \neq z$) $\wedge$ ($x_2 = y_1$))

     $\rightarrow$ ($w_2 = y_2$)))]$\bullet$,

$\lambda w_1 w_2 x_1 x_2 y_1 y_2 z \bullet$[(($1 < w_1 < 1\,000$) $\wedge$ ($1 < w_2 < 1\,000$)

   $\wedge$ ($1 < x_1 < 1\,000$) $\wedge$ ($1 < x_2 < 1\,000$)

   $\wedge$ ($1 < y_1 < 1\,000$) $\wedge$ ($1 < y_2 < 1\,000$)

   $\wedge$ ($1 < z < 1\,000$))]$\bullet$,

(Uni(*employee/responsible-to*)

$\qquad$ ∧ Can(*employee/responsible-to*, {*employee/supervisor, MD*})

$\qquad$)*[employee/responsible-to, employee/supervisor, MD]*

$\qquad$ ∧ (Can(*supervisor*, {*employee*}))*employee/supervisor*

$\qquad$ ∧ (Can(*responsible-to*, {*employee*}))*employee/responsible-to*

$\qquad$ ∧ (Card ≤ 500)*employee*]

3.7 Algebra of items

Data items, information items and knowledge items are discussed in Sects. 3.4–3.6 respectively. In general an item has the form:

$A[S_A, V_A, C_A]$

where S_A is the *item semantics* of A, V_A is the *item value constraints* of A and C_A is the *item set constraints* of A. If S_A does not represent an association them A is a data item. If S_A represents an implicit association then A is an information item. If S_A represents an explicit association then A is a knowledge item.

All things may be represented by items. In a trivial sense, a thing associates with itself. Informally, if an item's semantics represents the identity association between one or more things then that item is "tautological". A *tautological item* is an item that has the property that the value set of that item has the form:

{ (x, x,...,x) : x ∈ E }

where E is the value set of any one of that item's components. Information and knowledge items represent associations between data or information things. An information item with semantics:

λxy•[equal(x:P, y:Q)]•

is tautological if the value sets of P and Q are equal and if "equal(x, y)" means "x and y are equal". The information item *"understudies"* is *not* tautological if its semantics is:

λxy•[understudies(x:employee-id,y:employee-id)]•

where "understudies(x, y)" means "that person x understudies the duties of person y".

$\qquad$ In this section an algebra of items is defined. In this algebra there are four relations and one operation. These relations are called "identical", "equal".

"equivalent" and "weakly equivalent". In Sect. 3.3 the definitions are given of "identical" items and "equal" items. Given two items $A[\,S_A,\,V_A,\,C_A]$ and $B[\,S_B,\,V_B,\,C_B]$ A and B are *identical*, written $A \equiv B$, if S_A, S_B, V_A and V_B are all n argument λ-calculus expressions such that:

$$(\forall x_1 x_2 ... x_n)[S_A(x_1,x_2,...,x_n) \leftrightarrow S_B(x_1,x_2,...,x_n)]$$
$$(\forall x_1 x_2 ... x_n)[V_A(x_1,x_2,...,x_n) \leftrightarrow V_B(x_1,x_2,...,x_n)]$$
$$C_A \leftrightarrow C_B$$

A and B are *equal*, written $A = B$, if S_A and S_B are both n argument λ-calculus expressions such that:

$$(\forall x_1 x_2 ... x_n)[S_A(x_1,x_2,...,x_n) \leftrightarrow S_B(x_1,x_2,...,x_n)]$$

Given two n-adic items with the same set of components that are not necessarily in the same order:

$A[\,S_A,\,V_A,\,C_A]$ and
$B[\,S_B,\,V_B,\,C_B]$

A and B are *equivalent*, written $A \simeq B$, if there exists a permutation π such that:

$$(\forall x_1 x_2 ... x_n)[S_A(x_1,x_2,...,x_n) \leftrightarrow S_B(\pi(x_1,x_2,...,x_n))]$$
$$(\forall x_1 x_2 ... x_n)[V_A(x_1,x_2,...,x_n) \leftrightarrow V_B(\pi(x_1,x_2,...,x_n))]$$
$$C_A \leftrightarrow C_B$$

where the x_i are the n_i variables associated with the i'th component of A. A and B are *weakly equivalent*, written $A \simeq_w B$, if there exists a permutation π such that:

$$(\forall x_1 x_2 ... x_n)[S_A(x_1,x_2,...,x_n) \leftrightarrow S_B(\pi(x_1,x_2,...,x_n))]$$

where the x_i are the n_i variables associated with the i'th component of A. If A is a sub-item of B and if B is a sub-item of A then items A and B are weakly equivalent.

The algebra of items contains one operation on items. This operation is "item join". Item join is thought of as a "horizontal" operation. The motivation behind the term "horizontal" is given in Chap. 4.

The definition of "item join" follows. Given two items:

$A[\,S_A,\,V_A,\,C_A\,]$ and
$B[\,S_B,\,V_B,\,C_B\,]$

Suppose that S_A has n variables, that is A is an n-adic item. Suppose that S_B has m variables, that is B is an m-adic item. Some of the components of A and B may be identical. Suppose that k pairs of components of A and B that are identical are identified, where $k \geq 0$. Let E be an ordered set of components where each is one of these identical pairs of components of both A and B. E may be empty. To ensure that the definition is well defined the order of the components in the set E is the same as order in which they occur as components of A. Suppose the semantics expressions of the components from item A (or item B) that are in the set E are expressed in terms of a total of p variables. Let $A*$ be an n-adic item that is identical to item A except for the order of its variables. The last p variables in $A*$ are those variables in A that belong to the components of A in the set E. Let $B*$ be an m-adic item that is identical to item B except for the order of its variables. The first p variables in $B*$ are those variables in B that belong to the components of B in the set E. Let π be a permutation that turns the ordered set of variables of $A*$ into the ordered set of variables of A. Let π' be a permutation that turns the ordered set of variables of $B*$ into the ordered set of variables of B. Suppose that 'x' is an (n - p)-tuple of free variables, 'y' is a p-tuple of free variables and 'z' is an (m - p)-tuple of free variables. Then the item with name $A \otimes_E B$ is the *join* of A and B on E and is defined to be the item:

$$(A \otimes_E B)[\ \lambda xyz \bullet [S_A(\pi(x,y)) \wedge S_B(\pi'(y,z))]\bullet,$$
$$\lambda xyz \bullet [V_A(\pi(x,y)) \wedge V_B(\pi'(y,z))]\bullet,$$
$$C_{A \otimes_E B}\ ]$$

where $C_{A \otimes_E B}$ is defined as follows. Suppose that C_A is an expression of the form $c_A \wedge G$ where c is that part of C_A that carries the subscript 'A' and G is that part of C_A that carries subscripts other than 'A'. Likewise suppose that C_B is an expression of the form $d_B \wedge H$. Then:

$$C_{A \otimes_E B} = (c \wedge d)_{A \otimes_E B} \wedge (G \wedge H)$$

The set E is *a* set of identical pairs of components of A and B. If E is the set of *all* identical pairs of components of A and B then $A \otimes_E B$ is written as $A \otimes B$.

If A and B are two information items, and if set E contains one component then $A \otimes_E B$ is the "join", in the conventional sense, of the relations related to A and B on the shared domain in the set E. Also, if A and B are two functional associations and if E contains a component that is both the domain of one of these functions and the range of the other then $A \otimes_E B$ is the functional composition of the two functions. The set E may be empty. If $E = \emptyset$ then $A \otimes_E B$ is the Cartesian product of A and B.

If two items A and B are such that for each component of A there exists an identical component of B and item B has at least one component that is not a component of item A, and $A \otimes_K B = B$, then the *component set* of item A is a proper subset of the component set of item B, written $A \subset B$. The join $A \otimes_E B$ is a *monotonic join* if $A \otimes_E B$ is *not* weakly equivalent with either A or B. If $A \otimes_E B$ is a monotonic join and the set E contains one component only of A and B then $A \otimes_E B$ is a *unit join*.

The following properties of $\otimes$ may be established:

- $A \otimes_K A = A$ where $K \subseteq K_A$ and K_A is the set of components of A
- $A \otimes_K B \simeq B \otimes_K A$ where $K \subseteq (K_A \cap K_B)$
- $A \otimes_K (B \otimes_L C) \simeq (A \otimes_K B) \otimes_L C$ where
  $$K \subseteq (K_A \cap K_B) \text{ and } L \subseteq (K_B \cap K_C)$$

If $A \otimes_K B = A$ then $K = K_B \subseteq K_A$.

Using the rule of composition $\otimes$, knowledge items, information items and data items may be combined with one another. The type of the composition of two items is shown in Fig. 3.14. Consider the compound data item:

part_machine[λxy•[is-a[x:part-number] $\wedge$ is-a[y:machine-name]]•,
$\quad$ λxy•[(1 000 < x < 9 999) $\wedge$ (y = AB $\vee$ y = CD)]•,
$\quad$ (Uni(*part*) $\wedge$ Uni(*machine*))$_{part\_machine}$ $\wedge$
$\quad\quad$ (Card $\leq$ 100)$_{part}$ $\wedge$ (Card $\geq$ 2)$_{machine}$)]

$\otimes$	data	information	knowledge
data	data	information	knowledge
information	information	information	information
knowledge	knowledge	information	knowledge

Fig. 3.14 The type of the item $A \otimes$

machine/type

machine-number	type-description
AB	lathe
CD	press

part_machine/type

part-number_ machine-number	type-description
1234_AB	lathe
2468_AB	lathe
3579_AB	lathe
1234_CD	press
2468_CD	press
3579_CD	press

Fig. 3.15 The machine/type and part_machine/type relations

and the information item:

machine/type[λxy•[has-type(x:machine-name, y:type-description)]•,
    λxy•[(x = AB ∨ x = CD) ∧ (y = lathe ∨ y = press)]•,
    (Uni(*machine*) ∧ Can(*type*, {*machine*}))$_{machine/type}$ ∧
        (Card ≥ 2)$_{machine}$ ∧ (Card = 2)$_{type}$]

These two items may be joined on the set {*machine*}to obtain the information item:

part_machine/type[λxyz•[is-a[x:part-number] ∧
        has-type(y:machine-name, z:type-description)]•,
    λxyz•[(1 000 < x < 9 999) ∧
        (y = AB ∨ y = CD) ∧   (z = lathe ∨ z = press)]•,
    (Uni(*part*) ∧ Uni(*machine*) ∧
        Can(*type*, {*machine*}))$_{part\_machine/type}$ ∧
        (Card ≤ 100)$_{part}$ ∧ (Card ≥ 2)$_{machine}$ ∧ (Card = 2)$_{type}$]

where the resulting item has the name "*part_machine/type*". In summary:

part_machine ⊗$_{\{machine\}}$ *machine/type* = *part_machine/type*

In terms of the non-unified representation described in Chap. 2, the compound population "part_machine" whose value set is shown in Fig. 3.11 has been joined with the relation "machine/type" shown in Fig. 3.15 on the domain "machine" to give the relation "part_machine/type".
    Recall the information item:

part/sale-price[λxy•[sells-for(x:part-number, y:dollar-amount)]•,
    λxy•[(1 000 < x < 9 999)]•,
    (Uni(part) ∧ Can(sale-price, {part}))$_{part/sale-price}$ ∧
        (Card ≤ 100)$_{part}$]

and consider the knowledge item:

[sale-price, sales-tax, tax-rate][
    λxyz•[is-a[x:dollar-amount] ∧ is-a[y:dollar-amount]
        ∧ is-a[z:factor] ∧ (y = x × z)]•,
    λxyz•[(1 < x) ∧ (x > y) ∧ (0 < z < 1)]•,

(Uni(*sale-price*) ∧ Uni(*sales-tax*) ∧ Uni(*tax-rate*)
   ∧ Can(*sale-price*, {*sales-tax, tax-rate*})
   ∧ Can(*sales-tax*, {*sale-price, tax-rate*})
   ∧ Can(*tax-rate*, {*sale-price, sales-tax*})
)*[sale-price, sales-tax, tax-rate]*]

This expression represents the rule that sales-tax is associated with any sale-price and is calculated at a fixed rate. These two items may be joined on the set {*sale-price*} to obtain the information item:

part/sale-price/sales-tax/tax-rate[
   λvxyz•[sells-for(v:part-number, x:dollar-amount) ∧
     is-a[y:dollar-amount] ∧ is-a[z:factor] ∧
     $(y = x \times z)$]•,
   λvxyz•[$(1\,000 < v < 9\,999)$ ∧ $(1 < x)$ ∧
     $(x > y)$ ∧ $(0 < z < 1)$]•,
   (Uni(part) ∧ Can(sale-price, {part})))*part/sale-price* ∧
     (Card ≤ 100)*part* ∧
     (Uni(*sale-price*) ∧ Uni(*sales-tax*) ∧ Uni(*tax-rate*)
     ∧ Can(*sale-price*, {*sales-tax, tax-rate*})
     ∧ Can(*sales-tax*, {*sale-price, tax-rate*})
     ∧ Can(*tax-rate*, {*sale-price, sales-tax*})
)*[sale-price, sales-tax, tax-rate]*]

where the resulting item has the name "*part/sale-price/sales-tax/tax-rate*". In summary:

part/sale-price ⊗{*sale-price*} *[sale-price, sales-tax, tax-rate]* =
part/sale-price/sales-tax/tax-rate

In terms of the non-unified representation described in Chap. 2, the relation "part/sale-price" has been joined with the cluster "[sale-price, sales-tax, tax-rate]" on the domain "sale-price" to give the relation "part/sale-price/sales-tax/tax-rate".

part/sale-price/sales-tax/tax-rate

part-number	dollar-amount	dollar-amount	factor
1234	1.20	0.06	0.05
2468	2.40	0.12	0.05
3579	3.40	0.17	0.05
8642	4.60	0.23	0.05
7531	5.60	0.28	0.05
1470	6.80	0.34	0.05

Fig. 3.16 Relation part/sale-price/sales-tax/tax-rate

A possible set of tuples for this relation are shown in Fig. 3.16.

An item A is *decomposable* into $D = \{A_1, A_2, .., A_n\}$ if

- A_i is not tautological for all i,
- $A = A_1 \otimes A_2 \otimes ... \otimes A_n$, where
- each join is monotonic

If further each join in the definition of the term "decomposable" is a unit join then the decomposition is a *unit decomposition*. The "part_machine/type" relation shown in Fig. 3.15 is decomposable. The "cost-price/tax/part" relation shown in Fig. 3.16 is decomposable.

If item A is decomposable then it does not necessarily have a unique decomposition. In Sect. 3.8 that the operations of item join and decomposition are used to build and decompose complex items. In Chap. 6 the concept of decomposition is used to provide the foundation for a theory of normalisation.

3.8 System items

In the definition of the join of two items A and B on the set E, E can be the empty set. Further *any* two items can be "joined" on the empty set. For example:

part/sale-price $\otimes_\emptyset$ *employee/address =*

  part/sale-price/employee/address

The *part/sale-price/employee/address* item is decomposable. This idea may be extended further. Consider a large collection of items that represents a whole elaborate knowledge-based system. If the items in this collection are joined, two at a time, using the item join operator on the empty set then the final result would be one complex item. Such an item is a *system item*. It represents an entire system. The business of joining a number of simple items together to obtain a complex item may seem rather pointless, but it shows how the notion of an item can be used to represent complex systems as well as the simple items that are given as examples in this chapter. Chapter 7 begins with the loose description of a single system item and describes a procedure that continually decomposes this item until it has been broken down into non-decomposable items.

3.9 Summary

- A unified representation can be defined by defining "meaning" in terms of recognising functions for value sets.
- Items can model all the things in an application in a homogeneous way no matter whether those things are data things, information things or knowledge things.
- An item is a named triple consisting of an item name, item semantics, item value constraints and item set constraints.
- All items, including knowledge items, contain two powerful classes of constraints.
- The algebra of items contains four relations "identical", "equal", "equivalent" and "weakly equivalent".
- The algebra of items contains one operation "join".
- Using the join operator, items of different types may be joined together to form other items.
- Item decomposition is defined in terms of item join.
- Items can represent either simple things or complex things such as a whole knowledge-based system.

4 Objects

4.1 Introduction

In Chap. 3 a unified representation for conceptual modelling was described in which data things, information things and knowledge things are all represented in the same way as "items". An *item* is a named triple consisting of a "name", "semantics", "value constraints" and "set constraints". At any particular time an item has a particular value set. Unification of the representation is achieved by defining the semantics of items as recognising functions for their value set.

This chapter extends the ideas introduced in Chap. 3 so that they can be applied to the construction of a unified model that may be readily maintained [Aakvik et al., 1991]. In Sect. 4.2 the limitations of items are discussed. Items are limited because they alone cannot support a complete investigation of maintenance. This limitation can be removed by the introduction of "objects". Objects are "item building operators". An object is an operator that when applied to a set of items generates another item. Objects are defined formally in Sect. 4.3. Sections 4.4–4.6 consider respectively data objects, information objects and knowledge objects. An algebra of objects, including two rules of composition for objects, is given in Sect. 4.7. One of these rules of composition, object join, enables data, information and knowledge objects to be joined with one another regardless of their type.

Practical notations for both items and objects are given in Chap. 5. Object join together with item join (described in Sect. 3.7) is applied in Chap. 6 to simplify the unified conceptual model.

4.2 Limitations of items

Items may be used as a formalism for unified representation. They have three properties. First, items have a homogeneous format no matter whether they represent data, information or knowledge things. Second, all items incorporate two powerful classes of constraints. Third, as is shown in Chap. 6, a single rule of "normalisation" can be specified for items. Despite these three properties, items, together with the notion of item decomposition introduced in Sect. 3.7, fail to provide an adequate basis for a complete investigation of maintenance. This limitation of items is described in this section.

Three examples follow that illustrate why items and item decomposition fail to provide an adequate basis for investigating maintenance. First consider the information item:

part/cost-price[λxy•[costs(x:part-number, y:dollar-amount)]•,

$\quad$ λxy•[(1 000 < x < 9 999) ∧ (0 < y) ∧ ((x < 1 999) → (y ≤ 300))]•,

$\quad$ (Uni(*part*) ∧ Can(*cost-price*, {*part*}))$_{part/cost-price}$ ∧ (Card ≤ 100)$_{part}$]

This item is described in Sect. 3.5. Suppose that the meaning of the predicate "costs" is defined by "costs(x, y)" means "x costs y". The semantics of this item associates parts with their cost price. Suppose that the cost prices are obtained in the form of a price list from the supplier of the parts. Further suppose that the supplier modifies that price list. Then the meaning of the predicate costs has been modified and the value set of the item *part/cost-price* will change. This modification is not a problem in itself, but consider also the information item:

machine/cost-price[λxy•[costs(x:machine-number, y:dollar-amount)]•,

$\quad$ λxy•[(0 < x < 99) ∧ (0 < y) ∧ ((x < 10) → (y ≤ 5 000))]•,

$\quad$ (Uni(*machine*) ∧

$\quad\quad$ Can(*cost-price*, {*machine*}))$_{machine/cost-price}$ ∧

$\quad\quad$ (Card ≤ 20)$_{machine}$]

The semantics of the item *machine/cost-price* is also expressed in terms of the predicate "costs". If the meaning of "costs" is also to be modified due to the adoption of a new price list for machines then the value set of the *machine/cost-price* item will also have to be modified. A modification to the value set of the item *part/cost-price* may require that the value set of the item *machine/cost-price* will have at least to be checked for correctness if the modification is to be implemented. The semantics of both items contains the "costs" predicate and therefore the semantics of these two items are linked. The decomposition of items introduced in Sect. 3.7 does not reveal this link as neither of these items are decomposable. In this chapter "objects" are introduced. Objects enable the link between the items *part/cost-price* and *machine/cost-price* to be readily identified.

For a second example that illustrates why items and item decomposition fail to provide an adequate basis for investigating maintenance consider the knowledge item:

[part/profit, part/cost-price, part/mark-up-factor][
    λuvwxyz•[profit-of(u:part-number, v:dollar-amount) ∧
        costs(w:part-number, x:dollar-amount) ∧
        mark-up(y:part-number, z:factor) ∧
        $((u = w) \wedge (u = y) \wedge (v = x \times (z - 1)))$]•, **T**, $\emptyset$]

and consider the knowledge item:

[part/sale-price, part/cost-price, part/mark-up-factor][
    λuvwxyz•[sells-for(u:part-number, v:dollar-amount) ∧
        costs(w:part-number, x:dollar-amount) ∧
        mark-up(y:part-number, z:factor) ∧
        $((u = w) \wedge (u = y) \wedge (v = x \times z))$]•, **T**, $\emptyset$]

The notion of "profit" relies on the notion of "sale price" so the semantics of the second item *[part/sale-price, part/cost-price, part/mark-up-factor]* is buried within the semantics of the first item *[part/profit, part/cost-price, part/mark-up-factor]*. If the semantics of the second of these two items is modified then the semantics of the first item should at least be checked for correctness. Neither of these two items are decomposable. So items and item decomposition do not permit a sufficiently penetrating analysis to identify this potential maintenance hazard. If the item *[part/profit, part/cost-price, part/mark-up-factor]* is re-expressed as:

[part/profit, part/cost-price, part/sale-price][
    λuvwxyz•[profit-of(u:part-number, v:dollar-amount) ∧
        costs(w:part-number, x:dollar-amount) ∧
        sells-for(y:part-number, z:dollar-amount) ∧
        $((u = w) \wedge (u = y) \wedge (v = z - x))$]•, **T**, $\emptyset$]

then the semantics of this item *[part/profit, part/cost-price, part/sale-price]* is independent of the semantics of the item *[part/sale-price, part/cost-price, part/mark-up-factor]*.

For a third example of why items and item decomposition fail to provide an adequate basis for investigating maintenance consider the information item *part/cost-price/sale-price* that is:

part/cost-price/sale-price[
    λxyz•[prices(x:part-number, y:dollar-amount, z:dollar-amount)]•,
    λxy•[$(1\,000 < x < 9\,999) \wedge (0 < y) \wedge (y < z)$]•,
    (Uni(*part*) ∧ Can(*cost-price*, {*part*})
        ∧ Can(*sale-price*, {*part*}))*part/cost-price/sale-price*
        $\wedge$ (Card $\leq$ 100)*part*]

and the knowledge item *[cost-price, sale-price, mark-up]* that represents the knowledge thing that "the sale price is the cost price marked up by a universal mark-up factor":

[cost-price, sale-price, mark-up][
    λxyz•[is-a[x:dollar-amount] ∧ is-a[y:dollar-amount]
            ∧ is-a[z:factor] ∧ (y = x × z)]•,
    λxy•[(0 < x) ∧ (x < y) ∧ (0 < z < 3)]•,
    (Can(*cost-price*, {*sale-price, mark-up*})
            ∧ Can(*sale-price*, {*cost-price, mark-up*}))*[cost-price, sale-price, mark-up]*
    ]

The information item *part/cost-price/sale-price* and the knowledge item *[cost-price, sale-price, mark-up]* both share wisdom in common in that both items represent in different ways the wisdom that "the sale price is the cost price marked up by a universal mark-up factor". If this chunk of shared wisdom is to change and is replaced by a new knowledge thing that is used to calculate the sale price of parts then both of these items should be modified.

The trouble with items is that they are built up from components. The component structure of the items given above prevents the fact that two items share a chunk of wisdom from being represented simply. The three examples above illustrate how the replication of chunks of wisdom may be the source of potential maintenance hazards. Those examples are simple. Replications of this kind are difficult to detect and can be a cause of problems during maintenance.

To address the maintenance problems caused by the replication of chunks of wisdom within items a more detailed representation than items is required. Objects provide such a detailed representation [Henderson-Sellers, 1992]. In Chap. 6 "objects" are shown to be sufficiently detailed to provide a complete analysis of this kind of maintenance problem. "Objects" are item building operators. Using the object **price-of** the information item *part/cost-price/sale-price* may be built as follows:

part/cost-price/sale-price = **price-of**(*part, cost-price, sale-price*)

and using the object **mark-up-rule** the knowledge item *[cost-price, sale-price, mark-up]* may be built as follows:

[cost-price, sale-price, mark-up] =
    mark-up-rule(*cost-price, sale-price, mark-up*)

The objects **price-of** and **mark-up-rule** do not contain a reference to any particular components. They represent the "essence" of these two associations. Objects enable the maintenance hazards inherent in the above items to be represented explicitly. Those maintenance hazards may be removed from these object operators before they are used to construct items.

An item contains embedded within it the full specification of its constituent components. Items contain more detail than objects. Complex items may be expressed as a sequence of object operators applied to simple items. To analyse the item *[part/sale-price, part/cost-price, mark-up]* consider:

[part/sale-price, part/cost-price, mark-up] =
  mark-up-rule*(part/sale-price, part/cost-price, mark-up) =*
  mark-up-rule*(**sells-for***(part, **sale-price***(price)),*
     *costs(part, **cost-price***(price)), mark-up)*

The knowledge item *[part/sale-price, part/cost-price, mark-up]* may be represented as the application of a knowledge object to a data item and two information objects each of which in turn are applied to two data items. Like items, objects are defined using a single framework in which no distinction is made between data, information and knowledge. Like items, objects are capable of representing value and set constraints in a homogeneous way.

4.3 Object structure

Objects are item building operators. They have four properties. They have a homogeneous format no matter whether they represent data, information or knowledge things. They incorporate two powerful classes of constraints. They enable items to be built in such a way as to inherit naturally the characteristics of their components. And a single rule of normalisation can be specified for objects. If an item is built with "normal" object operators then that item is "normal".

The formal definition of an object is similar to that of an item. Each object has an argument type. The *argument type* of an object is a specification of the "types" of argument that that object may operate on. An object of argument type $(\mathbf{D}^1, \mathbf{I}^2, \mathbf{I}^2)$ may operate on any 1-adic data item followed by any 2-adic information item followed by another 2-adic information item. Informally "objects" are named triples, and consist of four parts:

- a unique object name,
- object semantics,
- object value constraints and
- object set constraints.

The object *name* is a unique letter string that, by convention, is written in bold, italic script. The object *semantics* is an n-argument typed λ-calculus expression that represents an association between the arguments of that object. The object *value constraints* is an n-argument typed λ-calculus expression that is satisfied by the members of the value set of any item constructed by applying that object to a set of items. The object *set constraints* is an n-argument typed λ-calculus expression constructed from the three primitives "Card", "Uni" and "Can". The object set constraints are structural constraints on the value set of any item constructed by applying that object to a set of items. These three primitives are defined below. An object with name A, object semantics E, object value constraints F and object set constraints G is written as the named triple $A[E,F,G]$, or as the object A.

Objects are operators that turn one or more items into another item. A "data object" is an operator that creates a data item from one or more data items. An "information object" is an operator that creates an information item from two or more data items. A "knowledge object" is an operator that creates a knowledge item from two or more data or information items. Each object is an operator that turns n items into an item for some value of n. The specification of each object requires that the set of items to which that object may be applied are of a specific "type". The *type* of an m-adic item is determined both by whether it is a data item, an information item or a knowledge item and by the value of m. The *argument type* of an n-adic object is an n-tuple that specifies the types of the n items to which that object may be applied. Each of the n elements in an argument type are either "free" or "fixed". A *free argument type* is denoted by $\mathbf{X}^n$ and indicates that the object may be applied to any type of n-adic item. $\mathbf{X}^n$ specifies the arity of that item. If an object has the argument type $(\mathbf{X}^2, \mathbf{X}^2, \mathbf{X}^1)$ then it may be applied to any 2-adic item, followed by any other 2-adic item that is followed by any 1-adic item. A *fixed argument type* is denoted by $\mathbf{D}^n$ (standing for single "data" elements), $\mathbf{I}^n$ (standing for single "integer" elements), $\mathbf{Q}^n$ (standing for single "rational number" elements), $\mathbf{R}^n$ (standing for single "real number" elements), $\mathbf{L}^n$ (standing for "lists of data elements"), $\mathbf{I}^n$ (standing for "information") or $\mathbf{K}^n$ (standing for "knowledge"). A fixed argument type indicates that the object may be applied to an n-adic item of the nominated type. A fixed argument type specifies both the arity of each argument and the type of that argument. If an object has argument type $(\mathbf{I}^2, \mathbf{I}^2, \mathbf{D}^1)$ then it may be applied to any 2-adic information item, followed by any other 2-adic information item that is followed by any 1-adic data item.

In Sect. 3.3 the terms "essentially m-argument predicate" and a "separable predicate" are defined. Both of those terms are employed here. Formally, given a unique name A, a j-tuple $(i_1, i_2,..., i_j)$, j variables $(Q_1, Q_2,..., Q_j)$ of type $(X_1^{i_1}, X_2^{i_2},..., X_j^{i_j})$ respectively where each X_k represents a type such as $\mathbf{X}, \mathbf{D}, \mathbf{I}$ or $\mathbf{K}$, an n-tuple $(m_1, m_2,..., m_n)$, $n \geq j$, $M = \sum_{i=1}^{n} m_i$, n not necessarily distinct variables $(P_1, P_2,..., P_n)$ such that $(\forall x: 1 \leq x \leq n)(\exists y)(P_x = Q_y$ *and* $m_x = i_y)$:

- E is a j-argument typed λ-calculus expression of type $(X_1^{i_1}, X_2^{i_2},..., X_j^{i_j})$:

$$\lambda Q_1:X_1^{i_1}Q_2:X_2^{i_2}...Q_j:X_j^{i_j}\bullet\lambda y_1^1...y_{m_1}^1...y_{m_n}^n\bullet[S_{P_1}(y_1^1,...,y_{m_1}^1)$$
$$\wedge \ S_{P_2}(y_1^2,...,y_{m_2}^2) \ \wedge \ .... \ \wedge \ S_{P_n}(y_1^n,...,y_{m_n}^n)$$
$$\wedge \ J(y_1^1...y_{m_1}^1...y_{m_n}^n)]\bullet\bullet$$

where S_B is the semantics of item B, and J is *not* a "separable" predicate. S_B is a λ-calculus expression that recognises the members of the value set of item B as defined in Chap. 3.

- F is a j-argument typed λ-calculus expression of type $(X_1^{i_1}, X_2^{i_2},..., X_j^{i_j})$:

$$\lambda Q_1:X_1^{i_1}Q_2:X_2^{i_2}...Q_j:X_j^{i_j}\bullet\lambda y_1^1...y_{m_1}^1...y_{m_n}^n\bullet[V_{P_1}(y_1^1,...,y_{m_1}^1)$$
$$\wedge \ V_{P_2}(y_1^2,...,y_{m_2}^2) \ \wedge \ .... \ \wedge \ V_{P_n}(y_1^n,...,y_{m_n}^n)$$
$$\wedge \ K(y_1^1,...y_{m_1}^1...y_{m_n}^n)]\bullet\bullet$$

where V_B denotes the value constraints of item B, and K is essentially an m-argument predicate where $\min(M,2) \le m \le M$. V_B is a λ-calculus expression that is satisfied by the members of the value set of item B as defined in Chap. 3.

- G is a j-argument typed λ-calculus expression of type $(X_1^{i_1}, X_2^{i_2},..., X_j^{i_j})$:

$$\lambda Q_1:X_1^{i_1}Q_2:X_2^{i_2}...Q_j:X_j^{i_j}\bullet[C_{Q_1} \ \wedge \ .... \ \wedge \ C_{Q_j}$$
$$\wedge \ (L(Q_1,...,Q_j))_{\nu(A,Q_1,...,Q_j)}]\bullet$$

where C_B denotes the item set constraints of item B as defined in Chap. 3. $\nu(A,Q_1,...,Q_j)$ is the name of the item that results from the application of object A to items $\{Q_1,...,Q_j\}$. L consists of a logical combination of:

- Card lies in some numerical range;
- $Uni(Q_k)$ for some k, $1 \le k \le n$, and
- $Can(Q_k, X)$ for some k, $1 \le k \le j$, where X is a non-empty subset of
  $\{Q_1,Q_2,...,Q_j\} - \{Q_k\}$

then the named triple:

$A[E,F,G]$

is an n-adic *object* with *object name A*, of argument type $(X_1^{i_1}, X_2^{i_2},..., X_j^{i_j})$. E is the *object semantics* of *A*. F is the *object value constraints* of *A*. G is the *object set constraints* of *A*.

There are a number of different senses in which two objects can be considered to be "equal". Two of these senses of "object equality" are described now. Given two n-adic objects of identical argument type $(X^{m_1}, X^{m_2},..., X^{m_n})$ where each X is a type such as **X**, **K**, **I** or **D** (standing respectively for "free", "knowledge", "information" or "data"):

$A[\ E_A, F_A, G_A\ ]$ and
$B[\ E_B, F_B, G_B\ ]$

A and *B* are *identical*, written $A \equiv B$, if:

$$(\forall Q_1,Q_2,...,Q_j)[E_A(Q_1,Q_2,...,Q_j) \leftrightarrow E_B(Q_1,Q_2,...,Q_j)]$$
$$(\forall Q_1,Q_2,...,Q_j)[F_A(Q_1,Q_2,...,Q_j) \leftrightarrow F_B(Q_1,Q_2,...,Q_j)]$$
$$(\forall Q_1,Q_2,...,Q_j)[G_A(Q_1,Q_2,...,Q_j) \leftrightarrow G_B(Q_1,Q_2,...,Q_j)]$$

A and *B* are *equal*, written $A = B$, if:

$$(\forall Q_1,Q_2,...,Q_j)[E_A(Q_1,Q_2,...,Q_j) \leftrightarrow E_B(Q_1,Q_2,...,Q_j)]$$

If two objects are either identical or equal then they will not necessarily have the same name.

Objects are item building operators. The action of an object when applied to a set of items is described below. First examples of object semantics, value constraints and set constraints are given.

The object *semantics* is a typed expression that represents an association between the arguments of that object. The object semantics E_A describes the association, if any, between the set of items to which the object may be applied. If E_A describes an implicit association then object *A* is an *information object*. If E_A describes an explicit association then object *A* is a *knowledge object*. If E_A describes no association at all then object *A* is a *data object*. The *type* of an object is the type of any item that may be generated by applying that object to other items of valid argument type.

The data object *part* is an operator of argument type $(\mathbf{D}^1)$ that when applied to any data item generates another data item. The semantics of the data object *part* could be:

$$\lambda P{:}\mathbf{D}^1{\bullet}\lambda x{\bullet}[\ S_P(x) \wedge \text{with-part}(x)\ ]{\bullet\bullet}$$

where the predicate "with-part(x)" means "x is to do with parts". The information object *costs* is an operator of argument type $(\mathbf{D}^1, \mathbf{D}^1)$ that when applied to two data items generates an information item that represents the association that "one of the items costs the other item". The semantics of the information object *costs* could be:

$$\lambda P:\mathbf{D}^1 Q:\mathbf{D}^1 \bullet \lambda xy \bullet [S_P(x) \wedge S_Q(y) \wedge costs(x, y)] \bullet \bullet$$

The knowledge object *mark-up-1* is an operator of argument type $(\mathbf{I}^2, \mathbf{I}^2, \mathbf{D}^1)$ that when applied to two information items and a data item generates a knowledge item that represents the association that "one of the information items can be derived from the other information item by marking up their second domains by a mark-up factor determined by the label related to that data item". The semantics of the knowledge object *mark-up-1* could be:

$$\lambda P:\mathbf{I}^2 Q:\mathbf{I}^2 R:\mathbf{D}^1 \bullet \lambda x_1 x_2 y_1 y_2 z \bullet [\ S_P(x1, x2) \wedge S_Q(y1, y2) \wedge S_R(z) \wedge$$
$$((x_1 = y_1) \rightarrow (x_2 = z \times y_2))\ ] \bullet \bullet$$

The above examples illustrate the semantics for the three types of object. An object can have recursive semantics. The following object has recursive semantics:

$$\lambda P:\mathbf{I}^2 Q:\mathbf{I}^3 R:\mathbf{D}^1 \bullet \lambda x_1 x_2 y_1 y_2 z_1 z_2 z_3 \bullet [$$
$$(\ S_P(x1, x2) \wedge S_P(y1, y2) \wedge S_R(z1, z2, z3) \wedge$$
$$(x_2 = z_3) \wedge (y_1 = z_1) \wedge (x_1 = z_2) \wedge$$
$$(x_1 = 1 + y_1) \wedge (x_1 \geq 1)\ )\ \vee$$
$$(\ S_P(1, 0))] \bullet \bullet$$

The object *value constraints* is an n-argument typed λ-calculus expression that is satisfied by the members of the value set of any item constructed by applying that object to a set of items. The object value constraints is a statement of any constraints on the combined value sets of the argument items. In the data object *part* considered above, the constraint that "any number associated with parts is positive" can be expressed as:

$$\lambda P:\mathbf{D}^1 \bullet \lambda x \bullet [\ V_P(x) \wedge (x \geq 0)\ ] \bullet \bullet$$

In the information object *costs* considered above, the constraint that "for things whose identifier lies between 1 000 and 1 999 the cost of that thing is less than 300 units" can be expressed as:

$$\lambda P:\mathbf{D}^1 Q:\mathbf{D}^1 \bullet \lambda xy \bullet [\ V_P(x) \wedge V_Q(y) \wedge ((1\,000 < x < 1\,999) \rightarrow (y \leq 300))\ ] \bullet \bullet$$

In the knowledge object *mark-up-1* considered above, the constraint that "labels in the second domain related to the first argument are greater than the corresponding labels related with the second domain of the second argument" can be expressed as:

$$\lambda P{:}I^2Q{:}I^2R{:}D^1 \bullet \lambda x_1 x_2 y_1 y_2 z \bullet [\ V_P(x_1, x_2) \wedge V_Q(y_1, y_2) \wedge$$
$$V_R(z) \wedge ((\ x_1 = y_1\ ) \rightarrow (\ x_2 > y_2\ ))\ ]\bullet\bullet$$

The above examples illustrate object value constraints for the three types of object.

The object *set constraints* is an n-argument typed λ-calculus expression that represents structural constraints on the value set of any item constructed by applying that object to a set of items. The object set constraints is an expression of the form:

$$\lambda Q_1{:}X_1^{i_1} Q_2{:}X_2^{i_2}...Q_j{:}X_j^{i_j} \bullet [C_{Q_1} \wedge \ .... \wedge C_{Q_j}$$
$$\wedge\ (L(Q_1,...,Q_j))_{v\,(A,Q_1,...,Q_j)}]\bullet$$

where L is expressed in terms of the primitives "Card", "Uni" and "Can". The meaning of these primitives is defined as follows:

- Card means "the number of members of the value set of any item generated by that object". The object set constraints may contain an arithmetic expression involving "Card".
- $Uni(Q_k)$ that means that Q_k is a "universal argument". A *universal argument* is an argument that when instantiated becomes a component of the item generated so that every permissible member of its value set must be in the value set of that item.
- $Can(Q_k, X)$ where X is a non-empty subset of:

$$\{Q_1, Q_2,...,Q_j\} - \{Q_k\}$$

this expression means that the set of arguments X is a "candidate" for Q_k. Given an argument, a *candidate* is minimal sets of (other) arguments such that the labels in the value sets of those arguments when instantiated, functionally determine the labels in the value set of the given argument when instantiated.

The items to which an object is applied contain set constraints of their own. The object set constraints is a statement of any additional constraints on the structure of the value set of the item generated by the application of that object to a set of items. In the data object *part* considered above, the constraint that "any item to do with part has at least one label in its value set" can be expressed as:

$\lambda P : \mathbf{D}^1 \cdot [\ C_P \wedge (\text{Card} \geq 1)_{V \, (part, P)} \ ] \cdot$

In the information object *costs* considered above, the constraint that "all labels related to the first argument must be in this association, and any label related to the second argument corresponds to at most one label related to the first argument" can be expressed as:

$\lambda P : \mathbf{D}^1 Q : \mathbf{D}^1 \cdot [\ C_P \wedge C_Q \wedge (\text{Uni}(P) \wedge \text{Can}(Q, \{P\}))_{V \, (costs, P, Q)} \ ] \cdot$

In the knowledge object *mark-up-1* considered above, the constraint that "all tuples related to the first and second argument must be in this relationship, and each pair of arguments is sufficient to determine the third" can be expressed as:

$\lambda P : \mathbf{I}^2 Q : \mathbf{I}^2 R : \mathbf{D}^1 \cdot [\ C_P \wedge C_Q \wedge C_R \wedge (\ \text{Uni}(P) \wedge \text{Uni}(Q)$
$\wedge \ \text{Can}(P, \{Q, R\}) \wedge \text{Can}(Q, \{P, \ R\})$
$\wedge \ \text{Can}(R, \{P, \ Q\}))_{V \, (mark\text{-}up\text{-}1, P, Q, R)} \ ] \cdot$

The above examples illustrate object set constraints for the three types of object.

Objects are functions that operate on items. This operation is defined as follows. Given the j items:

$I_1 [\ S_{I_1}, \ V_{I_1}, \ C_{I_1} \ ]$
$I_2 [\ S_{I_2}, \ V_{I_2}, \ C_{I_2} \ ]$
$\cdot \cdot \cdot \cdot \cdot \cdot \cdot \cdot \cdot \cdot \cdot \cdot \cdot$
$I_j [\ S_{I_j}, \ V_{I_j}, \ C_{I_j} \ ]$

where $j > 0$, and each item is either a data item, and information item or a knowledge item. Suppose that each I_k is a m_k-adic item. Given an n-adic object A with argument type $(X_1^{i_1}, \ X_2^{i_2}, ..., \ X_k^{i_k})$ where each X_i are a type such as $\mathbf{X}$, $\mathbf{D}$, $\mathbf{I}$ or $\mathbf{K}$ (standing respectively for "free", "data", "information" or "knowledge"):

$A [\ E_A, \ F_A, \ G_A \ ]$

in this object E_A, and F_A are expressions in terms of both the variables $\lambda Q_1 Q_2 ... Q_j$ and $\lambda y_1^1 ... y_{m_1}^1 ... y_{m_n}^n$, and G_A is an expression in terms of the variables $\lambda Q_1 Q_2 ... Q_j$ then:

$A [\ E_A, \ F_A, \ G_A \ ] (I_1, I_2, ..., I_j)$

is an *item instance* of object A. This item instance of object A is defined as follows. Suppose that:

$$E_A = \lambda Q_1 : X_1^{i_1} Q_2 : X_2^{i_2} ... Q_j : X_j^{i_j} \bullet \lambda y_1^1 ... y_{m_1}^1 ... y_{m_n}^n \bullet [S_{P_1}(y_1^1,...,y_{m_1}^1)$$
$$\wedge \ S_{P_2}(y_1^2,...,y_{m_2}^2) \wedge .... \wedge S_{P_n}(y_1^n,...,y_{m_n}^n)$$
$$\wedge \ J(y_1^1 ... y_{m_1}^1 ... y_{m_n}^n)]\bullet\bullet$$

$$F_A = \lambda Q_1 : X_1^{i_1} Q_2 : X_2^{i_2} ... Q_j : X_j^{i_j} \bullet \lambda y_1^1 ... y_{m_1}^1 ... y_{m_n}^n \bullet [V_{P_1}(y_1^1,...,y_{m_1}^1)$$
$$\wedge \ V_{P_2}(y_1^2,...,y_{m_2}^2) \wedge .... \wedge V_{P_n}(y_1^n,...,y_{m_n}^n)$$
$$\wedge \ K(y_1^1,...y_{m_1}^1 ... y_{m_n}^n)]\bullet\bullet$$

$$G_A = \lambda Q_1 : X_1^{i_1} Q_2 : X_2^{i_2} ... Q_j : X_j^{i_j} \bullet [C_{Q_1} \wedge .... \wedge C_{Q_j}$$
$$\wedge \ (L(Q_1,...,Q_j))_{\nu (A,Q_1,...,Q_j)}]\bullet$$

Then the item instance of object A is the item with name $\nu (A, I_1, I_2,..., I_j)$ say:

$$A[E_A, F_A, G_A](I_1, I_2,..., I_j) =$$
$$\nu (A,I_1, I_2,..., I_j)[E_A(I_1, I_2,..., I_j),$$
$$F_A(I_1, I_2,..., I_j), G_A(I_1, I_2,..., I_j)]$$

Consider the 3-adic knowledge object *mark-up-1* with argument type (X^2, X^2, X^1):

mark-up-1$[\lambda P:X^2 Q:X^2 R:X^1 \bullet \lambda x_1 x_2 y_1 y_2 z \bullet [S_P(x1, x2)$
$$\wedge \ S_Q(y1, y2) \wedge S_R(z)$$
$$\wedge \ ((x_1 = y_1) \to (x_2 = z \times y_2))]\bullet\bullet,$$
$$\lambda P:X^2 Q:X^2 R:X^1 \bullet \lambda x_1 x_2 y_1 y_2 z \bullet [V_P(x_1,x_2) \wedge V_Q(y_1,y_2) \wedge V_R(z) \wedge$$
$$((x_1 = y_1) \to (x_2 > y_2))]\bullet\bullet,$$
$$\lambda P:X^2 Q:X^2 R:X^1 \bullet [C_P \wedge C_Q \wedge C_R \wedge (Uni(P) \wedge Uni(Q)$$
$$\wedge \ Can(P, \{Q, R\}) \wedge Can(Q, \{P, R\})$$
$$\wedge \ Can(R, \{P, Q\}))_{\nu (mark\text{-}up\text{-}1,P,Q,R)}]\bullet]$$

The following is an item instance of the object *mark-up-1*:

mark-up-1(*part/sale-price, part/cost-price, mark-up*)

giving this knowledge item the name *[part/sale-price, part/cost-price, mark-up]*:

mark-up-1(*part/sale-price, part/cost-price, mark-up*) =

[part/sale-price, part/cost-price, mark-up][

$\lambda P:\mathbf{X}^2 Q:\mathbf{X}^2 R:\mathbf{X}^1 \bullet \lambda x_1 x_2 y_1 y_2 z \bullet [\ S_P(x_1,x_2) \wedge S_Q(y_1,y_2) \wedge S_R(z)$

$\wedge\ ((\ x_1 = y_1\ ) \rightarrow (x_2 = z \times y_2))\ ]^{\bullet\bullet}$

(part/sale-price, part/cost-price, mark-up),

$\lambda P:\mathbf{X}^2 Q:\mathbf{X}^2 R:\mathbf{X}^1 \bullet \lambda x_1 x_2 y_1 y_2 z \bullet [\ V_P(x_1,x_2) \wedge V_Q(y_1,y_2) \wedge V_R(z)\ \wedge$

$((\ x_1 = y_1\ ) \rightarrow (\ x_2 > y_2\ ))\ ]^{\bullet\bullet}$

(part/sale-price, part/cost-price, mark-up),

$\lambda P:\mathbf{X}^2 Q:\mathbf{X}^2 R:\mathbf{X}^1 \bullet [C_P \wedge C_Q \wedge C_R \wedge (\mathrm{Uni}(P) \wedge \mathrm{Uni}(Q)$

$\wedge\ \mathrm{Can}(P,\ \{Q,\ R\}) \wedge \mathrm{Can}(Q,\ \{P,\ R\})$

$\wedge\ \mathrm{Can}(R,\ \{P,\ Q\}))_{\nu\,(\textbf{\textit{mark-up-1}},P,Q,R)}\ ]^{\bullet}$

(part/sale-price, part/cost-price, mark-up)] =

[part/sale-price, part/cost-price, mark-up][

$\lambda x_1 x_2 y_1 y_2 z \bullet [(\ \text{sells-for}(x_1:\text{part-number},\ x_2:\text{dollar-amount})$

$\wedge\ \text{costs}(y_1:\text{part-number},\ y_2:\text{dollar-amount})$

$\wedge\ \text{is-a}[z:\text{mark-up-factor}]\ )$

$\wedge\ ((\ x_1 = y_1\ ) \rightarrow (x_2 = z \times y_2))\ ]^{\bullet},$

$\lambda x_1 x_2 y_1 y_2 z \bullet [\ ((1\,000 < x_1 < 9\,999) \wedge (1 < x_2) \wedge$

$(1\,000 < y_1 < 9\,999) \wedge (0 < y_2) \wedge$

$((y_1 < 1\,999) \rightarrow (y_2 \leq 300)) \wedge (0 < z < 3) \wedge$

$((\ x_1 = y_1\ ) \rightarrow (\ x_2 > y_2\ ))]^{\bullet},$

$(\mathrm{Uni}(\textit{part/sale-price}) \wedge \mathrm{Uni}(\textit{part/cost-price})$

$\wedge\ \mathrm{Can}(\textit{part/sale-price},\ \{\textit{part/cost-price, mark-up}\})$

$\wedge\ \mathrm{Can}(\textit{part/cost-price},\ \{\textit{part/sale-price, mark-up}\})$

$\wedge\ \mathrm{Can}(\textit{mark-up},\ \{\textit{part/sale-price, part/cost-price}\})$

$)_{[\textit{part/sale-price, part/cost-price, mark-up}]}$

$\wedge\ (\mathrm{Uni}(\textit{part}) \wedge \mathrm{Can}(\textit{sale-price},\ \{\textit{part}\}))_{\textit{part/sale-price}}\ \wedge$

$(\mathrm{Uni}(\textit{part}) \wedge \mathrm{Can}(\textit{cost-price},\ \{\textit{part}\}))_{\textit{part/cost-price}}\ \wedge$

$(\mathrm{Card} \leq 100)_{\textit{part}}\ ]$

In Chap. 3 it is noted that the basic structure of data items, information items and knowledge items is the same. Items can provide the basis for a unified approach to conceptual modelling of knowledge-based systems. This property is also shared by objects. In addition, objects have the further property that they provide a structured view in the sense that an item instance of an object inherits all the properties, including the constraints, of the items that are that object's arguments.

4.4 Data objects

Objects are operators that may be used to generate items. A *data item* is a named triple consisting of item semantics, item value constraints and item set constraints. The *semantics* of a data item is an expression that recognises the members of the value set of that data item at any time. The semantics of a data item is a λ-calculus expression. The *item value constraints* of a data item is a λ-calculus expression that should be satisfied by the members of the value set of that data item at any time. The *item set constraints* of a data item is an expression that constrains the structure of the value set of that data item at any time.

The "identity data object" is the identity object operator. The data object with $n = 1$, that is a 1-adic object, with argument type ($\mathbf{X}^1$), named I and written:

$$I[\lambda P{:}\mathbf{X}^1{\bullet}\lambda x{\bullet}[S_p(x)]{\bullet\bullet}, \lambda P{:}\mathbf{X}^1{\bullet}\lambda x{\bullet}[V_p(x)]{\bullet\bullet}, \lambda P{:}\mathbf{X}^1{\bullet}[C_p]{\bullet}]$$

is the *identity data object*. The identity data object has as its semantics the λ-calculus expression $\lambda P{:}\mathbf{X}^1{\bullet}\lambda x{\bullet}[S_p(x)]{\bullet\bullet}$. Any item generated by applying the identity data object to a given item has the same semantics as that given item. Likewise any item generated by applying the identity data object to a given item has the same value constraints and set constraints as that given item. The identity data object is an object that when applied to an item leaves that item unchanged.

A data object with $n = 1$, that is a 1-adic object, is a *simple object*. The identity data object is a simple object. Simple data objects provide a neat representation of the type hierarchy. An application could contain "parts" where each part is identified by a "part-number". The business of being "to do with parts" can be represented by a data object named *part*:

$$part[\lambda P{:}\mathbf{D}^1{\bullet}\lambda x{\bullet}[\ S_p(x) \wedge \text{with-part}(x)\ ]{\bullet\bullet},$$
$$\lambda P{:}\mathbf{D}^1{\bullet}\lambda x{\bullet}[\ V_p(x) \wedge (x \geq 0)\ ]{\bullet\bullet},$$
$$\lambda P{:}\mathbf{D}^1{\bullet}[\ C_p \wedge (\text{Card} \geq 1)_{v\,(part,P)}\ ]{\bullet}\ ]$$

This object is a simple data object. Other simple data objects are:

$$cost[\lambda P{:}\mathbf{D}^1{\bullet}\lambda x{\bullet}[\ S_p(x) \wedge \text{for-costing}(x)\ ]{\bullet\bullet},$$
$$\lambda P{:}\mathbf{X}^1{\bullet}\lambda x{\bullet}[\ V_p(x) \wedge (0 \neq x)\ ]{\bullet\bullet}, \lambda P{:}\mathbf{X}^1{\bullet}[\ C_p\ ]{\bullet}\ ]$$
$$sell[\lambda P{:}\mathbf{D}^1{\bullet}\lambda x{\bullet}[\ S_p(x) \wedge \text{for-selling}(x)\ ]{\bullet\bullet},$$
$$\lambda P{:}\mathbf{X}^1{\bullet}\lambda x{\bullet}[\ V_p(x) \wedge (0 \neq x)\ ]{\bullet\bullet}, \lambda P{:}\mathbf{X}^1{\bullet}[\ C_p\ ]{\bullet}\ ]$$
$$tax[\lambda P{:}\mathbf{D}^1{\bullet}\lambda x{\bullet}[\ S_p(x) \wedge \text{with-tax}(x)\ ]{\bullet\bullet},$$
$$\lambda P{:}\mathbf{X}^1{\bullet}\lambda x{\bullet}[\ V_p(x) \wedge (0 \leq x)\ ]{\bullet\bullet}, \lambda P{:}\mathbf{X}^1{\bullet}[\ C_p\ ]{\bullet}\ ]$$

mark-up$[\lambda P:\mathbf{D}^1\bullet\lambda x\bullet[\ S_P(x) \wedge \text{with-mark-up}(x)\ ]\bullet\bullet,$

$\qquad \lambda P:\mathbf{X}^1\bullet\lambda x\bullet[\ V_P(x) \wedge (0 < x < 3)\ ]\bullet\bullet,\ \lambda P:\mathbf{X}^1\bullet[\ C_P\ ]\bullet\ ]$

machine$[\lambda P:\mathbf{D}^1\bullet\lambda x\bullet[\ S_P(x) \wedge \text{with-machine}(x)\ ]\bullet\bullet,$

$\qquad \lambda P:\mathbf{X}^1\bullet\lambda x\bullet[\ V_P(x) \wedge (x = AB \vee x = CD)]\bullet\bullet,$

$\qquad \lambda P:\mathbf{X}^1\bullet[\ C_P \wedge (\text{Card} \geq 2)_{v\,(\mathbf{\mathit{machine}},P)}\ ]$

type$[\lambda P:\mathbf{D}^1\bullet\lambda x\bullet[\ S_P(x) \wedge \text{with-type}(x)\ ]\bullet\bullet,$

$\qquad \lambda P:\mathbf{X}^1\bullet\lambda x\bullet[\ V_P(x) \wedge (x = \text{lathe} \vee x = \text{press})]\bullet\bullet,$

$\qquad \lambda P:\mathbf{X}^1\bullet[\ C_P \wedge (\text{Card} \geq 2)_{v\,(\mathbf{\mathit{type}},P)}\ ]$

employee$[\lambda P:\mathbf{D}^1\bullet\lambda x\bullet[\ S_P(x) \wedge \text{with-employee}(x)\ ]\bullet\bullet,$

$\qquad \lambda P:\mathbf{X}^1\bullet\lambda x\bullet[\ V_P(x) \wedge (100 < x \leq 499)]\bullet\bullet,$

$\qquad \lambda P:\mathbf{X}^1\bullet[\ C_P \wedge (\text{Card} \geq 10)_{v\,(\mathbf{\mathit{employee}},P)}\ ]$

A *compound data item* is a data item that is constructed from a set of *component data items* and the "compound data object" in the following way. Given a set of n (component) simple data items:

$$I_1[\ S_{I_1}, V_{I_1}, C_{I_1}\ ]$$
$$I_2[\ S_{I_2}, V_{I_2}, C_{I_2}\ ]$$
$$\dots\dots\dots\dots$$
$$I_n[\ S_{I_n}, V_{I_n}, C_{I_n}\ ]$$

where $n > 0$, I_k is a 1-adic data item. The n-adic *compound data object* **comp** of argument type $(\mathbf{D}^1, \mathbf{D}^1,..., \mathbf{D}^1)$ where **D** stands for "data" is:

comp$[\lambda Q_1:\mathbf{D}^1 Q_2:\mathbf{D}^1....Q_n:\mathbf{D}^1\bullet\lambda x_1 x_2...x_n\bullet[\ S_{Q_1}(x_1) \wedge ... \wedge\ S_{Q_n}(x_n)\ ]\bullet\bullet,$

$\qquad \lambda Q_1:\mathbf{D}^1 Q_2:\mathbf{D}^1....Q_n:\mathbf{D}^1\bullet\lambda x_1 x_2...x_n\bullet[\ V_{Q_1}(x_1)$

$\qquad\qquad \wedge\ ...\ \wedge\ V_{Q_n}(x_n)\ ]\bullet,$

$\qquad \lambda Q_1:\mathbf{D}^1 Q_2:\mathbf{D}^1....Q_n:\mathbf{D}^1\bullet[C_{Q_1} \wedge ... \wedge C_{Q_n}$

$\qquad\qquad \wedge\ (\text{Uni}(Q_1) \wedge ... \wedge\ \text{Uni}(Q_n))_{v\,(\mathbf{\mathit{comp}},Q_1,..,Q_n)}]\bullet]$

The compound data item:

comp$(I_1, I_2,..., I_n)$

is often written with the name:

$I_1\_I_2\_...\_I_n$

provided that there is only one such compound data object constructed from the components $\{I_1, I_2, ..., I_n\}$.

As an example of a compound data item built using the **comp** object consider the two 1-adic data items:

$part[\lambda x \bullet [\text{is-a}[x:\text{part-number}]] \bullet,\ \lambda x \bullet [\ (1\,000 < x < 9\,999)\ ] \bullet,\ (\text{Card} \le 100)_{part}\ ]$
$machine[\lambda x \bullet [\text{is-a}[x:\text{machine-name}]] \bullet,$
$\qquad \lambda x \bullet [\ x = \text{AB} \lor x = \text{CD}\ ] \bullet,\ (\text{Card} \le 2)_{machine}\ ]$

then the compound dyadic data item:

$$comp[\ \lambda P{:}\mathbf{D}^1 Q{:}\mathbf{D}^1 \bullet \lambda xy \bullet [\ S_P(x) \land S_Q(y)\ ] \bullet \bullet,$$
$$\lambda P{:}\mathbf{D}^1 Q{:}\mathbf{D}^1 \bullet \lambda xy \bullet [\ V_P(x) \land V_Q(y)\ ] \bullet \bullet,$$
$$\lambda P{:}\mathbf{D}^1 Q{:}\mathbf{D}^1 \bullet [C_P \land C_Q$$
$$\land\ (\text{Uni}(P) \land \text{Uni}(Q))_{v(comp,P,Q)}\ ] \bullet\ ](part,\ machine)$$

is equivalent to the compound dyadic data item:

$$part\_machine[\lambda xy \bullet [\ S_{part}(x) \land S_{machine}(y)\ ] \bullet,$$
$$\lambda xy \bullet [\ (1\,000 < x < 9\,999)\ \land$$
$$(\ y = \text{AB} \lor y = \text{CD}\ )\ ] \bullet),$$
$$(\text{Uni}(part) \land \text{Uni}(machine))_{part\_machine}\ \land$$
$$(\text{Card} \le 100)_{part} \land (\text{Card} \ge 2)_{machine}\ ] =$$
$$part\_machine[\ \lambda xy \bullet [\text{is-a}[x:\text{part-number}] \land \text{is-a}[y:\text{machine-name}]\ ] \bullet,$$
$$\lambda xy \bullet [\ (1\,000 < x < 9\,999)\ \land$$
$$(\ y = \text{AB} \lor y = \text{CD}\ )\ ] \bullet),$$
$$(\text{Uni}(part) \land \text{Uni}(machine))_{part\_machine}\ \land$$
$$(\text{Card} \le 100)_{part} \land (\text{Card} \ge 2)_{machine}\ )\ ]$$

where *part_machine* is an item name.

At any particular time, the members of the value set of a compound data item are the Cartesian product of the members of the value sets of the component data items taken in sequence. The members of the value set of a compound data item are usually denoted by a sequence of component label names each separated by an underscore. See Fig. 4.1 for an example of a compound data item, corresponding name-population and value set. In this example the compound item *part_machine* has the two component items, namely *part* and *machine*. Likewise, the compound name-population part-number_machine-name is constructed from two component name-populations, namely part-number and machine-name. Further, the members of the value set of the item *part_machine* are the Cartesian product of pairs of members of the value sets of the items *part* and *machine*.

part_machine	part	machine
part-number_machine-number	part-number	machine-number
1234_AB	1234	AB
2468_AB	2468	CD
3579_AB	3579	
1234_CD		
2468_CD		
3579_CD		

Fig. 4.1 Compound data item, component data items and value sets

Data objects can be employed to represent the type hierarchy. Suppose that in an application there are things called machines and things called lathes, and suppose that all lathes are machines. This fact can be represented by representing lathe by the item *lathe* that is a sub-item of the item *machine*:

$lathe[\lambda x \bullet [is\text{-}a[x:lathe\text{-}name]] \bullet,$
$\quad \lambda x \bullet [\ x = AB\ ] \bullet,$
$\quad (Card \geq 1)_{lathe}\ ]$
$machine[\lambda x \bullet [is\text{-}a[x:machine\text{-}name]] \bullet,\ \lambda x \bullet [x = AB \lor x = CD] \bullet,$
$\quad (Card \geq 2)_{machine}]$

The relationship between these two items can be established by an object **lathe**:

$\textbf{lathe}[\ \lambda P:\textbf{D}^1 \bullet \lambda x \bullet [\ S_P(x) \land with\text{-}lathe(x)\ ] \bullet\bullet,$
$\quad \lambda P:\textbf{X}^1 \bullet \lambda x \bullet [\ V_P(x) \land (name(x) \rightarrow (x = AB))\ ] \bullet\bullet,$
$\quad \lambda P:\textbf{X}^1 \bullet [\ C_P \land (Card \geq 1)_{v\,(\textbf{lathe},P)}\ ] \bullet\ ]$

To show that "*lathe*" is a sub-type of "*machine*" apply the object **lathe** to the item *machine*. The resulting compound data item is equivalent to the data item with name $lathe = v\,(\textbf{lathe}, machine)$:

$\textbf{lathe}[\ \lambda P:\textbf{D}^1 \bullet \lambda x \bullet [\ S_P(x) \land with\text{-}lathe(x)\ ] \bullet\bullet,$
$\quad \lambda P:\textbf{X}^1 \bullet \lambda x \bullet [\ V_P(x) \land (name(x) \rightarrow (x = AB))\ ] \bullet\bullet,$
$\quad \lambda P:\textbf{X}^1 \bullet [\ C_P \land (Card \geq 1)_{v\,(\textbf{lathe},P)}\ ] \bullet\ ](machine)\ =$
$lathe[\ \lambda x \bullet [\ S_{machine}(x) \land with\text{-}lathe(x)\ ] \bullet,$
$\quad \lambda x \bullet [\ V_{machine}(x) \land (name(x) \rightarrow (x = AB))\ ] \bullet,$
$\quad (Card \geq 1)_{lathe} \land (Card \leq 2)_{machine}\ ]\ =$
$lathe[\ \lambda x \bullet [\ is\text{-}a[x:lathe\text{-}name]\ ] \bullet,$
$\quad \lambda x \bullet [\ x = AB\ ] \bullet,$
$\quad (Card \geq 1)_{lathe} \land (Card \leq 2)_{machine}\ ]$

Another example of the representation of the type hierarchy is given by the fact that "all cost-prices are prices". This fact can be represented by representing "cost-price" by the item *cost-price* that is a sub-item of the item *price*:

price$[\lambda x \bullet [\text{is-a}[x:\text{dollar-amount}]] \bullet, \lambda x \bullet [\ 0 \le x\ ] \bullet, \varnothing\ ]$

where the sub-type relationship is established by the object ***cost***:

cost$[\lambda P:\mathbf{D}^1 \bullet \lambda x \bullet [\ S_p(x) \wedge \text{for-costing}(x)\ ] \bullet \bullet,$

$\quad \lambda P:\mathbf{X}^1 \bullet \lambda x \bullet [\ V_p(x) \wedge (0 \ne x)\ ] \bullet \bullet,$

$\quad \lambda P:\mathbf{X}^1 \bullet [\ C_p\ ] \bullet\ ](price)$

This compound data item is equivalent to the data item with name *cost-price* = ν(***cost, price***):

cost-price$[\lambda x \bullet [x:\text{dollar-amount}] \bullet, \lambda x \bullet [\ 0 < x\ ] \bullet, \varnothing\ ]$

The semantics of any data item, including compound data items, is an expression that does not represent an association. Given an object ***object-name*** the semantics of the item generated by applying that object to n items:

object-name$[I_1, I_2,..., I_n]$

does not represent an association under two circumstances. First, if $n > 1$ and the semantics of the object ***object-name*** is the trivial expression:

$\lambda Q_1 Q_2...Q_n \bullet \lambda x_1 x_2...x_n \bullet [\ S_{Q_1}(x_1) \wedge .... \wedge\ S_{Q_n}(x_n)\ ] \bullet \bullet$

as in the ***comp*** object introduced above. Second, if $n = 1$ and the semantics represents a restriction to be applied to the semantics of its single component. So a data object is either the compound object or is a 1-adic object that represents sub-typing.

4.5 Information objects

An *information item* is a named triple consisting of item semantics, item value constraints and item set constraints. The *semantics* of an information item is an expression that recognises the members of the value set of that information item at any time. The *item value constraints* of an information item is an expression that should be satisfied by the members of the value set of that information item at any time. The *item set constraints* of an information item is an expression that constrains the structure of the value set of that item.

Given a set of n data items:

$$I_1[\ S_{I_1},\ V_{I_1},\ C_{I_1}\ ]$$
$$I_2[\ S_{I_2},\ V_{I_2},\ C_{I_2}\ ]$$
$$\ldots\ldots\ldots\ldots\ldots$$
$$I_n[\ S_{I_n},\ V_{I_n},\ C_{I_n}\ ]$$

where $n > 0$, I_k is a i_k-adic item, and the n-adic object A with argument type $(X_1^{i_1},\ X_2^{i_2},\ldots,\ X_j^{i_j})$ where the X_k are types such as **X, D, I** or **K**:

$$A[\ E_A,\ F_A,\ G_A\ ]$$

in this object E_A and F_A are typed λ-calculus expressions in terms of the variables $\lambda Q_1{:}X_1^{i_1}Q_2{:}X_2^{i_2}\ldots Q_j{:}X_j^{i_j}{\bullet}\lambda y_1^1\ldots y_{m_1}^1\ldots y_{m_n}^n{\bullet}$, and G_A is a typed λ-calculus expression expressed in terms of the variables $\lambda Q_1{:}X_1^{i_1}Q_2{:}X_2^{i_2}\ldots Q_j{:}X_j^{i_j}{\bullet}$:

$$E_A = \lambda Q_1:X_1^{i_1}Q_2:X_2^{i_2}\ldots Q_j:X_j^{i_j}{\bullet}\lambda y_1^1\ldots y_{m_1}^1\ldots y_{m_n}^n{\bullet}[S_{P_1}(y_1^1,\ldots,y_{m_1}^1)$$
$$\wedge\ S_{P_2}(y_1^2,\ldots,y_{m_2}^2)\ \wedge\ \ldots\ldots\ \wedge\ S_{P_n}(y_1^n,\ldots,y_{m_n}^n)$$
$$\wedge\ J(y_1^1\ldots y_{m_1}^1\ldots y_{m_n}^n)]{\bullet\bullet}$$

and where J represents an implicit association, then the object:

$$A[\ E_A,\ F_A,\ G_A\ ]$$

is an n-adic *information object* with argument type $(X_1^{i_1},\ X_2^{i_2},\ldots,\ X_j^{i_j})$ where the X_k are types such as **X, D, I** or **K**. Further, the item instance of object A:

$$A[\ E_A,\ F_A,\ G_A\ ](I_1, I_2,\ldots, I_n)\ =$$
$$v(A,I_1, I_2,\ldots, I_n)[\ E_A(I_1, I_2,\ldots, I_n),\ F_A(I_1, I_2,\ldots, I_n),\ G_A(I_1, I_2,\ldots, I_n)\ )$$

is an information item. It is usual to write the name $v(A,I_1, I_2,\ldots, I_n)$ of this item as:

$$I_1/I_2/\ldots/I_n$$

provided that there is only one such information item constructed from the components $\{I_1, I_2, \ldots, I_n\}$. The object set constraint, G_A, of the information

object *A* should include the identification of any universal arguments and the identification of the set of candidates, if any, for each argument.

Consider the three data items:

part[λx•[is-a[x:part-number]]•, λx•[(1 000 < x < 9 999)]•,
    (Card ≤ 100)$_{part}$]
cost-price[λx•[is-a[x:dollar-amount]]•, λx•[0 ≤ x]•, ∅]
sale-price[λx•[is-a[x:dollar-amount]]•, λx•[1 ≤ x]•, ∅]

and the information object:

costs[λP:X^1Q:X^1•λxy•[S$_P$(x) ∧ S$_Q$(y) ∧ costs(x, y)]••,
    λP:X^1Q:X^1•λxy•[V$_P$(x) ∧ V$_Q$(y) ∧
        ((1 000 < x < 1 999) → (y ≤ 300))]••,
    λP:X^1Q:X^1•[C$_P$ ∧ C$_Q$
        ∧ (Uni(P) ∧ Can(Q, {P}))$_{v\,(costs,P,Q)}$]•]

where the predicate "costs(x, y)" means "x costs y". Consider the item instance of
the object *costs*:

costs(*part*, *cost-price*)

Giving this information item the name *part/cost-price*:

costs(*part*, *cost-price*) =
part/cost-price[λxy•[S$_{part}$(x) ∧ S$_{cost-price}$(y) ∧ costs(x, y)]•,
    λxy•[V$_{part}$(x) ∧ V$_{cost-price}$(y) ∧
        (1 000 < x < 1 999) → (y ≤ 300)]•
    (Uni(*part*) ∧ Can(*cost-price*, {*part*})$_{part/cost-price}$ ∧
        C$_{part}$ ∧ C$_{cost-price}$] =
part/cost-price[λxy•[costs(x:part-number, y:dollar-amount)]•,
    λxy•[(1 000 < x < 9 999) ∧ (0 < y) ∧
        ((x < 1 999) → (y ≤ 300))]•,
    (Uni(*part*) ∧ Can(*cost-price*, {*part*})$_{part/cost-price}$ ∧
        (Card ≤ 100)$_{part}$]

In Sect. 3.5 the inverse of an information item is introduced. The *inverse
operator*, is an object operator that when applied to an item generates the inverse
of that item. The inverse operator is an object. The inverse operator for binary
items *inv-2* is defined by:

inv-2$[\lambda P:\mathbf{D}^2\bullet\lambda xy\bullet[\ S_P^{-1}(x,\ y)\ ]\bullet\bullet,$

$\quad\lambda P:\mathbf{D}^2\bullet\lambda xy\bullet[\mathbf{T}]\bullet\bullet,\ \lambda P:\mathbf{D}^2\bullet[C_P\ \wedge\ (\varnothing)_{\nu\,(inv\text{-}2,P)}\ ]\bullet]$

where $S_P^{-1}(x,\ y)$ is defined to be "for all x, y is a list of all elements z such that $S_P(z,\ x)$". For example:

inv-2(*part/cost-price*) = *cost-price/part-list*

This item is defined in Sect. 3.5.

At any particular time, the value set of an information item is a subset of the Cartesian product of the value sets of the component data items taken in sequence. The members of the value set of an information item are usually denoted by a sequence of labels from the value sets of each component data item separated by obliques '/'. If an n-adic information item *A* has as its components the 'n' data items $\{B_1,...,B_n\}$ then the following relationship holds between the value set of *A* and the value set of *comp*$(B_1,...,B_n)$:

$$\gamma(A)\ \subset\ \gamma(comp(B_1,...,B_n))$$

In Sect. 4.4 objects are used to represent sub-type relationships between data items. In Sect. 3.3 the sub-type relationship is generalised to the sub-item relationship. Given two items *A* and *B*, if item *B* is subject to the constraint that at any time τ the value set of item *B* is a subset of the value set of item *A* then item *B* is a *sub-item* of item *A*. That is, item *B* is a sub-item of item *A* if:

$$(\forall\tau)\ [\ \gamma^\tau(B)\subset\gamma^\tau(A)\ ]$$

The idea of a sub-item may be employed to extend the notion of sub-typing so that it applies to information items. Consider the information item *person/house*:

person/house$[\ \lambda xy\bullet[owns(x:person\text{-}id,\ y:house\text{-}id)]\bullet,\ \lambda xy\bullet[\ \varnothing\ ]\bullet,\ \varnothing\ ]$

and the information object:

lives-at$[\lambda P:\mathbf{X}^2\bullet\lambda xy\bullet[S_P(x,\ y)\ \wedge\ lives\text{-}at(x,\ y)]\bullet\bullet,$

$\quad\lambda P:\mathbf{X}^2\bullet\lambda xy\bullet[V_P(x,\ y)]\bullet\bullet,$

$\quad\lambda P:\mathbf{X}^2\bullet[C_P\ \wedge\ (\varnothing)_{\nu\,(lives\text{-}at,P)}\ ]\bullet]$

The *lives-at* object may be applied to the *person/house* item to construct:

lives-at(*person/house*) =
person/own-home[λxy•[owns(x:person-id, y:house-id)
             ∧ lives-at(x:person-id, y:house-id)]•,
   λxy•[**T**]•, ∅]

Consider the item:

employee/department[λx₁x₂•[works-in(x₁:person-id, x₂:dept-desc)]•,
   λx₁x₂•[(1 < x₁ < 100)]•,
   (Uni(*employee*) ∧ Can(*department*, {*employee*}))/*employee/department*
          ∧ (Card ≤ 50)*employee*]

Apply the object:

manages[λP:**X**²•λxy•[Sₚ(x, y) ∧ manages(x, y)]••,
   λP:**X**²•λxy•[Vₚ(x, y)]••,
   λP:**X**²•[Cₚ ∧ (∅)ᵥ(*manages*,P)]•]

to the *employee/department* item to obtain:

manages(*employee/department*) =
manager/department[λxy•[work-in(x:person-id, y:dept-desc)
          ∧ manages(x:person-id,y:dept-desc)]•,
   λxy•[(1 < x < 100)]•, (Card ≤ 50)*manager*]

Objects can be used to generalise the data sub-typing relationship to sub-typing
between information items. In Sect. 4.6 objects are employed to generalise the
sub-item relationship so that it applies to knowledge items.

4.5.1 Further examples

Another example of an information object is:

sells-for[λP:**X**¹Q:**X**¹•λxy•[Sₚ(x) ∧ S_Q(y) ∧ sells-for(x, y)]••,
   λP:**X**¹Q:**X**¹•λxy•[Vₚ(x) ∧ V_Q(y) ∧ **T**]••,
   λP:**X**¹Q:**X**¹•[Cₚ ∧ C_Q
          ∧ (Uni(P) ∧ Can(Q, {P}))ᵥ(*sells-for*,P,Q)]•]

where the predicate "sells-for(x, y)" means "x sells for y". The item instance of
the object *sells-for*:

sells-for(*part, sale-price*)

is an information item. Giving this information item the name *part/sale-price*:

sells-for(*part, sale-price*) =
part/sale-price[λxy•[sells-for(x:part-number, y:dollar-amount)]•,
   λxy•[(1 000 < x < 9 999) ∧ (1 < y)]•,
   (Uni(*part*) ∧ Can(*sale-price*, {*part*}))_{*part/sale-price*} ∧
       (Card ≤ 100)_{*part*}]

Another example of an information object is:

has-type[λP:$\mathbf{X}^1$Q:$\mathbf{X}^1$•λxy•[$S_P(x)$ ∧ $S_Q(y)$ ∧ has-type(x, y)]••,
   λP:$\mathbf{X}^1$Q:$\mathbf{X}^1$•λxy•[$V_P(x)$ ∧ $V_Q(y)$ ∧ **T**]••,
   λP:$\mathbf{X}^1$Q:$\mathbf{X}^1$•[C_P ∧ C_Q
      ∧ (Uni(P) ∧ Can(Q, {P}))_{*v (**has-type**,P,Q)*}]•]

where the predicate "has-type(x, y)" means "x has type y". The item instance of
the object **has-type**:

has-type(*machine, type*)

is an information item. Giving this information item the name *machine/type*:

has-type(*machine, type*) =
machine/type[λxy•[has-type(x:machine-name, y:type-description)]•,
   λxy•[(x=AB ∨ x=CD) ∧ (y=lathe ∨ y=press)]•,
   (Uni(*machine*) ∧ Can(*type*, {*machine*}))_{*machine/type*} ∧
      (Card ≥ 2)_{*machine*} ∧ (Card ≥ 2)_{*type*}]

The item instance of the object **has-type**:

has-type(*part, type*)

is an information item. Giving this information item the name *part/type*:

has-type(*part, type*) =
part/type[λxy•[has-type(x:part-number, y:type-description)]•,
   λxy•[(1 000 < x < 9 999) ∧ (y=lathe ∨ y=press)]•,
   (Uni(*part*) ∧ Can(*type*, {*part*}))_{*part/type*} ∧
      (Card ≤ 100)_{*part*} ∧ (Card ≥ 2)_{*type*}]

Another example of an information object is:

factor-of[λP:$\mathbf{X}^1$Q:$\mathbf{X}^1$•λxy•[S_P(x) ∧ S_Q(y) ∧ factor-of(x, y)]••,

   λP:$\mathbf{X}^1$Q:$\mathbf{X}^1$•λxy•[V_P(x) ∧ V_Q(y) ∧ **T**]••,

   λP:$\mathbf{X}^1$Q:$\mathbf{X}^1$•[C_P ∧ C_Q

      ∧ (Uni(P) ∧ Can(Q, {P}))$_{v\,(factor\text{-}of,P,Q)}$]•]

where the predicate "factor-of(x, y)" means "y is a factor associated with x". The item instance of the object *factor-of*:

factor-of(*type, mark-up-factor*)

is an information item.   Giving this information item the name *type/mark-up-factor*:

factor-of(*type, mark-up-factor*) =
type/mark-up-factor[λxy•[factor-of(x:type-description, y:mark-up-factor)]•,

   λxy•[(x=lathe ∨ x=press) ∧ (0 < y < 3)]•,

   (Uni(*type*) ∧ Can(*mark-up-factor*, {*type*}))$_{type/mark\text{-}up\text{-}factor}$

      ∧ (Card ≥ 2)$_{type}$]

Another example of an information object is:

owns[λP:$\mathbf{X}^1$Q:$\mathbf{X}^1$•λxy•[S_P(x) ∧ S_Q(y) ∧ owns(x, y)]••,

   λP:$\mathbf{X}^1$Q:$\mathbf{X}^1$•λxy•[V_P(x) ∧ V_Q(y) ∧ (x ≠ y)]••,

   λP:$\mathbf{X}^1$Q:$\mathbf{X}^1$•[C_P ∧ C_Q ∧ (∅)$_{v\,(owns,P,Q)}$]•]

where the predicate "owns(x, y)" means "x owns y". The item instance of the object *owns*:

owns(*person, house*)

is an information item. Giving this information item the name *person/house*:

owns(*person, house*) =
person/house[λxy•[owns(x:person-id, y:house-id)]•, λxy•[∅]•, ∅]

4.6 Knowledge objects

A *knowledge item* is a named triple consisting of item semantics, item value constraints and item set constraints.   The *semantics* of a knowledge item is an expression that recognises the members of the value set of that knowledge item at any time. The *item value constraints* of a knowledge item is an expression that should be satisfied by the members of the value set of that knowledge item at any time. The *item set constraints* of a knowledge item is an expression that constrains the structure of the value set of the item.

Given a set of n (information or data) items:

$$I_1[\ S_{I_1},\ V_{I_1},\ C_{I_1}\ ]$$
$$I_2[\ S_{I_2},\ V_{I_2},\ C_{I_2}\ ]$$
$$\dots\dots\dots\dots\dots$$
$$I_n[\ S_{I_n},\ V_{I_n},\ C_{I_n}\ ]$$

where $n > 0$, I_k is a i_k-adic item, and the n-adic object of argument type $(X_1^{i_1}, X_2^{i_2}, \dots, X_j^{i_j})$, where the X_k are types such as **X, D, I** or **K**:

$$A[\ E_A,\ F_A,\ G_A\ ]$$

in this object E_A and F_A are typed λ-calculus expressions in terms of the variables $\lambda Q_1{:}X_1^{i_1}Q_2{:}X_2^{i_2}\dots Q_j{:}X_j^{i_j}{\bullet}\lambda y_1^1\dots y_{m_1}^1\dots y_{m_n}^n{\bullet}$. G_A is a typed λ-calculus expression expressed in terms of the variables $\lambda Q_1{:}X_1^{i_1}Q_2{:}X_2^{i_2}\dots Q_j{:}X_j^{i_j}{\bullet}$:

$$E_A = \lambda Q_1{:}X_1^{i_1}Q_2{:}X_2^{i_2}\dots Q_j{:}X_j^{i_j}{\bullet}\lambda y_1^1\dots y_{m_1}^1\dots y_{m_n}^n{\bullet}[S_{P_1}(y_1^1,\dots,y_{m_1}^1)$$
$$\wedge\ S_{P_2}(y_1^2,\dots,y_{m_2}^2)\ \wedge\ \dots\dots\dots\ \wedge\ S_{P_n}(y_1^n,\dots,y_{m_n}^n)$$
$$\wedge\ J(y_1^1\dots y_{m_1}^1\dots y_{m_n}^n)]{\bullet\bullet}$$

J represents an explicit association. Then the object:

$$A[\ E_A,\ F_A,\ G_A\ ]$$

is an n-adic *knowledge object*. The item instance of the object A:

$$A[\ E_A,\ F_A,\ G_A\ ](I_1, I_2,\dots, I_n)\ =$$
$$\nu(A, I_1, I_2,\dots, I_n)[\ E_A(I_1, I_2,\dots, I_n),\ F_A(I_1, I_2,\dots, I_n),\ G_A(I_1, I_2,\dots, I_n)\ )$$

is a knowledge item. It is often written with the name:

$$[I_1, I_2,\ \dots,\ I_n]$$

provided that there is only one such knowledge item constructed from the components $\{I_1, I_2, \dots, I_n\}$. The object set constraint, G_A, of the knowledge object A

includes the identification of any universal arguments and the identification of the set of candidates, if any, for each argument.

Consider the 3-adic knowledge object with argument type $(\mathbf{X}^2, \mathbf{X}^2, \mathbf{X}^1)$:

mark-up-1$[\lambda P{:}\mathbf{X}^2 Q{:}\mathbf{X}^2 R{:}\mathbf{X}^1{\bullet}\lambda x_1 x_2 y_1 y_2 z{\bullet}[\ S_P(x_1,x_2) \wedge S_Q(y_1,y_2) \wedge S_R(z)$
$\wedge\ ((\ x_1 = y_1\ ) \rightarrow (x_2 = z \times y_2))\ ]{\bullet\bullet},$
$\lambda P{:}\mathbf{X}^2 Q{:}\mathbf{X}^2 R{:}\mathbf{X}^1{\bullet}\lambda x_1 x_2 y_1 y_2 z{\bullet}[\ V_P(x_1,x_2) \wedge V_Q(y_1,y_2) \wedge V_R(z)\ \wedge$
$((\ x_1 = y_1\ ) \rightarrow (\ x_2 > y_2\ ))\ ]{\bullet\bullet},$
$\lambda P{:}\mathbf{X}^2 Q{:}\mathbf{X}^2 R{:}\mathbf{X}^1{\bullet}[C_P \wedge C_Q \wedge C_R \wedge (\mathrm{Uni}(P) \wedge \mathrm{Uni}(Q)$
$\wedge\ \mathrm{Can}(P, \{Q, R\}) \wedge \mathrm{Can}(Q, \{P, R\})$
$\wedge\ \mathrm{Can}(R, \{P, Q\}))_{\nu\,(\textbf{\textit{mark-up-1}},P,Q,R)}\ ]{\bullet}\ ]$

Consider the item instance of the knowledge object **mark-up-1**:

mark-up-1(*part/sale-price, part/cost-price, mark-up*)

giving this knowledge item the name *[part/sale-price, part/cost-price, mark-up]*:

mark-up-1(*part/sale-price, part/cost-price, mark-up*) =
[part/sale-price, part/cost-price, mark-up][
$\quad\lambda P{:}\mathbf{X}^2 Q{:}\mathbf{X}^2 R{:}\mathbf{X}^1{\bullet}\lambda x_1 x_2 y_1 y_2 z{\bullet}[\ S_P(x_1,x_2) \wedge S_Q(y_1,y_2) \wedge S_R(z)$
$\quad\wedge\ ((\ x_1 = y_1\ ) \rightarrow (x_2 = z \times y_2))\ ]{\bullet\bullet}$
$\quad$(*part/sale-price, part/cost-price, mark-up*),
$\quad\lambda P{:}\mathbf{X}^2 Q{:}\mathbf{X}^2 R{:}\mathbf{X}^1{\bullet}\lambda x_1 x_2 y_1 y_2 z{\bullet}[\ V_P(x_1,x_2) \wedge V_Q(y_1,y_2) \wedge V_R(z)\ \wedge$
$\quad((\ x_1 = y_1\ ) \rightarrow (\ x_2 > y_2\ ))\ ]{\bullet\bullet}$
$\quad$(*part/sale-price, part/cost-price, mark-up*),
$\quad\lambda P{:}\mathbf{X}^2 Q{:}\mathbf{X}^2 R{:}\mathbf{X}^1{\bullet}[\ C_P \wedge C_Q \wedge C_R \wedge (\mathrm{Uni}(P) \wedge \mathrm{Uni}(Q)$
$\quad\wedge\ \mathrm{Can}(P, \{Q, R\}) \wedge \mathrm{Can}(Q, \{P, R\})$
$\quad\wedge\ \mathrm{Can}(R, \{P, Q\}))_{\nu\,(\textbf{\textit{mark-up-1}},P,Q,R)}\ ]{\bullet}$
$\quad$(*part/sale-price, part/cost-price, mark-up*)] =
[part/sale-price, part/cost-price, mark-up][
$\lambda x_1 x_2 y_1 y_2 z{\bullet}[\ \text{sells-for}(x_1{:}\text{part-number}, x_2{:}\text{dollar-amount})$
$\quad\wedge\ \text{costs}(y_1{:}\text{part-number}, y_2{:}\text{dollar-amount})$
$\quad\wedge\ \text{is-a}[z{:}\text{mark-up-factor}]$
$\quad\wedge\ ((\ x_1 = y_1\ ) \rightarrow (x_2 = z \times y_2))\ ]{\bullet},$
$\lambda x_1 x_2 y_1 y_2 z{\bullet}[\ (1\,000 < x_1 < 9\,999) \wedge (1 < x_2) \wedge$
$\quad(1\,000 < y_1 < 9\,999) \wedge (0 < y_2) \wedge$
$\quad((y_1 < 1\,999) \rightarrow (y_2 \leq 300)) \wedge (0 < z < 3) \wedge$
$\quad((\ x_1 = y_1\ ) \rightarrow (\ x_2 > y_2\ ))\ ]{\bullet},$

(Uni(*part/sale-price*) ∧ Uni(*part/cost-price*)

    ∧ Can(*part/sale-price*, {*part/cost-price, mark-up*})

    ∧ Can(*part/cost-price*, {*part/sale-price, mark-up*})

    ∧ Can(*mark-up*, {*part/sale-price, part/cost-price*})

)*[part/sale-price, part/cost-price, mark-up]*

        ∧ (Uni(*part*) ∧ Can(*sale-price*, {*part*}))*part/sale-price* ∧

        (Uni(*part*) ∧ Can(*cost-price*, {*part*}))*part/cost-price* ∧

        (Card ≤ 100)*part*]

The above knowledge item is constructed as an instance of a knowledge object. That item inherits the semantics and constraints of its component information and data items. That is:

[part/sale-price, part/cost-price, mark-up] =
   mark-up-1(*part/sale-price, part/cost-price, mark-up*) =
   mark-up-1(**sells-for**(*part, sale-price*),
       costs(*part, cost-price*), *mark-up*)

Objects are a powerful and succinct notion for representing the structure of items.

In Sect. 4.5 objects are used to generalise the notion of sub-type relationships so that it applied to information items. This generalisation of "sub-typing" is the sub-item relationship. The sub-item relationship may be generalised further so that it applies to knowledge items [Russell & Norvig, 1995]. Consider the knowledge item *[part/sale-price, part/cost-price, mark-up]* introduced above and the knowledge object:

low[$\lambda P:X^3 \cdot \lambda x_1 x_2 y_1 y_2 z \cdot$[$S_P(x_1, x_2, y_1, y_2, z)$ ∧
      $x_1 < 2\,000$ ∧ $y_1 < 2\,000$]••,
  $\lambda P:X^3 \cdot \lambda x_1 x_2 y_1 y_2 z \cdot [V_P(x_1, x_2, y_1, y_2, z)$ ∧ **T**]••,
  $\lambda P:X^3 \cdot [C_P$ ∧ $(\mathbf{T})_{v\,(low, P)}$]•]

The *low* object may be applied to the *[part/sale-price, part/cost-price, mark-up]* item to construct:

low(*[part/sale-price, part/cost-price, mark-up]*) =
[lpart/sale-price, lpart/cost-price, mark-up][
   $\lambda x_1 x_2 y_1 y_2 z \cdot$[sells-for($x_1$:part-number, x_2:dollar-amount)
        ∧ costs(y_1:part-number, y_2:dollar-amount)
        ∧ is-a[z:mark-up-factor] ∧ $x_1 < 2\,000$ ∧ $y_1 < 2\,000$
        ∧ (($x_1 = y_1$) → ($x_2 = z \times y_2$))]•,

$$\lambda x_1 x_2 y_1 y_2 z \bullet [\ (1\,000 < x_1 < 9\,999) \wedge (1 < x_2) \wedge$$
$$(1\,000 < y_1 < 9\,999) \wedge (0 < y_2) \wedge$$
$$((y_1 < 1\,999) \rightarrow (y_2 \leq 300)) \wedge (0 < z < 3) \wedge$$
$$((\ x_1 = y_1\ ) \rightarrow (\ x_2 > y_2\ ))\ ]\bullet,$$

$$(\text{Uni}(part/sale\text{-}price) \wedge \text{Uni}(part/cost\text{-}price)$$
$$\wedge \text{Can}(part/sale\text{-}price, \{part/cost\text{-}price, mark\text{-}up\})$$
$$\wedge \text{Can}(part/cost\text{-}price, \{part/sale\text{-}price, mark\text{-}up\})$$
$$\wedge \text{Can}(mark\text{-}up, \{part/sale\text{-}price, part/cost\text{-}price\})$$
$$)[part/sale\text{-}price, part/cost\text{-}price,\ mark\text{-}up]$$
$$\wedge\ (\text{Uni}(part) \wedge \text{Can}(sale\text{-}price, \{part\}))_{part/sale\text{-}price}\ \wedge$$
$$(\text{Uni}(part) \wedge \text{Can}(cost\text{-}price, \{part\}))_{part/cost\text{-}price}\ \wedge$$
$$(\text{Card} \leq 100)_{part}\ ]$$

In the above information items *lpart/sale-price* and *lpart/cost-price* the component data item '*lpart*' represents a "low part number". The value set of the knowledge item above contains those values in the value set of the knowledge item *[part/sale-price, part/cost-price, mark-up]* whose part-numbers are less than 2 000. Objects can be used to represent the sub-item relationship between knowledge items.

4.6.1 Further examples

Consider the 4-adic knowledge object with argument type $(\mathbf{X}^2, \mathbf{X}^2, \mathbf{X}^2, \mathbf{X}^2)$:

$$\textbf{mark-up-rule-2}[\lambda P{:}\mathbf{X}^2 Q{:}\mathbf{X}^2 R{:}\mathbf{X}^2 S{:}\mathbf{X}^2 \bullet \lambda w_1 w_2 x_1 x_2 y_1 y_2 z_1 z_2 \bullet [$$
$$S_P(w_1, w_2) \wedge S_Q(x_1, x_2) \wedge S_R(y_1, y_2) \wedge S_S(z_1, z_2) \wedge$$
$$(((\ w_1 = x_1 = y_1\ ) \wedge (\ y_2 = z_1\ ))$$
$$\rightarrow (x_2 = z_2 \times y_2))\ ]\bullet\bullet,$$
$$\lambda P{:}\mathbf{X}^2 Q{:}\mathbf{X}^2 R{:}\mathbf{X}^2 S{:}\mathbf{X}^2 \bullet \lambda w_1 w_2 x_1 x_2 y_1 y_2 z_1 z_2 \bullet [\ V_P(w_1, w_2) \wedge$$
$$V_Q(x_1, x_2) \wedge V_R(y_1, y_2) \wedge V_S(z_1, z_2) \wedge$$
$$((\ w_1 = x_1\ ) \rightarrow (\ w_2 > x_2\ ))\ ]\bullet\bullet,$$
$$\lambda P{:}\mathbf{X}^2 Q{:}\mathbf{X}^2 R{:}\mathbf{X}^2 S{:}\mathbf{X}^2 \bullet [C_P \wedge C_Q \wedge C_R \wedge C_S \wedge (\text{Uni}(P) \wedge \text{Uni}(Q)$$
$$\wedge \text{Can}(P, \{Q, R, S\})$$
$$\wedge\ \text{Can}(Q, \{P, R, S\}))_{v\,(\textbf{mark-up-2}, P, Q, R, S)}]\bullet\ ]$$

The item instance of the object **mark-up-rule-2**:

mark-up-rule-2(*part/sale-price, part/cost-price, part/type,*
   type/mark-up-factor)

is a knowledge item. This knowledge item corresponds to the knowledge item:

[part/sale-price, part/cost-price, part/type, type/mark-up-factor][

$\lambda w_1 w_2 x_1 x_2 y_1 y_2 z_1 z_2 \bullet$[sells-for($w_1$:part-number, w_1:dollar-amount)

$\wedge$ costs(x_1:part-number, x_2:dollar-amount)

$\wedge$ has-type(y_1:part-number, y_2:type-description)

$\wedge$ factor-of(z_1:type-description, z_2:factor)) $\wedge$

$(((w_1 = x_1 = y_1) \wedge (y_2 = z_1))$

$\rightarrow (x_2 = z_2 \times y_2))]\bullet,$

$\lambda w_1 w_2 x_1 x_2 y_1 y_2 z_1 z_2 \bullet [(1\ 000 < w_1 < 9\ 999) \wedge (1 < w_2) \wedge$

$(1\ 000 < x_1 < 9\ 999) \wedge (0 < x_2) \wedge$

$((x_1 < 1\ 999) \rightarrow (x_2 \le 300)) \wedge$

$(1\ 000 < y_1 < 9\ 999) \wedge (y_2 = \text{lathe} \vee y_2 = \text{press}) \wedge$

$(z_1 = \text{lathe} \vee z_1 = \text{press}) \wedge (0 < z_2 < 3) \wedge$

$((w_1 = x_1) \rightarrow (w_2 > x_2))]\bullet,$

(Uni(*part/sale-price*) $\wedge$ Uni(*part/cost-price*) $\wedge$

Can(*part/sale-price*,

{*part/cost-price, part/type, type/mark-up-factor*}) $\wedge$

Can(*part/cost-price*,

{*part/sale-price, part/type, type/mark-up-factor*})

)*[part/sale-price, part/cost-price, part/type,*

type/mark-up-factor] $\wedge$

(Uni(*part*) $\wedge$ Can(*sale-price*, {*part*})$_{part/sale-price}$ $\wedge$

(Card $\le$ 100)$_{part}$ $\wedge$

(Uni(*part*) $\wedge$ Can(*cost-price*, {*part*})$_{part/cost-price}$ $\wedge$

(Card $\le$ 100)$_{part}$ $\wedge$

(Uni(*part*) $\wedge$ Can(*type*, {*part*})$_{part/type}$ $\wedge$

(Card $\le$ 100)$_{part}$ $\wedge$ (Card $\ge$ 2)$_{type}$ $\wedge$

(Uni(*type*) $\wedge$ Can(*mark-up-factor*, {*type*})$_{type/mark-up-factor}$

$\wedge$ (Card $\ge$ 2)$_{type}$]

Consider the 2-adic knowledge object with argument type $(\mathbf{X}^2, \mathbf{X}^2)$:

live-together$[\lambda P{:}\mathbf{X}^2 Q{:}\mathbf{X}^2 \bullet \lambda x_1 x_2 y_1 y_2 z_1 z_2 \bullet [S_P(x_1, x_2) \wedge S_Q(y_1, y_2)$

$\wedge S_Q(z_1, z_2)$

$\wedge (((x_1 = y_1) \wedge (x_2 = z_1) \wedge (x_1 \ne x_2)) \rightarrow (y_2 = z_2))]\bullet\bullet,$

$\lambda P{:}\mathbf{X}^2 Q{:}\mathbf{X}^2 \bullet \lambda x_1 x_2 y_1 y_2 z_1 z_2 \bullet [V_P(x_1, x_2) \wedge V_Q(y_1, y_2)$

$\wedge V_Q(z_1, z_2) \wedge \mathbf{T}]\bullet\bullet,$

$\lambda P{:}\mathbf{X}^2 Q{:}\mathbf{X}^2 \bullet [C_P \wedge C_Q$

$\wedge (\text{Uni}(P) \wedge \text{Can}(P, \{Q\}))_{V (\textbf{\textit{live-together}},P,Q)}]\bullet]$

The item instance of the object *live-together*:

live-together(*person/cohabitant, person/address*)

Is a knowledge item. Giving this knowledge item the name *[person/cohabitant, person/address]*:

live-together(*person/cohabitant, person/address*) =
[person/cohabitant, person/address][

$\quad \lambda P{:}\mathbf{X}^2 Q{:}\mathbf{X}^2 {\bullet} \lambda x_1 x_2 y_1 y_2 z_1 z_2 {\bullet}[\ S_P(x_1, x_2) \wedge S_Q(y_1, y_2)$

$\qquad \wedge\ S_Q(z_1, z_2)$

$\qquad \wedge\ (((\ x_1 = y_1\ ) \wedge (\ x_2 = z_1\ ) \wedge (\ x_1 \neq x_2\ ))$

$\qquad\quad \rightarrow (y_2 = z_2))\ ]{\bullet\bullet}$

$\qquad$ *(person/cohabitant, person/address),*

$\quad \lambda P{:}\mathbf{X}^2 Q{:}\mathbf{X}^2 {\bullet} \lambda x_1 x_2 y_1 y_2 z_1 z_2 {\bullet}[\ V_P(x_1, x_2) \wedge V_Q(y_1, y_2)$

$\qquad \wedge\ V_Q(z_1, z_2) \wedge \mathbf{T}]{\bullet\bullet}$

$\qquad$ *(person/cohabitant, person/address),*

$\quad \lambda P{:}\mathbf{X}^2 Q{:}\mathbf{X}^2 {\bullet}[C_P \wedge C_Q$

$\qquad \wedge\ (\text{Uni}(P) \wedge \text{Can}(P,\ \{Q\}))_{V\,(\textbf{\textit{live-together}},P,Q)}\ ]{\bullet}$

$\qquad$ *(person/cohabitant, person/address)*] =
[person/cohabitant, person/address][

$\quad \lambda x_1 x_2 y_1 y_2 z_1 z_2 {\bullet}[\ \text{lives-with}(x_1{:}\text{person-id}, x_2{:}\text{person-id})$

$\qquad \wedge\ \text{has-address}(y_1{:}\text{person-id}, y_2{:}\text{address-desc})$

$\qquad \wedge\ \text{has-address}(z_1{:}\text{person-id}, z_2{:}\text{address-desc})$

$\qquad \wedge\ (((\ x_1 = y_1\ ) \wedge (\ x_2 = z_1\ ) \wedge (\ x_1 \neq x_2\ ))$

$\qquad\quad \rightarrow (y_2 = z_2))\ ]{\bullet},$

$\quad \lambda x_1 x_2 y_1 y_2 z_1 z_2 {\bullet}[\ (1 < x_1 < 1\ 000) \wedge (1 < x_2 < 1\ 000) \wedge$

$\qquad (1 < y_1 < 1\ 000) \wedge (1 < z_1 < 1\ 000)\ ]{\bullet},$

(Uni(*person/cohabitant*)

$\qquad \wedge\ \text{Can}(\textit{person/cohabitant}, \{\textit{person/address}\})$

$\qquad)\textit{[person/cohabitant, person/address]}$

$\qquad \wedge\ (\text{Uni}(\textit{person})$

$\qquad\quad \wedge\ \text{Can}(\textit{address}, \{\textit{person}\})_{\textit{person/address}}$

$\qquad \wedge\ (\text{Card} \leq 500)_{\textit{person}}\ ]$

Consider the 3-adic knowledge object with argument type $(\mathbf{X}^2, \mathbf{X}^2, \mathbf{X}^1)$:

responsibility[λP:$\mathbf{X}^2$Q:$\mathbf{X}^2$R:$\mathbf{X}^1 \cdot \lambda$w$_1w_2x_1x_2y_1y_2z\cdot$[S$_P$(w$_1$, w$_2$)

$\wedge$ S$_Q$(x$_1$, x$_2$) $\wedge$ S$_P$(y$_1$, y$_2$) $\wedge$ S$_R$(z)

$\wedge$ ((((w$_1$ = x$_1$) $\wedge$ (x$_2$ = z) $\wedge$ (y$_1$,y$_2$ <u>are</u> $\perp$))

$\rightarrow$ (w$_2$ = z))

$\vee$ (((w$_1$ = x$_1$) $\wedge$ (x$_2$ $\neq$ z) $\wedge$ (x$_2$ = y$_1$))

$\rightarrow$ (w$_2$ = y$_2$)))]$\cdot$$\cdot$,

λP:$\mathbf{X}^2$Q:$\mathbf{X}^2$R:$\mathbf{X}^1 \cdot \lambda$w$_1w_2x_1x_2y_1y_2z\cdot$[V$_P$(w$_1$, w$_2$) $\wedge$ V$_Q$(x$_1$, x$_2$)

$\wedge$ V$_P$(y$_1$, y$_2$) $\wedge$ V$_R$(z) $\wedge$ **T**]$\cdot$$\cdot$,

λP:$\mathbf{X}^2$Q:$\mathbf{X}^2$R:$\mathbf{X}^1 \cdot$[C$_P$ $\wedge$ C$_Q$ $\wedge$ C$_R$

$\wedge$ (Uni(P) $\wedge$ Can(P, {Q, R}))$_{v (responsibility,\text{P,Q,R})}$]$\cdot$]

The item instance of the object *responsibility*:

responsibility(*employee/responsible-to, employee/supervisor, MD*)

is a knowledge item. Giving this knowledge item the name:
[employee/responsible-to, employee/supervisor, MD]

responsibility(*employee/responsible-to, employee/supervisor, MD*) =
[employee/responsible-to, employee/supervisor, MD][

λP:$\mathbf{X}^2$Q:$\mathbf{X}^2$R:$\mathbf{X}^1 \cdot \lambda$w$_1w_2x_1x_2y_1y_2z\cdot$[S$_P$(w$_1$, w$_2$)

$\wedge$ S$_Q$(x$_1$, x$_2$) $\wedge$ S$_P$(y$_1$, y$_2$) $\wedge$ S$_R$(z)

$\wedge$ ((((w$_1$ = x$_1$) $\wedge$ (x$_2$ = z) $\wedge$ (y$_1$,y$_2$ <u>are</u> $\perp$))

$\rightarrow$ (w$_2$ = z))

$\vee$ (((w$_1$ = x$_1$) $\wedge$ (x$_2$ $\neq$ z) $\wedge$ (x$_2$ = y$_1$))

$\rightarrow$ (w$_2$ = y$_2$)))]$\cdot$$\cdot$

(employee/responsible-to, employee/supervisor, MD),

λP:$\mathbf{X}^2$Q:$\mathbf{X}^2$R:$\mathbf{X}^1 \cdot \lambda$w$_1w_2x_1x_2y_1y_2z\cdot$[V$_P$(w$_1$, w$_2$) $\wedge$ V$_Q$(x$_1$, x$_2$)

$\wedge$ V$_P$(y$_1$, y$_2$) $\wedge$ V$_R$(z) $\wedge$ **T**]$\cdot$$\cdot$

(employee/responsible-to, employee/supervisor, MD),

λP:$\mathbf{X}^2$Q:$\mathbf{X}^2$R:$\mathbf{X}^1 \cdot$[C$_P$ $\wedge$ C$_Q$ $\wedge$ C$_R$

$\wedge$ (Uni(P) $\wedge$ Can(P, {Q, R}))$_{v (responsibility,\text{P,Q,R})}$]$\cdot$

(employee/responsible-to, employee/supervisor, MD)] =

[employee/responsible-to, employee/supervisor, MD][

$\lambda w_1 w_2 x_1 x_2 y_1 y_2 z \bullet$[responsible-to($w_1$:employee-id, w_2:employee-id)

$\land$ has-supervisor(x_1:employee-id, x_2:employee-id)

$\land$ responsible-to(y_1:employee-id, y_2:employee-id)

$\land$ is-a[z:MD-id]

$\land$ (((($w_1 = x_1$) $\land$ ($x_2 = z$) $\land$ (y_1, y_2 <u>are</u> $\perp$))

$\qquad \rightarrow$ ($w_2 = z$))

$\qquad \lor$ ((($w_1 = x_1$) $\land$ ($x_2 \neq z$) $\land$ ($x_2 = y_1$))

$\qquad \rightarrow$ ($w_2 = y_2$)))]$\bullet$,

$\lambda w_1 w_2 x_1 x_2 y_1 y_2 z \bullet$[$(1 < w_1 < 1\,000)$ $\land$ $(1 < w_2 < 1\,000)$

$\land$ $(1 < x_1 < 1\,000)$ $\land$ $(1 < x_2 < 1\,000)$

$\land$ $(1 < y_1 < 1\,000)$ $\land$ $(1 < y_2 < 1\,000)$

$\land$ $(1 < z < 1\,000)$]$\bullet$,

(Uni(*employee/responsible-to*)

$\land$ Can(*employee/responsible-to*, {*employee/supervisor, MD*})

)*[employee/responsible-to, employee/supervisor, MD]*

$\land$ (Can(*supervisor*, {*employee*}))_*employee/supervisor*

$\land$ (Can(*responsible-to*, {*employee*}))_*employee/responsible-to*

$\land$ (Card $\leq$ 500)_*employee*]

4.7 Algebra of objects

Examples of data objects, information objects and knowledge objects are given in
Sects. 4.4–4.6 respectively. Objects are named triples. Objects are operators that
turn a given set of items into another item. An object has the form:

A[E,F,G]

where E is the *object semantics* of A, F is the *object value constraints* of A and G
is the *object set constraints* of A. If E represents no particular association them A
is a data object. If E represents an implicit association then A is an information
object. If E represents an explicit association then A is a knowledge object.

In Chap. 3 real things are represented by items. If an item's semantics represents the identity association between one or more things then that item is
"tautological". A *tautological item* has the property that the value set of that item
has the form:

$\{ (x, x,...,x) : x \in S \}$

where S is the value set of any one of its components. An information or knowledge object represents an association between the arguments of that object. Extending the notion of a tautological item, a *tautological object* is an object that has the property that any instance of that object is a tautological item. An information object of argument type $(\mathbf{X}^1, \mathbf{X}^1, \mathbf{X}^1)$ is tautological if its semantics is:

$$\lambda P:\mathbf{X}^1 Q:\mathbf{X}^1 R:\mathbf{X}^1 \bullet \lambda xyz \bullet [\; S_P(x) \wedge S_Q(y) \wedge S_R(z) \wedge equal(x,\ y,\ z)\;] \bullet \bullet$$

where "equal(x, y, z)" means that "x, y and z are all equal". The information object "**understudies**" of argument type $(\mathbf{X}^1, \mathbf{X}^1)$ is not tautological if its semantics is:

$$\lambda P:\mathbf{X}^1 Q:\mathbf{X}^1 \bullet \lambda xy \bullet [\; S_P(x) \wedge S_Q(y) \wedge understudies(x,\ y)\;] \bullet \bullet$$

where "understudies(x, y)" means that "x understudies the duties of y". The "**understudies**" object is not tautological despite the fact that it can be applied to the two items *employee* and *employee* to give:

employee/employee[
    $\lambda xy \bullet [\; understudies(x:employee\text{-}id,\ y:employee\text{-}id)\;] \bullet,\ ...,\ ...]$

Consider the knowledge object of argument type $(\mathbf{X}^2, \mathbf{X}^2)$ whose semantics is:

$$\lambda P:\mathbf{X}^2 Q:\mathbf{X}^2 \bullet \lambda wxyz \bullet [\; S_P(w,\ x) \wedge S_Q(y,\ z) \wedge (w = y) \wedge (x = z)\;] \bullet \bullet$$

this object is also tautological.
    Given two n-adic objects:

$$A[\; E_A,\ F_A,\ G_A\;]\ \text{and}$$
$$B[\; E_B,\ F_B,\ G_B\;]$$

A and B are *identical*, written $A \equiv B$, if they are both of the same argument type and if:

$$(\forall Q_1, Q_2, ..., Q_j)[E_A(Q_1, Q_2, ..., Q_j) \leftrightarrow E_B(Q_1, Q_2, ..., Q_j)]$$
$$(\forall Q_1, Q_2, ..., Q_j)[F_A(Q_1, Q_2, ..., Q_j) \leftrightarrow F_B(Q_1, Q_2, ..., Q_j)]$$
$$(\forall Q_1, Q_2, ..., Q_j)[G_A(Q_1, Q_2, ..., Q_j) \leftrightarrow G_B(Q_1, Q_2, ..., Q_j)]$$

A and B are *equal*, written $A = B$, if:

$$(\forall Q_1, Q_2, ..., Q_j)[E_A(Q_1, Q_2, ..., Q_j) \leftrightarrow E_B(Q_1, Q_2, ..., Q_j)]$$

Given two n-adic objects:

$$A[\ E_A,\ F_A,\ G_A\ ]\ \text{and}$$
$$B[\ E_B,\ F_B,\ G_B\ ]$$

A and B are *equivalent*, written $A \simeq B$, if they are both of the same argument type and there exists a permutation π such that:

$$(\forall Q_1,Q_2,...,Q_j)[E_A(Q_1,Q_2,...,Q_j) \leftrightarrow E_B(\pi(Q_1,Q_2,...,Q_j))]$$
$$(\forall Q_1,Q_2,...,Q_j)F_A(Q_1,Q_2,...,Q_j) \leftrightarrow F_B(\pi(Q_1,Q_2,...,Q_j))]$$
$$(\forall Q_1,Q_2,...,Q_j)[G_A(Q_1,Q_2,...,Q_j) \leftrightarrow G_B(\pi(Q_1,Q_2,...,Q_j))]$$

A and B are *weakly equivalent*, written $A \simeq_w B$, if they are both of the same argument type and there exists a permutation π such that:

$$(\forall Q_1,Q_2,...,Q_j)[E_A(Q_1,Q_2,...,Q_j) \leftrightarrow E_B(\pi(Q_1,Q_2,...,Q_j))]$$

Two operations on objects are described in Sects. 4.7.1–4.7.2 respectively. The first operation "object composition" is thought of as a "vertical" operation. The second operation "object join" is thought of as a "horizontal" operation. The motivation behind the terms "vertical" and "horizontal" is given below.

An n-adic object is an operator that given a set of n items of the correct type generates a new item. Consider the knowledge object:

$$\textbf{\textit{mark-up-1}}[\lambda P{:}I^2 Q{:}I^2 R{:}D^1 \bullet \lambda x_1 x_2 y_1 y_2 z \bullet [\ S_P(x_1,x_2) \wedge S_Q(y_1,y_2) \wedge S_R(z)$$
$$\wedge\ ((\ x_1 = y_1\ ) \rightarrow (x_2 = z \times y_2))\ ]\bullet\bullet,$$
$$\lambda P{:}I^2 Q{:}I^2 R{:}D^1 \bullet \lambda x_1 x_2 y_1 y_2 z \bullet [\ V_P(x_1,x_2) \wedge V_Q(y_1,y_2) \wedge V_R(z) \wedge$$
$$((\ x_1 = y_1\ ) \rightarrow (\ x_2 > y_2\ ))\ ]\bullet\bullet,$$
$$\lambda P{:}I^2 Q{:}I^2 R{:}D^1 \bullet [C_P \wedge C_Q \wedge C_R \wedge (\text{Uni}(P) \wedge \text{Uni}(Q)$$
$$\wedge\ \text{Can}(P,\ \{Q,\ R\}) \wedge \text{Can}(Q,\ \{P,\ R\})$$
$$\wedge\ \text{Can}(R,\ \{P,\ Q\}))_{V(\textbf{\textit{mark-up-1}},P,Q,R)}\ ]\bullet\ ]$$

The first and second argument of this object are required to be 2-adic information items and the third argument is required to be a 1-adic data item.

4.7.1 Object composition

In this section the "object composition" operation is defined. In what follows, given a λ-calculus expression E the notation $E^\dagger$ means "expression E less its initial string of lambdas". The definition of object composition that follows is long and complicated. The reader way wish to study first the examples given at the end of this section. Those examples should convey the essence of "object composition". "Object join" is described in Sect. 4.7.2. Object join is used to develop the "normalisation" operation in Chap. 6. "Object composition" is not used in subsequent chapters. Given a f-adic object:

$$A[\ E_A,\ F_A,\ G_A\ ]$$

of argument type $(X_1^{p_1},\ X_2^{p_2},...,\ X_f^{p_f})$ where the X_k are types such as **X**, **D**, **I** or **K** (standing respectively for "free", "data", "information" or "knowledge"), in which E_A and F_A are typed λ-calculus expressions expressed in terms of the variables $\lambda P_1:X_1^{p_1}P_2:X_2^{p_2}...P_f:X_f^{p_f}$ and $\lambda x_1^1...x_{r_1}^1...x_{r_m}^m$ and G_A is a typed λ-calculus expression expressed in terms of the variables $\lambda P_1:X_1^{p_1}P_2:X_2^{p_2}...P_f:X_f^{p_f}$:

$$E_A = \lambda P_1:X_1^{p_1}P_2:X_2^{p_2}...P_f:X_f^{p_f} \bullet \lambda x_1^1...x_{r_1}^1...x_{r_m}^m \bullet [\ S_{R_1}(x_1^1,...,x_{r_1}^1)$$
$$\wedge\ S_{R_2}(x_1^2,...,x_{r_2}^2)\ \wedge\ ....\ \wedge\ S_{R_m}(x_1^m,...,x_{r_m}^m)$$
$$\wedge\ J_A(x_1^1...x_{r_1}^1...x_{r_m}^m)\ ]^{\bullet\bullet}$$
$$= \lambda P_1:X_1^{p_1}P_2:X_2^{p_2}...P_f:X_f^{p_f} \bullet E_A^\dagger \bullet$$
$$F_A = \lambda P_1:X_1^{p_1}P_2:X_2^{p_2}...P_f:X_f^{p_f} \bullet \lambda x_1^1...x_{r_1}^1...x_{r_m}^m \bullet [\ V_{R_1}(x_1^1,...,x_{r_1}^1)$$
$$\wedge\ V_{R_2}(x_1^2,...,x_{r_2}^2)\ \wedge\ ....\ \wedge\ V_{R_m}(x_1^m,...,x_{r_m}^m)$$
$$\wedge\ K_A(x_1^1...x_{r_1}^1...x_{r_m}^m)\ ]^{\bullet\bullet}$$
$$= \lambda P_1:X_1^{p_1}P_2:X_2^{p_2}...P_f:X_f^{p_f} \bullet F_A^\dagger \bullet$$
$$G_A = \lambda P_1:X_1^{p_1}P_2:X_2^{p_2}...P_f:X_f^{p_f} \bullet [C_{P_1}\ \wedge\ ....\ \wedge\ C_{P_f}$$
$$\wedge\ (L_A(P_1,...,P_f))_{v(A,P_1,...,P_f)}]^\bullet$$
$$= \lambda P_1:X_1^{p_1}P_2:X_2^{p_2}...P_f:X_f^{p_f} \bullet G_A^\dagger \bullet$$

where $(\forall x: 1 \leq x \leq m)(\exists y)(R_x = P_y$ *and* $r_x = p_y)$. Given a set:

$$C = \{c_1,...,c_k\} \subseteq \{1,2,...,f\}$$

of *identified indices* in object *A*. The set $D = \{P_i : i \in C\}$ is the *identified arguments* in object *A*. Given a g-adic object:

$$B[\ E_B,\ F_B,\ G_B\ ]$$

of argument type $(Y_1^{q_1},\ Y_2^{q_2},...,\ Y_g^{q_g})$ where the Y_k are types such as **X**, **D**, **I** or **K**, in which E_B and F_B are typed expressions expressed in terms of the variables

$\lambda Q_1:Y_1^{q_1}Q_2:Y_2^{q_2}...Q_g:Y_g^{q_g}$ and $\lambda y_1^1...y_{s_1}^1...y_{s_n}^n$ and G_A is a typed expression expressed in terms of the variables $\lambda Q_1:Y_1^{q_1}Q_2:Y_2^{q_2}...Q_g:Y_g^{q_g}$:

$$
\begin{aligned}
E_B &= \lambda Q_1:Y_1^{q_1}Q_2:Y_2^{q_2}...Q_g:Y_g^{q_g}\bullet\lambda y_1^1...y_{s_1}^1...y_{s_n}^n\bullet[\ S_{S_1}(y_1^1,...,y_{s_1}^1) \\
&\qquad \wedge\ S_{S_2}(y_1^2,...,y_{s_2}^2)\ \wedge\ ....\ \wedge\ S_{S_n}(y_1^n,...,y_{s_n}^n) \\
&\qquad \wedge\ J_B(y_1^1,...,y_{s_1}^1,...,y_{s_n}^n)\ ]\bullet\bullet \\
&= \lambda Q_1:Y_1^{q_1}Q_2:Y_2^{q_2}...Q_g:Y_g^{q_g}\bullet E_B^\dagger\bullet \\
F_B &= \lambda Q_1:Y_1^{q_1}Q_2:Y_2^{q_2}...Q_g:Y_g^{q_g}\bullet\lambda y_1^1...y_{s_1}^1...y_{s_n}^n\bullet[\ V_{S_1}(y_1^1,...,y_{s_1}^1) \\
&\qquad \wedge\ V_{S_2}(y_1^2,...,y_{s_2}^2)\ \wedge\ ....\ \wedge\ V_{S_n}(y_1^n,...,y_{s_n}^n) \\
&\qquad \wedge\ K_B(y_1^1,...,y_{s_1}^1,...,y_{s_n}^n)\ ]\bullet\bullet \\
&= \lambda Q_1:Y_1^{q_1}Q_2:Y_2^{q_2}...Q_g:Y_g^{q_g}\bullet F_B^\dagger\bullet \\
G_B &= \lambda Q_1:Y_1^{q_1}Q_2:Y_2^{q_2}...Q_g:Y_g^{q_g}\bullet[C_{Q_1}\ \wedge\ ....\ \wedge\ C_{Q_g} \\
&\qquad \wedge\ (L_B(Q_1,...,Q_g))_{V(B,Q_1,...,Q_g)}]\bullet
\end{aligned}
$$

where $(\forall x:\ 1\leq x\leq n)(\exists y)(S_x = Q_y\ \text{and}\ s_x = q_y)$, and the types of the arguments of object B are "compatible with" the types of the identified arguments of object A. The types of the set of typed variables B are *compatible with* the types of the set of typed variables A if:

$B = \{B_1:X_1^{b_1},...,B_n:X_n^{b_n}\}$

$A = \{A_1:Y_1^{a_1},...,A_m:Y_m^{a_m}\}$ and

$\exists d_1$ such that $b_1 = a_1 + a_2 +...+ a_{d_1}$

and if $X_1 \neq X$ then $Y_1 =...= Y_{d_1} = X_1$

$\exists d_2 > d_1$ such that $b_2 = a_{d_1+1} +...+ a_{d_2}$

and if $X_2 \neq X$ then $Y_{d_1+1} =...= Y_{d_2} = X_2$

and so on, so that each B_i corresponds to a set of A_j's.

If the types of the arguments of object B are compatible with the types of the identified arguments of object A then:

$$
\sum_{j=1}^{g} q_j = \sum_{i\in C} p_i = \sum_{i=1}^{k} p_{c_i} = \sum_{i=1}^{n} s_i
$$

The object with name $A\ _C\oplus\ B$ is defined to be:

$$A \ _C{\oplus}\ B[\ S{\bullet}E^{\dagger}_{A,B}{\bullet},\ S{\bullet}F^{\dagger}_{A,B}{\bullet},\ S{\bullet}G^{\dagger}_{A,B}{\bullet}\ ]$$

the string S is constructed as follows:

take the string $\lambda P_1{:}X_1^{p_1}P_2{:}X_2^{p_2}...P_f{:}X_f^{p_f}$

  delete $P_i{:}X_i^{p_i}$ if $i{\in}C$

to the resulting string

  add $Q_1{:}Y_1^{q_1}Q_2{:}Y_2^{q_2}...Q_g{:}Y_g^{q_g}$

the expression $E^{\dagger}_{A,B}$ is constructed from the expression $E^{\dagger}_{A}$ as follows:

take the expression $E^{\dagger}_{A}$

  delete $S_{R_i}(x_1^i,...,x_{r_i}^i)$ if $i{\in}C$

to the resulting expression

  conjoin the term $\lambda x_1^{c_1}..x_{p_{c_1}}^{c_1}..x_1^{c_k}..x_{p_{c_k}}^{c_k}{\bullet}E^{\dagger}_{B}(x_1^{c_1},...,x_{p_{c_1}}^{c_1},...,x_1^{c_k},..,x_{p_{c_k}}^{c_k}){\bullet}$

the expression $F^{\dagger}_{A,B}$ is constructed from the expression $F^{\dagger}_{A}$ as follows:

take the expression $F^{\dagger}_{A}$

  delete $V_{R_i}(x_1^i,...,x_{r_i}^i)$ if $i{\in}C$

to the resulting expression

  conjoin the term $\lambda x_1^{c_1}..x_{p_{c_1}}^{c_1}..x_1^{c_k}..x_{p_{c_k}}^{c_k}{\bullet}F^{\dagger}_{B}(x_1^{c_1},...,x_{p_{c_1}}^{c_1},...,x_1^{c_k},..,x_{p_{c_k}}^{c_k}){\bullet}$

where the expression $G^{\dagger}_{A,B}$ is constructed from the expression $G^{\dagger}_{A}$ as follows:

take the expression $G^{\dagger}_{A}$

  delete C_{P_i} if $i{\in}C$

  delete $(L_A(P_1,...,P_f))_{V(A,P_1,...,P_f)}$

  conjoin the term $C_{Q_1}\wedge\ ....\ \wedge C_{Q_g}$

  conjoin the term $(L_{A,B})_{V(A\ _C{\oplus}\ B,\ S^V)}$

where S^V is a list of the variable names in the list S separated by commas and $L_{A,B}$ is constructed as follows:

  let $L_{A,B}$ be $\emptyset$ the empty expression

    if $L_A(P_1,...,P_f)$ contains $Uni(P_i)$ where $i{\notin}C$ then conjoin $Uni(P_i)$

      to $L_{A,B}$

if $L_A(P_1,...,P_f)$ contains $Can(P_i,X)$ where $i \notin C$ and $(\forall j)(\text{if } P_j \in X$ then $j \notin C)$ then conjoin $Can(P_i,X)$ to $L_{A,B}$

if $L_A(P_1,...,P_f)$ contains $Can(P_{c_1},X)$ then if $k = 1$ and $L_B(Q_1,...,Q_g)$ contains $Can(Q_k,\{Q_j\})$ for every $k \neq j$ and $1 \leq k \leq g$ then conjoin $Can(Q_j,X)$ to $L_{A,B}$

if $k = 1$ and P_{c_1} has argument type $\mathbf{X}^1, \mathbf{D}^1, \mathbf{I}^1$ or $\mathbf{K}^1$ then if $L_A(P_1,...,P_f)$ contains $Can(P_i,X)$ or $Uni(P_j)$ then replace P_{c_1} by Q_1 wherever it occurs in the $Can(P_i,X)$ or $Uni(P_j)$ and conjoin the result to $L_{A,B}$

if $L_A(P_1,...,P_f)$ contains a sub-expression containing 'Card' and if $L_A(P_1,...,P_f)$ contains $Can(P_i,X)$ where $(\forall j)(\text{if } P_j \in X$ then $j \notin C)$ then conjoin that sub-expression containing 'Card' to $L_{A,B}$

if $L_B(Q_1,...,Q_g)$ contains $Uni(Q_j)$ then if $L_A(P_1,...,P_f)$ contains $Can(P_i,\{P_{c_1},...,P_{c_k}\})$ where $i \notin C$ then conjoin $Uni(Q_j)$ to $L_{A,B}$

if $L_B(Q_1,...,Q_g)$ contains $Uni(Q_j)$ then if $k = 1$ and $L_A(P_1,...,P_f)$ contains $Uni(P_{c_1})$ then conjoin $Uni(Q_j)$ to $L_{A,B}$

if $L_B(Q_1,...,Q_g)$ contains $Can(Q_j,X)$ then conjoin $Can(Q_j,X)$ to $L_{A,B}$

if $L_B(Q_1,...,Q_g)$ contains a sub-expression containing 'Card' then if $L_A(P_1,...,P_f)$ contains $Can(P_i,\{P_{c_1},...,P_{c_k}\})$ where $i \notin C$ then conjoin that sub-expression containing 'Card' to $L_{A,B}$

The expressions $E_B^{\dagger}$ and $F_B^{\dagger}$ are defined to be E_B and F_B respectively except for the initial string of lambdas, as shown above. This operation is *object composition*. Object A is said to have been combined on set C with object B using object composition.

Using the rule of object composition $\oplus$, knowledge objects, information objects and data objects may be combined with one another. If a knowledge object is combined with an information object using $\oplus$ then the resulting object has mixed type.

The object composition:

mark-up-1 $\{1\} \oplus$ *sells-for*[
$\lambda P{:}\mathbf{X}^1 Q{:}\mathbf{X}^1 R{:}\mathbf{X}^2 S{:}\mathbf{X}^1 \bullet \lambda wxy_1y_2z\bullet[\ S_P(w) \wedge S_Q(x) \wedge S_R(y_1, y_2) \wedge$
$S_S(z) \wedge \text{sells-for}(w,x) \wedge ((w = y_1) \rightarrow (x = z \times y_2))\ ]^{\bullet\bullet},$
$\lambda P{:}\mathbf{X}^1 Q{:}\mathbf{X}^1 R{:}\mathbf{X}^2 S{:}\mathbf{X}^1 \bullet \lambda wxy_1y_2z\bullet[\ V_P(w) \wedge V_Q(x) \wedge V_R(y_1, y_2) \wedge$
$V_S(z) \wedge ((w = y_1) \rightarrow (x > y_2))\ ]^{\bullet\bullet},$

$$\lambda P : X^1 Q : X^1 R : X^2 S : X^1 \bullet [\ C_P \wedge C_Q \wedge C_R \wedge C_S \wedge$$
$$(Uni(R) \wedge Uni(P) \wedge Can(Q, \{P\}) \wedge$$
$$Can(P, \{R, S\}))_{v\,(\textbf{\textit{mark-up-1}}_{\ \{1\}}\oplus\ \textbf{\textit{sells-for}}, P, Q, R, S)}\ ]^\bullet\ ]$$

has argument type (X^1, X^1, X^2, X^1). The object composition:

mark-up-1 $_{\{3\}} \oplus$ **_mark-up_**[
$\quad \lambda P : X^2 Q : X^2 R : X^1 \bullet \lambda x_1 x_2 y_1 y_2 z \bullet [\ S_P(x_1, x_2) \wedge S_Q(y_1, y_2) \wedge S_R(z) \wedge$
$\quad\quad$ is-a[z:mark-up-factor] $\wedge\ ((\ x_1 = y_1\ ) \rightarrow (x_2 = z \times y_2))\ ]^\bullet,$
$\quad \lambda P : X^2 Q : X^2 R : X^1 \bullet \lambda x_1 x_2 y_1 y_2 z \bullet [\ V_P(x_1, x_2) \wedge V_Q(y_1, y_2) \wedge V_R(z) \wedge$
$\quad\quad (0 < z < 3) \wedge ((\ x_1 = y_1\ ) \rightarrow (\ x_2 > y_2\ ))\ ]^{\bullet\bullet},$
$\quad \lambda P : X^2 Q : X^2 R : X^1 \bullet [C_P \wedge C_Q \wedge C_R \wedge (Uni(P) \wedge Uni(Q)$
$\quad\quad \wedge Can(P, \{Q, R\}) \wedge Can(Q, \{P, R\})$
$\quad\quad \wedge Can(R, \{P, Q\}))_{v\,(\textbf{\textit{mark-up-1}}_{\ \{3\}}\oplus\ \textbf{\textit{mark-up}}, P, Q, R)}]^\bullet\ ]$

has argument type (X^2, X^2, X^1). The object composition:

sells-for $_{\{1\}} \oplus$ **_part_**[
$\quad \lambda P : X^1 Q : X^1 \bullet \lambda xy \bullet [\ S_P(x) \wedge S_Q(y) \wedge$ is-a[x:part-number] $\wedge$
$\quad\quad$ sells-for(x, y) $]^{\bullet\bullet},$
$\quad \lambda P : X^1 Q : X^1 \bullet \lambda xy \bullet [\ V_P(x) \wedge V_Q(y) \wedge (1\,000 < x < 9\,999)\ ]^{\bullet\bullet},$
$\quad \lambda P : X^1 Q : X^1 \bullet [C_P \wedge C_Q \wedge (Uni(P) \wedge Can(Q, \{P\}) \wedge$
$\quad\quad$ Card $\leq 100)_{v\,(\textbf{\textit{sells-for}}_{\ \{1\}}\oplus\ \textbf{\textit{part}}, P, Q)}]^\bullet\ ]$

has argument type (X^1, X^1).

The object composition operator is particularly useful when both objects have the same type. Consider the 2-adic object:

lives-at[$\lambda P : X^1 Q : X^1 \bullet \lambda xy \bullet [\ S_P(x) \wedge S_Q(y) \wedge$ lives-at(x, y) $]^{\bullet\bullet},$
$\quad \lambda P : X^1 Q : X^1 \bullet \lambda xy \bullet [\ V_P(x) \wedge V_Q(y) \wedge (x \neq y)\ ]^{\bullet\bullet},$
$\quad \lambda P : X^1 Q : X^1 \bullet [C_P \wedge C_Q \wedge (\mathbf{T})_{v\,(\textbf{\textit{lives-at}}, P)}\ ]^\bullet]$

and the 2-adic object:

owns[$\lambda P : X^1 Q : X^1 \bullet \lambda xy \bullet [\ S_P(x) \wedge S_Q(y) \wedge$ owns(x, y) $]^{\bullet\bullet},$
$\quad \lambda P : X^1 Q : X^1 \bullet \lambda xy \bullet [\ V_P(x) \wedge V_Q(y) \wedge (x \neq y)\ ]^{\bullet\bullet},$
$\quad \lambda P : X^1 Q : X^1 \bullet [C_P \wedge C_Q \wedge (\mathbf{T})_{v\,(\textbf{\textit{owns}}, P, Q)}\ ]^\bullet]$

The object composition **_lives-at_** $_{\{1,2\}} \oplus$ **_owns_** is:

lives-at $_{\{1,2\}}\oplus$ *owns* $[\lambda P:X^1Q:X^1\bullet\lambda xy\bullet[\ S_P(x)\wedge S_Q(y)$

$\wedge$ lives-at$(x,\ y)\wedge$ owns$(x,\ y)\ ]\bullet\bullet,$

$\lambda P:X^1Q:X^1\bullet\lambda xy\bullet[\ V_P(x)\wedge V_Q(y)\wedge(x\neq y)\ ]\bullet\bullet,$

$\lambda P:X^1Q:X^1\bullet[C_P\wedge C_Q\wedge(T)_{\vee\,(\textit{lives-at}\ _{\{1,2\}}\oplus\ \textit{owns},P,Q)}\ ]\bullet]$

This construct is the *"lives-at-and-owns"* 2-adic object. In a sense the *lives-at* object has been employed to refine the *owns* object. When an n-adic object *A* is employed in this way to refine an n-adic object *B* of identical type instead of representing the result as:

A $_{\{1,2,...,n\}}\oplus$ *B*

the more compact notation:

A $\oplus$ *B*

may be used. Object composition can be used to build complex objects from simple objects. Alternatively object composition can form the basis of an approach to decompose objects into a sequence of simple objects.

4.7.2 Object join

In this section the "object join" operation is defined. Object join is closely related to item join that is described in Sect. 3.7. Given two objects:

A[E_A, F_A, G_A] and
B[E_B, F_B, G_B]

then E_A, F_A, E_B and F_B all have the form:

λ<string of typed outer variables>$\bullet\lambda$<string of inner variables>$\bullet$[...]$\bullet\bullet$

Both G_A and G_B have the form:

λ<string of typed outer variables>$\bullet$[...]$\bullet$

Suppose that E_A has n typed outer variables, and that E_B has m typed outer variables. Some of the outer arguments of *A* and *B* may have identical argument types. Suppose that k pairs of outer arguments of *A* and *B* that have identical argument types are identified, where k $\geq$ 0. Let C be a set of k pairs of indices where the first index in each pair identifies an outer variable of *A* and the second identifies an outer variable of *B* of identical type. C may be empty. To ensure that C is well defined the pairs of indices in C occur in ascending order of the first index of each pair. Let $A*$ be an object that is identical to object A except for the order of its outer and inner variables. The last k outer variables in $A*$ are those outer variables in A that are referred to by the indices of A that are in the set C. The inner variables of $A*$ are a permutation of the inner variables of A to ensure that $A*$ is identical to A, except for the order of its variables. Let $B*$ be an object that is identical to object B except for the order of its outer and inner variables. The first k outer variables in $B*$ are those outer variables in B that are referred to by the indices of B that are in the set C. The inner variables of $B*$ are a permutation of the inner variables of B to ensure that $B*$ is identical to B, except for the order of its variables. Let π be a permutation that turns the ordered set of outer variables of $A*$ into the ordered set of outer variables of A. Let π' be a permutation that turns the ordered set of outer variables of $B*$ into the ordered set of outer variables of B. Let ρ be a permutation that turns the ordered set of inner variables of $A*$ into the ordered set of inner variables of A. Let ρ' be a permutation that turns the ordered set of inner variables of $B*$ into the ordered set of inner variables of B. Suppose that 'P' is an (n - k)-tuple of typed variables, 'Q' is a k-tuple of typed variables and 'R' is an (m - k)-tuple of typed variables. Suppose that 'x' is a string of inner variables that correspond to 'P', 'y' is a string of inner variables that correspond to 'Q' and 'z' is a string of inner variables that correspond to 'R'. Then the object with name $A \otimes_C B$ is the *join* of A and B on C and is defined to be:

$$(A \otimes_C B)[$$
$$\lambda P{:}T_P Q{:}T_Q R{:}T_R \bullet \lambda xyz \bullet [E_A(\rho(P,Q))(\pi(x,y)) \wedge E_B(\rho'(Q,R))(\pi'(x,y))]\bullet,$$
$$\lambda P{:}T_P Q{:}T_Q R{:}T_R \bullet \lambda xyz \bullet [F_A(\rho(P,Q))(\pi(x,y)) \wedge F_B(\rho'(Q,R))(\pi'(x,y))]\bullet,$$
$$[G_A(\rho(P,Q)) \wedge G_B(\rho'(Q,R))]\bullet \;]$$

If A and B are two information objects with a single shared argument in the set C then $A \otimes_C B$ is their "join", in the conventional sense, on the domain represented by the single shared argument. Also, if A and B are two functional associations and if C represents both the argument of one of these functions and the range of the other then $A \otimes_C B$ is the functional composition of these two functions. C may be empty. If $C = \emptyset$ then $A \otimes_C B$ is the Cartesian product of A and B.

If two objects A and B are such that for each argument of A there exists an argument of B with identical type and object B has at least one argument that is not an argument of object A, and $A \otimes_C B = B$, then object A is a *sub-object* of object B, written $A \subset B$. The composition $A \otimes_C B$ is a *monotonic composition* if $A \otimes_C B$ is not weakly equivalent with either A or B. If $A \otimes_C B$ is a monotonic composition and the set C identifies one argument only of A and B then $A \otimes_C B$ is a *unit composition*.

The following are properties of $\otimes$:

$\otimes$	data	information	knowledge
data	data	information	knowledge
information	information	information	information
knowledge	knowledge	information	knowledge

Fig. 4.2 The type of the object $A \otimes B$

- $A \otimes_K A = A$ where $K \subseteq K_A$ and K_A is the set of arguments of A
- $A \otimes_K B \simeq B \otimes_K A$ where $K \subseteq (K_A \cap K_B)$
- $A \otimes_K (B \otimes_L C) \simeq (A \otimes_K B) \otimes_L C$ where
  $$K \subseteq (K_A \cap K_B) \text{ and } L \subseteq (K_B \cap K_C)$$

If $A \otimes_K B = A$ then $K = K_B \subseteq K_A$.

Using the rule of composition $\otimes$, knowledge objects, information objects and data objects may be combined with one another. The type of the composition of two objects is shown in Fig. 4.2.

The compound data object:

$$comp[\ \lambda P:\mathbf{D}^1 Q:\mathbf{D}^1 \bullet \lambda xy \bullet [\ S_P(x) \wedge S_Q(y)\ ]\bullet\bullet,$$
$$\lambda P:\mathbf{D}^1 Q:\mathbf{D}^1 \bullet \lambda xy \bullet [\ V_P(x) \wedge V_Q(y)\ ]\bullet\bullet,$$
$$\lambda P:\mathbf{D}^1 Q:\mathbf{D}^1 \bullet [C_P \wedge C_Q$$
$$\wedge\ (Uni(P) \wedge Uni(Q))_{v(comp,P,Q)}\ ]\bullet\ ]$$

has argument type $(\mathbf{D}^1, \mathbf{D}^1)$. The information object:

$$has\text{-}type[\lambda P:\mathbf{X}^1 Q:\mathbf{X}^1 \bullet \lambda xy \bullet [S_P(x) \wedge S_Q(y) \wedge has\text{-}type(x,\ y)]\bullet\bullet,$$
$$\lambda P:\mathbf{X}^1 Q:\mathbf{X}^1 \bullet \lambda xy \bullet [V_P(x) \wedge V_Q(y) \wedge T]\bullet\bullet,$$
$$\lambda P:\mathbf{X}^1 Q:\mathbf{X}^1 \bullet [C_P \wedge C_Q$$
$$\wedge\ (Uni(P) \wedge Can(Q,\ \{P\}))_{v(has\text{-}type,P,Q)}\ ]\bullet]$$

has argument type $(\mathbf{X}^1, \mathbf{X}^1)$. These two objects may be combined using object join on the set containing the second argument of *comp* and the first argument of *has-type* to obtain the information object:

$$comp \otimes_{\{(2,1)\}} has\text{-}type[\ \lambda P:\mathbf{D}^1 Q:\mathbf{D}^1 R:\mathbf{X}^1 \bullet \lambda xyz \bullet [\ S_P(x) \wedge S_Q(y) \wedge$$
$$S_R(z) \wedge has\text{-}type(y,\ z)\ ]\bullet\bullet,$$
$$\lambda P:\mathbf{D}^1 Q:\mathbf{D}^1 R:\mathbf{X}^1 \bullet \lambda xyz \bullet [\ V_P(x) \wedge V_Q(y) \wedge V_R(y)\ ]\bullet\bullet,$$
$$\lambda P:\mathbf{D}^1 Q:\mathbf{D}^1 R:\mathbf{X}^1 \bullet [C_P \wedge C_Q \wedge C_R\ (Uni(P) \wedge Uni(Q) \wedge Uni(Q) \wedge$$
$$Can(R,\ \{Q\}))_{v(comp\ \otimes_{\{(2,1)\}}\ has\text{-}type,P,Q)}]\bullet]$$

machine/type	
machine-number	type-description
AB	lathe
CD	press

part_machine/type	
part-number_ machine-number	type-description
1234_AB	lathe
2468_AB	lathe
3579_AB	lathe
1234_CD	press
2468_CD	press
3579_CD	press

Fig. 4.3 The machine/type and part_machine/type relations

This information object has argument type $(\mathbf{D}^1, \mathbf{D}^1, \mathbf{X}^1)$. This object has an instance:

$comp \otimes_{\{(2,1)\}} \textbf{\textit{has-type}}[\ \lambda P:\mathbf{D}^1 Q:\mathbf{D}^1 R:\mathbf{X}^1 \cdot \lambda xyz \cdot [\ S_P(x) \wedge S_Q(y) \wedge$
$\qquad S_R(z) \wedge has\text{-}type(y, z)\ ]\cdot\cdot,$
$\quad \lambda P:\mathbf{D}^1 Q:\mathbf{D}^1 R:\mathbf{D}^1 \cdot \lambda xyz \cdot [\ V_P(x) \wedge V_Q(y) \wedge V_R(y)\ ]\cdot\cdot,$
$\quad \lambda P:\mathbf{D}^1 Q:\mathbf{D}^1 R:\mathbf{D}^1 \cdot [C_P \wedge C_Q \wedge C_R\ (Uni(P) \wedge Uni(Q) \wedge$
$\qquad Can(R, \{Q\}))_{V (comp \otimes_{\{(2,1)\}} \textbf{\textit{has-type}}, P, Q)}\cdot]$
$\quad (part, machine, type) =$
$part\_machine/type[\ \lambda xyz \cdot [\ is\text{-}a[x:part\text{-}number] \wedge is\text{-}a[y:machine\text{-}name] \wedge$
$\qquad has\text{-}type(y:machine\text{-}name, z:type\text{-}description)\ ]\cdot,$
$\quad \lambda xyz \cdot [\ (1\,000 < x < 9\,999) \wedge$
$\qquad (y = AB \vee y = CD) \wedge (z = lathe \vee z = press)\ ]\cdot,$
$\quad (Uni(part) \wedge Uni(machine) \wedge$
$\qquad Can(type, \{machine\}))_{part\_machine/type} \wedge$
$\qquad (Card \leq 100)_{part} \wedge (Card \geq 2)_{machine} \wedge$
$\qquad (Card = 2)_{type}\ ]$

where the resulting item is named "*part_machine/type*". This corresponds to the compound population "part_machine" shown in Fig. 4.1 being joined with the relation "machine/type" shown in Fig. 4.3 on the domain "machine" to give the relation "part_machine/type". In terms of the corresponding items:

$part\_machine \otimes_{\{machine\}} machine/type = part\_machine/type$

The knowledge object:

$\textbf{\textit{mark-up-1}}[\lambda P{:}X^2Q{:}X^2R{:}X^1{\bullet}\lambda x_1x_2y_1y_2z{\bullet}[\ S_P(x_1,\,x_2)\wedge S_Q(y_1,\,y_2)$
$\qquad\wedge\ S_R(z)\wedge((\,x_1=y_1\,)\to(x_2=z\times y_2))\ ]{\bullet\bullet},$
$\quad\lambda P{:}X^2Q{:}X^2R{:}X^1{\bullet}\lambda x_1x_2y_1y_2z{\bullet}[\ V_P(x_1,\,x_2)\wedge V_Q(y_1,\,y_2)\wedge V_R(z)$
$\qquad\wedge((\,x_1=y_1\,)\to(\,x_2>y_2\,))\ ]{\bullet\bullet},$
$\quad\lambda P{:}X^2Q{:}X^2R{:}X^1{\bullet}[C_P\wedge C_Q\wedge C_R\wedge(\mathrm{Uni}(P)\wedge\mathrm{Uni}(Q)$
$\qquad\wedge\ \mathrm{Can}(P,\,\{Q,\,R\})\wedge\mathrm{Can}(Q,\,\{P,\,R\})$
$\qquad\wedge\ \mathrm{Can}(R,\,\{P,\,Q\}))_{V(\textbf{\textit{mark-up-1}},P,Q,R)}\ ]{\bullet}\ ]$

has argument type $(X^2,\,X^2,\,X^1)$. The information object:

$\textbf{\textit{valid}}[\lambda P{:}X^1Q{:}X^2{\bullet}\lambda xy_1y_2{\bullet}[\ S_P(x)\wedge S_Q(y_1,\,y_2)\wedge\mathrm{valid}(x,\,y_1,\,y_2)\ ]{\bullet\bullet},$
$\quad\lambda P{:}X^1Q{:}X^1R{:}X^1{\bullet}\lambda xy_1y_2{\bullet}[\ V_P(x)\wedge V_Q(y_1,\,y_2)\wedge\mathbf{T}\ ]{\bullet\bullet},$
$\quad\lambda P{:}X^1Q{:}X^1R{:}X^1{\bullet}[C_P\wedge C_Q$
$\qquad\wedge\ (\mathrm{Can}(P,\,\{Q\}))_{V(\textbf{\textit{valid}},P,Q)}{\bullet}]$

has argument type $(X^1,\,X^2)$ where "valid(x, y, z)" means "x is valid at y and z". These two objects may be combined using object join on the set containing the third argument of $\textbf{\textit{mark-up-1}}$ and the first argument of $\textbf{\textit{valid}}$ to obtain the object:

$\textbf{\textit{mark-up-1}}\otimes_{\{(3,1)\}}\textbf{\textit{valid}}[$
$\quad\lambda P{:}X^2Q{:}X^2R{:}X^1S{:}X^2{\bullet}\lambda x_1x_2y_1y_2zv_1v_2{\bullet}[\ S_P(x_1,\,x_2)\wedge$
$\qquad S_Q(y_1,\,y_2)\wedge S_R(z)\wedge S_S(v_1,\,v_2)\wedge$
$\qquad((\,x_1=y_1\,)\to(x_2=z\times y_2))\wedge\mathrm{valid}(z,\,v_1,\,v_2)\ ]{\bullet\bullet},$
$\quad\lambda P{:}X^2Q{:}X^2R{:}X^1S{:}X^2{\bullet}\lambda x_1x_2y_1y_2zv_1v_2{\bullet}[$
$\qquad((\,x_1=y_1\,)\to(\,x_2>y_2\,))\ ]{\bullet\bullet},$
$\quad\lambda P{:}X^2Q{:}X^2R{:}X^1S{:}X^2{\bullet}[C_P\wedge C_Q\wedge C_R\wedge C_S$
$\qquad\wedge\ \mathrm{Uni}(P)\wedge\mathrm{Uni}(Q)\wedge\mathrm{Can}(P,\,\{Q,\,R\})$
$\qquad\wedge\ \mathrm{Can}(Q,\,\{P,\,R\})\wedge\mathrm{Can}(R,\,\{P,\,Q\})$
$\qquad\wedge\ \mathrm{Can}(R,\,\{S\}))_{V(\textbf{\textit{mark-up-1}}\otimes_{\{(3,1)\}}\textbf{\textit{valid}},P,Q,R)}{\bullet}\ ]$

This information object has argument type $(X^2,\,X^2,\,X^1,\,X^2)$. This object has an instance:

mark-up-1 $\otimes_{\{(3,1)\}}$ **valid**(
        part/sale-price, part/cost-price, mark-up, month_year)
= *[part/sale-price, part/cost-price, mark-up, month_year]*[
    $\lambda x_1 x_2 y_1 y_2 z v_1 v_2 \bullet$[
        sells-for(x_1:part-number, x_2:dollar-amount) $\wedge$
        costs(y_1:part-number, y_2:dollar-amount) $\wedge$
        valid(z:mark-up-factor,
            v_1:month-number, v_2:year-number) $\wedge$
        $((x_1 = y_1) \to (x_2 = z \times y_2))] \bullet$
    $\lambda x_1 x_2 y_1 y_2 z v_1 v_2 \bullet$[
        $(1\,000 < y_1 < 9\,999) \wedge (0 < y_2) \wedge$
        $((y_1 < 1\,999) \to (y_2 \leq 300)) \wedge (z > 0) \wedge$
        $((x_1 = y_1) \to (x_2 > y_2))] \bullet$,
    (Uni(*part/sale-price*) $\wedge$ Uni(*part/cost-price*) $\wedge$
        Can(*part/sale-price*, {*part/cost-price, mark-up*}) $\wedge$
        Can(*part/cost-price*, {*part/sale-price, mark-up*}) $\wedge$
        Can(*mark-up*, {*part/sale-price, part/cost-price*}) $\wedge$
        Can(*mark-up*, {*date*})
)*[part/sale-price,part/cost-price, mark-up, date]* $\wedge$
    (Uni(*part*) $\wedge$ Can(*sale-price*, {*part*})$_{part/sale-price}$ $\wedge$
    (Uni(*part*) $\wedge$ Can(*cost-price*, {*part*})$_{part/cost-price}$ $\wedge$
        (Card $\leq$ 100)$_{part}$]

where the resulting item is named "*[part/sale-price,part/cost-price, mark-up, month_year]*". This corresponds to the cluster "[part/sale-price, part/cost-price, mark-up]" being joined with the relation "mark-up/month_year" on the domain "mark-up" to give the cluster "[part/sale-price, part/cost-price, mark-up, month_year]". In terms of the corresponding items:

[part/sale-price,part/cost-price, mark-up] $\otimes_{\{mark-up\}}$ *mark-up/month_year* =
    [part/sale-price, part/cost-price, mark-up, month_year]

Object **O** is *decomposable* into **D** = {**O₁, O₂, ..,Oₙ**} if

- **O**$_i$ is not tautological for all i,
- **O** = **O₁** $\otimes$ **O₂** $\otimes$ ... $\otimes$ **O**$_n$, where
- each composition is monotonic

If further each composition in the definition of the term "decomposable" is a unit composition then the decomposition is a *unit decomposition*.

If object O is decomposable then it does not necessarily have a unique decomposition. In Chap. 6 that the concept of decomposition provides the foundation for a theory of normalisation of objects. The objects:

$$comp \otimes_{\{(2,1)\}} \textit{has-type}$$
$$\textit{mark-up-1} \otimes_{\{(3,1)\}} \textit{valid}$$

are decomposable.

4.8 Inheritance

Objects are operators that may be used to construct complex items from a set of simpler items. Objects and items together are related closely both to the *frame-based* and to the *rule-based* paradigm. An item represents a chunk of "knowledge". A chunk of knowledge is related to a collection of "rules" [Blair, 1994c]. Objects represent the inheritance of properties between items.

The semantics of an item is an expression that recognises the members of the value set of that item. The semantics of the item *[part/sale-price, part/cost-price, part/type, type/mark-up]* discussed in Sect. 3.6 is:

$$\lambda w_1 w_2 x_1 x_2 y_1 y_2 z_1 z_2 \bullet [\ S_{part/sale-price}(w_1, w_2) \wedge S_{part/cost-price}(x_1, x_2) \wedge$$
$$S_{part/type}(y_1, y_2) \wedge S_{type/mark-up}(z_1, z_2) \wedge$$
$$(((\ w_1 = x_1 = y_1\ ) \wedge (\ y_2 = z_1\ )) \to (x_2 = z_2 \times y_2))\ ] \bullet$$

This expression is a generalisation of the following collection of two rules that are represented below as logic programs:

part/sale-price(x, y) ← part/cost-price(x, z), part/type(x, t),
    type/mark-up(t, u), y = z × u

part/cost-price(x, z) ← part/sale-price(x, y), part/type(x, t),
    type/mark-up(t, u), y = z × u

In this example, the item's semantics represents a chunk of *knowledge*. The "if-then" interpretations of this chunk be represented as *rules* in logic programming.

Object operators may be used to represent sub-tying between data items. In that way objects represent *inheritance*. The *cost* and *sell* objects described in Sect. 4.4:

cost[$\lambda P{:}X^1{\bullet}\lambda x{\bullet}[S_P(x) \wedge \text{for-costing}(x)]{\bullet\bullet}$,

   $\lambda P{:}X^1{\bullet}\lambda x{\bullet}[\ V_P(x) \wedge (0 \neq x)\ ]{\bullet\bullet}, \lambda P{:}X^1{\bullet}[\ C_P\ ]{\bullet}\ ]$

sell[$\lambda P{:}X^1{\bullet}\lambda x{\bullet}[S_P(x) \wedge \text{for-selling}(x)]{\bullet\bullet}$,

   $\lambda P{:}X^1{\bullet}\lambda x{\bullet}[\ V_P(x) \wedge (0 \neq x)\ ]{\bullet\bullet}, \lambda P{:}X^1{\bullet}[\ C_P\ ]{\bullet}\ ]$

can be used to construct the items *cost-price* and *sale-price* as sub-items of the item *price*. In this way, the items *cost-price* and *sale-price* inherit all the properties of the item *price*. The use of objects to represent inheritance extends beyond data to inheritance between information items and between knowledge items. The object **works-at** of type (X^1, X^1):

works-in[$\lambda P{:}X^1 Q{:}X^1{\bullet}\lambda xy{\bullet}[S_P(x) \wedge S_Q(y) \wedge \text{works-in}(x,\ y)]{\bullet\bullet}$,

   $\lambda P{:}X^1 Q{:}X^1{\bullet}\lambda xy{\bullet}[V_P(x) \wedge V_Q(y) \wedge T]{\bullet\bullet}$,

   $\lambda P{:}X^1 Q{:}X^1{\bullet}[C_P \wedge C_Q\ ]{\bullet}\ ]$

may be applied to the two data items *employee* and *department* to generate:

employee/department = **works-in**(*employee, department*)

If "the manager of a department is also an employee who works in that department" then the object of type X^2:

manages[$\lambda P{:}X^2{\bullet}\lambda xy{\bullet}[S_P(x,\ y) \wedge \text{manages}(x,\ y)]{\bullet\bullet}$,

   $\lambda P{:}X^2{\bullet}\lambda xy{\bullet}[V_P(x,\ y)]{\bullet\bullet}$,

   $\lambda P{:}X^2{\bullet}[C_P \wedge (\emptyset)_{v(\textbf{\textit{manages}},P)}\ ]{\bullet}\ ]$

may be applied to the information item *employee/department* to obtain the information item:

manages(*employee/department*) =
manager/department[$\lambda xy{\bullet}[$ work-in(x:person-id, y:dept-desc)

      $\wedge$ manages(x:person-id, y:dept-desc)]$\bullet$,

   $\lambda xy{\bullet}[\ (1 < x < 100)\ ]{\bullet},\ (\text{Card} \leq 50)_{manager}\ ]$

Hence the information item *manager/department* inherits all the properties of the information item *employee/department*. Likewise the object **sub** of type X^8:

$sub[\lambda P:X^8 \bullet \lambda w_1 w_2 x_1 x_2 y_1 y_2 z_1 z_2 \bullet [$

$\quad S_P(w_1, w_2, x_1, x_2, y_1, y_2, z_1, z_2,) \wedge (w_1 = x_1 = y_1 < 1\ 000)] \bullet \bullet,$

$\quad \lambda P:X^8 \bullet \lambda w_1 w_2 x_1 x_2 y_1 y_2 z_1 z_2 \bullet [V_P(w_1, w_2, x_1, x_2, y_1, y_2, z_1, z_2,)] \bullet \bullet,$

$\quad \lambda P:X^8 \bullet [C_P \wedge (\emptyset)_{v(sub,P)}] \bullet]$

may be applied to the knowledge item *[part/sale-price, part/cost-price, part/type, type/mark-up]* to generate a knowledge item that may only be used on part numbers that are less than one thousand. This example illustrates how the knowledge item generated by applying the **sub** object inherits all the properties of its argument. Hence objects may be used to represent inheritance between data items, information items and knowledge items.

4.9 Summary

- The unified representation based on items is too limited to provide an adequate basis for investigating maintenance.
- Objects are item building operators.
- Objects enable items to be constructed in a homogeneous way no matter whether those items represent data things, information things or knowledge things.
- An object is a named triple. An object consists of an object name, object semantics, object value constraints and object set constraints.
- All objects, including knowledge objects, contain two powerful classes of constraints.
- The algebra of objects contains four relations "identical", "equal", "equivalent" and "weakly equivalent".
- The algebra of objects contains two operations "composition" and "join".
- Using either the composition operator or the join operator, objects of different types may be combined to form other objects.
- Object decomposition is defined in terms of object join.

5 Schemas

5.1 Introduction

Chapters 3–4 described a unified representation for conceptual modelling in which data things, information things and knowledge things are all represented in the same way as "items". Complex items may be constructed by applying objects to simpler items. Items and objects are named triples consisting of a "name", "semantics", "value constraints" and "set constraints". At any particular time an item is associated with a particular value set.

This chapter describes practical notations for use when applying the unified methodology. These practical notations include schemas for representing items, objects and transactions. Two different notations are introduced to represent items, one to represent objects and one to represent transactions. The two notations for representing items are the "i-schema notation" and the "r-schema notation". The notation for representing objects is the "o-schema notation". That for representing transactions is the "t-schema notation". These various schemas are used when the unified knowledge engineering methodology is applied. The various relations and operations in the algebras of items and objects apply to items and objects expressed in these schema representations.

Chapter 6 will consider the simplification of the unified conceptual model.

5.2 i-schemas

Items (introduced in Chap. 3) are a unified representation for the real data, information and knowledge things in an application. The structure of the data as represented both by sub-typing and by compound data items can be represented by items. Items also contain two powerful classes of constraints that apply equally to data, information and knowledge.

The formal, λ-calculus presentation of items is cumbersome. The "i-schema" notation is comparatively simple. The general *i-schema* format for representing an item is shown in Fig. 5.1. In this i-schema format a graphic notation is employed to represent the item set constraints. This graphic notation is illustrated by examples below. The i-schema notation may be used to represent all items including data, information and knowledge items. In Sect. 3.3 the general λ-calculus form for an item is:

$$A[\ \lambda y_1^1...y_{m_1}^1...y_{m_n}^n \bullet [\ S_{A_1}(y_1^1,...,y_{m_1}^1)$$
$$\wedge\ S_{A_2}(y_1^2,...,y_{m_2}^2)\ \wedge\ ....\ \wedge\ S_{A_n}(y_1^n,...,y_{m_n}^n)$$
$$\wedge\ J(y_1^1...y_{m_1}^1...y_{m_n}^n)\ ]\bullet,$$
$$\lambda y_1^1...y_{m_1}^1...y_{m_n}^n \bullet [\ V_{A_1}(y_1^1,...,y_{m_1}^1)$$
$$\wedge\ V_{A_2}(y_1^2,...,y_{m_2}^2)\ \wedge\ ....\ \wedge\ V_{A_n}(y_1^n,...,y_{m_n}^n)$$
$$\wedge\ K(y_1^1,...y_{m_1}^1...y_{m_n}^n)\ ]\bullet,$$
$$C_{A_1} \wedge C_{A_2} \wedge...\wedge C_{A_n} \wedge (L)_A\ ]$$

An item presented in this way is in *item standard form*. Figure 5.2 shows this item *A* in item standard form using the i-schema format.

If an item is in item standard form then the i-schema representation of that item can be unnecessarily complex. The item:

[employee/supervisor, employee/department, person/job]

$[\lambda qrstuvwxyz \bullet [\ S_{employee/supervisor}(q,\ r) \wedge S_{person/job}(s,\ t)$

$\wedge\ S_{person/job}(u,\ v) \wedge S_{employee/department}(w,\ x)$

$\wedge\ S_{employee/department}(y,\ z)$

$\wedge\ (\ (((q = s) \wedge (t = \text{'manager'}) \wedge (v = \text{'gen mngr'})$

$\wedge\ (w,x,y,z\ \underline{are}\ \perp)) \rightarrow\ (r = u))$

$\vee\ (((q = s) \wedge (q = w) \wedge (r = y) \wedge (x = z)$

$\wedge\ (t = \text{'worker'}) \wedge (v = \text{'manager'})) \rightarrow\ (r = u))\ )\ ]\bullet,$

$\lambda qrstuvwxyz \bullet [\ \mathbf{T}\ ]\bullet,\ \emptyset\ ]$

is in the item standard form. The i-schema for this item is shown in Fig. 5.3. The representation in Fig. 5.3 is complex. The basic structure of the knowledge represented as the semantics of this item is comparatively simple.

A canonical form for items is developed. This canonical form leads to a simpler i-schema representation than that derived from items in item standard form. The canonical form for an item is introduced with an example. This canonical form is achieved by two transformations of the item standard form. In the first of these transformations the item above is re-written as:

name		item name
name1	name2	item components
x	y	dummy variables
item semantics expressed in terms of the dummy variables		item semantics
constraints on values of the dummy variables		item value constraints
constraints on value set in graphic notation		item set constraints

Fig. 5.1 i-schema for representing items

A		
A_1	. . . .	A_n
$y_1^1,...,y_{m_1}^1$	. . . .	$y_1^n,...,y_{m_n}^n$
$J(y_1^1...y_{m_1}^1...y_{m_n}^n)$		
$K(y_1^1,...y_{m_1}^1...y_{m_n}^n)$		
graphic form for 'L'		

Fig. 5.2 i-schema for item A

[employee/supervisor, employee/department, person/job]

$[\lambda qrstuvwxyz \bullet [(S_{employee/supervisor}(q, r) \wedge S_{person/job}(s, t)$
$\wedge S_{person/job}(u, v) \wedge S_{employee/department}(w, x)$
$\wedge S_{employee/department}(y, z)$
$\wedge (((q = s) \wedge (t = \text{'manager'}) \wedge (v = \text{'gen mngr'})$
$\wedge (w,x,y,z \underline{are} \perp)) \rightarrow (r = u)))$
$\vee (S_{employee/supervisor}(q, r) \wedge S_{person/job}(s, t)$
$\wedge S_{person/job}(u, v) \wedge S_{employee/department}(w, x)$
$\wedge S_{employee/department}(y, z)$
$\wedge (((q = s) \wedge (q = w) \wedge (r = y) \wedge (x = z)$
$\wedge (t = \text{'worker'}) \wedge (v = \text{'manager'})) \rightarrow (r = u)))]\bullet,$
$\lambda qrstuvwxyz \bullet [\mathbf{T}]\bullet, \emptyset]$

In the above form the two disjunctive sub-cases of the item's semantics are shown explicitly as two separate expressions. The i-schema for this item is shown in Fig. 5.4. That i-schema contains two separate blocks to represent the item's semantics and value constraints. It represents the result of the first transformation.

[employee/supervisor, employee/department, person/job]		
employee/supervisor	*employee/department*	*person/job*
(q, r)	(w, x)	(s, t)
	(y, z)	(u, v)
$(((q = s) \wedge (t = $ 'manager'$) \wedge (v = $ 'gen mngr'$)$ $\wedge (w,x,y,z \ \underline{are} \ \bot)) \rightarrow (r = u))$ $\vee (((q = s) \wedge (q = w) \wedge (r = y) \wedge (x = z)$ $\wedge (t = $ 'worker'$) \wedge (v = $ 'manager'$)) \rightarrow (r = u))$		
T		
$\emptyset$		

Fig. 5.3 i-schema for *[employee/supervisor, employee/department, person/job]*

Following the first transformation above, the item semantics contains a number of equalities. In the second transformation these equalities are made explicit:

[employee/supervisor, employee/department, person/job]

$[\lambda qrstuvwxyz \bullet [\ ((S_{employee/supervisor}(q = s, r)$

$\wedge \ S_{person/job}(s, \ t = $ 'manager'$)$

$\wedge \ S_{person/job}(u, \ v = $ 'gen mngr'$)$

$\wedge \ S_{employee/department}(w \ \underline{is} \ \bot, \ x \ \underline{is} \ \bot)$

$\wedge \ S_{employee/department}(y \ \underline{is} \ \bot, \ z \ \underline{is} \ \bot))$

$\rightarrow (r = u))$

$\vee \ ((S_{employee/supervisor}(q = s, \ r = y)$

$\wedge \ S_{person/job}(s, \ t = $ 'worker'$)$

$\wedge \ S_{person/job}(u, \ v = $ 'manager'$)$

$\wedge \ S_{employee/department}(w = s, \ x = z)$

$\wedge \ S_{employee/department}(y, \ z))$

$\rightarrow (r = u)) \ ] \bullet,$

$\lambda qrstuvwxyz \bullet [\ \mathbf{T} \ ] \bullet, \ \emptyset \ ]$

The i-schema for this item is shown in Fig. 5.5. This i-schema includes the explicit representation of constants and equivalent variables. It represents the result of the second transformation. In the i-schema shown in Fig. 5.5 the conclusion of each inference is identified using a "→" sign. The i-schema shown in Fig. 5.5 is in canonical form. This example demonstrates that the i-schema format can be economical and easy to use. The representation of value constraints and the graphical notation for representing the set constraints have yet to be considered.

[employee/supervisor, employee/department, person/job]		
employee/supervisor	employee/department	person/job
(q, r)	(w, x)	(s, t)
	(y, z)	(u, v)
((q = s) ∧ (t = 'manager') ∧ (v = 'gen mngr') ∧ (w,x,y,z <u>are</u> ⊥)) → (r = u)		
T		
(q, r)	(w, x)	(s, t)
	(y, z)	(u, v)
((q = s) ∧ (q = w) ∧ (r = y) ∧ (x = z) ∧ (t = 'worker') ∧ (v = 'manager')) → (r = u)		
T		
∅		

Fig. 5.4 i-schema for item in Fig. 5.3

[employee/supervisor, employee/department, person/job]		
employee/supervisor	employee/department	person/job
(s, r)	(⊥, ⊥)	(s, 'manager')
	(⊥, ⊥)	(u, 'gen mngr')
→ (r = u)		
T		
(s, r)	(s, x)	(s, 'worker')
	(u, x)	(u, 'manager')
→ (r = u)		
T		
∅		

Fig. 5.5 Canonical i-schema for item in Fig. 5.3

In general the *canonical form* of an item is constructed by:

- taking an item in item standard form;
- splitting up the semantics and value constraints to reflect disjunctive divisions in the value set;
- explicitly representing any constants in the semantics, and
- explicitly representing any equalities between variables in the antecedent of the semantics.

The following item is in item standard form:

[part/sale-price, part/cost-price, mark-up]		
part/sale-price	part/cost-price	mark-up
(x, w)	(x, y)	z
$\rightarrow$ (w = z × y)		
T		
$\emptyset$		

Fig. 5.6 i-schema for *[part/sale-price, part/cost-price, mark-up]*

[person/cohabitant, person/address]	
person/cohabitant	person/address
(x, y)	(x, z) (y, z)
x ≠ y	
T	
$\emptyset$	

Fig. 5.7 i-schema for *[person/cohabitant, person/address]*

[part/sale-price, part/cost-price, mark-up][
 $\lambda x_1 x_2 y_1 y_2 z \bullet [\ S_{part/sale-price}(x_1, x_2)\ \wedge\ S_{part/cost-price}(y_1, y_2)$
  $\wedge\ S_{mark-up}(z) \wedge ((\ x_1 = y_1\ ) \rightarrow (x_2 = z \times y_2))\ ]\bullet,$
 $\lambda x_1 x_2 y_1 y_2 z \bullet [\ \mathbf{T}\ ]\bullet,\ \emptyset\ ]$

The canonical form for this item is:

[part/sale-price, part/cost-price, mark-up][
 $\lambda x_1 x_2 x_1 y_2 z \bullet [\ (\ S_{part/sale-price}(x_1, x_2)$
  $\wedge\ S_{part/cost-price}(y_1 = x_1, y_2) \wedge S_{mark-up}(z)\ )$
  $\rightarrow (x_2 = z \times y_2)\ ]\bullet,$
 $\lambda x_1 x_2 y_1 y_2 z \bullet [\ \mathbf{T}\ ]\bullet,\ \emptyset\ ]$

The i-schema for this canonical form is shown in Fig. 5.6.
 The following item is in item standard form:

[person/cohabitant, person/address][
 $\lambda x_1 x_2 y_1 y_2 z_1 z_2 \bullet [\ S_{person/cohabitant}(x_1, x_2)$
  $\wedge\ S_{person/address}(y_1, y_2) \wedge S_{person/address}(z_1, z_2)$
  $\wedge\ ((\ x_1 = y_1\ ) \wedge (\ x_2 = z_1\ ) \wedge (\ x_1 \neq x_2\ )$
   $\wedge\ (y_2 = z_2))\ ]\bullet,\ \lambda x_1 x_2 y_1 y_2 z_1 z_2 \bullet [\ \mathbf{T}\ ]\bullet,\ \emptyset\ ]$

The canonical form for this item is:

[person/cohabitant, person/address][
  $\lambda x_1 x_2 y_1 y_2 z_1 z_2 \bullet [\ S_{person/cohabitant}(x_1, x_2)$
    $\wedge\ S_{person/address}(y_1 = x_1, y_2)$
    $\wedge\ S_{person/address}(z_1 = x_2, z_2 = y_2) \wedge (\ x_1 \neq x_2\ )\ ]\bullet,$
  $\lambda x_1 x_2 y_1 y_2 z_1 z_2 \bullet [\ \mathbf{T}\ ]\bullet,\ \emptyset\ ]$

The i-schema for this canonical form is shown in Fig. 5.7.
  The following item is in item standard form:

[employee/responsible-to, employee/supervisor, MD][
  $\lambda x_1 x_2 y_1 y_2 z_1 z_2 w \bullet [\ S_{employee/responsible-to}(x_1, x_2)$
    $\wedge\ S_{employee/supervisor}(y_1, y_2)$
    $\wedge\ S_{employee/supervisor}(z_1, z_2) \wedge S_{MD}(w)$
    $\wedge\ ((((\ x_1 = y_1\ ) \wedge (\ y_2 = w\ )) \rightarrow (\ x_2 = w\ )) \vee$
    $(((\ x_1 = y_1\ ) \wedge (\ y_2 \neq w\ ) \wedge (\ y_2 = z_1\ ))$
    $\rightarrow (\ x_2 = z_2\ )))\ ]\bullet,$
  $\lambda w_1 w_2 x_1 x_2 y_1 y_2 z \bullet [\ \mathbf{T}\ ]\bullet,\ \emptyset\ ]$

The canonical form for this item is:

[employee/responsible-to, employee/supervisor, MD][
  $\lambda x_1 x_2 y_1 y_2 z_1 z_2 w \bullet [$
    $(\ (S_{employee/responsible-to}(x_1, x_2)$
    $\wedge\ S_{employee/supervisor}(y_1 = x_1, y_2 = w)$
    $\wedge\ S_{employee/supervisor}(z_1\ \underline{is}\ \bot, z_2\ \underline{is}\ \bot) \wedge S_{MD}(w))$
    $\rightarrow (\ x_2 = w\ )\ )$
    $\vee\ (\ (S_{employee/responsible-to}(x_1, x_2)$
    $\wedge\ S_{employee/supervisor}(y_1 = x_1, y_2 = z_1)$
    $\wedge\ S_{employee/supervisor}(z_1, z_2) \wedge S_{MD}(w)$
    $\wedge\ (\ y_2 \neq w\ )) \rightarrow (\ x_2 = z_2\ )\ )\ ]\bullet,$
  $\lambda w_1 w_2 x_1 x_2 y_1 y_2 z \bullet [\ \mathbf{T}\ ]\bullet,\ \emptyset\ ]$

The i-schema for this canonical form is shown in Fig. 5.8.
  i-schemas can represent simple items. The i-schema representations of the data
items:

part[$\lambda x \bullet$[is-a[x:part-number]]$\bullet$, $\lambda x \bullet$[(1 000 < x < 9 999)]$\bullet$,
  (Card $\leq$ 100)$_{part}$]

[employee/responsible-to, employee/supervisor, MD]		
employee/respons-to	*employee/supervisor*	*MD*
(x, z)	(x, w) (⊥, ⊥)	(w)
→ (z = w)		
T		
(x, z)	(x, y) (y, v)	(w)
(y ≠ w) → (z = v)		
T		
∅		

Fig. 5.8 i-schema for *[employee/responsible-to,   employee/supervisor, MD]*

price[λx•[is-a[x:dollar-amount]]•, λx•[0 ≤ x]•, ∅]
cost-price[λx•[is-a[x:dollar-amount]]•, λx•[0 < x]•, ∅]

are shown in Fig. 5.9. Given the information item:

part/cost-price[λxy•[costs(x:part-number, y:dollar-amount)]•,
    λxy•[(1 000 < x < 9 999) ∧ (0 < y)
        ∧ ((x < 1 999) → (y ≤ 300))]•,
    (Uni(*part*) ∧ Can(*cost-price*, {*part*}))*part/cost-price*
        ∧ (Card ≤ 100)*part*]

its canonical form is:

part/cost-price[λxy•[S_{part}(x) ∧ $S_{cost-price}$(y) ∧ costs(x, y)]•,
    λxy•[V_{part}(x) ∧ $V_{cost-price}$(y)
        ∧ ((x < 1 999) → (y ≤ 300))]•,
    C_{part} ∧ $C_{cost-price}$
        ∧ (Uni(*part*) ∧ Can(*cost-price*, {*part*}))*part/cost-price*]

The i-schema for this canonical form is shown in Fig. 5.10. In Fig. 5.10 '∀'
represents the 'Uni' item set constraint, and '-' and 'o' represent the 'Can'
constraint. Consider the following knowledge item. This item is similar to the
item illustrated in Fig. 5.6 with the inclusion of non-trivial value constraints and
set constraints:

[part/sale-price, part/cost-price, mark-up][
   $\lambda x_1 x_2 y_1 y_2 z$•[sells-for($x_1$:part-number, x_2:dollar-amount)

       ∧ costs(y_1:part-number, y_2:dollar-amount)

       ∧ is-a[z:mark-up-factor]

       ∧ $((x_1 = y_1) \to (x_2 = z \times y_2)) $]•,

   $\lambda x_1 x_2 y_1 y_2 z$•[$(1\,000 < x_1 < 9\,999) \wedge (1 < x_2) \wedge$

       $(1\,000 < y_1 < 9\,999) \wedge (0 < y_2) \wedge$

       $((y_1 < 1\,999) \to (y_2 \le 300)) \wedge (0 < z < 3) \wedge$

       $((x_1 = y_1) \to (x_2 > y_2))$]•,

   (Uni(*part/sale-price*) ∧ Uni(*part/cost-price*)

       ∧ Can(*part/sale-price*, {*part/cost-price, mark-up*})

       ∧ Can(*part/cost-price*, {*part/sale-price, mark-up*})

       ∧ Can(*mark-up*, {*part/sale-price, part/cost-price*})

)*[part/sale-price, part/cost-price, mark-up]*

          ∧ (Uni(*part*) ∧ Can(*sale-price*, {*part*}))*part/sale-price* ∧

          (Uni(*part*) ∧ Can(*cost-price*, {*part*}))*part/cost-price* ∧

          (Card $\le$ 100)*part*]

its canonical form is:

[part/sale-price, part/cost-price, mark-up][
   $\lambda x_1 x_2 y_1 y_2 z$•[$(S_{part/sale-price}(x_1 = y_1, x_2)$

      $\wedge\ S_{part/cost-price}(y_1, y_2) \wedge S_{mark-up}(z))$

       $\to (x_2 = z \times y_2)$]•,

   $\lambda x_1 x_2 y_1 y_2 z$•[$(V_{part/sale-price}(x_1 = y_1, x_2)$

      $\wedge\ V_{part/cost-price}(y_1, y_2) \wedge \wedge V_{mark-up}(z))$

       $\to (x_2 > y_2)$]•,

   (Uni(*part/sale-price*) ∧ Uni(*part/cost-price*)

       ∧ Can(*part/sale-price*, {*part/cost-price, mark-up*})

       ∧ Can(*part/cost-price*, {*part/sale-price, mark-up*})

       ∧ Can(*mark-up*, {*part/sale-price, part/cost-price*})

)*[part/sale-price, part/cost-price, mark-up]*

          ∧ (Uni(*part*) ∧ Can(*sale-price*, {*part*}))*part/sale-price* ∧

          (Uni(*part*) ∧ Can(*cost-price*, {*part*}))*part/cost-price* ∧

          (Card $\le$ 100)*part*]

The i-schema for this canonical form is shown in Fig. 5.11. Consider the following knowledge item. This item is similar to the item illustrated in Fig. 5.7 with the inclusion of non-trivial set constraints:

[person/cohabitant, person/address][

$\lambda x_1 x_2 y_1 y_2 z_1 z_2 \bullet [\ S_{person/cohabitant}(x_1 = y_1, x_2 = z_1)$

$\wedge\ S_{person/address}(y_1, y_2 = z_2) \wedge S_{person/address}(z_1, z_2)$

$\wedge\ (\ x_1 \neq x_2\ )\ ]\bullet,$

$\lambda x_1 x_2 y_1 y_2 z_1 z_2 \bullet [\ V_{person/cohabitant}(x_1 = y_1, x_2 = z_1)$

$\wedge\ V_{person/address}(y_1, y_2 = z_2) \wedge V_{person/address}(z_1, z_2)\ ]\bullet,$

$C_{person/cohabitant} \wedge C_{person/address}$

$\wedge (\mathrm{Uni}(person/cohabitant)$

$\wedge\ \mathrm{Can}(person/cohabitant, \{person/address\})$

$)_{[person/cohabitant, \ person/address]}\ ]$

The i-schema for this canonical form is shown in Fig. 5.12. The following knowledge item is similar to the item illustrated in Fig. 5.8 with the inclusion of non-trivial set constraints:

[employee/responsible-to, employee/supervisor, MD][

$\lambda w_1 w_2 x_1 x_2 y_1 y_2 z \bullet [$

$(\ (S_{employee/supervisor}(w_1 = x_1, w_2)$

$\wedge\ S_{employee/supervisor}(x_1, x_2 = z)$

$\wedge\ S_{employee/responsible\text{-}to}(y_1, y_2) \wedge S_{MD}(z))$

$\rightarrow (\ w_2 = z\ )\ )$

$\vee\ (\ (S_{employee/supervisor}(w_1 = x_1, w_2)$

$\wedge\ S_{employee/supervisor}(x_1, x_2 = y_1)$

$\wedge\ S_{employee/responsible\text{-}to}(y_1, y_2) \wedge S_{MD}(z)$

$\wedge\ (\ x_2 \neq z\ ))$

$\rightarrow (\ w_2 = y_2\ )\ )\ ]\bullet,$

$\lambda w_1 w_2 x_1 x_2 y_1 y_2 z \bullet [\ V_{employee/supervisor}(w_1 = x_1, w_2)$

$\wedge\ V_{employee/supervisor}(x_1, x_2 = z)$

$\wedge\ V_{employee/responsible\text{-}to}(y_1, y_2) \wedge V_{MD}(z)\ ]\bullet,$

$C_{employee/supervisor} \wedge C_{employee/supervisor} \wedge C_{MD}$

$\wedge (\mathrm{Uni}(employee/responsible\text{-}to)$

$\wedge\ \mathrm{Can}(employee/responsible\text{-}to, \{employee/supervisor, MD\})$

$)_{[employee/responsible\text{-}to, \ employee/supervisor, \ MD}\ ]$

The i-schema for this canonical form is shown in Fig. 5.13.

part
$\emptyset$
x
is-a[x:part-number]
1 000 <x< 9 999
≤100

price
$\emptyset$
x
is-a[x:dollar-amount]
0≤x
$\emptyset$

cost-price
$\emptyset$
x
is-a[x:dollar-amount]
0<x
$\emptyset$

Fig. 5.9 i-schemas for data items '*part*' '*price*' and '*cost-price*'

part/cost-price	
part	*cost-price*
x	y
costs(x, y)	
x < 1 999 → y ≤ 300	
∀	
----------------	O

Fig. 5.10 i-schema for information item '*part/cost-price*'

[part/sale-price, part/cost-price, mark-up]		
part/sale-price	*part/cost-price*	*mark-up*
(x, w)	(x, y)	z
→ (w = z × y)		
→ w > y		
∀	∀	
---		O
O	---	
------------------------	O	------------------------

Fig. 5.11 i-schema for knowledge item '*[part/sale-price, part/cost-price, mark-up]*'

[person/cohabitant, person/address]	
person/cohabitant	*person/address*
(x, y)	(x, z)
	(y, z)
x ≠ y	
T	
∀	
O	-----------------------------

Fig. 5.12 i-schema for knowledge item '*[person/cohabitant, person/address]*'

[employee/responsible-to, employee/supervisor, MD]		
employee/respons-to	employee/supervisor	MD
(x, z)	(x, w)	(w)
	(⊥, ⊥)	
→ (z = w)		
T		
(x, z)	(x, y)	(w)
	(y, v)	
(y ≠ w) → (z = v)		
T		
∀		
O	---	

Fig. 5.13 i-schema for '[employee/responsible-to, employee/supervisor, MD]'

In Sect. 3.7 an operation on items is discussed. That operation is "item join". Item join can be applied to generate an item from two given items. This operation can be applied to the i-schema representation of items. Item join generates an i-schema from two given i-schemas. Figure 5.14 and Fig. 5.15 respectively show the i-schemas for the items $part\_machine \otimes_{\{machine\}} machine/type$ and $part/sale\text{-}price \otimes_{\{sale\text{-}price\}} [sale\text{-}price, sales\text{-}tax, tax\text{-}rate]$.

5.3 r-schemas

Illustrations are given in Chap. 3 of "data items", "information items" and "knowledge items". In Sect. 3.8 it is noted that the definition of an item as given in Sect. 3.3 *does not require* an item to be either a data item, information item or knowledge item. Further, the definition of an item given in Sect. 3.3 *does not require* items to be non-decomposable in the sense defined in Sect. 3.7. The item *"part/cost-price"* whose i-schema is shown in Fig. 5.10 is non-decomposable as it cannot be broken down into "simpler" items using the item join operator. In Sect. 3.8 it is noted that a complex item can represent a whole system, a whole knowledge base or a whole database. Such a complex item might be large and clumsy but would still be an item. If an item is sufficiently elaborate that it is infeasible to represent that item succinctly using either the λ-calculus form or the i-schema format then that item is described informally as being "complex".

The λ-calculus form and the i-schema format are sufficiently explicit to specify how an item may be implemented within a knowledge-based system without additional information. If a view of an item contains sufficient detail about *how* that item may be implemented without additional information then that view is a *low level view*. i-schemas provide a detailed representation for items. i-schemas are a

part_machine	
part	machine
x	y
∅	
T	
∀	∀

$\otimes_{\{machine\}}$

machine/type	
machine	type
x	y
has-type(x, y)	
∅	
∀	
--------------	**O**

=

part_machine $\otimes_{\{machine\}}$ machine/type		
part	machine	type
x	y	z
has-type(y, z)		
∅		
∀	∀	
	--------------------	**O**

Fig. 5.14   i-schema for item *part_machine* $\otimes_{\{machine\}}$ *machine/type*

low-level view of items. The i-schema representation of an item specifies *how* the item should do what it may be asked to do, and hence is a *declarative view* of items. The i-schema notation is introduced in Sect. 5.2.

Neither the λ-calculus form nor the i-schema format can represent complex items succinctly. A succinct form of representation for complex items can not be "low level" in the sense described above. A *high-level view* of an item is a representation that provides a succinct view of some features only of a complex item. A high level view does not contain sufficient detail to specify completely the way in which that item might be implemented. A high-level view does not provide a complete specification. The "r-schema" notation gives a high-level view of items. The 'r' in r-schema stands for "requirements". r-schemas are used during the first "requirements specification" design step in the unified design methodology. Requirements specification is the subject of Chap. 7. A high level view of an item can only present some features of that item. The particular feature presented by r-schemas is "item behaviour". The "behaviour" of an item is an informal description of *what* that item is expected to do when it is implemented, but not *how* it will do it. Item behaviour is discussed below. The r-schema view specifies *what* the item should be able to do but not *how* it should do it. The r-schema view is an *imperative view*. That is, r-schemas give an imperative, high-level view of items. A single r-schema can be used to provide a high-level, imperative view of a *set of* one or more items. By contrast, a single i-schema provides a low-level, declarative view of a single item. The r-schema notation provides a more succinct and less precise view of items than i-schemas.

part/sale-price	
part	sale-price
v	x
sells-for(v, x)	
∅	
∀	
-------------	O

$\otimes_{\{sale\text{-}price\}}$

[sale-price, sales-tax, tax-rate].		
sale-price	sales-tax	tax-rate
x	y	z
(y = x × z)		
x > y		
∀	∀	∀
O	------------------------------	
------------------------	O	-------------

=

part/sale-price $\otimes_{\{sale\text{-}price\}}$ [sale-price, sales-tax, tax-rate].			
part	sale-price	sales-tax	tax-rate
v	x	y	z
sells-for(v, x) ∧ (y = x × z)			
x > y			
∀	∀		
	---------------------	O	

Fig. 5.15 Item *part/sale-price* $\otimes_{\{sale\text{-}price\}}$ *[sale-price, sales-tax, tax-rate]*

The requirements specification step is the first step in the unified design methodology and is discussed in Chap. 7. The r-schema notation is used during this requirements specification step. During the initial requirements specification step the degree of understanding of the application is necessarily rather vague. The high-level nature of the r-schema notation accommodates this lack of detailed understanding. In Chap. 7 the requirements specification step begins with the construction of a context diagram. From this context diagram a single "system r-schema" is extracted. This single r-schema represents the entire system. The item represented by this single r-schema is typically complex. During requirements specification this single system r-schema is repeatedly decomposed until non-decomposable, simple r-schemas are constructed. This cascade decomposition of r-schemas establishes a framework of r-schemas. After the initial "requirements specification" step has been performed, the structure of this framework is employed to guide the next step that is a detailed analysis of the system. An "r-schema" can be used to provide a succinct, high-level, imperative view of a complex item. A complex item may be constructed by using the item join operator on a number of simpler items.

An r-schema has an *r-schema name*. The r-schema name is chosen to be intuitively associated with the item or set of items that it represents. An *optional* part of the r-schema view is a description of that r-schema's "mission". The *r-schema mission* is a succinct statement of what the item represented by that r-schema is supposed to achieve within the general operation of the system. The inclusion of the r-schema mission is particularly valuable for the representation of complex items, and is a useful tool for focusing discussion during the requirements specification process. The low-level i-schema view of an item includes the names of *all* of that item's components. The specification of an item's components provides structural information about that item. Likewise the r-schema view includes the specification of as many components as can be readily identified. It would be unreasonable at a high-level view to expect *all* of the components to be correctly identified. The identification of the components of r-schemas is described in Chap. 7. The components of a given r-schema are the names of other r-schemas that when taken together should substantially support the behaviours required of that given r-schema.

The "r-schema" view of an item refers to that item's "behaviour" rather than its semantics. Item behaviour is discussed in detail in Sect. 7.3. A brief introduction to "behaviour" that is sufficient to understand the r-schema view of an item is presented below.

A key output from the unified design methodology is a physical model. In a physical model derived by the unified methodology, an item might, for example, be implemented within a relational database management system or within an expert system shell coupled to that database management system [Goul & Tonge, 1987]. No matter how an item is implemented, its implementation is expected to be able to do something. A description of something that an item is expected to do when it has been implemented is an example of its "behaviour". The item "*part/cost-price*" may have the behaviour "when the implemented item is given the number of a part it should respond by providing that part's cost-price". Section 7.3 contains a more detailed presentation of "behaviour" than that given here. For the purpose of this chapter, *item behaviour* is an informal description of *what* an implementation of that item is expected to do in response to a particular type of request.

An r-schema's behaviour specifies "what" an implementation of the item described by that r-schema should do in response to a particular type of request, but not "how" it is expected to do it. If an item is expected to respond to more than one type of request then it may have more than one "behaviour". A description of a comprehensive set of behaviours for an item provides a functional, or "input/output" view of that item. The distinction between an item's "behaviour" and its "semantics" is fundamental. An item's semantics specifies "how" the implemented item is expected to do what it has to do, and is independent of "what" that item may be called upon to do, if anything. An item's behaviours specifies the "what". The semantics specifies the "how".

In an r-schema, item behaviour is an informal notion. Informality is appropriate during requirements specification as requirements specification is an informal exercise. Item behaviour *could* be defined formally. Consider the knowledge item *[part/sale-price, part/cost-price, mark-up]*. A behaviour of this item could be described informally as "calculate the sale price of a given part". This behaviour could be described formally using the λ-calculus as follows:

$\lambda x \bullet [= y \times z$ where find y such that part/cost-price(x, y) and
   find z such that mark-up(z)]•

This expression returns a value equal to the sale price of a given part. From here on item behaviour is treated informally.

Constraints are also a part of the "r-schema" view of items. In the i-schema view a distinction is drawn between the item's value constraints and the item's set constraints. Both of these forms of constraints are represented formally in the i-schema view. In the r-schema view a less prescriptive approach is taken to constraints. An r-schema constraint is an informal statement of a constraint on the way in which an implementation of the item described by that r-schema should behave. Only those r-schema constraints that are seen to be "important" during the requirements specification step are included.

The *r-schema* representation of an item consists of:

• the r-schema name;
• the names of (at least some of) the r-schema's components;
• (at least one of) the r-schema's behaviours;
• (some of) the r-schema's constraints, and
• (optional) the r-schema's mission.

In the r-schema notation, it is not necessarily required to quote *all* of the r-schema's components, behaviours or constraints. This degree of imprecision is intended to reflect the lack of understanding that necessarily pervades the requirements specification step in the design process. The high-level, imperative r-schema notation is illustrated in Fig. 5.16.

The r-schema view has five sections. The sequence of these sections is chosen to preserve consistency with the i-schema view. The i-schema's "item semantics", that specifies *how* the item is to do whatever is required of it, is related to the r-schema's "behaviour", that specifies *what* the item described by the r-schema should be capable of doing. When constructing an r-schema, the "r-schema mission" is completed before the "r-schema behaviour", and the "r-schema behaviour" is often completed before the "r-schema components".

5.4 From r-schemas to i-schemas

Section 5.3 introduced the r-schema notation. Chapter 7 will discuss the requirements specification step. Requirements specification is the first step of the unified methodology. Requirements specification commences by constructing a context diagram. A single r-schema is then extracted from this context diagram. This single r-schema is then repeatedly decomposed to form a cascade decomposition of r-schemas. Chapter 8 discusses the "system analysis" design step.

name
name1
name2
informal description
informal description

"informal description"

r-schema name
r-schema components

r-schema behaviour
r-schema constraints
r-schema mission

Fig. 5.16 The high-level r-schema view of a set of items

name	
name1	name2
x	y
meaning of the item expressed in terms of the dummy variables	
constraints on values of the dummy variables	
set constraints in graphic notation	

item name
item components
dummy variables
item semantics

item value constraints

item set constraints

Fig. 5.17 The low-level i-schema view of items

System analysis is the second step of the unified methodology. System analysis uses the structure of the cascade decomposition constructed during requirements specification as a guide. System analysis is partly concerned with the construction of i-schema representations of the items that were identified during requirements specification. This section contains a discussion of what is involved in constructing an i-schema view of a given r-schema.

There are three difference between r-schemas and i-schemas. First, r-schemas are informal and i-schemas are formal. Second, r-schemas give a high-level view of items, and i-schemas give a low-level view of items. Third, r-schemas are imperative and describe *what* a set of items will be required to do, and i-schemas are declarative and describe *how* an item will do whatever it may be asked to do. Setting these differences aside for the moment, the specification of the name, components and constraints in both an r-schema and an i-schema has the same general intention. The mission statement in the r-schema notation has no parallel in the i-schema notation. It is sometimes worth adding the mission statement to an item's i-schema to convey the general role of that item.

The set of item behaviours specified in an r-schema is related to the item semantics in the corresponding i-schemas. There are two differences between behaviour and semantics. First the item semantics expresses *how* that item might do something that it is called upon to do. The item behaviour describes *what* the item described by that r-schema is expected to be able to do. A fair amount of work can be involved in developing the *how* from the *what*. An item's behaviour might require that an item sort a list. The specification of that item's behaviour

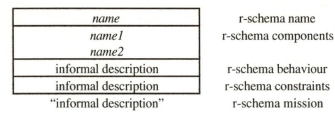

Fig. 5.18   The high-level r-schema view

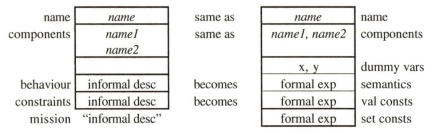

Fig. 5.19   Rough correspondence between r-schemas and i-schemas

does not specify *how* a list should be sorted. The specification of the "how" is the business of the system analysis step that is discussed in Chap. 8. The second difference between semantics and behaviour is that there is a lot of information in the behaviour that does not find its way into the semantics. The item semantics does not contain any statement of what that item is required to do. The i-schemas in the conceptual model are linked to the corresponding r-schemas in the requirements model. In this way the *what* is linked to the *how*.

The general form of the i-schema notation is shown in Fig. 5.17. The general form of the r-schema notation is shown in Fig. 5.18. A rough correspondence between r-schemas and i-schemas is shown in Fig. 5.19.

An r-schema can be used to represent either a simple item, a set of items or a complex item. r-schemas present a more succinct and less detailed view than i-schemas. The following points summarise the relationships between items, schemas and their implementation.

- each r-schema represents either a simple item, a set of items or a complex item;
- each complex item corresponds to a set of simpler items;
- each simple item may be described succinctly by an i-schema;
- each i-schema's semantics represents a chunk of knowledge;
- each chunk of knowledge may be interpreted as a set of rules; and
- each rule may be implemented either as a set of logic clauses or as programs in some other programming language.

5.5 o-schemas

Items are more detailed than objects in that each item contains an explicit reference to its particular component items. The level of detail in an item limits the usefulness of items as a basis for analysing maintenance. Two distinct knowledge items can represent the same essential rule but have different components. In Sect. 4.2 the limitations of items are discussed. It is noted there that items together with the item join operator are too limited to provide a suitable basis for analysing maintenance.

Objects are operators for building items. They enable the relationships between data, information and knowledge items to be represented explicitly in a uniform way. These relationships include the sub-typing relationship and compound data item relationship. Objects include two powerful classes of constraints. Items and objects together are more powerful as a basis for the analysis of maintenance than items alone because objects are not associated with particular components. In Chap. 8 items and objects together with their respective join operators provide the basis for a rigorous analysis of the maintenance of knowledge-based systems.

The formal, λ-calculus presentation of objects is cumbersome. The "o-schema" notation is presented shortly. It is comparatively simple. The general *o-schema* format for representing an object is shown in Fig. 5.20. In this o-schema format a graphic notation is employed to represent the object set constraints. This graphic notation is the same as the notation used for items. This graphic notation is illustrated by examples below. The o-schema notation may be used to represent all objects including data, information and knowledge objects. In Sect. 4.3 the general λ-calculus form for an object is:

$$
\begin{aligned}
A[\ \lambda Q_1 &: X_1^{i_1} Q_2 : X_2^{i_2} ... Q_j : X_j^{i_j} \bullet \lambda y_1^1 ... y_{m_1}^1 ... y_{m_n}^n \bullet [\ S_{P_1}(y_1^1,...,y_{m_1}^1) \\
&\wedge \ S_{P_2}(y_1^2,...,y_{m_2}^2) \wedge .... \wedge S_{P_n}(y_1^n,...,y_{m_n}^n) \\
&\wedge \ J(y_1^1...y_{m_1}^1...y_{m_n}^n) \ ]\bullet\bullet, \\
\lambda Q_1 &: X_1^{i_1} Q_2 : X_2^{i_2} ... Q_j : X_j^{i_j} \bullet \lambda y_1^1 ... y_{m_1}^1 ... y_{m_n}^n \bullet [\ V_{P_1}(y_1^1,...,y_{m_1}^1) \\
&\wedge \ V_{P_2}(y_1^2,...,y_{m_2}^2) \wedge .... \wedge V_{P_n}(y_1^n,...,y_{m_n}^n) \\
&\wedge \ K(y_1^1...y_{m_1}^1...y_{m_n}^n) \ ]\bullet\bullet, \\
\lambda Q_1 &: X_1^{i_1} Q_2 : X_2^{i_2} ... Q_j : X_j^{i_j} \bullet [C_{Q_1} \wedge .... \wedge C_{Q_j} \\
&\wedge \ (L(Q_1,...,Q_j))_{V(A,Q_1,...,Q_j)}]\bullet \ ]
\end{aligned}
$$

An object presented in this way is in *object standard form*. This object is shown in Fig. 5.21 in its o-schema form.

As for items, if an object is in object standard form then the o-schema representation of that object can be unnecessarily complex. The "canonical form" of an

name		object name
type1	type2	argument type
(tuple1)	(tuple2)	dummy variables
meaning of the object expressed in terms of the dummy variables		object semantics
constraints on values of the dummy variables		object value constraints
set constraints		object set constraints

Fig. 5.20 The o-schema for representing objects

A		
$X^{m_1}_1$	. . . .	$X^{m_n}_n$
$(y^1_1,...,y^1_{m_1})$	. . . .	$(y^n_1,...,y^n_{m_n})$
$J(y^1_1...y^1_{m_1}...y^n_{m_n})$		
$K(y^1_1,...y^1_{m_1}...y^n_{m_n})$		
graphic form for 'L'		

Fig. 5.21 The o-schema for object A

object is defined in a similar way to the canonical form of an item. The *canonical form* of an object is constructed by:

- taking an object in object standard form;
- splitting up the semantics and value constraints to reflect disjunctive divisions in the value set of items generated by that object;
- explicitly representing any constants in the semantics, and
- explicitly representing any equalities between variables in the antecedent of the semantics.

Illustrations follow of the use of the o-schema notation to represent objects in their canonical form. The o-schema representation of the canonical form of the data objects:

$part[\lambda P:X^1 \bullet \lambda x \bullet [S_p(x) \wedge \text{with-part}(x)] \bullet \bullet,$

$\quad \lambda P:X^1 \bullet \lambda x \bullet [V_p(x) \wedge (x \geq 0)] \bullet \bullet,$

$\quad \lambda P:X^1 \bullet [C_p \wedge (\text{Card} \geq 1)_v (part,P)] \bullet]$

$cost[\lambda P:X^1 \bullet \lambda x \bullet [S_p(x) \wedge \text{for-costing}(x)] \bullet \bullet,$

$\quad \lambda P:X^1 \bullet \lambda x \bullet [V_p(x) \wedge (0 \neq x)] \bullet \bullet, \lambda P:X^1 \bullet [C_p] \bullet]$

mark-up$[\lambda P:\mathbf{X}^1 \cdot \lambda x \cdot [\ S_P(x) \wedge \text{with-mark-up}(x)\ ] \cdot\cdot,$

   $\lambda P:\mathbf{X}^1 \cdot \lambda x \cdot [\ V_P(x) \wedge (0 < x < 3)\ ] \cdot\cdot, \quad \lambda P:\mathbf{X}^1 \cdot [\ C_P\ ] \cdot\ ]$

is shown in Fig. 5.22. The o-schema representation of the canonical form of the information objects:

costs$[\lambda P:\mathbf{X}^1 Q:\mathbf{X}^1 \cdot \lambda xy \cdot [\ S_P(x) \wedge S_Q(y) \wedge \text{costs}(x,\ y)\ ] \cdot\cdot,$

   $\lambda P:\mathbf{X}^1 Q:\mathbf{X}^1 \cdot \lambda xy \cdot [\ V_P(x) \wedge V_Q(y) \wedge$

      $((1\ 000 < x < 1\ 999) \rightarrow (y \leq 300))\ ] \cdot\cdot,$

   $\lambda P:\mathbf{X}^1 Q:\mathbf{X}^1 \cdot [C_P \wedge C_Q \wedge (\text{Uni}(P) \wedge \text{Can}(Q,\ \{P\}))_{v\,(costs,P,Q)}\ ] \cdot]$

sells-for$[\lambda P:\mathbf{X}^1 Q:\mathbf{X}^1 \cdot \lambda xy \cdot [\ S_P(x) \wedge S_Q(y) \wedge \text{sells-for}(x,\ y)\ ] \cdot\cdot,$

   $\lambda P:\mathbf{X}^1 Q:\mathbf{X}^1 \cdot \lambda xy \cdot [\ V_P(x) \wedge V_Q(y) \wedge \mathbf{T}\ ] \cdot\cdot,$

   $\lambda P:\mathbf{X}^1 Q:\mathbf{X}^1 \cdot [C_P \wedge C_Q$

      $\wedge (\text{Uni}(P) \wedge \text{Can}(Q,\ \{P\}))_{v\,(sells\text{-}for,P,Q)}\ ] \cdot]$

is shown in Fig. 5.23. The o-schema representation of the canonical form of the knowledge object:

mark-up-1$[\lambda P:\mathbf{X}^2 Q:\mathbf{X}^2 R:\mathbf{X}^1 \cdot \lambda x_1 x_2 y_1 y_2 z \cdot [\ S_P(x_1,\ x_2) \wedge S_Q(y_1,\ y_2)$

      $\wedge S_R(z) \wedge ((\ x_1 = y_1\ ) \rightarrow (x_2 = z \times y_2))\ ] \cdot\cdot,$

   $\lambda P:\mathbf{X}^2 Q:\mathbf{X}^2 R:\mathbf{X}^1 \cdot \lambda x_1 x_2 y_1 y_2 z \cdot [\ V_P(x_1,x_2) \wedge V_Q(y_1,y_2) \wedge V_R(z) \wedge$

      $((\ x_1 = y_1\ ) \rightarrow (\ x_2 > y_2\ ))\ ] \cdot\cdot,$

   $\lambda P:\mathbf{X}^2 Q:\mathbf{X}^2 R:\mathbf{X}^1 \cdot [C_P \wedge C_Q \wedge C_R \wedge (\text{Uni}(P) \wedge \text{Uni}(Q)$

      $\wedge \text{Can}(P,\ \{Q,\ R\}) \wedge \text{Can}(Q,\ \{P,\ R\})$

      $\wedge \text{Can}(R,\ \{P,\ Q\}))_{v\,(mark\text{-}up\text{-}1,P,Q,R)}\ ] \cdot]$

is shown in Fig. 5.24. The o-schema representation of the canonical form of the knowledge object:

live-together$[\lambda P:\mathbf{X}^2 Q:\mathbf{X}^2 \cdot \lambda x_1 x_2 y_1 y_2 z_1 z_2 \cdot [\ S_P(x_1,\ x_2) \wedge S_Q(y_1,\ y_2)$

      $\wedge S_Q(z_1,\ z_2)$

      $\wedge (((\ x_1 = y_1\ ) \wedge (\ x_2 = z_1\ ) \wedge (\ x_1 \neq x_2\ ))$

         $\rightarrow (y_2 = z_2))\ ] \cdot\cdot,$

   $\lambda P:\mathbf{X}^2 Q:\mathbf{X}^2 \cdot \lambda x_1 x_2 y_1 y_2 z_1 z_2 \cdot [\ V_P(x_1,x_2) \wedge V_Q(y_1,y_2)$

      $\wedge V_Q(z_1,\ z_2) \wedge \mathbf{T}] \cdot\cdot,$

   $\lambda P:\mathbf{X}^2 Q:\mathbf{X}^2 \cdot [C_P \wedge C_Q$

      $\wedge (\text{Uni}(P) \wedge \text{Can}(P,\ \{Q\}))_{v\,(live\text{-}together,P,Q)}\ ] \cdot]$

part
X^1
(x)
with-part(x)
x ≥ 0
≤100

cost
X^1
(x)
for-costing(x)
0 ≠ x
∅

mark-up
X^1
(x)
with-mark-up(x)
0<x<3
∅

Fig. 5.22   o-schemas for data objects *'part'*, *'cost-price'* and *'mark-up'*

costs	
X^1	X^1
(x)	(y)
costs(x, y)	
x<1 999 → y≤300	
∀	
-----------------	O

sells-for	
X^1	X^1
(x)	(y)
sells-for(x, y)	
T	
∀	
-----------------	O

Fig. 5.23   o-schema for information objects *'costs'* and *'sells-for'*

mark-up-1		
X^2	X^2	X^1
(x, w)	(x, y)	(z)
→ (w = z × y)		
→ w > y		
∀	∀	
---------------------------------------		O
O	---	
-----------------	O	-----------------

Fig. 5.24   o-schema for knowledge object *'mark-up-1'*

is shown in Fig. 5.25. The *live-together* object does not have an elementary semantics. The o-schema representation of the canonical form of the knowledge object:

responsibility$[\lambda P:X^2Q:X^2R:X^1 \bullet \lambda w_1 w_2 x_1 x_2 y_1 y_2 z \bullet [S_P(w_1, w_2)$

$\wedge S_Q(x_1, x_2) \wedge S_P(y_1, y_2) \wedge S_R(z)$

$\wedge ((((w_1 = x_1) \wedge (x_2 = z)) \rightarrow (w_2 = z)) \vee$

$(((w_1 = x_1) \wedge (x_2 \neq z) \wedge (x_2 = y_1))$

$\rightarrow (w_2 = y_2)))]\bullet\bullet,$

$$\lambda P{:}\mathbf{X}^2 Q{:}\mathbf{X}^2 R{:}\mathbf{X}^1 \cdot \lambda w_1 w_2 x_1 x_2 y_1 y_2 z \cdot [\ V_P(w_1,\ w_2)\ \wedge\ V_Q(x_1,\ x_2)$$
$$\wedge\ V_P(y_1,\ y_2)\ \wedge\ V_R(z)\ \wedge\ \mathbf{T}]^{\bullet\bullet},$$
$$\lambda P{:}\mathbf{X}^2 Q{:}\mathbf{X}^2 R{:}\mathbf{X}^1 \cdot [C_P\ \wedge\ C_Q\ \wedge\ C_R$$
$$\wedge\ (\text{Uni}(P)\ \wedge\ \text{Can}(P,\ \{Q,R\}))_{v\ (responsibility,P,Q,R)}\ ]^\bullet\ ]$$

is shown in Fig. 5.26. The *responsibility* object is recursive and does not have an elementary semantics.

The specification of items as the product of object operators applied to simpler items provides a natural representation of inheritance. o-schemas may be used to represent this sequence of object operators. i-schemas may be used to represent those simpler items.

In Sect. 4.7 two operations on objects are defined in terms of the λ-calculus form for objects. Those two operations are "object composition" and "object join". Both of these operations can be used to generate an object from two given objects. Those two operations can also be applied to the o-schema representation of objects. Those two operations generate an o-schema from two o-schemas.

live-together	
$\mathbf{X}^2$	$\mathbf{X}^2$
(x, y)	(x, z)
	(y, z)
$x \neq y$	
T	
$\forall$	
O	-------------------------

Fig. 5.25   o-schema for knowledge object *'live-together'*

responsibility		
$\mathbf{X}^2$	$\mathbf{X}^2$	$\mathbf{X}^1$
(x, z)	(x, w)	(w)
	($\perp, \perp$)	
$\rightarrow\ (z = w)$		
T		
(x, z)	(x, y)	(w)
	(y, v)	
(y $\neq$ w) $\rightarrow$ (z = v)		
T		
$\forall$		
O	--------------------------------------	

Fig. 5.26   o-schema for knowledge object *'responsibility'*

mark-up-1

X²	X²	X¹
(x, w)	(x, y)	(z)
→ (w = z × y)		
→ w > y		
∀	∀	
--------------------------------		O
O	--------------------------------	
--------------	O	--------------

sells-for

X¹	X¹
(x)	(y)
sells-for(x, y)	
T	
∀	
---------------	O

$\{1\}^{\oplus}$

=

mark-up-1 $_{\{1\}}^{\oplus}$ **sells-for**

X¹	X¹	X²	X¹
(x)	(w)	(x, y)	(z)
→ sells-for(x, w) ∧ (w = z × y)			
→ w > y			
∀		∀	
-----------------	O		
O		--	

Fig. 5.27   o-schema for the object **mark-up-1** $_{\{1\}}^{\oplus}$ **sells-for**

mark-up-1

X²	X²	X¹
(x, w)	(x, y)	(z)
→ (w = z × y)		
→ w > y		
∀	∀	
--------------------------------		O
O	--------------------------------	
--------------	O	--------------

mark-up

X¹
(x)
with-mark-up(x)
0<x<3
∅

$\{3\}^{\oplus}$

=

mark-up-1 $_{\{3\}}^{\oplus}$ **mark-up**

X²	X²	X¹
(x, w)	(x, y)	(z)
→ with-mark-up(x) ∧ (w = z × y)		
→ w > y ∧ 0<z<3		
∀	∀	
--		O
O	--	
--------------	O	--------------

Fig. 5.28   o-schema for the object **mark-up-1** $_{\{3\}}^{\oplus}$ **mark-up**

sells-for	
$\mathbf{X}^1$	$\mathbf{X}^1$
(x)	(y)
sells-for(x, y)	
T	
∀	
------------	**O**

part
$\mathbf{X}^1$
(x)
with-part(x)
x ≥ 0
≤100

$\{1\}^\oplus$

=

sells-for $\{1\}^\oplus$ part	
$\mathbf{X}^1$	$\mathbf{X}^1$
(x)	(y)
with-part(x) ∧ sells-for(x, y)	
x ≥ 0	
≤ 100	
∀	
----------------------	**O**

Fig. 5.29   o-schema for the object *sells-for* $\{1\}^\oplus$ *part*

comp	
$\mathbf{D}^1$	$\mathbf{D}^1$
(x)	(y)
∅	
T	
∀	∀

$\otimes_{\{(2,1)\}}$

has-type	
$\mathbf{X}^1$	$\mathbf{X}^1$
(x)	(y)
has-type(x, y)	
T	
∀	
---------------	**O**

=

comp $\otimes_{\{(2,1)\}}$ has-type		
$\mathbf{D}^1$	$\mathbf{D}^1$	$\mathbf{X}^1$
(x)	(y)	(z)
has-type(y, z)		
T		
∀	∀	
	---------------	**O**

Fig. 5.30   o-schema for the object *comp* $\otimes_{\{(2,1)\}}$ *has-type*

Consider the object composition operation. Figure 5.27 shows the o-schema for the object *mark-up-1* $\{1\}^\oplus$ *sells-for*. Figure 5.28 shows the o-schema for the object *mark-up-1* $\{3\}^\oplus$ *mark-up*. Figure 5.29 shows the o-schema for the object *sells-for* $\{1\}^\oplus$ *part*.

mark-up-1		
X^2	X^2	X^1
(x, w)	(x, y)	(z)
→ (w = z × y)		
→ w > y		
∀	∀	
--------------------------------		O
O	--------------------------------	
--------------	O	--------------

$\otimes_{\{(3,1)\}}$

valid	
X^1	X^2
(x)	(y, z)
valid(x, y, z)	
T	
O	--------------

=

mark-up-1 $\otimes_{\{(3,1)\}}$ valid			
X^2	X^2	X^1	X^2
(x, w)	(x, y)	(z)	(s, t)
→ (w = z × y) and valid(z, s, t)			
→ (w > y)			
∀	∀		
-----------------------------------		O	
O	-----------------------------------		
--------------	O	--------------	
		O	--------------

Fig. 5.31   o-schema for the object **mark-up-1** $\otimes_{\{(3,1)\}}$ **valid**

Consider the object join operation. Figure 5.30 shows the o-schema for the object **comp** $\otimes_{\{(2,1)\}}$ **has-type** where {(2,1)} identifies the second argument of **comp** and the first argument of **has-type**. Figure 5.31 shows the o-schema for the object **mark-up-1** $\otimes_{\{(3,1)\}}$ **valid**. where {(3,1)}) identifies the third argument of **mark-up-1** and the first argument of **valid**.

5.6 o-schemas as operators

Section 5.5 defined the o-schema notation for representing objects. An object is an operator that turns a set of items into an item. Objects may be represented either formally as λ-calculus expressions or informally as o-schemas. In Sect. 4.3 the resulting item obtained applying an object to a set of items was defined formally in the λ-calculus notation. The o-schema representations of objects enables the result of the application of an object to a set of items of be

part
∅
x
is-a[x:part-number]
1 000<x<9 999
≤100

cost-price
∅
x
is-a[x:dollar-amount]
0<x
∅

costs	
X¹	**X**¹
(x)	(y)
costs(x, y)	
x<1 999 → y≤300	
∀	
-----------------	O

part/cost-price	
part	cost-price
x	y
costs(x, y)	
x<1 999 → y≤300	
∀	
-----------------	O

Fig. 5.32   The application of the object **costs** to two items

calculated by hand in the schema notation. Figure 5.32 shows the **costs** object, the *part* and *cost-price* items and the result of the application of this object to these two items.

5.7 t-schemas

Chapter 9 will discuss t-schemas in detail. The 't' in t-schema stands for "transaction". A t-schema is constructed for each transaction type. The aim of this chapter is to describe the schemas that are used when the unified methodology is applied. For completeness the t-schema notation is described briefly here.

A *player* in a knowledge-based system is an entity that interacts with the system. The players are identified in the context diagram. A player can be a person, a computer system, a robot or anything capable of generating or receiving a request. Informally a "transaction" of a knowledge-based system is any behaviour initiated by a request from one player or group of players, and resulting in the delivery of a response to another player or group of players. A *transaction* consists of:

- a transaction *name* (the names of system transactions are usually specified in the high-level r-schema);
- a transaction *specification* (an informal description of what the transaction does);

- the *request players* that are the set of players who deliver the request to the system, and the *request name* of the request used by those players;
- the name of the *system* to which the request is delivered and the name (*sys_req* in Fig. 5.33) given to that request by that system;
- the name of the *response players* to whom the system delivers its response, and the *response name* given to that response by those players;
- the name (*sys_resp* in Fig. 5.33) given to the response by the system, and
- the high-level *instruction* that the system executes on receiving the request.

In terms of the jargon identified above, the general format of a *t-schema* is shown in Fig. 5.33. A sample t-schema is shown in Fig. 5.34.

name		
specification		
request player	*system*	response player
request name	*sys_req*	
	sys_resp	response name
instruction		

Fig. 5.33 t-schema format

find_sal-bill		
find the salary bill for a given department		
Accounts Clerk	*personnel management system*	Accounts Clerk
department name	dept_name	
	(sal-bill, ok)	(salary bill, ok)
FIND_SAL-BILL(dept_name, sal-bill, ok)		

Fig. 5.34 Sample t-schema

5.8 Summary

- Schemas are practical representations that are used when the unified methodology is applied.
- i-schemas provide a low-level, declarative representation of single items.
- If an item is in item standard form then the i-schema representation of that item can be unnecessarily complex.
- The canonical form of an item is designed to lead to a simple representation of that item using an i-schema.
- r-schemas provide a high-level, imperative view of a *set of* one or more items.
- There is a rough correspondence between the structure of r-schemas and the structure of i-schemas.
- o-schemas provide a low-level, declarative representation of single objects.
- If an object is in object standard form then the o-schema representation of that object can be unnecessarily complex.
- The canonical form of an object is designed to lead to a simple representation of that object using an o-schema.
- t-schemas represent transactions. A t-schema is constructed for each transaction type.

6 Normalisation

6.1 Introduction

In the unified representation for conceptual modelling described in Chaps. 3 and 4, data things, information things and knowledge things are all represented in the same way as "items". Items may be constructed by applying objects to simpler items. In Chap. 5 a variety of schemas were described including schemas for describing items and objects. Items and objects are named triples consisting of a "name", "semantics", "value constraints" and "set constraints". At any particular time an item is associated with a particular value set. In Sect. 3.7 the notion of a "decomposable" item and in Sect. 4.7 the notion of a "decomposable" object were defined.

This chapter discusses the "normalisation" of the "conceptual model". The conceptual model is defined in Sect. 6.2. It is constructed during the second "system analysis" step in the unified design methodology. System analysis is discussed in detail in Chap. 8. Normalisation is a process that simplifies the conceptual model by decomposing the items and objects in it [Debenham, 1996c]. The significance of normalisation for maintenance is discussed in Chap. 8. Section 6.2 explores the different meanings that the term "normal" has in common usage, and the relationships between these different meanings. The normalisation of items and objects is described in Sects. 6.3 and 6.4 respectively. Some of the normalisation forms derived are generalisations of the well known normal forms for relational database. These well known normal forms are the *"classical normal forms"* which can be applied to data, information and knowledge [Debenham, 1997b]. Normalisation forms that are not generalisations of the well known normal forms for relational database are the "non-classical normal forms". In Sect. 6.6 some non-classical normal forms are discussed. In Sect. 6.7 a variant of normalisation is applied to the structure of groups. In Chap. 8 "normalisation" is described as a process performed during system analysis.

6.2 Meaning of normal

Chapter 8 will describe the "system analysis" step of the unified design methodology. The principal product of the "system analysis" step is the construction of a "conceptual model". The conceptual model is defined here (it is described in greater detail in Chap. 8). A *conceptual model* consists of:

- a conceptual library, and
- a conceptual map.

The *conceptual library* is a collection of items each of which represents a real thing in the application. The *conceptual map* is a vertex labelled graph. For each item in the conceptual library there is a vertex in the conceptual map labelled with that item's name. An arc joins a pair of vertices in the conceptual map if there is a "coupling relationship" between the items whose names are attached to those vertices. If one item in the conceptual library is modified in any way then certain other items may have to be modified as well if the correctness of the conceptual model is to be preserved. A *coupling relationship* links two items in the conceptual map if modification to one of those items requires that the other item be checked for correctness. Coupling relationships provide the basic structure that supports the maintenance process (they are described in detail in Chap. 8). The set of items comprising the conceptual library may *either* be defined explicitly using the λ-calculus or i-schema notation *or* implicitly by representing each item as the result of the application of a sequence of object operators to a fundamental set of items called the "basis". If the set of items comprising the conceptual library are defined explicitly then the resulting conceptual model is an *explicit conceptual model*. If the set of items comprising the conceptual library are defined implicitly then the resulting conceptual model is an *implicit conceptual model*. A conceptual model is a representation of an application together with a structure that supports the maintenance process [Martins & Reinfrank, 1991].

In traditional database technology a key goal of the normalisation of the conceptual models of data and information is to prevent the introduction of update anomalies. In the unified methodology a key goal of the normalisation of the conceptual model is also to prevent the introduction of update anomalies. In addition to the normalisation of the conceptual model, constraints, which are discussed in Chap. 8, provide a mechanism that enables the conceptual model to be protected against the introduction of anomalies during the execution of maintenance operations.

In common usage, the process of "database normalisation" has a variety of different meanings, three of which are:

- "normalisation" is a procedure that *replaces* a "bad" conceptual model with a "good" conceptual model. This is the spirit in which normalisation was originally presented. The five normal forms were promoted as tests that are applied to a relational model. If a relation failed any of these tests then it is replaced with a relation that is in normal form.

- "normalisation" is a selection criterion that enables a good conceptual model to be *selected* from a "complete" conceptual model. A *complete* conceptual model is a conceptual model with the property that nothing can be added to that model that represents a "valid thing" in the application. This is the meaning given to *normalisation* here.
- "normalisation" is a *goal* for an analysis method. That is, a good analysis method is one that generates a conceptual model that is in normal form. This is the role that the classical normal forms play in the Binary Relationship approach to modelling information. Models developed using the BR approach tend to be in normal form.

These three meanings for normalisation may not be complete, are not independent of each other, and merely indicate the variety of meanings that the term "normalisation" has in common usage.

The first two meanings for "normalisation" given above are related. In the first meaning, normalisation is a procedure that replaces a "bad" conceptual model with a "good" one. For the classical normal forms this process of replacement is presented in the form "given this form of representation, if such and such a test fails then the given representation should be replaced by this other representation". If this process to be effective then "all that is valid about the application" must be readily available to the process. Hence the first meaning of normalisation can be expressed as "given a bad model of an application, augment that model with a representation of all valid statements about the application, and then select a good model from this augmented representation of gathered statements". That is, the first meaning of normalisation consists of two steps. The first step is to *complete* the model, and the second step is to *select* a good model from this complete model. The second meaning of normalisation is contained within the first. The first meaning of normalisation is shown in Fig. 6.1 where γ is the "completion mapping" and σ is the "selection mapping".

In the unified methodology there is one principle of normalisation. All of the traditional normal forms for relational database may be derived from this single principle. The principle of normalisation may be applied to items and objects in the conceptual model no matter whether those items and objects are classified as data, information or knowledge. The problem of defining the concept of "normal" for the conceptual model is dealt with using this single principle. This principle is phrased in terms of the "decomposition" of items that is discussed in Sect. 3.7, and in terms of the "decomposition" of objects that is discussed in Sect. 4.7.

Fig. 6.1 Normalisation as a process of completing and selecting

---

Principle NF. Given a conceptual model discard any items, or objects, that are decomposable.

The general idea of the principle of normalisation is to break items and objects down into their simplest form. An item A is *decomposable* into $D = \{A_1, A_2, .., A_n\}$ if:

- A_i is not tautological for all i,
- $A = A_1 \otimes A_2 \otimes ... \otimes A_n$, where
- each composition is monotonic

Principle NF requires that item A should be replaced by a set of non-tautological, simpler items from which item A can be reconstructed. Nothing is lost by replacing item A by the set $\{A_1, A_2, .., A_n\}$. Having decomposed an item A, principle NF requires that the set $\{A_1, A_2, .., A_n\}$ should be inspected to determine whether any of its members are decomposable, and so on.

A conceptual model is *normal* if it contains no decomposable items. Items and objects consist of a name, semantics, value constraints and set constraints. In Sect. 6.7 further principles of normalisation for the implementation of knowledge items as groups are described. These principles are in addition to the principle of normalisation NF.

The principle of normalisation NF requires that all valid statements about the application are readily available. This is often not so. An example of the normalisation of information is given by the item:

person/street-address/town/post-code/state[
    λvwxyz•[is-address-of(v:person-number, w:street-address-sting,
        x:town-name, y:post-code-string, z:state-name)]•,
    λvwxyz•[(1 000 < y < 9 999)]•,
    (Uni(*person*) ∧ Can(*street-address*, {*person*}) ∧ Can(*town*, {*person*})
        ∧ Can(*post-code*, {*person*})∧ Can(*state*, {*person*})
)*person/street-address/town/post-code/state*]

The facts that "the name of the town determines the post code" and that "the post code determines the state" are valid but may not be readily available. The constraint:

Can(*post-code*, {*town*}) ∧ Can(*state*, {*post-code*})

should have been included in the item's set constraints. Hence the fact that this item is decomposable may not be realised.

Missing information can lead to the construction of databases that contain relations that are not normal. Likewise missing knowledge can lead to the construction of knowledge bases that contain clusters that are not normal. The following example illustrates the normalisation of knowledge. In that example two rules share an, as yet unstated, sub-rule between them. This situation is undesirable because if the knowledge implicit in the sub-rule should change then both of the rules should be modified. Consider the rule:

"the sale price of a part is calculated by taking the cost price of that part, marking that cost price up by the profit margin for that part and adding sales tax at the correct rate for that part"   [A]

This rule can be represented by the item *[part/sale-price, part/cost-price, part/sales-tax-rate, part/profit-margin]* shown in Fig. 6.2. Suppose that in addition the following rule is noted:

"the value added tax payable on a part is the product of the value added tax rate for that part and the difference between the pre-sales tax sale price and the cost price of that part"   [B]

This rule can be represented by the item *[part/value-added-tax, part/cost-price, part/profit-margin, part/value-added-tax-rate]* shown in Fig. 6.3. Further suppose that the following rule is noted:

"the pre-sales tax selling price of a part is the cost price of the part marked up by the profit margin for that part per cent"   [C]

This sub-rule can be represented by the item *[part/pre-sales-tax-selling-price, part/cost-price, part/profit-margin]* shown in Fig. 6.4. The problem with rules [A] and [B] is that rule [C] is buried within both of them. The items illustrated in Figs. 6.3–6.4 are not normal. To see this consider the rules:

"the sale price of a part is calculated by taking the pre-sales tax selling price of the part and marking it up by the sales tax rate for that part per cent"   [A*]

and

"the value added tax payable on a part is the product of the pre-sales tax selling price of the part less the cost price of the part and the value added tax rate for that part less 100"   [B*]

These rules can be represented by the items *[part/sale-price, part/pre-sales-tax-selling-price, part/sales-tax-rate]* and *[part/value-added-tax, part/pre-sales-tax-selling-price, part/cost-price, part/value-added-tax-rate]* shown in Figs. 6.5–6.6. It may be shown that:

[part/sale-price, part/cost-price, part/sales-tax-rate, part/profit-margin]
= *[part/sale-price, part/pre-sales-tax-selling-price, part/sales-tax-rate]*
$\otimes$ *{part/pre-sales-tax-selling-price}*
      [part/pre-sales-tax-selling-price, part/cost-price, part/profit-margin]

and that:

[part/value-added-tax, part/cost-price, part/profit-margin, part/value-added-tax-rate]
= *[part/value-added-tax, part/pre-sales-tax-selling-price, part/cost-price,*
        part/value-added-tax-rate]
$\otimes$ *{part/pre-sales-tax-selling-price}*
      [part/pre-sales-tax-selling-price, part/cost-price, part/profit-margin]

Hence Principle NF may be employed to remove the items shown in Figs. 6.2–6.3 from the conceptual library and to replace them with the items shown in Figs. 6.5–6.6.

[part/sale-price, part/cost-price, part/sales-tax-rate, part/profit-margin].			
part/sale-price	*part/cost-price*	*part/sales-tax-rate*	*part/profit-margin*
(x, y)	(x, z)	(x, v)	(x, w)
$\rightarrow$ y $=$ $(1 + w \div 100) \times (1 + v \div 100) \times z$			
y > z			
$\forall$	$\forall$		
O	--		

Fig. 6.2 Item *[part/sale-price, part/cost-price, part/sales-tax-rate, part/profit-margin]*

[part/value-added-tax, part/cost-price, part/profit-margin, part/value-added-tax-rate]			
part/value-added-tax	*part/cost-price*	*part/profit-margin*	*part/value-added-tax-rate*
(x, y)	(x, z)	(x, w)	(x, v)
$\rightarrow$ y $=$ $(z \times w \times v) \div 10\,000$			
$\emptyset$			
$\forall$	$\forall$		
O	--		

Fig. 6.3 Item *[part/value-added-tax, part/cost-price, part/profit-margin, part/value-added-tax-rate]*

[part/pre-sales-tax-selling-price, part/cost-price, part/profit-margin]		
part/pre-sales-tax-selling-price	part/cost-price	part/profit-margin
(x, y)	(x, z)	(x, w)
→ y = (1 + w ÷ 100) × z		
→ y > z		
∀	∀	
O	--	

Fig. 6.4 Item *[part/pre-sales-tax-selling-price, part/cost-price, part/profit-margin]*

[part/sale-price, part/pre-sales-tax-selling-price, part/sales-tax-rate]		
part/sale-price	part/pre-sales-tax-selling-price	part/sales-tax-rate
(x, y)	(x, z)	(x, w)
→ y = (1 + w ÷ 100) × z		
→ y > z		
∀	∀	
O	--	

Fig. 6.5 Item *[part/sale-price, part/pre-sales-tax-selling-price, part/sales-tax-rate]*

[part/value-added-tax, part/pre-sales-tax-selling-price, part/cost-price, part/value-added-tax-rate]			
part/value-added-tax	part/pre-sales-tax-selling-price	part/cost-price	part/value-added-tax-rate
(x, y)	(x, z)	(x, w)	(x, v)
→ y = (v ÷ 100) × (z − w)			
→ z > w			
∀	∀		
O	---		

Fig. 6.6 Item *[part/value-added-tax, part/cost-price, part/profit-margin,*
part/value-added-tax-rate]

The example of normalisation considered above concerns knowledge. It has implications for the structure of rules that can be derived from that knowledge. Consider the following clause groups that implement the items in that example. Rule [A] can be implemented as the clause group:

part/sale-price(x, y) ← part/cost-price(x, z), part/sales-tax-rate(x, v),
   part/profit-margin(x, w),
   u = (1 + w ÷ 100) × (1 + v ÷ 100), y = u × z   [1]

where both the sales tax rate and the profit margin are expressed as percentages. Group [1] can also be expressed more succinctly in the group notation:

part/sale-price $\Leftarrow$ part/cost-price, part/sales-tax-rate,
    part/profit-margin   [1']

Rule [B] can be implemented as the clause group:

part/value-added-tax(x, y) $\leftarrow$ part/cost-price(x, z), part/profit-margin(x, w),
    part/value-added-tax-rate(x, v), y $= (z \times w \times v) \div 10\,000$ [2]

or more succinctly in the group notation:

part/value-added-tax $\Leftarrow$ part/cost-price, part/profit-margin,
    part/value-added-tax-rate   [2']

The problem with group [1] and group [2] is that buried within both groups is the sub-rule, Rule [C], that "the pre-sales tax selling price of a part is the cost price of the part marked up by the profit margin for that part per cent". Rule [C] can be implemented as:

part/pre-sales-tax-selling-price(x, y) $\leftarrow$ part/cost-price(x, z),
    part/profit-margin(x, w), y $= (1 + w \div 100) \times z$ [3]

or more succinctly in the group notation:

part/pre-sales-tax-selling-price $\Leftarrow$ part/cost-price,
    part/profit-margin   [3']

Suppose that rule [C] changes and is replaced by the rule "the pre-sales-tax selling price of a part is a fixed $5 charge plus the cost price of the part marked up by the profit margin for that part per cent". This new rule can be implemented as the clause group:

part/pre-sales-tax-selling-price(x, y) $\leftarrow$ part/cost-price(x, z),
    part/profit-margin(x, w),
    y $= 5 + (1 + w \div 100) \times z$ [4]

The change in rule [C] means that rules [A] and [B] should both be modified as they both depend implicitly on the notion of the "pre-sales tax selling price". This problem can be serious because the implicit dependence of rules [A] and [B] on the concept of "pre-sales tax selling price" may not be identified in the implementation of those rules. There is a potential "maintenance hazard" in the expression of the two rules [A] and [B]. This hazard could be avoided by identifying the sub-rule [C], extracting rule [C] from rules [A] and [B], and hence obtaining rules [A*] and [B*]. Rules [A*] and [B*] implemented as clause groups could be:

part/sale-price(x, y) ← part/pre-sales-tax-selling-price(x, z),
   part/sales-tax-rate(x, w),
   $y = (1 + w \div 100) \times z$ [1*]

and:

part/value-added-tax(x, y) ← part/pre-sales-tax-selling-price(x, z),
   part/cost-price(x, w),
   part/value-added-tax-rate(x, v),
   $y = (v \div 100) \times (z - w)$ [2*]

respectively, or more succinctly in the group notation:

part/sale-price ⇐ part/pre-sales-tax-selling-price,
   part/sales-tax-rate   [1*']

and:

part/value-added-tax ⇐ part/pre-sales-tax-selling-price, part/cost-price,
   part/value-added-tax-rate   [2*']

The two groups [1*] and [2*] are insulated against changes in group [3].

The above example concerns the situation when two rules share an, as yet unstated, sub-rule between them. In theory "unstated rules" can be disposed of by assuming that *all* valid rules have been gathered and stated. This assumption is not reasonable. The existence of unstated sub-rules may be the cause of update anomalies for knowledge bases.

The concept of a "normal" conceptual model is defined above. In the following sections particular "normal forms" and "strategies for normalisation" are described. The definition of "normal" given above specifies what a "normal" conceptual model is. A normal conceptual model can be constructed by removing decomposable items and objects. The identification of items and objects that are not normal is hard. Tests of normality help to identify items and objects that are not normal. The "normal forms" that are discussed throughout this chapter are tests of normality that are intended to be pointers to ways in which the items and objects in a conceptual model may not be normal. That is, the normal forms provide an indication of some of the ways in which an entire conceptual model may not be normal.

6.3 Normalisation of items

In Sect. 6.2 the meaning of normalisation is discussed and a general principle of normalisation Principle NF is stated. In Sect. 8.5 the value of normalisation to the reduction of maintenance costs is discussed. The general principle of normalisation Principle NF is expressed in terms of the notion of decomposition [Debenham, 1996b]. It applies to both items in an explicit conceptual model as well as to both objects and items in an implicit conceptual model. In this section the normalisation of the items in an explicit conceptual model is discussed. In Sect. 6.4 the normalisation of objects is discussed. To construct an explicit conceptual model that is in normal form first gather all relevant facts about the application and represent them as a set of items. Second discard any items from this set that are decomposable. Then the remaining set of items constitutes the conceptual library of a normal conceptual model.

In this section various strategies for normalisation are described. These strategies are all of the form "if this test is satisfied by an item then investigate whether the given item can be decomposed". They are all special cases of the general principle of normalisation. The satisfaction of all of these strategies is not sufficient to ensure that an explicit conceptual model is "normal". They are intended to capture some of the ways in which a collection of items may not be normal.

The general principle of normalisation Principle NF requires that decomposable items should be discarded. Using the notation of Sect. 3.7, this principle requires that:

$$(A \otimes_E B)[\; \lambda xyz \bullet [S_A(\pi(x, \; y)) \wedge S_B(\pi'(y, \; z)) \;] \bullet,$$
$$\lambda xyz \bullet [\; V_A(\pi(x, \; y)) \wedge V_B(\pi'(y, \; z)) \;] \bullet,$$
$$C_A^{\pi} \wedge C_B^{\pi'} \;]$$

should be discarded in favour of both:

$$A[\; S_A, \; V_A, \; C_A \;] \text{ and}$$
$$B[\; S_B, \; V_B, \; C_B \;]$$

provided that the composition is monotonic and that items A and B are not tautological.

The general principle of normalisation requires that:

$$part\_machine/type[\; \lambda xyz \bullet [\text{is-a}[x\text{:part-number}] \wedge$$
$$\text{has-type}(y\text{:machine-name}, \; z\text{:type-description}) \;] \bullet,$$
$$\lambda xyz \bullet [\; (1\,000 < x < 9\,999) \wedge$$
$$(y = AB \vee y = CD) \wedge \quad (z = \text{lathe} \vee z = \text{press}) \;] \bullet,$$

(Uni(*part*) ∧ Uni(*machine*) ∧
 Can(*type*, {*machine*}))$_{part\_machine/type}$ ∧
 (Card ≤ 100)$_{part}$ ∧ (Card ≥ 2)$_{machine}$ ∧ (Card = 2)$_{type}$]

should be discarded in favour of both the data item:

part_machine[λxy•[is-a[x:part-number] ∧ is-a[y:machine-name]]•,
 λxy•[(1 000 < x < 9 999) ∧ (y = AB ∨ y = CD)]•,
 (Uni(*part*) ∧ Uni(*machine*))$_{part\_machine}$ ∧
  (Card ≤ 100)$_{part}$ ∧ (Card ≥ 2)$_{machine}$)]

and the information item:

machine/type[λxy•[has-type(x:machine-name, y:type-description)]•,
 λxy•[(x = AB ∨ x = CD) ∧   (y = lathe ∨ y = press)]•,
 (Uni(*machine*) ∧ Can(*type*, {*machine*}))$_{machine/type}$ ∧
  (Card ≥ 2)$_{machine}$ ∧ (Card = 2)$_{type}$]

This example is shown in the i-schema notation in Fig. 6.7.

 Given an item, a *component set* of that item is a subset of the set of that item's components. In Fig. 6.8 *A*, *B* and *C* are three item names, and D, E and F are the names of three component sets of item *C* that may not be disjoint. Item *C* may be generated from items *A* and *B* by a *single* application of the join operator

part_machine/type			
part	*machine*	*type*	
(x)	(y)	(z)	
has-type(y, z)			=
1 000 < x < 9 999	y = AB ∨ y = CD	z=lathe ∨ z=press	
∀	∀		
	----------------------	O	

part_machine			
part	*machine*		
(x)	(y)	⊗{*machine*}	
∅			
∅			
∀	∀		

machine/type		
machine	*type*	
(x)	(y)	
has-type(x, y)		
∅		
∀		
----------------	O	

Fig. 6.7 Decomposition of the item *part_machine/type*

C		
D	E	F
S_C		
V_C		
C_C		

$=$

A	
D	E
S_A	
V_A	
C_A	

$\otimes_E$

B	
E	F
S_B	
V_B	
C_B	

Fig. 6.8 General structure of a single join decomposition

using the component set E. If the decomposition of an item can be effected by a *single* application of the join operator then that decomposition is a *single join decomposition*.

One strategy for applying the general principle of normalisation to items in the i-schema notation is first to try to identify structures of the form shown in Fig. 6.8. Having identified such structures then investigate whether the semantics, value constraints and set constraints of item C permit that item to be represented as the join of items A and B,. That is, investigate whether $A \otimes_E B = C$. The general structure of Fig. 6.8 helps to identify candidate items to normalise. The order of the components within the component sets E, F and G is of no significance.

The recognition of decomposable items may not be difficult. Given an item if it is decomposable then its semantics permits that item to be represented as the join of two other items. An example is given below to show that a decomposable item's semantics can be phrased in such a way as to hide the fact that the item is decomposable. A strategy for the identification of decomposable items is to examine each item's semantics expression and to note the extent to which the predicate in that expression is "separable". The notion of a "separable" predicate is defined in Sect. 3.3. That definition is repeated here. Given a predicate J of the form:

$$J(y_1^1,...,y_{m_1}^1,y_1^2,...,y_{m_2}^2,..........,y_1^n,...,y_{m_n}^n)$$

Define the set $\{Y_1, Y_2,..., Y_n\}$ by $Y_i = \{y_1^i,...,y_{m_i}^i\}$. If J can be written in the form:

$$J_1 \wedge J_2 \wedge ... \wedge J_m$$

where each J_i is a predicate in terms of the set of variables X_i with:

$X_i \subset Y_1 \cup Y_2 \cup ... \cup Y_n$, and

for each X_i $(\exists j)$ such that X_i does *not* contain any of the variables in Y_j

then predicate J is *separable* into the partition $\{X_1, X_2,..., X_m\}$. Given the predicate $J(y_1^1, y_2^1, y_1^2, y_2^2, y_1^3, y_2^3)$ that means:

$$(y_2^2 = y_1^1 + y_2^1) \wedge (y_2^3 > y_1^3)$$

J is separable into the partition $\{ \{y_1^1, y_2^1, y_1^2, y_2^2\}, \{y_1^3, y_2^3\} \}$ by:

$$J_1(y_1^1, y_2^1, y_1^2, y_2^2) \wedge J_2(y_1^3, y_2^3)$$

where $J_1(y_1^1, y_2^1, y_1^2, y_2^2)$ means $(y_2^2 = y_1^1 + y_2^1)$ and $J_2(y_1^3, y_2^3)$ means $(y_2^3 > y_1^3)$.

Normalisation Strategy I:1. If the predicate in an item's semantics expression is separable then investigate whether that item is decomposable into items containing the component sets identified by the separability of that predicate.

The semantics of the *part_machine/type* item is:

$$\lambda xyz \bullet [\ S_{part} \wedge S_{machine} \wedge S_{type} \wedge \text{has-type}(y,\ z)\ ] \bullet$$

The predicate "has-type" in this expression is separable into the disjoint partition $\{(y, z)\}$ because:

$$J_1(y, z) = \text{has-type}(y,\ z)$$

If the predicate in an item's semantics is separable into a partition then the next step is determine whether the entire item is separable into the component sets identified by that partition. It may be shown that:

$$part\_machine/type\ =\ part \otimes_{\{\emptyset\}} machine/type$$

This decomposition is shown in Fig. 6.9. This decomposition is simpler than the decomposition shown in Fig. 6.7. The decomposition shown in Fig. 6.7 may be derived from the non-disjoint partition $\{(x, y), (y, z)\}$ where 'y', as the common variable between the two elements in the partition, determines the form of the decomposition that is $\otimes_{\{machine\}}$.

A decomposable item's semantics can be phrased in such a way as to hide the fact that the item is decomposable. An example follows to illustrate this. Consider the item semantics:

$$\lambda xyz \bullet [\ \text{is-a}[x:\text{person-number}] \wedge \text{is-a}[y:\text{street-address}] \wedge \text{is-a}[z:\text{postcode}]$$
$$\wedge\ \text{has-address}(x, y, z)\ ] \bullet$$

part
part
∅
(x)
is-a[x:part-number]
1 000<x<9 999
≤ 100

⊗{∅}

machine/type	
machine	*type*
(x)	(y)
has-type(x, y)	
x=AB ∨ x=CD	y=lathe ∨ y=press
∀	
--------------------	O

Fig. 6.9 Another decomposition of the item *part_machine/type*

where "has-address(x, y, z)" means "person 'x' has a house with street address 'y' and the post-code that applies to this persons house is 'z'". The way in which the expression is phrased masks the fact that postcode might be dependent on street address. If this item's semantics is expressed as:

λxyz•[is-a[x:person-number] ∧ is-a[y:street-address] ∧ is-a[z:postcode]
    ∧ address-of(x, y) ∧ postcode-of(y, z)]•

then the predicate in this item's semantics is separable into the partition {(x,y),(y,z)}. This partition leads to an investigation of the decomposability of the item. This example is used frequently in discussions on functional dependencies in databases.

The example considered above illustrates that the apparent separability of the predicate in an item's semantics can not be relied on as a pointer to that item's decomposability. When looking for decomposable items it is useful to have strategies that are based on other parts of an item's specification besides the semantics. In the remainder of this section strategies are discussed that are based on the item's set constraints.

There is a fundamental distinction that determines two different types of item. This distinction is based on whether or not a given item represents an association. If an item does *not* represent an association then that item is a data item. An example of the normalisation of a data item is given above. If an item *does* represent an association then that item is either an information item or a knowledge item. Suppose that a given item represents an association and that the association is functional. Items of this type may be classified by considering the structure of their set constraints. They may be classified by considering the candidate constraints that occur within their set constraints.

Principle NF applies to items in general. If an item is an information item or a knowledge item then it represents an association. Associations are sometimes functional. Explicit associations represented as "if-then rules" are functional. Implicit associations represented as relations with a key are functional. Hence the implications of the general Principle NF for those items that contain functional associations is relevant to conceptual models of real applications.

The second strategy for identifying decomposable items from Principle NF is described. This strategy is Normalisation Strategy I:2. Two other strategies are then derived from Principle NF. These strategies are related to the classical normal forms for information. No distinction is drawn between implicit and explicit functional associations. The Normalisation Strategy I:2, and the two other strategies that follow it can be employed, for example, to normalise an information item using a knowledge item or vice versa.

Items are classified below using the structure of the candidate constraints within their set constraints. Once again, the letters D, E and F represent the names of component sets. Suppose that:

$$D = \{D_1, D_2,..., D_p\}$$
$$E = \{E_1, E_2,..., E_q\}$$
$$F = \{F_1, F_2,..., F_r\}$$

Suppose that item A has the two component sets D and E. Item A is then denoted by $A(D, E)$. The notation $D \Leftarrow E$ denotes that:

$$\{ \text{Can}(D_i, \{E_1, E_2,..., E_q\}): \text{ for all } i = 1,..,p \}$$

The notation $C_A[G_1, G_2,..., G_k]$ where each G_i is a term of the form $Y \Leftarrow X$ denotes that the set $\{G_1, G_2,..., G_k\}$ consists of *all* of the valid candidate constraints on item A. Suppose that item C is decomposable by:

$$C(D, E, F) = A(D, E) \otimes_E B(E, F)$$

where $C_A[D \Leftarrow E]$ and $C_B[E \Leftarrow F]$. Then, using Principle NF on this single join decomposition gives Normalisation Strategy I:2:

Normalisation Strategy I:2. Given item C, if the items A and B are not tautological, and the component sets D, E and F all non-empty with:

$$C_C[D \Leftarrow E, \ E \Leftarrow F]$$
$$C_A[D \Leftarrow E]$$
$$C_B[E \Leftarrow F]$$

then check whether:

$$C(D, E, F) = A(D, E) \otimes_E B(E, F)$$

If it does then discard item C in favour of items A and B.

Normalisation Strategy I:2 is illustrated in Fig. 6.10. If D, E and F are domains in a "three columned relation" called C then Normalisation Strategy I:2 is a generalisation of the classical third normal form. The wisdom behind this normalisation strategy is that item C contains items A and B implicitly embedded within it. The tedious aspect of applying Normalisation Strategy I:2 is checking whether:

$$C(D, E, F) = A(D, E) \otimes_E B(E, F)$$

is valid. If:

$$(\text{Uni(D)} \wedge \text{Uni(E)})_C \in C_C$$
$$(\text{Uni(D)})_A \in C_A$$
$$(\text{Uni(E)})_B \in C_B$$

then item C may well be decomposable in this way.

A special case of Normalisation Strategy I:2 is derived. This special case is a generalisation of the second classical normal form. To derive this special case from I:2, let $E \subseteq F$ and item C becomes $C_C[D \Leftarrow F]$ and item B becomes $C_B[\varnothing]$.

Normalisation Strategy I:3. Given item C, if the items A and B are not tautological, and the component sets D, E and F all non-empty with $E \subseteq F$ and:

$$C_C[D \Leftarrow F]$$
$$C_A[D \Leftarrow E]$$
$$C_B[\varnothing]$$

then check whether:

$$C(D, F) = A(D, E) \otimes_E B(F)$$

If it does then discard item C in favour of items A and B.

Normalisation Strategy I:3 is illustrated in Fig. 6.11. When applied to information, this strategy is the second classical normal form. Consider the special case when the semantics of item A is equivalent to the semantics of item C. In this special case Strategy I:3 reduces to "...then discard item C in favour of item A.". If $(\text{Uni(D)})_C \in C_C$ and $(\text{Uni(D)})_A \in C_A$ then this special case may well apply. This special case is applied to an example below.

Normalisation Strategy I:3 can be applied equally either to knowledge alone, to a mixture of knowledge and information, or to information alone. An example of

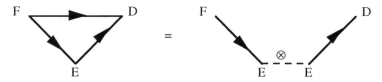

Fig. 6.10 Representation of the Normalisation Strategy I:2

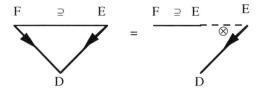

Fig. 6.11 Representation of the Normalisation Strategy I:3

the application of this strategy to knowledge follows. Consider the two items *item1* and *item2*. The item value constraints and the item set constraints of *item1* and *item2* have been deliberately made simple.

item1[$\lambda v_1 v_2 w_1 w_2 x_1 x_2 y_1 y_2 z_1 z_2$•[(

sells-for(x_1:part-number, x_2:dollar-amount)

$\wedge$ costs(y_1:part-number, y_2:dollar-amount)

$\wedge$ has-type(z_1:part-number, z_2:type-description)

$\wedge$ part-mark-up(v_1:part-number, v_2:mark-up-factor)

$\wedge$ type-mark-up(w_1:type-description, w_2:mark-up-factor)

$\wedge$ (($x_1 = y_1$) $\wedge$ ($x_1 = z_1$) $\wedge$ ($x_1 = v_1$)

$\wedge$ ((($z_2 = $ 'tractor') $\wedge$ ($w_1 = z_2$)) $\rightarrow$ ($x_2 = w_2 \times y_2$))

$\wedge$ (($z_2 = $ 'car') $\rightarrow$ ($x_2 = v_2 \times y_2$))

$\wedge$ ((($y_2 > 100$) $\wedge$ ($1\,000 \leq z_1 < 2\,000$))

$\rightarrow$ ($z_2 = $ 'tractor'))]•,

$\lambda v_1 v_2 w_1 w_2 x_1 x_2 y_1 y_2 z_1 z_2$•[**T**]•,

(Can(*part/sale-price*, {*part/cost-price, part/type,*

part/mark-up-factor, type/mark-up-factor}))$_{item1}$]

item2[$\lambda x_1 x_2 y_1 y_2 z_1 z_2$•[(

sells-for(x_1:part-number, x_2:dollar-amount)

$\wedge$ costs(y_1:part-number, y_2:dollar-amount)

$\wedge$ part-mark-up(z_1:part-number, z_2:mark-up-factor)

$\wedge$ ((($x_1 = y_1$) $\wedge$ ($x_1 = z_1$)) $\rightarrow$ ($x_2 = z_2 \times y_2$))]•,

$\lambda x_1 x_2 y_1 y_2 z_1 z_2$•[**T**]•,

(Uni(*part/sale-price*) $\wedge$

Can(*part/sale-price*, {*part/cost-price, part/mark-up-factor*}))$_{item2}$]

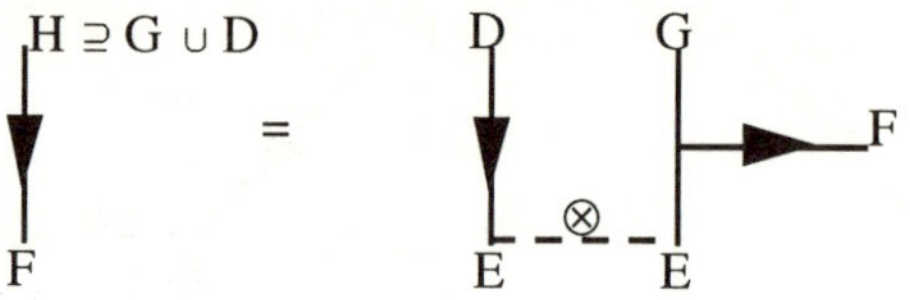

Fig. 6.12   Representation of the Normalisation Strategy I:4

The two items *item1* and *item2* are interesting for three reasons. First, the component set of *item2* is a proper subset of the component set of *item1*. If the two items are being used to deduce the selling price of parts then *item2* is more general than *item1* because *item2* can be used for all types of part whereas *item1* only works for car parts and tractor parts. Second, if the two items are being used to deduce the selling price of parts then *item1* can be replaced by the simpler, and more general, *item2*. Third, *item1* contains the knowledge that "a part whose number is in the region (1 000, 1 999) and whose cost is more than 100 is a tractor part", but *item2* does not contain this piece of knowledge.

The fourth normalisation strategy for items that contain functional associations is given. Like Normalisation Strategy I:2 it is a generalisation of third classical normal form.

Normalisation Strategy I:4. Given item C, if the items A and B are not tautological, and the component sets D, E, F and G all non-empty with $H \supseteq G \cup D$ and:

$$C_C[F \Leftarrow H]$$
$$C_A[F \Leftarrow G, E]$$
$$C_B[E \Leftarrow D]$$

then check whether:

$$C(F, H) = A(E, F, G) \otimes_E B(E, D)$$

if it does then discard item C in favour of items A and B.

Normalisation Strategy I:4 is illustrated in Fig. 6.12. It can be applied equally to information or to knowledge. The wisdom behind this strategy is that item C contains items A and B implicitly embedded within it. If either items A or B are to change then, to preserve consistency, item C should be changed as well. Items A and B alone may not suffer from this difficulty.

Normalisation Strategy I:4 is a generalisation of the classical third normal form rule that is illustrated in Fig. 6.28. If $G = \emptyset$ and $H = D$ in the rule illustrated in Fig. 6.12 then the structure of that rule reduces to the structure illustrated in Fig. 6.28.

item3		
original-price	*period-held*	*sale-price*
(x)	(y)	(z)
sell-now(x,y,z)		
Ø		
--		O

Fig. 6.13 The information item *item3*

item3		
original-price	period-held	sale-price
dollar-amount	years	dollar-amount
2.00	1	5.00
2.00	2	7.00
5.00	1	9.50

Fig. 6.14 The value set of item *item3*

item4		
original-price	*period-held*	*value*
(x)	(y)	(z)
$z = x \times 1.2^{(y)}$		
Ø		
--		O

Fig. 6.15 The knowledge item *item4*

Normalisation can be applied to data, information or knowledge items, or to any combination of these. An example of how a knowledge item can be used to normalise an information item follows. This example is concerned with a wine shop's pricing strategy. The sale price of a wine is related to the original cost price of that wine and to the period for which that wine has been held in stock. A wine that originally cost $2 and had been held for two years could now have an asking price of $7. This relationship could be represented by the information item *item3* shown in Fig. 6.13 where "sell-now(x,y,z)" means "a wine that originally cost $x and has been held for y years sells now for $z". The value set of this item could be as shown in Fig. 6.14.

Suppose that the price that a wine sells for now is also dependent on the "value" of the wine, where the value is determined by the original cost and by the years for which the wine has been held. The relationship between 'value', 'cost' and 'period held' can be represented by the knowledge item *item4* shown in Fig. 6.15. Further the relationship between 'value' and 'sale price' can be represented by the information item *item5* shown in Fig. 6.16. The value set of this item could be as shown in Fig. 6.17.

item5	
value	sale-price
(x)	(y)
price-of(x, y)	
∅	
---------------	O

Fig. 6.16 The information item item5

item5	
value	sale-price
dollar-amount	dollar-amount
2.40	5.00
2.88	7.00
6.00	9.50

Fig. 6.17 The value set of item item5

Information *item3* fails to satisfy Principle NF and should be replaced by the information item *item5* and the knowledge item *item4*.

If a set of items satisfies the four normalisation strategies described above then that set of items does not necessarily satisfy the general Principle NF. Satisfaction of the four normalisation strategies introduced here does not necessarily lead to a normal conceptual model. It is natural to consider the extent to which satisfaction of Normalisation Strategy I:2, Normalisation Strategy I:3 and Normalisation Strategy I:4 achieves a normal conceptual model. Normalisation Strategy I:3 is concerned with removing functional associations that are subsumed by other functional associations, and Normalisation Strategy I:2 is concerned with removing functional associations that can be constructed by combining two other functional associations. Hence Normalisation Strategy I:2 and Normalisation Strategy I:3 together insist that the functional associations chosen from those that have been identified for the normal model are the most fundamental of those identified functional associations. These normalisation strategies are intended to draw attention to structures that may prevent a conceptual model from being normal.

6.4 Normalisation of objects

Section 6.3 discusses the normalisation of items and the explicit conceptual model. In this section the normalisation of objects is discussed. So Sect. 6.3 and this section together describe the normalisation of the implicit conceptual model.

The general principle of normalisation Principle NF is expressed in terms of decomposition. It applies to both items, as discussed in Sect. 6.3, and to objects that are discussed here [Debenham, 1993b]. Chapter 8 describes the construction of a normalised implicit conceptual model. To construct an implicit conceptual model that is in normal form. First gather all relevant facts about the application and represent them as a set of basis items and as a set of object operators. Second discard any items from the basis that are decomposable and discard any objects from the set of object operators that are decomposable. The remaining basis and set of object operators constitutes a normal implicit conceptual model.

In this section various strategies for the normalisation of objects are described. These strategies are all of the form "if this test is satisfied by an object then investigate whether that object can be decomposed". They are all special cases of the general principle of normalisation. If all of these strategies are satisfied then this does *not* imply that the resulting implicit conceptual model is "normal". These strategies are intended to capture some of the ways in which a collection of objects may not be normal.

The general principle of normalisation requires that decomposable objects should be discarded. Using the notation of Sect. 4.7, this principle requires that:

$$(A \otimes_C B)[\lambda xyz\bullet[E_A(\pi(x,\ y)) \wedge BE(\pi'(y,\ z))\ ]\bullet,$$
$$\lambda xyz\bullet[F_A(\pi(x,\ y)) \wedge F_B(\pi'(y,\ z))\ ]\bullet,$$
$$\lambda xyz\bullet[G_A(\pi(x,\ y)) \wedge G_B(\pi'(y,\ z))]\bullet]$$

should be discarded in favour of:

$$A[\ E_A,\ F_A,\ G_A\ ]\ \text{and}$$
$$B[\ E_B,\ F_B,\ G_B\ ]$$

provided that this composition is monotonic and that objects A and B are not tautological.

The general principle of normalisation requires that:

$$\textit{two-type}[\ \lambda P:D^1Q:D^1R:X^1\bullet\lambda xyz\bullet[\ S_P(x) \wedge S_Q(y) \wedge$$
$$S_R(z) \wedge \text{has-type}(y,\ z)\ ]\bullet\bullet,$$
$$\lambda P:D^1Q:D^1R:X^1\bullet\lambda xyz\bullet[\ V_P(x) \wedge V_Q(y) \wedge V_R(z)\ ]\bullet\bullet,$$
$$\lambda P:D^1Q:D^1R:X^1\bullet[C_P \wedge C_Q \wedge C_R\ (\text{Uni}(P) \wedge \text{Uni}(Q) \wedge$$
$$\text{Can}(R,\ \{Q\}))_{v\,(\textit{two-type},P,Q)}]\bullet]$$

should be discarded in favour of both the data object:

$$\textit{comp}[\ \lambda P:D^1Q:D^1\bullet\lambda xy\bullet[\ S_P(x) \wedge S_Q(y)\ ]\bullet\bullet,$$
$$\lambda P:D^1Q:D^1\bullet\lambda xy\bullet[\ V_P(x) \wedge V_Q(y)\ ]\bullet\bullet,$$
$$\lambda P:D^1Q:D^1\bullet[C_P \wedge C_Q \wedge (\text{Uni}(P) \wedge \text{Uni}(Q))_{v\,(\textit{comp},P,Q)}\ ]\bullet\ ]$$

and the information object:

$$has\text{-}type[\lambda P:X^1Q:X^1 \bullet \lambda xy \bullet [\ S_P(x) \wedge S_Q(y) \wedge has\text{-}type(x,\ y)\ ]^{\bullet\bullet},$$
$$\lambda P:X^1Q:X^1 \bullet \lambda xy \bullet [\ V_P(x) \wedge V_Q(y)\ ]^{\bullet\bullet},$$
$$\lambda P:X^1Q:X^1 \bullet [C_P \wedge C_Q$$
$$\wedge\ (Uni(P) \wedge Can(Q,\ \{P\}))_{V\,(has\text{-}type,P,Q)}\ ]^\bullet]$$

This example is shown in the o-schema notation in Fig. 6.18.

Given an object, an *argument set* of that object is a subset of the set of dummy tuple argument type pairs of that object. In Fig. 6.19 A, B and C are three object names, and X, Y and Z are the names of three argument sets of object C that may not be disjoint. Object C may be generated from objects A and B by a *single* application of the join operator using the argument set indices $\{(2,1)\}$. If the decomposition of an object can be effected by a *single* application of the join operator then that decomposition is a *single join decomposition*. One strategy for applying the general principle of normalisation to an object in the o-schema notation is to look for structures of the form shown in Fig. 6.19. If such structures are identified then investigate whether the semantics, value constraints and set constraints of object C permit that object to be represented as the join of objects A and B. That is, investigate whether $A \otimes_{\{(2,1)\}} B = C$. The general structure of Fig. 6.19 can help to identify candidate objects to normalise. The ordering of the arguments within the argument sets X, Y and Z is of no significance.

two-type		
D^1	D^1	D^1
(x)	(y)	(z)
has-type(y, z)		
$\emptyset$		
$\forall$	$\forall$	
	--------------	O

$=$

comp	
D^1	D^1
(x)	(y)
$\emptyset$	
$\emptyset$	
$\forall$	$\forall$

$\otimes_{\{(2,1)\}}$

has-type	
D^1	D^1
(x)	(y)
has-type(x, y)	
$\emptyset$	
$\forall$	
--------------	O

Fig. 6.18   Decomposition of the object *two-type*

C		
X	Y	Z
E_C		
F_C		
G_C		

A	
X	Y
E_A	
F_A	
G_A	

B	
Y	Z
E_B	
F_B	
G_B	

$$= \qquad \otimes_{\{(2,1)\}}$$

Fig. 6.19 General structure of a single join decomposition

The recognition of decomposable objects may not be difficult. If a given object is decomposable then its semantics permits that object to be represented as the join of two other objects. As for items, it is shown below that a decomposable object's semantics can be phrased in such a way as to hide the fact that the object is decomposable. A strategy for the identification of decomposable objects is to examine an object's semantics expression and to note the extent to which the predicate in that expression is separable. An object's semantics is an expression of the form:

$$\lambda Q_1{:}X_1^{i_1}Q_2{:}X_2^{i_2}...Q_j{:}X_j^{i_j}{\bullet}\lambda y_1^1...y_{m_1}^1...y_{m_n}^n{\bullet}[\ S_{P_1}(y_1^1,...,y_{m_1}^1)$$
$$\wedge\ S_{P_2}(y_1^2,...,y_{m_2}^2)\ \wedge\ ....\ \wedge\ S_{P_n}(y_1^n,...,y_{m_n}^n)$$
$$\wedge\ J(y_1^1...y_{m_1}^1...y_{m_n}^n)\ ]^{\bullet\bullet}$$

where the X_k are one of **X, D, I** or **K** for $1{\leq}k{\leq}j$. The predicate J may be separable in the sense defined in Sect. 6.3.

Normalisation Strategy O:1. If the predicate in an object's semantics is separable then investigate whether that object is decomposable into objects containing the argument sets identified by the separability of that predicate.

The semantics of the *two-type* object is:

$$\lambda P{:}D^1 Q{:}D^1 R{:}X^1{\bullet}\lambda xyz{\bullet}[\ S_P(x)\ \wedge\ S_Q(y)\ \wedge\ S_R(z)\ \wedge\ \text{has-type}(y,\ z)\ ]^{\bullet\bullet}$$

The predicate in this expression is separable into the partition $\{(x, y), (y, z)\}$ because:

$$J_1(x) = T(x,\ y)$$
$$J_2(y,\ z) = \text{has-type}(y,\ z)$$

where **T** is the constant true predicate. If the predicate in an object's semantics is separable into a partition then the next step is determine whether the entire object

thing
$\mathbf{D}^1$
(x)
$\emptyset$
$\emptyset$
$\forall$

$\otimes_{\{\emptyset\}}$

has-type	
$\mathbf{X}^1$	$\mathbf{X}^1$
(x)	(y)
has-type(x, y)	
$\emptyset$	
$\forall$	
----------------	O

Fig. 6.20   Another decomposition of the object *two-type*

address-is		
$\mathbf{D}^1$	$\mathbf{D}^1$	$\mathbf{X}^1$
(x)	(y)	(z)
has-address(x,y,z)		
$\emptyset$		
----------------	O	
	----------------	O
----------------		O
--		O

Fig. 6.21   The object *address-is*

is decomposable using the argument set indices identified by that partition. As is shown above:

$$two\text{-}type \;=\; comp \;\otimes_{\{(2,1)\}} \; has\text{-}type$$

This decomposition is shown in Fig. 6.18.   Another decomposition may be derived from the partition $\{(y, z)\}$ because $J_1(y, z) = \text{has-type}(y, z)$.   This decomposition is simpler than the decomposition shown in Fig. 6.18.   This decomposition is shown in Fig. 6.20.

A decomposable object's semantics can be phrased in such a way as to hide the fact that the object is decomposable. Consider the object *address-is* illustrated in Fig. 6.21. The predicate "has-address(x, y, z)" means "person 'x' has a house with street address 'y' and the post-code that applies to this persons house is 'z'". The way in which the semantics expression is phrased masks fact that postcode is functionally dependent on street address. Alternatively if this object's semantics is expressed as shown in Fig. 6.22, where 'address-of' and 'postcode-of' are as defined in Sect. 6.3, then the predicate in this object's semantics is separable. The observation that this predicate is separable leads to an investigation of the decomposability of this object. The decomposition of the semantics of an item instance of the object *address-is* is discussed in Sect. 6.3.

address-is		
D^1	D^1	X^1
(x)	(y)	(z)
address-of(x, y) ∧ postcode-of(y, z)		
∅		
------------------	O	
	------------------	O
------------------		O
------------------------------------		O

Fig. 6.22   The object *address-is* showing an alternative semantics

If the predicate in an object's semantics is separable then this does not necessarily mean that that object is decomposable. So when looking for decomposable objects it is useful to have strategies that are based on other parts of an object's specification besides its semantics. The remainder of this section discusses other strategies that are based on the object's set constraints.

There is a fundamental distinction between two different types of object. This distinction is based on whether or not an object represents an association. If an object does *not* represent an association then that object is a data object. If an object *does* represent an association then that object is either an information object or a knowledge object. The special case is considered when an object represents an association and that association is functional. Objects in this special case can be classified by the structure of their set constraints. They can be classified by the structure of the candidate constraints that occur within their set constraints.

Principle NF applies to objects in general. If an object is an information object or a knowledge object then it represents an association. Associations are sometimes functional. Explicit functional associations can be represented as "if-then rules". Implicit functional associations can be represented as relations with a key. The general Principle NF is applied to those objects that contain functional associations. A second strategy for identifying decomposable objects is derived from Principle NF. This strategy is Normalisation Strategy O:2. Two other strategies are derived from Principle NF. These other strategies are related to the classical normal forms for information. No distinction is drawn here between implicit and explicit functional associations. So the Normalisation Strategy O:2, and the two other strategies that follow it can be employed, for example, to normalise an information object using a knowledge object or vice versa.

Objects are classified below according to the structure of the candidate constraints within their set constraints. X, Y and Z are the names of argument sets. Suppose that:

$X = \{X_1, X_2,..., X_p\}$
$Y = \{Y_1, Y_2,..., Y_q\}$
$Z = \{Z_1, Z_2,..., Z_r\}$

Suppose that object A has the two argument sets X and Y. Object A is then denoted by $A(X, Y)$. The notation $X \Leftarrow Y$ denotes that:

$\{ \text{Can}(X_i, \{Y_1, Y_2,..., Y_q\}):$ for all $i = 1,..,p \}$

The notation $C_A[G_1, G_2,..., G_k]$ where each G_i is a term of the form $Y \Leftarrow X$ denotes that the set $\{G_1, G_2,..., G_k\}$ consists of *all* of the valid candidate constraints on object A. Suppose object C is decomposable by:

$C(X, Y, Z) = A(X, Y) \otimes_{\{(2,1)\}} B(Y, Z)$

where $C_A[X \Leftarrow Y]$ and $C_B[Y \Leftarrow Z]$. Normalisation Strategy O:2 is derived by applying Principle NF to this single join decomposition.

Normalisation Strategy O:2. Given object C, if the objects A and B are not tautological, and the argument sets X, Y and Z all non-empty with:

$C_C[X \Leftarrow Y, Y \Leftarrow Z]$
$C_A[X \Leftarrow Y]$
$C_B[Y \Leftarrow Z]$

then check whether:

$C(X, Y, Z) = A(X, Y) \otimes_{\{(2,1)\}} B(Y, Z)$

If it does then discard object C in favour of objects A and B.

Normalisation Strategy O:2 is a generalisation of classical third normal form because any item instance of it becomes Normalisation Strategy I:2. The wisdom behind this normalisation strategy is that object C contains objects A and B implicitly embedded within it. A special case of Normalisation Strategy O:2 is derived. This special case is a generalisation of second classical normal form. To derive this special case from Normalisation Strategy O:2, let Z be $Y \cup W$ and object C becomes $C_C[X \Leftarrow (Y, W)]$ and object B becomes $C_B[\emptyset]$.

Normalisation Strategy O:3. Given object C, if the objects A and B are not tautological, and the argument sets X, Y and W all non-empty and:

$$C_C[X \Leftarrow (Y, W)]$$

$$C_A[X \Leftarrow Y]$$

$$C_B[\emptyset]$$

then check whether:

$$C(X, Z) = A(X, Y) \otimes_{\{(2,1)\}} B(Y, W)$$

If it does then discard object C in favour of objects A and B.

When applied to information, Normalisation Strategy O:3 is the second classical normal form. Consider the special case when the semantics of object A is equivalent to the semantics of object C. In this special case Strategy O:3 reduces to "...then discard object C in favour of object A.". The application of this special case is illustrated below.

Normalisation Strategy O:3 applies equally to knowledge, to a mixture of knowledge and information, and to information alone. An example of the application of this strategy to knowledge follows. Consider the two objects shown in Fig. 6.23. The object value constraints and the object set constraints for those two objects have been deliberately made simple.

The two objects shown in Fig. 6.23 are interesting for three reasons. First, the argument set of *object2* is a proper subset of the argument set of *object1*. If the two objects are being used to deduce values of the first argument then *object2* is more general than *object1* because *object2* does not refer to any constants whereas *object1* refers to 'car' and 'tractor'. Second, if the two objects are being used to deduce values of the first argument then *object1* can be replaced by the simpler, and more general, *object2*. Third, *object1* contains the knowledge that:

$$((x> 100) \wedge (1\,000 \leq y < 2\,000)) \rightarrow (z='tractor')$$

but *object2* does not contain this piece of knowledge.

object1				
$\mathbf{X}^2$	$\mathbf{X}^2$	$\mathbf{X}^2$	$\mathbf{X}^2$	$\mathbf{X}^2$
(y, r)	('tractor', t)	(y, v)	(y, x)	(y, 'tractor')
$\to (v = t \times x)$				
$\emptyset$				
(y, r)	(s, t)	(y, v)	(y, x)	(y, 'car')
$\to (v = r \times x)$				
$\emptyset$				
(y, r)	(s, t)	(y, v)	(y, x)	(y, z)
$((x > 100) \wedge (1\,000 \le y < 2\,000)) \to (z = \text{'tractor'})$				
$\emptyset$				
O	--			

object2		
$\mathbf{X}^2$	$\mathbf{X}^2$	$\mathbf{X}^2$
(y, v)	(y, x)	(y, z)
$\to (v = z \times x)$		
$\emptyset$		
$\forall$		
O	---	

Fig. 6.23 The objects *object1* and *object2*

The fourth normalisation strategy for objects that contain functional associations is described. Like Normalisation Strategy O:2 it is a generalisation of third classical normal form.

Normalisation Strategy O:4. Given object C, if the objects A and B are not tautological, and the argument sets V, W, X, Y and Z all non-empty with $W \supseteq V \cup X$ and:

$C_C[Z \Leftarrow W]$
$C_A[Z \Leftarrow V, Y]$
$C_B[Y \Leftarrow X]$

then check whether:

$C(Z, W) = A(Y, Z, V) \otimes_{\{(1,1)\}} B(Y, X)$

If it does then discard object C in favour of objects A and B.

---

object3		
$\mathbf{D}^1$	$\mathbf{D}^1$	$\mathbf{X}^1$
(x)	(y)	(z)
sell-now(x,y,z)		
$\emptyset$		
--		O

Fig. 6.24   The information object *object3*

Normalisation Strategy O:4 can be applied equally to information or to knowledge. The wisdom behind this strategy for normalisation is that object *C* contains objects *A* and *B* implicitly embedded within it.   If either objects *A* or *B* are modified then, to preserve consistency, object *C* would have to be modified as well.   Objects *A* and *B* alone may not suffer from this difficulty.

Normalisation Strategy O:4 is a generalisation of the classical third normal form rule that is illustrated in Fig. 6.28.   If $V = \emptyset$ and $W = X$ in Normalisation Strategy O:4 then the structure of that strategy reduces to:

$$C_C[Z \Leftarrow X]$$
$$C_A[Z \Leftarrow Y]$$
$$C_B[Y \Leftarrow X]$$

This structure is the structure of the classical third normal form as illustrated in Fig. 6.28.

Normalisation can be applied to data, information or knowledge objects, or to any combination of these.   An example of how a knowledge object can be used to normalise an information object follows.   This example is concerned with a wine shop's pricing strategy.   The sale price of a wine is related to the original cost price of that wine and to the period for which that wine has been held in stock. This relationship can be represented by the information object *object3* shown in Fig. 6.24 where "sell-now(x,y,z)" means "a thing that originally cost $x and has been held for y years sells now for $z".

Suppose that the price that a wine sells for now is also dependent on the "value" of the wine.   The value of a wine is determined by the original cost and by the years for which that wine has been held.   The relationship between 'value', 'cost' and 'period held' is represented by the knowledge object *object4* shown in Fig. 6.25.   The relationship between 'value' and 'sale price' is represented by the information object *object5* shown in Fig. 6.26.   So the knowledge *object3* fails to satisfy Principle NF and should be replaced by the information object *object5* and the knowledge object *object4*.

If a set of objects satisfies the four normalisation strategies described above then that set of objects does not necessarily satisfy the general Principle NF. Satisfaction of these four normalisation strategies does not necessarily lead to a

object4		
$\mathbf{D}^1$	$\mathbf{D}^1$	$\mathbf{X}^1$
(x)	(y)	(z)
$z = x \times 1.2^{(y)}$		
$\emptyset$		
---		O

Fig. 6.25   The knowledge object *object4*

object5	
$\mathbf{D}^1$	$\mathbf{D}^1$
(x)	(y)
price-of(x, y)	
$\emptyset$	
----------------	O

Fig. 6.26   The information object *object5*

normal conceptual model. It is natural to consider the extent to which satisfaction of Normalisation Strategy O:2, Normalisation Strategy O:3 and Normalisation Strategy O:4 achieves a normal conceptual model. Normalisation Strategy O:3 is concerned with removing functional associations that are subsumed by other functional associations, and Normalisation Strategy O:2 is concerned with removing functional associations that can be constructed by combining two other functional associations. So Normalisation Strategy O:2 and Normalisation Strategy O:3 together insist that the functional associations chosen from those that have been identified for the normal model are the most fundamental of those identified functional associations. These normalisation strategies are intended to draw attention to structures that may prevent a conceptual model from being normal.

Given a basis of normal data items and a set of normal object operators then the resulting set of items that can be constructed from this basis and those object operators is normal.

6.5 Classical normal forms

In this section the "Classical Normal Forms" are discussed. This discussion is illustrated using items, objects and traditional representation formalisms.

Suppose that item I has the three component sets D, E and F. Item I is denoted by $I(D, E, F)$. Consider the different ways in which the item $I = I(D, E, F)$ can be decomposed into two sub-items I_1 and I_2 by:

$I(D, E, F) = I_2(D, E) \otimes_E I_1(E, F)$.

If two items are joined on the component set that consists of *all* of their identical components then the subscript of the join operator may be omitted. If this is so then the above expression may be presented simply as:

$I(D, E, F) = I_2(D, E) \otimes I_1(E, F)$.

Section 6.3 describes various strategies for the normalisation of items. Three of those strategies are characterised by the different ways in which the candidate constraints are present in an item's set constraints. This section describes other ways in which an item I can be decomposed. These other ways are also categorised by the different candidate constraints that are present in the set constraints of I.

If item I has two component sets:

$$D = \{D_1, D_2,.., D_p\}$$
$$E = \{E_1, E_2,.., E_q\}$$

then the notation $D \Leftarrow E$ denotes $Can(D_i, \{E_1, E_2,.., E_q\})$ for all $i = 1,..,p$. The notation $C_I[H_1, H_2,.., H_k]$ where each H_i is a term of the form $Y \Leftarrow X$ denotes that the set $\{H_1, H_2,.., H_k\}$ contains *all* of the valid candidate constraints on item A.

If an item has two component sets such that one of these component sets is in a candidate constraint for the other component set then that item is said to contain a *functional association*. If the component sets D and E in item I are candidates for component F then item I contains a functional association between its components. If the set constraints of I contains the expression $Can(F, D \cup E)$ then this is denoted by $C_I[F \Leftarrow (D, E)]$.

Given an item I with three component sets D, E and F, such that:

$I(D, E, F) = I_2(D, E) \otimes I_1(E, F)$.

three different cases are identified:

- there are no functional associations in I;
- the functional associations in I are only between pairs of D, E and F, and
- there is at least one functional association in I of the form $Z \Leftarrow (X, Y)$.

Consider the first case, if there are no functional associations in I then:

$$C_I[\, \emptyset \,], \quad C_{I_1}[\, \emptyset \,], \quad C_{I_2}[\, \emptyset \,]$$

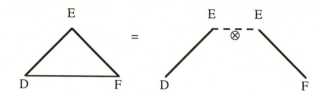

Fig. 6.27 Second case for decomposition of a three component item

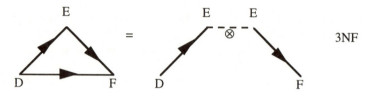

Fig. 6.28 Classical third normal form

and the decomposition:

$$I(D, E, F) \;=\; I_2(D, E) \otimes I_1(E, F) \qquad\qquad\text{4NF}$$

is *classical fourth normal form*.

Consider the second case when the functional associations in I are only between pairs of D, E and F. The specification of functional associations between pairs of D, E and F may be represented by entering arrows on the arcs shown in Fig. 6.27. Removing unnecessary duplications, these arrows may be entered in five different ways:

$$C_I[\, E \Leftarrow D\,], \quad C_{I_1}[\, E \Leftarrow D\,], \quad C_{I_2}[\,\varnothing\,]$$
$$C_I[\, D \Leftarrow E\,], \quad C_{I_1}[\, D \Leftarrow E\,], \quad C_{I_2}[\,\varnothing\,]$$
$$C_I[\, E \Leftarrow F,\, E \Leftarrow D\,], \quad C_{I_1}[\, E \Leftarrow D\,], \quad C_{I_2}[\, E \Leftarrow F\,]$$
$$C_I[\, F \Leftarrow D,\, F \Leftarrow E,\, E \Leftarrow D\,], \quad C_{I_1}[\, E \Leftarrow D\,], \quad C_{I_2}[\, F \Leftarrow E\,] \qquad \text{3NF}$$
$$C_I[\, F \Leftarrow E,\, D \Leftarrow E\,], \quad C_{I_1}[\, D \Leftarrow E\,], \quad C_{I_2}[\, F \Leftarrow E\,]$$

These five different ways each represent a valid decomposition but only the fourth is non-trivial. It is the well known classical third normal form and is illustrated in Fig. 6.28.

Consider the third case in which there is at least one functional association in I of the form $Z \Leftarrow (X, Y)$. Removing unnecessary duplications, this may occur in three different ways:

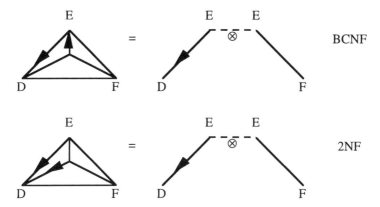

Fig. 6.29 Classical Boyce-Codd and second normal forms

$$C_I[\ E \Leftarrow (F, D),\ D \Leftarrow E\ ],\quad C_{I_1}[\ D \Leftarrow E\ ],\quad C_{I_2}[\ \emptyset\ ] \qquad \text{BCNF}$$

$$C_I[\ F \Leftarrow (D, E),\ D \Leftarrow E\ ],\quad C_{I_1}[\ D \Leftarrow E\ ],\quad C_{I_2}[\ \emptyset\ ]$$

$$C_I[\ D \Leftarrow (E, F),\ D \Leftarrow E\ ],\quad C_{I_1}[\ D \Leftarrow E\ ],\quad C_{I_2}[\ \emptyset\ ] \qquad \text{2NF}$$

These three different ways each represent a valid decomposition but only the first and the third are non-trivial. They are the well known classical *Boyce-Codd normal form* and the classical *second normal form* respectively. They are illustrated in Fig. 6.29.

The different ways in which an item of three component sets can be decomposed into two items each of which has two component sets by:

$$I(D, E, F) = I_2(D, E) \otimes I_1(E, F).$$

are given above. The only other way that an item of three component sets can be decomposed is by:

$$I(D, E, F) = I_3(F, D) \otimes I_2(D, E) \otimes I_1(E, F).$$

If there are no functional associations present in I then this decomposition becomes:

$$C_I[\ \emptyset\ ],\quad C_{I_1}[\ \emptyset\ ],\quad C_{I_2}[\ \emptyset\ ],\quad C_{I_3}[\ \emptyset\ ] \qquad \text{5NF}$$

This decomposition is the classical *fifth normal form*. Further if there are functional associations present in I then it may be shown that the decomposition

$$I(D, E, F) = I_3(F, D) \otimes I_2(D, E) \otimes I_1(E, F).$$

reduces to one of the decompositions given above.

In the preceding discussion four of the classical normal forms are derived from the decomposition:

$$I(D, E, F) = I_2(D, E) \otimes I_1(E, F).$$

as follows:

4NF $C_I[\ \emptyset\ ]$, $C_{I_1}[\ \emptyset\ ]$, $C_{I_2}[\ \emptyset\ ]$

3NF $C_I[\ F \Leftarrow D,\ F \Leftarrow E,\ E \Leftarrow D\ ]$, $C_{I_1}[\ E \Leftarrow D\ ]$, $C_{I_2}[\ F \Leftarrow E\ ]$

BCNF $C_I[\ E \Leftarrow (F, D),\ D \Leftarrow E\ ]$, $C_{I_1}[\ D \Leftarrow E\ ]$, $C_{I_2}[\ \emptyset\ ]$

2NF $C_I[\ D \Leftarrow (E, F),\ D \Leftarrow E\ ]$, $C_{I_1}[\ D \Leftarrow E\ ]$, $C_{I_2}[\ \emptyset\ ]$

and one of the classical normal forms was derived from the decomposition:

$$I(D, E, F) = I_3(F, D) \otimes I_2(D, E) \otimes I_1(E, F).$$

as follows:

5NF $C_I[\ \emptyset\ ]$, $C_{I_1}[\ \emptyset\ ]$, $C_{I_2}[\ \emptyset\ ]$, $C_{I_3}[\ \emptyset\ ]$

These classical normal forms apply equally well to knowledge as to information.

The different possible functional associations in the decomposition:

$$I(D, E, F) = I_2(D, E) \otimes I_1(E, F).$$

lead to the classical second, third, fourth and Boyce-Codd normal forms. The only way that the decomposition:

$$I(D, E, F) = I_3(F, D) \otimes I_2(D, E) \otimes I_1(E, F).$$

does not decompose into two components leads to the classical fifth normal form. So the classical normal forms provide a complete characterisation of the ways that an item of three component sets may be decomposed.

The principle of normalisation applies to data, information and knowledge. The classical normal forms may be applied to the normalisation of knowledge. The knowledge in a conceptual model is a representation of the explicit functional associations in the application. The first, second and third classical normal forms concern items that contain functional associations. So they may be applied to knowledge that is in an "if-then" form. The dependency diagram notation may be used to represent functional associations present in knowledge in an "if-then" form. So the first three classical normal forms, when applied to knowledge,

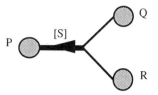

Fig. 6.30 An explicit functional association shown on a dependency diagram

restrict the form that the explicit functional associations may have. Such an association denoted on the dependency diagram in Fig. 6.30.

Before giving examples of how the classical normal forms may be applied to knowledge some fundamental correspondences between information and knowledge are considered. First, both information and knowledge are representations of functional associations. Information is concerned with *implicit* functional associations. Knowledge is concerned with *explicit* functional associations. So the notion of a relation in a database corresponds to the notion of a group in a knowledge base. A domain in a relation corresponds to a predicate in a group. A key of a relation corresponds to a set of body predicates of a group. The non-key domain in a relation corresponds to the head predicate of a group. The set of tuples that belong to a relation corresponds to the members of the value set of a group. These fundamental correspondences between information and knowledge show how the classical normal forms for information may by analogy be applied to knowledge.

The classical normal forms for information are well established. See [Date, 1995] and [Kent, 1983]. The notions of "normal" and "normal form" as they are defined in Sect. 6.2 may not appear to be related to the result of applying the classical normal forms to a relational model. If a database is normal in the sense that it contains the representation of normal items then it satisfies the classical normal forms. If a database satisfies the classical normal forms then it is not necessarily normal in the sense defined here. The notion of normal given here is stronger than the classical concept of normality. Further, the notion of normal given here applies to knowledge-based systems as well as to conventional database systems.

With respect to the role of normalisation discussed in Sect. 6.2 the classical normal forms are a process of "selection". That is, classical normalisation is a process of selecting the acceptable facts from a pool of all valid facts. So from a pool of "all valid facts" a subset is chosen. This subset contains those facts that have been selected from the pool to become part of the "normalised" model.

The prevention of update anomalies is a key motivation for the normalisation of knowledge-based systems. The basic rationale behind the specification of normal forms for data, information and knowledge is that in a "good" model (but not necessarily in a good implementation) of an application, the execution of a maintenance task should be simple. A modification to any particular item in the conceptual model, together with corresponding modifications to any other items to which that particular item is joined by a coupling relationship, should not violate the consistency of that model. If the conceptual model is normal then the only coupling relationships in it are those relationships that cannot be removed. In that sense the normalised conceptual model is a "good" model to support maintenance.

A loose interpretation follows of the "classical" normal forms. In this context a *classical model* consists of a data model and an information model only. Information is implicit functional associations between items of data. The problem of modelling the information in an application is the problem of representing "well" the real, implicit functional associations in that application using relations.

A real, implicit functional association may be represented using a relation. If an implicit functional association has a uniqueness constraint on all but one of its component data items then the domains corresponding to those data items may be selected as the key and that implicit functional association may be represented as a function passing from those key domains to the single non-key domain of the relation. This is shown in Fig. 6.31 where r is the "representation mapping". In this example the "real" functional association is represented in the relation as a functional association *from* the two key domains *to* the single non-key domain. The classical normal forms are principally concerned with the functional structure of the selected functional associations. The first, second and third classical normal forms are concerned with the properties of the function from the key domains to the non-key domain, and the fourth and fifth classical normal forms are concerned with the structure of the key domains. This is shown in Fig. 6.32.

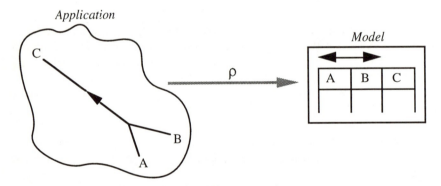

Fig. 6.31   Relations represent "real" explicit functional associations

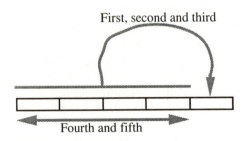

Fig. 6.32   Role of the classical normal forms

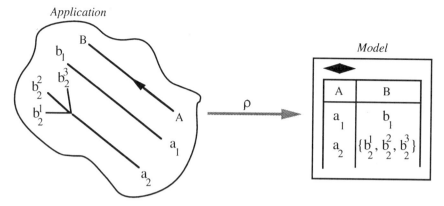

Fig. 6.33 First "classical" normal form

[part/sale-price, part/cost-price, mark-up]		
part/sale-price	*part/cost-price*	*mark-up*
(x, v)	(x, y)	(z)
$\rightarrow$ v = z × y		
$\rightarrow$ v > y		
∀	∀	
--		O
O	--	
------------------------------	O	------------------------------

Fig. 6.34 Knowledge item '*[part/sale-price, part/cost-price, mark-up]*'

6.5.1 First classical normal form

In traditional database technology, the first classical normal form asserts that the representation of a functional association between a collection of real things must itself be a function. The represented function can only have single things as values. In the example shown in Fig. 6.33 there are three labels in population B corresponding to the label a_2 in population A. So the first classical normal form requires that the association shown in Fig. 6.33 should not be selected.

In terms of items and objects, the first classical normal form states that candidate constraints may only represent single valued functions. Consider the knowledge item *[part/sale-price, part/cost-price, mark-up]* illustrated in Fig. 6.34. One of three functional interpretations of this item can be implemented as the group:

part/sell-price $\Leftarrow$ part/buy-price, mark-up

This group can be realised as the single clause:

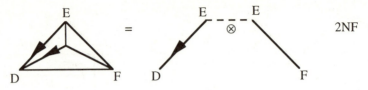

Fig. 6.35 Second classical normal form

part/sell-price(x, y) ← part/buy-price(x, z), is-a[w:mark-up-factor]
    y = z × w

For this item the first classical normal form requires that its value set contains at most one member containing any given values for both "part/cost-price" and "mark-up".

6.5.2 Second classical normal form

The second classical normal form as it is usually presented for relations asserts that in the representation of an implicit functional association, the functional association must not contain another "sub" functional association that is *from* a subset of what is to be represented as the key domains *to* the non-key domains. This is generalised to the form for items:

2NF $C_I[\ D \Leftarrow (E, F),\ D \Leftarrow E\ ],\ \ C_{I_1}[\ D \Leftarrow E\ ],\ \ C_{I_2}[\ \emptyset\ ]$

This form is illustrated in Fig. 6.35. This normal form requires that item I should be replaced by items I_1 and I_2 if the stated conditions hold.

Examples illustrating the application of the second classical normal form to database relations may be found in any good book on database design. Consider the items illustrated in Fig. 6.36. The second classical normal form requires that item I should be replaced by items I_1 and I_2.

The second classical normal form applied to knowledge objects states, for example, that *object1* shown in Fig. 6.37 should be replaced by *object2*. The second classical normal form applied to groups states, for example, that if the group $P \Leftarrow Q, R$ is equivalent to the group $P \Leftarrow Q$ then the first group should be discarded in favour of the second group.

6.5.3 Third classical normal form

The third classical normal form as it is usually presented for relations asserts that in the representation of a functional association, the functional association must not contain another "sub" functional association that is *from* a set of non-key domains *to* another non-key domain. This normal form is generalised to:

I		
D	E	F
x	y	z
S_I		
V_I		
	$\forall$	$\forall$
O	--	
O	---------------------	

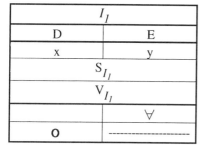

I_1	
D	E
x	y
S_{I_1}	
V_{I_1}	
	$\forall$
O	----------------------

I_2	
E	F
x	y
S_{I_2}	
V_{I_2}	
$\forall$	$\forall$

Fig. 6.36 Item template for second classical normal form

object1		
$\mathbf{X}^2$	$\mathbf{X}^2$	$\mathbf{X}^1$
(x, v)	(x, y)	(z)
$\rightarrow$ v = x × y		
$\emptyset$		
	$\forall$	
O	---	

object2	
$\mathbf{X}^2$	$\mathbf{X}^2$
(x, v)	(x, y)
$\rightarrow$ v = x × y	
$\emptyset$	
	$\forall$
O	------------------------

Fig. 6.37 Second classical normal form applied to objects

3NF $C_I[\, F \Leftarrow D,\ F \Leftarrow E,\ E \Leftarrow D\,]$, $C_{I_1}[\, E \Leftarrow D\,]$, $C_{I_2}[\, F \Leftarrow E\,]$

This form is illustrated in Fig. 6.38. This normal form requires that item I should be replaced by items I_1 and I_2 if the stated conditions hold.

Examples of the application of the classical third normal form to information can be found in any good book on database design. The third classical normal form applied to knowledge objects states, for example, that **object1** shown in Fig. 6.39 should be replaced by **object2** and **object3**. That is:

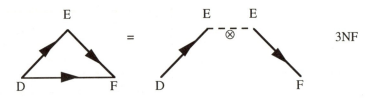

Fig. 6.38   Classical third normal form

object1				
X^2	X^2	X^2	X^2	X^2
(w, q)	(w, t)	(w, z)	(w, y)	(y, z)
		$\rightarrow$ (q $= t \times v$)		
		$\emptyset$		
		$\forall$		
		O	- - - - - - - - - - - - - - - -	
	$\forall$			
O	- - - - - - - - - - - - -			
$\forall$				
O	- -			

object2		
X^2	X^2	X^2
(w, z)	(w, y)	(y, z)
	$\emptyset$	
	$\emptyset$	
$\forall$		
O	- - - - - - - - - - - - - -	

object3		
X^2	X^2	X^2
(y, v)	(y, x)	(y, z)
	$\rightarrow$ (v $= x \times z$)	
	$\emptyset$	
$\forall$		
O	- - - - - - - - - - - - - -	

Fig. 6.39   Classical third normal form applied to three objects

$$object1 = object3 \otimes_{\{(3,1)\}} object2$$

Fig. 6.39 is complex. The clue to identifying classical third normal form is in the structure of the object set constraints that are a representation of the arrows on the diagram shown in Fig. 6.38.

The third classical normal form applied to groups states, for example, that given the three groups:

P   ⇐   R
P   ⇐   Q
Q   ⇐   R

the first group should be discarded in favour of both the second group and the third group. Consider the clause group:

part/sale-price(x, y) ← part/cost-price(x, z), part/type(x, v),
type/mark-up(v, w), y = (z × w)

Suppose that buried within this clause group is the sub-rule that "the mark-up factor for a spare part is the mark-up factor associated with that spare part's type". This sub-rule can be implemented as:

part/mark-up(x, y) ← part/type(x, z), type/mark-up(z, y)

This clause shows that the first clause group breaches the third classical normal form and should be replaced by the second clause group and the following third clause group:

part/sale-price(x, y) ← part/cost-price(x, z),
part/mark-up(x, w), y = (z × w)

The first of these three clause groups can be re-generated from the second and the third by resolution. This example corresponds to the structure illustrated in Fig. 6.39. To establish this correspondence, in *object1* let the first argument correspond to "part/sale-price", the second to "part/cost-price", the third to "part/mark-up", the fourth to "part/type" and the fifth to "type/mark-up". The item form for this example is shown in Fig. 6.40.

6.5.4 Boyce-Codd classical normal form

The Boyce-Codd classical normal form as it is usually presented for relations asserts that in the representation of a functional association, the only functional association present must be *from* the key domains *to* a non-key domain. This normal form is generalised to:

[part/sell, part/cost, part/type, type/m-up]			
part/sell	part/cost	part/type	type/m-up
(x, y)	(x, z)	(x, v)	(v, w)
$\rightarrow$ (y = z × w)			
∅			
∀			
O	--		

=

[part/m-up, part/type, type/m-up]		
part/m-up	part/type	type/m-up
(x, y)	(x, z)	(z, y)
∅		
∅		
∀		
O	-------------------------	

⊗

[part/sell, part/cost, part/m-up]		
part/sell	part/cost	part/m-up
(x, y)	(x, z)	(x, w)
$\rightarrow$ (y = z × w)		
∅		
∀		
O	-------------------------	

Fig. 6.40 Classical third normal form applied to three items

BCNF $C_I[\,E \Leftarrow (F, D),\; D \Leftarrow E\,]$, $C_{I_1}[\,D \Leftarrow E\,]$, $C_{I_2}[\,\emptyset\,]$

This form is illustrated in Fig. 6.41. The left diagram in Fig. 6.41 can not be generated from the right diagram. This normal form advises that if the stated conditions hold then investigate whether $I = I_1 \otimes I_2$.

Examples illustrating the application of the Boyce-Codd classical normal form to database relations may be found in any good book on database design. Consider the items illustrated in Fig. 6.42. The Boyce-Codd normal form advises that the possibility of replacing item I by items I_1 and I_2 should be investigated.

Consider the fact "An organisation is staffed by 'persons (pers)'. Each person holds one of three 'jobs (job)': 'General Manager (GM)', 'Department Manager (DM)' or 'Worker (W)'. A person who holds the job of DM or W is an 'employee (emp)'. Employees work in 'departments (dep)'. There is one GM, and each department has one DM. Each employee has a 'supervisor (super)'. The GM supervises the DMs. Each DM supervises the Ws who work in that DM's department." Suppose that four information items *emp/super*, *pers/job*, *emp/dep*

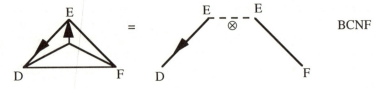

Fig. 6.41 Classical Boyce-Codd normal form

and *dep/man* are identified. Consider the knowledge item shown in Fig. 6.43.
The candidate constraints show a breach of Boyce-Codd normal form. Boyce-Codd
normal form advises that the possibility of replacing this item by the two items
shown in Fig. 6.44 should be investigated.

In terms of a logic program implementation, the Boyce-Codd example shown
in Fig. 6.43 and Fig. 6.44 may be interpreted as follows. If:

emp/super(x, y) ← pers/job(x, 'W'), emp/dep(x, z), dep/man(z, y)
emp/super(x, y) ← pers/job(x, 'DM'), pers/job(y, 'GM')   [A]

and:

pers/job(x, 'GM') ← emp/super(y, x), emp/super(z, y)
pers/job(x, 'DM') ← emp/super(y, x), emp/super(y, z)
pers/job(x, 'W') ← emp/super(x, y), emp/super(y, z)

then [A] breaches Boyce-Codd normal form. The replacement of [A] by:

emp/dep(x, y) ← dep/man(y, x)
emp/dep(x, y) ← emp/super(x, z), dep/man(y, z)   [B]

I		
D	E	F
x	y	z
S_I		
V_I		
∀	∀	
---------------	O	---------------
O	---------------	

I_1	
D	E
x	y
S_{I_1}	
V_{I_1}	
∀	∀
O	---------------

I_2	
E	F
x	y
S_{I_2}	
V_{I_2}	
∀	

Fig. 6.42 Item template for Boyce-Codd classical normal form

[emp/super, pers/job, emp/dep, dep/man]			
emp/super	pers/job	emp/dep	dep/man
(x, v) (⊥, ⊥)	(x, 'W') (⊥, ⊥)	(x, z)	(z, y)
→ (v = y)			
(x, v) (⊥, ⊥)	(x, 'DM') (y, 'GM')	(⊥, ⊥)	(⊥, ⊥)
→ (v = y) **T**			
(y, x) (z, y)	(x, w) (⊥, ⊥)	(⊥, ⊥)	(⊥, ⊥)
→ (w = 'GM')			
(y, x) (y, z)	(x, w) (⊥, ⊥)	(⊥, ⊥)	(⊥, ⊥)
→ (w = 'DM')			
(x, y) (y, z)	(x, w) (⊥, ⊥)	(⊥, ⊥)	(⊥, ⊥)
→ (w = 'W') **T**			
∀	∀	∀	∀
O	--		
∀	∀		
--------------------	**O**		

Fig. 6.43 Knowledge item that breaches Boyce-Codd normal form

[pers/job, emp/super]	
pers/job	emp/super
(x, w)	(y, x) (z, y)
→ (w = 'GM')	
(x, w)	(y, x) (y, z)
→ (w = 'DM')	
(x, w)	(x, y) (y, z)
→ (w = 'W') **T**	
∀	∀
O	---------------

[emp/dep, dep/man, emp/super]		
emp/dep	dep/man	emp/super
(x, w)	(y, x)	
→ (w = y)		
(x, w)	(y, z)	(x, z)
→ (w = y) **T**		
∀	∀	∀
O	-------------------------------------	

Fig. 6.44 Possible normalised form of item in Fig. 6.43

should be investigated. In general when the Boyce-Codd normal form is applied to conventional relations dependencies may be lost. The same is true when the Boyce-Codd normal form is applied to knowledge. If [A] is deleted in the above example then neither of the two groups that remain enable emp/super to be derived.

6.5.5 Fourth and fifth classical normal forms

The fourth and fifth classical normal forms assert that in the representation of a functional association, that functional association must not be derivable from two, or three respectively, "sub" functional associations within itself. This is generalised to:

4NF $C_I[\ \emptyset\ ]$, $C_{I_1}[\ \emptyset\ ]$, $C_{I_2}[\ \emptyset\ ]$

5NF $C_I[\ \emptyset\ ]$, $C_{I_1}[\ \emptyset\ ]$, $C_{I_2}[\ \emptyset\ ]$, $C_{I_3}[\ \emptyset\ ]$

A relation P is in fourth normal form if it is not possible to group its key domains into three compound domains so that for some relations Q and R the if-and-only-if clause:

$$P(\ x, y, z\ ) \leftrightarrow Q(\ x, y\ ), R(\ y, z\ )$$ [1]

defines all the tuples in relation P. If relation P contravenes fourth normal form, then it should be replaced by the two relations Q and R. The if-an-only-if clause [1] above can be represented as three single-clause groups:

$$P(\ x, y, z\ ) \leftarrow Q(\ x, y\ ), R(\ y, z\ )$$ [2]
$$Q(\ x, y\ ) \leftarrow P(\ x, y, z\ )$$ [3]
$$R(\ y, z\ ) \leftarrow P(\ x, y, z\ )$$ [4]

The three groups [2], [3] and [4] together form a complete cluster. This cluster can be represented as the item I shown in Fig. 6.45. There is nothing wrong with item I. Fourth normal form requires that because of the existence of item I item P should be discarded and should be replaced by items Q and R. Fourth normal form contains advice about the components of I and not about I itself.

A relation P is in fifth normal form if it is not possible to group its key domains into three compound domains so that for some relations Q, R and S, the if-and-only-if clause:

$$P(\ x, y, z\ ) \leftrightarrow Q(\ x, y\ ), R(\ y, z\ ), S(\ z, x\ )$$ [6]

defines all the tuples in relation P. If relation P contravenes fifth normal form, then it should be replaced by the three relations Q, R and S. The if-an-only-if clause [6] above can be represented as four single-clause groups:

I		
P	*Q*	*R*
(x, y, z)	(x, y)	(y, z)
P(t, u, v) ↔ (Q(w, x) ∧ R(y, z))		
∅		
∀	∀	∀
--------------------		O
--------------------	O	
O	--------------------	

Fig. 6.45 i-schema showing classical fourth normal form

$$P(x, y, z) \leftarrow Q(x, y), R(y, z), S(z, x) \tag{7}$$
$$Q(x, y) \leftarrow P(x, y, z) \tag{8}$$
$$R(y, z) \leftarrow P(x, y, z) \tag{9}$$
$$S(z, x) \leftarrow P(x, y, z) \tag{10}$$

The four groups [7], [8], [9] and [10] together form a complete cluster. This cluster can be represented as the item *I* shown in Fig. 6.46. There is nothing wrong with item *I*. Fifth normal form requires that because of the existence of item *I* item *P* should be discarded and should be replaced by items *Q*, *R* and *S*. Fifth normal form contains advice about the components of *I* and not about *I* itself.

Figs. 6.45–6.46 show items that describe classical fourth and fifth normal form. The items shown in both figures are complex. The clue to spotting fourth and fifth normal forms in both of these figures is in the unique pattern displayed by the item set constraints.

I			
P	*Q*	*R*	*S*
(x, y, z)	(x, y)	(y, z)	(z, x)
P(x,y,z) ↔ Q(x, y) ∧ R(y, z) ∧ S(z, x)			
∅			
∀	∀	∀	∀
--------------------	O		
--------------------		O	
--------------------			O

Fig. 6.46 i-schema showing classical fifth normal form

[P, Q, R]		
P	Q	R
(v, w)	(v, x)	(y, z)
(x = w × 1.2) ∧ (y = v+w) ∧ (z = w × 1.7)		
∅		
∀	∀	∀

[P, Q]	
P	Q
(v, w)	(v, x)
(x = w × 1.2)	
∅	
∀	∀

[P, R]	
P	R
(v, w)	(y, z)
(y = v+w) ∧ (z = w × 1.7)	
∅	
∀	∀

Fig. 6.47 i-schema that violates classical fourth normal form

A natural generalisation of fourth and fifth normal forms is "if any item *P* with three component sets is in turn a component of another item *I* whose set constraints are as shown either in Fig. 6.45 or Fig. 6.46 then item *P* should be discarded in favour of the other component items of item *I*".

To explore the implications of the fourth and fifth classical normal form to knowledge consider examples where the component items in Figs. 6.45–6.46 are knowledge items. The following example is in clausal logic. Suppose that:

$P(x,y,z)$ means "$2^x = y = z + 10$"
$Q(x, y)$ means "$y = 2^x$"
$R(y, z)$ means "$y = z + 10$"

then the logical relationship:

$$P(x, y, z) \leftrightarrow Q(x, y), R(y, z)$$

holds and the predicate P should be discarded in favour of the predicates Q and R. Also consider the item *[P, Q, R]* shown in Fig. 6.47. This item breaches fourth normal form and should be replaced by the items *[P, Q]* and *[P, R]*.

Examples can be constructed to illustrate the application of fifth normal form to knowledge items, or the application of fourth or fifth normal forms to a combination of information and knowledge items.

6.5.6 Summary of classical normal forms

Taken together, the first, second, third, fourth and fifth normal forms for the relational model attempt to assert that a relation should represent one and only one "real", implicit functional association that is between those things that are represented as the key domains and those things that are represented as the non-key domains. The first, second and third normal forms assert that each implicit functional association should not have buried within it another implicit functional association. The fourth and fifth normal forms assert that an implicit functional association should not have buried within it an explicit functional association.

The classical fourth and fifth normal forms may be generalised. They may be applied to examine how items of knowledge could be buried within items of information. In a real working system the presence of a derived relation in the information model can pose as serious a threat to maintenance as a breach of fourth normal form. Consider the two groups [1] and [2]:

$$\text{item/sale-price}(x, y) \leftarrow \text{item/cost-price} (x, z), \; y = z \times 1.2 \qquad [1]$$
$$\text{item/cost-price}(x, y) \leftarrow \text{item/sale-price} (x, z), \; z = y \times 1.2 \qquad [2]$$

The cluster diagram for these two groups is shown in Fig. 6.48. So even if realistic constraints have been specified, any attempt to modify either of the two relations 'item/sale-price' and 'item/cost-price' or the cluster shown in Fig. 6.48 could jeopardise the consistency of the model. In the absence of elaborate constraints, these two relations and the cluster taken together are not normal in the sense defined here. To obtain a normal model *either* the 'item/cost-price' relation together with group [1] *or* the 'item/sale-price' relation together with group [2] could be chosen. From either of these two choices a model can be selected that is compatible with the general deductive flow of the knowledge-based system. The deductive flow is established by the query and update types. So it is *not possible* to select a model for a knowledge-based system that is to support maintenance until the query and update types are specified and incorporated into the modelling process.

The classical normal forms are principally concerned with the functional structure of the represented implicit functional associations. Non-classical normal forms are discussed. These non-classical normal forms can be applied to data, information and knowledge, and to any combination of these.

Fig. 6.48 Cluster diagram for groups [1] and [2]

6.6 Non-classical normal forms

Section 6.5 describes the classical normal forms as a complete characterisation of the non-trivial decomposition of items with three component sets. By considering decompositions of items with more than three component sets new, "non-classical" normal forms can be derived for items [Debenham, 1993a]. The normal forms in this section are illustrated principally in terms of items. They could equally well be expressed in terms of objects.

Suppose that item I has the four component sets A, B, C and D. Consider the different ways in which this item $I(A, B, C, D)$ can be decomposed so that the decomposition does not reduce to the decomposition of items with three component sets. First consider the decomposition of item I into two sub-items I_1 and I_2. The decomposition of a four component set item I into two sub-items may be achieved in a number of ways. It may be achieved by:

$$I(A, B, C, D) = I_1(A, B) \otimes I_2(B, C, D), \text{ and}$$
$$I(A, B, C, D) = I_1(A, B, C) \otimes I_2(B, C, D).$$

Second consider the decomposition of item I into three sub-items I_1, I_2 and I_3. The decomposition of a four component set item I into three sub-items may be achieved in a number of ways. It may be achieved by:

$$I(A, B, C, D) = I_1(A, B) \otimes I_2(B, C) \otimes I_3(C, D), \text{ and}$$
$$I(A, B, C, D) = I_1(A, B, C) \otimes I_2(B, C, D) \otimes I_3(C, D, A)$$

Third consider the decomposition of item I into four sub-items I_1, I_2, I_3 and I_4. The decomposition of a four component set item I into four sub-items may be achieved in a number of ways. It may be achieved by:

$$I(A, B, C, D) = I_1(A, B) \otimes I_2(B, C) \otimes I_3(C, D) \otimes I_4(D, A)$$

Consider the first of the two decompositions of a four component set item I into two sub-items given above. The different ways in which the rule of decomposition:

$$I(A, B, C, D) = I_1(A, B) \otimes I_2(B, C, D)$$

can be employed may be categorised by the different ways in which functional associations are present in I. Three different cases are:

- there are no functional associations in I;
- the functional associations in I are only between pairs of A, B, C and D, and

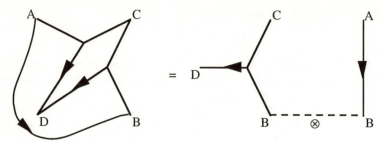

Fig. 6.49 The first decomposition of a four component set item

- there is at least one functional association in I of the form $Z \Leftarrow (X, Y)$.

The first and second of these cases reduce to classical normal forms. Consider the case when the functional association $D \Leftarrow (C, A)$ is present in I. If this functional association is present in I then one way in which functional associations may be present in I_1 and I_2 is:

$$C_I[D \Leftarrow (C, A),\ D \Leftarrow (C, B),\ B \Leftarrow A]$$
$$C_{I_1}[B \Leftarrow A]$$
$$C_{I_2}[D \Leftarrow (C, B)]$$

This rule of decomposition is not equivalent to any of the classical forms introduced above. It is illustrated in Fig. 6.49.

All of the above rules of decomposition for items can be applied to knowledge, information and data items. In the following example the rule illustrated in Fig. 6.49 is applied to knowledge items. Consider the item shown in Fig. 6.50. In this example the value constraints are trivial. To see that the rule illustrated in Fig. 6.49 applies to the item illustrated in Fig. 6.50 let 'A' be {*part/type, type/mark-up*}, 'B' be {*part/mark-up*}, 'C' be {*part/cost-price*} and 'D' be {*part/sale-price*}. That is '*part/mark-up*' is the item introduced by the normalisation process. The result of the normalisation process is shown in Fig. 6.51. The semantics of the *[part/mark-up, part/type, type/mark-up]* item in Fig. 6.51 is not trivial.

The example illustrated in Figs. 6.50–6.51 may be shown in its object representation. This is given in Fig. 6.52.

The non-classical normal form shown in Fig. 6.49 may be applied to less abstract representations than items and objects. First, applied to groups this normal form requires that the group:

part/sale-price $\Leftarrow$ part/cost-price, part/type, type/mark-up   [1]

should be replaced by the two groups:

[part/sale-price, part/cost-price, part/type, type/mark-up]			
part/sale-price	*part/cost-price*	*part/type*	*type/mark-up*
(x, u)	(x, v)	(x, y)	(y, z)
$u = v \times z$			
∅			
∀	∀		
O	--		
----------------------	O	--	

Fig. 6.50 Non-normal item to illustrate the rule in Fig. 6.49

[part/mark-up, part/type, type/mark-up]		
part/mark-up	*part/type*	*type/mark-up*
(x, z)	(x, y)	(y, z)
∅		
∅		
∀		
O	---	

[part/sale-price, part/cost-price, part/mark-up]		
part/sale-price	*part/cost-price*	*part/mark-up*
(w, x)	(w, y)	(w, z)
$x = y \times z$		
∅		
∀	∀	
O	---	
--------------------------	O	--------------------------

Fig. 6.51 Normal items for the item in Fig. 6.50

part/mark-up ⇐ part/type, type/mark-up   [2]
part/sale-price ⇐ part/cost-price, part/mark-up   [3]

The wisdom behind the above rule for normalisation is that rule [1] contains rule [2] and rule [3] implicitly embedded within it. If either rule [2] or rule [3] changes then, to preserve consistency, rule [1] should be changed as well. Rule [2] and rule [3] alone may not suffer from this difficulty.

Second applied to logic programming this normal form identifies the fact that the clause group:

mark-up-rule-1			
X^2	X^2	X^2	X^2
(x, u)	(x, v)	(x, y)	(y, z)
$u = v \times z$			
$\emptyset$			
$\forall$	$\forall$		
O	--		
--------------	O	--	

type-mark-up-rule		
X^2	X^2	X^2
(x, z)	(x, y)	(y, z)
$\emptyset$		
$\emptyset$		
$\forall$		
O	-------------------------------------	

mark-up-rule-2		
X^2	X^2	X^2
(w, x)	(w, y)	(w, z)
$x = y \times z$		
$\emptyset$		
$\forall$	$\forall$	
O	----------------------------	
--------------	O	-------------

Fig. 6.52   Object form of items in Figs. 6.50–6.51

part/sale-price(x, y) ← part/cost-price(x, z), part/part-type(x, v),
   type/mark-up(v, w), y = (z × w)   [A]

has buried within it the sub-rule that "the mark-up factor for a spare part is the mark-up factor associated with that spare part's type". This sub-rule can be represented as the clause group:

part/mark-up(x, y) ← part/type(x, z), type/mark-up(z, y)   [B]

Further clause group [A] also has buried within it the sub-rule that "the selling price of a spare part is the cost price of that spare part marked up by the mark-up factor associated with that spare part". This sub-rule can be represented as the clause group:

part/sale-price(x, y) ← part/cost-price(x, z),
   part/mark-up(x, w), y = (z × w)   [C]

The normal form requires that clause group [A] should be replaced by clause groups [B] and [C].

All of the rules of decomposition for items can be applied to knowledge, information and data items. The rule illustrated in Fig. 6.49 is applied to information. Consider the items shown in Fig. 6.53. In this example the value constraints are trivial. The predicate "applies(x,y,z)" means "'z' is the discount

part/customer/discount		
part	customer	discount
(x)	(y)	(z)
applies(x,y,z)		
Ø		
∀	∀	
---------------------------------------		O

customer/type/discount		
customer	type	discount
(x)	(y)	(z)
has-rate(x,y,z)		
Ø		
∀		
---------------------------------		O

part/type	
part	type
(x)	(y)
has-type(x, y)	
Ø	
∀	
-----------------	O

Fig. 6.53 Information items to illustrate the rule in Fig. 6.49

rate that applies to part 'x' when supplied to customer 'y'". The predicate "has-rate(x,y,z)" means "'z' is the discount rate that applies to part of type 'y' when supplied to customer 'x'". The predicate "has-type(x,y)" means "part 'x' has type 'y'". To see that the rule illustrated in Fig. 6.49 applies to the item illustrated in Fig. 6.53 let 'A' be {*part*}, 'B' be {*type*}, 'C' be {*customer*} and 'D' be {*discount*}. That is '*type*' is the item introduced by the normalisation process.

The rule shown in Fig. 6.49 may be applied to less abstract representations than items and objects. First, expressed in relational form this normal form requires that the first relation in Fig. 6.54 should be replaced with the second and the third. Second, the example in Fig. 6.53 in relational form is illustrated in Fig. 6.55. If all three of those relations are valid then the rule illustrated in Fig. 6.49 requires that the first should be discarded in favour of the second and the third. The relations shown in Fig. 6.55 are in classical normal form. In that figure underlining is used to identify key domains. To see the significance of this principle to maintenance consider the example shown in Fig. 6.55. Suppose that the three implicit functional associations shown are valid, and suppose that a part is re-classified as belonging to a new 'part-type', and that this new part-type attracts a different discount rate for some customers. Then the 'part-customer-discount' relation should be modified to reflect this change for every such part/customer pair.

Consider the second rule of decomposition of a four component set item *I* into two sub-items noted above. The different ways in which the rule of decomposition:

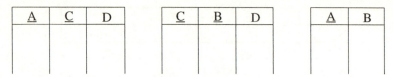

A	C	D

C	B	D

A	B

Fig. 6.54 Principle of Fig. 6.49 applied to relations

part/customer/discount

part-number	customer-number	rate-%

customer/type/discount

customer-number	type-description	rate-%

part/type

part-number	type-description

Fig. 6.55 Relations for the items in Fig. 6.53

$$I(A, B, C, D) = I_1(A, B, C) \otimes I_2(B, C, D)$$

can be employed may be categorised by the different ways in which functional associations are present in I. Three different cases are:

- there are no functional associations in I;
- the functional associations in I are only between pairs of A, B, C and D, and
- there is at least one functional association in I of the form $Z \Leftarrow (X, Y)$.

As with the previous rule of decomposition of a four component set item I into two sub-items, the first and second of these cases reduce to classical normal forms. Consider the case when the functional association $D \Leftarrow (C, A)$ is present in I. If this functional association is present in I then one way in which functional associations may be present in I_1 and I_2 is:

$$C_I[D \Leftarrow (B, A), \ D \Leftarrow (C, B), \ C \Leftarrow (B, A)]$$
$$C_{I_1}[C \Leftarrow (B, A)]$$
$$C_{I_2}[D \Leftarrow (C, B)]$$

This rule of decomposition is not equivalent to any of the classical forms introduced above. It is illustrated in Fig. 6.56.

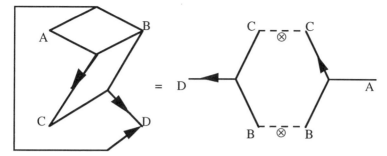

Fig. 6.56 The second decomposition of a four component set item

[part/profit, part/cost-price, part/mark-up]		
part/profit	*part/cost-price*	*part/mark-up*
(y, v)	(y, x)	(y, z)
$\rightarrow (v = x \times (z - 1))$		
$\emptyset$		
$\forall$		
O	---	

Fig. 6.57 Non-normal item to illustrate the rule in Fig. 6.56

The rule illustrated in Fig. 6.56 can applied to data, information or to knowledge items. In the following example that rule is applied to knowledge items. Consider the item shown in Fig. 6.57. In this example the value constraints are trivial. To see that the rule illustrated in Fig. 6.56 applies to the item illustrated in Fig. 6.57 to produce the items shown in Fig. 6.58 let 'A' be {*part/mark-up*}, 'B' be {*part/cost-price*}, 'C' be {*part/sale-price*} and 'D' be {*part/profit*}.

This second non-classical normal form may be applied to less abstract representations than items and objects. First, applied to groups this normal form requires that the group:

part/profit ⇐ part/cost-price, part/mark-up   [1]

should be replaced by the two groups:

part/sale-price ⇐ part/cost-price, part/mark-up   [2]
part/profit ⇐ part/sale-price, part/cost-price   [3]

The wisdom behind this rule for normalisation is that rule [1] contains rule [2] and rule [3] implicitly embedded within it. If either rule [2] or rule [3] changes then, to preserve consistency, rule [1] should be changed as well. Rule [2] and rule [3] alone may not suffer from this difficulty.

[*part/sale-price, part/cost-price, part/mark-up*]		
part/sale-price	*part/cost-price*	*part/mark-up*
(y, v)	(y, x)	(y, z)
$\to$ (v = x $\times$ z)		
Ø		
∀		
O	--	

[*part/profit, part/sale-price, part/cost-price*]		
part/profit	*part/sale-price*	*part/cost-price*
(y, v)	(y, x)	(y, z)
$\to$ (v = x − z)		
Ø		
∀		
O	--	

Fig. 6.58   Normal items for the item in Fig. 6.57

Second applied to logic programming this normal form identifies the fact that the clause group:

part/profit(x, y) ← part/cost-price(x, w),
  part/mark-up-factor(x, u), y = w $\times$ (u − 1)   [A]

has buried within it the sub-rule that "the sale price of a part is the cost price of that part multiplied by the mark-up-factor associated with that part". This sub-rule can be represented as the clause group:

part/sale-price(x, y) ← part/cost-price(x, z),
  part/mark-up-factor(x, w), y = (z $\times$ w)   [B]

Further clause group [A] also has buried within it the sub-rule that "the profit on a part is the difference between the sale price of that part and the cost price of that part". This sub-rule can be represented as the clause group:

part/profit(x, y) ← part/sale-price(x, z),
  part/cost-price(x, w), y = z − w   [C]

The normal form requires that clause group [A] should be replaced by clause groups [B] and [C].
   The normal form illustrated in Fig. 6.56 may also be applied to a mixture of information and knowledge. Suppose that in a retail organisation the (selling)

price/cost/demand/increase			
price	cost	demand	increase
(w)	(x)	(y)	(z)
price-movement(w, x, y, z)			
∅			
--			O

[price, cost, demand, value]			
price	cost	demand	value
(w)	(x)	(y)	(z)
z = y × (w - x)			
∅			
--			O

value/price/increase		
value	price	increase
(x)	(y)	(z)
price-increase(x,y,z)		
∅		
------------------------------------		O

Fig. 6.59   Retail example

price and cost of goods is recorded and data is kept on the demand for goods. Demand is measured by the mean number sold per day. At each review period the price of the goods is increased (or decreased) as specified by the information item '*price/cost/demand/increase*' shown in Fig. 6.59. Suppose that the concept of the "value" of a good is established by the knowledge item *[price, cost, demand, value]*. In Fig. 6.59 the knowledge item '*[price, cost, demand, value]*' and the information item '*value/price/increase*' are also shown. To see that the normal form illustrated in Fig. 6.56 can be applied to this example let 'A' be {*cost, demand*}, 'B' be {*price*}, 'C' be {*value*} and 'D' be {*increase*}. The normal form illustrated in Fig. 6.56 requires that the first item shown in Fig. 6.59 should be replaced by the second and third items shown in Fig. 6.59.

   In terms of relations and groups, the retail example given in Fig. 6.59 requires that the relation price/cost/demand/increase should be replaced by the group defined by the purely computational predicate:

value/demand/price/cost(w, x, y, z) ← w = x × (y − z)

together with the relation value/price/increase. The first item shown in Fig. 6.59 has the knowledge expressed in the second item implicitly buried within it. This normal form requires that the first item should be replaced by the information item '*value/price/increase*' also shown in Fig. 6.59.

Sections 6.3–6.6 present the normalisation of knowledge, and the unification of this notion with the ideas behind the normalisation of information. A question to consider is extent to which the normal forms for knowledge introduced in Sect. 6.5 are "complete". A set of normal forms for information (or knowledge) is a *complete set of normal forms* if any collection of information (or knowledge) that satisfies those normal forms is "normal" in the sense defined above.

6.7 Normal forms for groups

In terms of groups the rules for normalising knowledge described above are all concerned with the normalisation of the functional flow from the body of the group to the head of the group. There is another "function" associated with groups that should also be "normal" in some sense. That function is defined by the logical implication from a clause group to the clauses derivable, using resolution, from that group. The way in which the group is constructed and the way in which recursion operates should also be "normal". The normalisation of knowledge in this sense is considered briefly here.

A knowledge item may be implemented as one or more groups. Groups have an inherent structure of their own in that the set of clauses that comprise a group together logically imply all of the clauses that can be derived from that group using resolution. For "groups" normality has two levels of meaning. First the groups must be in normal form. This is concerned with the normality of the associations within each group as described above. Second the function is defined by the logical implication in the groups should be in normal form. This second sense is concerned with the normality of the implication from the clauses in the group to the clauses derivable from the group by resolution.

Consider the "normal form" that requires that "Any clause derivable from the clauses in a group using resolution should have a unique derivation". A derivable clause is said to have a *unique derivation* from a group if there is one way in which that derivable clause may be deduced from the group using the conventional "left-right/backtracking" execution strategy of Prolog [Clark, McCabe & Gregory, 1982]. If a clause can be derived from a given group in two different ways then it is possible that the group can be modified in a way that effects one of these derived clauses but not the other. Consider the group:

item/sell-price(x, y) ← item/cost-price(x, z), y = z × 1.2
item/sell-price('book', 1.44) ←   [1]

Suppose that elsewhere it is established that item/cost-price('book', 1.20). Using group [1] it is possible to deduce that 'book' sells for $1.44 in two different ways. Group [1] constitutes a maintenance hazard.

6.8 Summary

- The term "normalisation" has three different meanings in common usage.
- A single general principle of normalisation applies to items and to objects.
- The single general principle of normalisation is expressed in terms of the decomposition of items and objects.
- Strategies for normalising items and objects aim to identify those items and objects that are decomposable.
- The classical normal forms provide a complete characterisation of the ways in which an item of three component sets may be decomposed.
- Non-classical normal forms are rules of normalisation that do not reduce to the classical normal forms.
- The structure of groups may be "normalised".

7 Specification

7.1 Introduction

The non-unified design methodology for knowledge-based systems described in Chap. 2 employs a non-unified representation for the conceptual model. That conceptual model consists of two separate parts: a model of the data and information things and a model of the knowledge things. In that methodology data, information and knowledge things are modelled and treated differently from each other.

This chapter describes the first step in a unified design methodology. This step is "requirements specification" [Blair et al., 1994]. This unified methodology employs the unified representation for conceptual modelling developed in Chaps. 3 and 4. The requirements specification step makes extensive use of the r-schema format for describing items discussed in Sects. 5.3 and 5.4 [Debenham, 1997a].

The requirements specification step contains two tasks. The first task is the "application representation" task that generates a high level view of the application called the "application description" [Lee, 1993]. The second task is the "requirements identification" task that generates the "requirements model" [Fensel, 1995].

The application representation task consist of three sub-tasks. The first sub-task is the construction of the context diagram, which identifies the system boundary and the key players that interact with the system. These "players" may include other systems. The context diagram shows how "inputs" flow into the system, and how "outputs" flow out of the system. A strategy for constructing the context diagram is to identify the "major requirements". The major requirements are those requirements that are in some sense the "most important". When the design process for the major requirements is completed, the "next most important" set of requirements are identified. This process is not unduly repetitive. Having processed some of the requirements, the design of the system for subsequent sets of requirements is "hung onto" the design that has already been completed [Fensel

& Poeck, 1994]. Chapter 12 describes a case study. The design process in that case study makes two major passes through the design. The first pass is for a set of "major requirements" and the second pass is for the remaining requirements. The relevant sections of Chap. 12 may be read concurrently with Chaps. 7–11.

The requirements identification task consists of five sub-tasks. The principal product of the requirements identification task is the requirements model. The requirements model contains a description of the system requirements. This description gives a view of the general shape of the system. The requirements model contains details of the sections of that model:

- that can re-use existing systems or sub-systems;
- that should be implemented in an imperative programming language;
- that should be implemented as a knowledge-based system; and
- that should be implemented as traditional DSS system.

The requirements model contains other details too.

The structure of the whole methodology is described. Then the requirements specification step is discussed followed by the description of item behaviour and the construction of r-schemas. Finally the two tasks of the requirements specification step are described in detail.

7.2 Methodology structure

The overall structure of the unified methodology is shown in Fig. 7.1, at the highest level of which is the "lifecycle". The *lifecycle* is the way in which the "steps" of the methodology are applied throughout the whole design process. Each *step* involves as a series of "tasks". Each *task* involves a series of sub-tasks. The tasks and sub-tasks employ various methods, guidelines and algorithms. Each step, and each task has an identifiable *deliverable*.

"Incremental design" is a suitable life cycle model for large knowledge-based systems. *Incremental design* is the process of completely designing, and possibly implementing as well, a part of the system. Having dealt with that part the design process begins over again to include another part of the system and so on. Incremental design has the feature that part implemented systems are constructed and trialed comparatively quickly. "Incremental design" is seen in contrast to "sequential design". *Sequential design* is the process of applying each step in a design methodology to its full extent before proceeding to apply the next step.

In an incremental design a part of the system is identified and the whole design process is completed for it. Then another part is selected and the whole design process is completed for that part and so on. This leads to the description of the evolving design as being of the first, second, third, and so on, *generation*. The use of incremental design is particularly suitable for knowledge-based systems due to

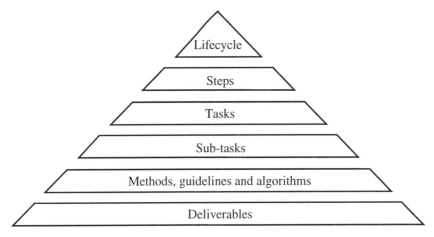

Fig. 7.1 Structure of the unified methodology

the "modular" nature of knowledge. Knowledge is *modular* in the sense that given an existing knowledge base, it is possible to add more rules to that knowledge base without necessarily modifying the existing rules.

Sections 7.5 and 7.6 describe the two tasks that make up the requirements specification step. These two tasks construct the high level structure that governs the incremental design process. In an incremental design the requirements specification step is completed for part of the application and then the rest of the design process is completed for that part. Then the requirements specification step is completed for another part of the application and so on until the whole design is complete. The parts of the system are prioritised. The design process is applied to those parts in that priority order. During requirements specification the focus is on what is important to the *structure* of the system. So one way to prioritise the importance of the parts of the system identified in the context diagram is by the extent of their influence on the structure of the system. Another way to prioritise the importance of the various parts of the system is based on an estimate of the inherent value of the expertise embedded within them. The way the various parts of the system are arranged in priority order is determined by the context of the application. The way this priority order is established is not relevant to the discussion here.

Section 7.5.2 describes the differentiation sub-task. The product of the differentiation sub-task is a set of "prime r-schemas", which form the basis for the incremental design. The choice of lifecycle is not *either* incremental *or* sequential. The choice is the extent to which the incremental design should be applied. It may be prudent to complete the entire first requirements specification step incrementally using the prime r-schemas as a guide before considering the second system analysis step.

An outline description of the steps in the unified knowledge engineering methodology follows. This description is independent of the choice of a sequential or incremental life cycle model.

- *requirements specification.* This step begins by constructing a rough, "broad brush" view of the application and ends with a "fairly complete" specification of the system requirements called the "requirements model". The requirements model specifies both *what* is functionally required of the system and *what* is required of the system design. The requirements model addresses the maintainability of the final system. The requirements specification step is the subject of this chapter.

- *system analysis.* This step begins with the requirements model and constructs a complete model of the system called the "conceptual model". The conceptual model contains details of *how* the system can do what it is required to do. The conceptual model does not include implementation details of the form "what parts of the model are required to do the job, and what should be stored and what should be deduced". The conceptual model is "non-functional and implementation independent". The conceptual model does not contain details of *what* the system is required to do. The specification of *what* the system is required to do is overlaid on the conceptual model using links from the requirements model. The system analysis step is the subject of Chap. 8.

- *system function.* This step begins with the requirements model and the conceptual model and constructs the "functional model". The functional model contains functional implementation details of the form "what parts of the conceptual model are required to do the job". The functional model does *not* contain layout implementation details of the form "what should be stored and what should be deduced". System function produces a model that can *do something*. That is, the functional model combines both the "what" and the "how" aspects of the system. The system function step is the subject of Chap. 9.

- *system layout.* This step begins with the functional model and constructs the "internal model". The internal model contains implementation details of the form "what should be stored and what should be deduced". The internal model is a complete specification for the programmer. Given an internal model the programmer should require no further information to implement the system on any given platform. The internal model contains the system constraints and a procedure for maintaining the system. The maintenance procedure is an integral part of the design. System layout is the subject of Chap. 10.

- *system implementation.* This step begins with the internal model and a specified implementation platform and constructs the "physical model". The physical model is an implementation of the system. This implementation may include an implementation of the maintenance procedure for the system as well as the implementation of the system itself. System implementation is not discussed here.

Each design step described above produces a deliverable that forms all or part of the input to the next design step. The entire unified methodology starts with an "application". It is assumed that as much wisdom about the application as is required is available. The methodology finishes with an implemented, maintainable system. The deliverables for each design step are:

- the *requirements model*, this is a functional and implementation independent representation of the system. The requirements model describes *what* the system should be able to do.
- the *conceptual model*, this is a non-functional and implementation independent representation of the system. The conceptual model describes *how* the system can do what is asked of it. The specification of *what* the system should be able to do is provided by links from the requirements model.
- the *functional model*, this is a functional and implementation independent representation of the system. The functional model describes how the wisdom in the conceptual model may be employed to do what is required as described by the requirements model.
- the *internal model*, this is a functional and implementation dependent representation of the system. The internal model describes how the functional model should be implemented.
- the *physical model* that is an implementation of the system.

The internal model provides a complete specification of the system and is the limit of the discussion here. The whole *knowledge engineering* process is shown in Fig. 7.2 [Gaines, 1987].

A principal concern of the unified methodology is to generate *maintainable* systems. A key decision that has to be made before commencing any knowledge engineering process is what, if any, of the product of the design will be retained and maintained to support system maintenance. At one extreme, the whole design, consisting here of the four design models, can be retained. At the other extreme, once completed the whole design can be discarded except for the physical model. This latter approach is sometimes known as the "seat of the pants" approach. This decision is primarily one of cost. The retention of the complete design as a superstructure to govern the maintenance process is desirable in theory. If one modification is made to the physical model that is not reflected in the design then the design may become inconsistent with the physical model. If a design is inconsistent with its physical model then the value of the design is reduced. If a decision is made to retain the complete design as a superstructure to govern the maintenance process then *all* maintenance operations should be fed through the design to emerge as maintenance tasks to be performed on the implemented system.

The requirements specification step is the first step in the unified design methodology for knowledge-based systems. This step is the subject of this chapter. This step begins with the construction of a rough view of the application and ends with a "fairly complete" specification of the system requirements called the "requirements model". This requirements specification step together with the second step in the methodology "system analysis" are illustrated in Fig. 7.3. For an incremental design, Fig. 7.3 is not a flow chart. In an incremental design the

Application

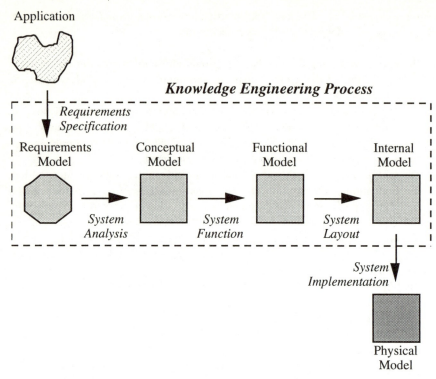

Fig. 7.2 The knowledge engineering process

specification of the application description is not finalised completely before work on the requirements model begins. Figure 7.3 shows that the requirements specification step consists of two tasks. These two tasks are:

- *application representation*. This task begins with the construction of an overview of the system requirements called the "context diagram". This overview is then expanded into a fairly complete view of the system requirements called the application description. The application description does not give all the details that would be required to implement the system.
- *requirements identification*. This task is concerned with the identification of those things in the application description that are relevant to the system, and with the "classification" of those things. Those things are classified as to be implemented "by re-using an existing component", or by constructing "a knowledge-based system component", "a conventional programmed component" or a component constructed in some other framework [Mili et al., 1995]. In addition, sections of the system that are subject to regular maintenance are identified. This classified sub-set of the application description is the *requirements model*.

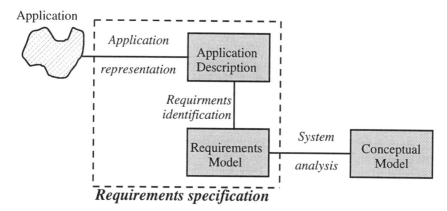

Fig. 7.3   The application description, requirements model and conceptual model

Both the application description and the requirements model represent the system requirements. The application description and the requirements model are composed substantially of the description of the application using the r-schema notation. The business of constructing models using r-schemas is described in Sects. 7.3–7.4. The structure of both the application description and the require-ments model are cascade decompositions of r-schemas. Each level in this cascade decomposition gives a view of more detailed features of the system requirements than the previous level.

7.3   Item behaviour

The r-schema view is introduced in Sect. 5.3.   This view is used during the requirements specification step.   An r-schema describes *what* a set of items is required to do [Dalal & Yadav, 1992].   Part of the r-schema representation is the r-schema's behaviour.   The concept of "behaviour" is introduced in Sect. 5.3. Section 5.3 defines an item's *behaviour* as a statement of "what" an implemen-tation of that item is to do in response to a particular type of request, but *not* "how" it is expected to do it.   "Item behaviour" is described in more detail than in Sect. 5.3.   This more detailed description is consistent with the "provisional" description given in Sect. 5.3..   Section 7.4 describes r-schema construction.   An r-schema describes a set of items.   A "behaviour" of an r-schema is a description of one variety of task that an implementation of the set of items described by that r-schema are expected to be able to perform.

When an item is implemented, the implementation will "sit there" until it is asked to do something.   A message that asks the implemented form of an item to do something is an *item request*.   When the implementation of an item receives an item request, it should *do something* specific and then should deliver an appropriate message in response. Such a response message is an *item response*. An item request may be received by the item over some period of time. Some time, at or after the time that the item request begins to arrive at the item, the item begins to generate the item response. The item request should be fully received before the item response can be considered to be completely delivered. From the time that the item request begins to arrive to the time that the item response is fully delivered the item is *active*. What the item does while it is active is the *item activity*. This description of item behaviour is illustrated in Fig. 7.4. This description leads to three inter-related but separate "aspects" of item behaviour. These three *aspects* of item behaviour are:

- the presentation of an item request;
- the item activity, and
- the delivery of an item response.

These three aspects are *not* considered to be sequential. That is, bits of the item request may be presented after the item has become active, and bits of the item response may be delivered before the item ceases to be active. The behaviour of an item is described by describing these three aspects of item behaviour [Davis, 1993]. The first aspect is the *item request presentation*, the second aspect is the *item activity*, and the third aspect is the *item response delivery*. The description of "item behaviour" is based on this idea.

The implementation of an item may be expected to do a number of different things. In general an item request should tell the item what it is supposed to do. In the formal λ-calculus form of an item, an "item request" is presented to an item in the form of a tuple in which certain elements are variables and others are constants. In this formal presentation, the sequence of variables and constants "tells" the item what to do. Presenting the tuple (1234, y) as a formal item request to the *part/cost-price* item, as introduced in Sect. 3.5, might return the item response (1234, $1.23). In this example the structure of the item request has "told" the item to "retrieve the cost of part number 1234". Another tuple might tell the *part/cost-price* item "to find a part that costs a given amount". There are at least two different item activities that the *part/cost-price* item could be asked to perform.

The collection of all item requests that ask an item to perform the same particular activity is an *item request type*. The one particular activity that an item performs as a result of receiving an item request of a certain item request type is an *item activity type*. An item may be presented with an unbounded number of different possible item requests but only a finite number of different possible item

Fig. 7.4 Item request, item activity and item response

request types. The collection of item responses to all of the item requests of a particular item request type is an *item response type*. An *item behaviour* is a description of the item request presentation, the corresponding item activity and the corresponding item response delivery for each item request type. Item behaviour is a set of linked triples of descriptions. There may be as many different item request types as there are different item behaviours. This definition of behaviour is consistent with the less detailed version given in Sect. 5.3. To complete the development of this description of "behaviour" requires a specification of how an item request presentation, an item activity and an item response delivery should be described. "Item behaviour" describes "what" an item is to do. "Item behaviour" does not describe "how" it is expected to do it.

Three "aspects" of an item's behaviour are identified above. There are five "perspectives" of each aspect that could be significant. These are the *behaviour perspectives*. The five behaviour perspectives are the five perspectives used customarily by journalists when describing things. Together the three aspects and five perspectives provide a complete framework within which item behaviour may be described. The five perspectives of each aspect of behaviour are:

- *what* is it? For example, the request might be either a string of ten numbers, the entire contents of thirteen relations in a relational database, a chunk of expertise or a string of words. The item request type presentation should "tell" the item what form the item request type has. For example, the request type might be an Order Form, the activity type might be an Ordering Process, and the response type might be a Goods Delivery. If the request is a Car Order Form then the activity may be a Car Ordering Process, and the response may be a Car Delivery.
- *why* is it happening? For example, the request might consist of a string of ten numbers and the reason that these numbers are being presented to the implemented item is because their mean and standard deviation is required. The item request type presentation should "tell" the item what to do.
- *who* else is involved? For example the item request type might have been generated by "the Managing Director", or by another item. For example, the item activity type may entail reference to a particular database. The "who" aspects of "item activity type" help to identify the item's components.
- *when* does it happen? For example a request might be generated on the first day of each month to produce a summary of the sales figures for the previous month. For example, the item activity type may have to be complete within a certain period of time.
- *where* does it happen? For example a request might have been generated at a branch office in a distributed system. For example, the item activity type may have to be completed by a particular secure mainframe.

The three aspects and five perspectives of item behaviour are summarised as a complete framework in Fig. 7.5. This complete framework can be used to describe "item behaviour". Item behaviour is a description of the item request

	Item request type presentation	Item activity type	Item response type delivery
What	What is the form of the item request type?	What is the item activity type?	What is the form of the item response type?
Why	Why is the item request type being presented?	Why is the activity being performed?	Why is the item response type being delivered?
Who	By whom will the item request type be presented?	Who else, including other system components, will contribute to the item activity type?	To whom should the item response type be delivered?
When	Will the item request type be presented at any particular time?	Is there any limit on the time taken for processing the item activity type?	Should the item response type be delivered at any particular time?
Where	Where will the item request type come from?	Does the item activity type need to take place anywhere in particular?	Where should the item response type be delivered?

Fig. 7.5 Perspectives and aspects of item behaviour

presentation, the corresponding item activity and the corresponding item response delivery for each item request type. The framework is comprehensive. The detailed description of the behaviour of an item within this framework could be very elaborate. The requirements specification step is "working on the fly", and may involve time spent in dialogue with the knowledge source [Samson & Wirth, 1991]. The aim of this dialogue is to determine the overall "shape" of the system. Some aspects of the system description are identified as aspects that "are to be worked out later". The resulting description of the system is necessarily incomplete, and is probably inaccurate. Requirements specification attends to those features of an item's behaviour *that appear to be important*. There is flexibility in the level of detail to which the framework may be applied to the description of an item's behaviour. The salient features of the three aspects of behaviour are identified for each item request type. Item behaviour only describes "what" an item is required to do and not "how" it might do it.

7.4 r-schema construction

The requirements specification step involves "fishing in the dark". Requirements specification tries to form a picture of something that is known to exist but the details of which are not known. The requirements specification process is often carried out together with the knowledge source. The knowledge source may have a view of what is required of the system. The knowledge source can be expected to know *what* the system should be able to do. The knowledge source does not necessarily know all the details of *how* the system might do it. The r-schema notation is suited to the description of the *what*.

Suppose that a name for a body of wisdom is at least tentatively adopted. This name might refer either to a complex body of wisdom that represents a whole system or to sub-system as described in Sect. 3.8. This name is recorded as an *r-schema's name*. Suppose that the name identified is the *"Tax Act knowledge base"*. This name could refer to a complex body of wisdom. As this body of wisdom could be complex requirements specification tries to identify a single, succinct statement of what this body of wisdom is supposed to do within the general operation of the proposed complete system. This succinct statement is recorded as the r-schema's *mission statement*. The mission statement identified for the *"Tax Act KB"* r-schema could be "To provide an implementation of the Tax Act to suit the general requirements of individuals, corporations and taxation specialists."

Having identified the r-schema's name and mission statement, requirements specification then focuses on the r-schema's behaviour. To determine the r-schema's behaviour construct descriptions of particular types of job that the *"Tax Act KB"* is expected to do. These descriptions are constructed in terms of the framework consisting of the "item request types" and corresponding "item activity types" and "item response types". This framework is described in Sect. 7.3. The detailed framework described should only be applied as far as it appears to be iden- tifying things of prime importance. There are no set criteria to decide which "things are of prime importance". This decision has to be left to experience and good judgement. For example, something is of prime importance if it could have a significant impact on the structure of the system. Suppose that the *"Tax Act KB"* is required to:

- advise on tax payable by an individual on the presentation of a correctly prepared profile of that individual;
- advise on tax payable by a corporation on the presentation of a correctly prepared profile of that corporation, and
- provide intelligent cross referencing to support requests to browse the Tax Act knowledge base.

These three statements are recorded as that r-schema's behaviour. In this example the "when" and "where" aspects of behaviour are ignored. The description of an r-schema's behaviour constructed during requirements specification may not be complete or correct. Additional behaviours may be identified and subsequently included as the application description is refined and developed. The descriptions of behaviours may not include all significant aspects of behaviour from the complete framework shown in Fig. 7.5.

Having identified the r-schema's behaviour then focus on the r-schema's components. An r-schema represents a system, or sub-system, that *does something*. Given an r-schema that represents a system, the things that that system is supposed to do are described in that r-schema's behaviour. An r-schema's components are the names of other r-schemas. An r-schema's components represent sub-systems that also do something. An r-schema's *components* are chosen to represent sub-systems that perform key sub-tasks of some or all of the tasks described in that r-schema's behaviour. So the identification of an r-schema's components provides a basis for the decomposition of the tasks described in the r-schema's behaviour. This is the approach taken to the decomposition of tasks. The choice of components determines the way in which tasks are decomposed. For example components can be chosen so that tasks are decomposed in the same manner as they are performed in an existing manual or automated system. Alternatively, components can be chosen so that tasks are decomposed in a manner that hopefully leads to an efficient physical model. Further, components can be chosen so that tasks are decomposed in such a manner as to accommodate existing software modules leading to their possible reuse. There is considerable flexibility in the choice of components. The choice of components is an architectural decision. During requirements specification a dialogue alternates between considering *what* has to be done and an outline specification of *what* is required to do it. The interpretation of the name, components and behaviour sections of an r-schema is described on Fig. 7.6.

An r-schema's behaviour describes *what* tasks that r-schema is required to do. The *r-schema's components* identify the sub-systems that can perform key sub-tasks of these tasks. An r-schema's components are not necessarily able to perform individually every behaviour of that r-schema. In general an r-schema's behaviour either:

- may be performed completely by one of that r-schema's components, or
- may be performed partially by one or more of that r-schema's components, or
- may be independent of that r-schema's components.

The decomposition process described in Sect. 7.5.3. Section 7.5.3 treats these three cases as follows. If an r-schema's behaviour may be performed completely by one of that r-schema's components then that behaviour is passed to that component. If an r-schema's behaviour may be performed partially by one or more of that r-schema's components then the contribution of those components to that behaviour is made explicit. If an r-schema's behaviour is independent of that

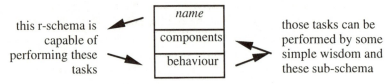

Fig. 7.6 Interpretation of r-schema

r-schema's components then this may indicate that more components should be identified.

Examples of the identification of r-schema components are given. The requirement "To relate cost and sale prices for parts." could form the mission of a simple r-schema. This r-schema might be required "To deduce sale price from cost price" and "To deduce cost price from sale price". These two requirements are two behaviours of that r-schema. The identification of the r-schema components follows from a view on the structure that can perform these two tasks. During requirements specification items are not described in detail. The identification of *item structure* is concerned with the identification of those things that the item "associates". Suppose that in this example "buying price can be deduced from selling price using a universal mark-up factor, and vice versa" then three components could be identified that are *"part/sale-price"*, *"part/cost-price"* and *"mark-up"*. The requirement "To estimate the income tax payable by an individual" could form the mission of an r-schema. This r-schema might be required to "Given access to an individual to interactively generate an estimate of the income tax payable by that individual.". This requirement is a behaviour of that r-schema. The r-schema components are identified by forming a view on the structure that can perform this task. Suppose that the decomposition of tasks is to be based on the way in which these tasks are presently performed in an existing manual system. In that manual system, to estimate the income tax payable by an individual "first prepare a standard proforma for that individual and then analyse this proforma to estimate the income tax payable". This rule associates the preparation of a proforma with the analysis of that proforma. This leads to the identification of the components that might be named *"proforma construction"*, *"proforma analysis"*. In this example, the contribution of those components to that behaviour is made explicit by adding to the r-schema the rule "To estimate the income tax payable by an individual first invoke the proforma construction sub-system and second to present the product of this sub-system to the proforma analysis sub-system".

The components identified for an r-schema represent sub-systems that perform key sub-tasks of some or all of that r-schema's behaviours. If a given r-schema possesses two sets of behaviours that are supported by distinct sets of components then the r-schema may be split into two simpler r-schema each of which one has one of these sets of behaviours and its corresponding set of components.

The behaviours identified for an r-schema should not be "parallel". Two behaviours are described as being *parallel* if they both employ the same set of components in the same way. Following the above taxation example, the behaviours "to estimate the income tax paid by a male person" and "to estimate the income tax paid by a female person" are parallel behaviours if they both employed the same set of components in the same way. If two parallel behaviours are identified then they should be generalised to a single behaviour.

A strategy for the identification of components is to identify a few "important" components. The term "important" is described. Suppose that an r-schema A contains components B, C and D. Further, suppose that r-schema B has components E, F and G, and so on as illustrated in Fig. 7.7. One possible choice of

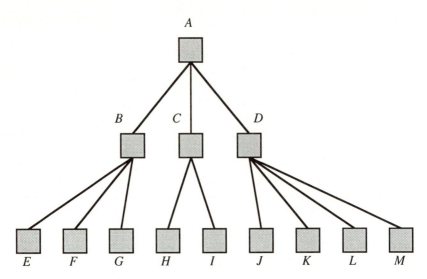

Fig. 7.7 One decomposition of complex r-schema *A*

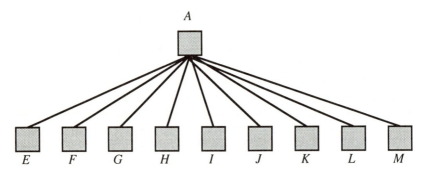

Fig. 7.8 Another decomposition of complex r-schema *A*

components for r-schema *A* is illustrated in Fig. 7.7. Another possible choice of components for r-schema *A* is illustrated in Fig. 7.8.

Both of the sets of components of r-schema *A* as illustrated in Figs. 7.7–7.8 could be "correct". The diagram in Fig. 7.7 involves the identification of fewer components for each r-schema than the diagram in Fig. 7.8. This poses the problem of determining an "acceptable" number of components for an r-schema. Some author's advocate the "7±2" rule. That is, they advocate between 5 and 9 components as being a "good" choice. In this context "7±2" can be too high because during requirements specification components are frequently omitted. The range "between 2 and 6 components" is a useful rule of thumb.

Using the rule of thumb stated in the previous paragraph, Fig. 7.7 shows a good choice of components for r-schema *A* but that Fig. 7.8 does not show such a good choice of components for r-schema *A*. A set of components of r-schema *A* is an *important* set of components *if* there are between 2 and 6 of them *and* none

Tax Act KB
Individual Tax KB *Corporation Tax KB*
• Advise on tax payable by an individual on the presentation of a correctly prepared profile of that individual. • Advise on tax payable by a corporation on the presentation of a correctly prepared profile of that corporation. • Provide intelligent cross referencing to support requests to browse the knowledge base.
• If two different profiles can be prepared for a given individual or corporation then the advice given on the basis of those two different profiles should be the same.

"To provide an implementation of the Tax Act to
suit the general requirements of individuals,
corporations and taxation specialists."

Fig. 7.9 r-schema for *"Tax Act KB"*

of the components in the set could be derived as a component of another member of the set. The set $\{B, C, D\}$ is a set of important components of A, and so is $\{B, H, I, D\}$. The set $\{C, E, F, G, H, K, L, M\}$ is *not* a set of important components of A for two reasons. First, this set contains eight members. Second, H is a component of C. This definition of an important set of components is only meaningful if all component relationships are known.

Within the necessarily vague context of requirements specification, the definition of "important" should not be taken *too* seriously. It is not intended that a given set of components that has a good intuitive appeal should necessarily satisfy the definition of "important". Requirements specification attempts to identify a set of components that appears at first glance to satisfy the rule of thumb and in which each component is "meaningful" in the context of the application. In the above example suppose that the Tax Act in question refers separately to individuals and to corporations then it might be reasonable to identify two components of the *"Tax Act KB"* that could be *"Individual Tax KB"* and *"Corporation Tax KB"*.

Having determined the r-schema's components, there remains only the r-schema constraints to be completed. The present example could include the constraint that "If two different profiles can be prepared for a given individual or corporation then the advice given on the basis of those two different profiles should be the same". All of this leads to the r-schema for the *"Tax Act KB"* as shown in Fig. 7.9.

For the purpose of providing a summary only, Fig. 7.10 shows a simplified picture of the business of r-schema construction. This simplified picture shows only the r-schema's name, the r-schema's components and the r-schema's behaviour. The r-schema's constraints and mission are omitted.

7.5 Application representation

The requirements specification step consists of two tasks [Karunananda et al., 1994]. These two tasks are "application representation" and "requirements identification". The application representation task begins with the construction of an overview of the system requirements called the "context diagram". This overview is then expanded into a fairly complete view of the system requirements called the application description [Sharp, 1994]. The application description does not give all the details necessary to implement the system. The application description is usually constructed in the context of an incremental design lifecycle.

The application representation task is a top-down procedure. This task is performed by three sub-tasks. These three sub-tasks are:

- construction of the context diagram;
- differentiation of the context diagram, and
- decomposition.

The construction of the context diagram sub-task constructs a succinct view of the environment of the whole application including the proposed system. The differentiation of the context diagram sub-task is concerned with the extraction and prioritisation of a set of one or more *prime r-schema* from the context diagram. This set of prime r-schemas taken together describes the operation of the system as shown in the context diagram. Further, the behaviours in each of these prime r-schemas should not "overlap" the behaviours in the other prime r-schemas. The prime r-schemas form the basis of the incremental design. The set of prime r-schemas is prioritised. The incremental design selects the r-schema of highest priority that has not yet been processed, and a complete design is constructed for that r-schema. The complete design for that r-schema may well make use of completed sections of the design constructed during previous generations of the incremental design [Sølvberg et al., 1988]. Having selected the r-schema of highest priority the decomposition sub-task is applied to it. The decomposition sub-task decomposes the selected prime r-schema into a cascade decomposition of r-schemas that may include r-schemas that have already been derived. The decom-

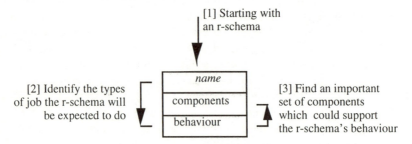

Fig. 7.10 Simplified approach to r-schema construction

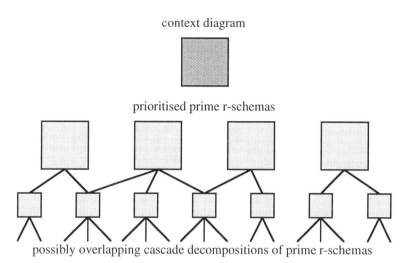

context diagram

prioritised prime r-schemas

possibly overlapping cascade decompositions of prime r-schemas

Fig. 7.11 The application representation task

position sub-task for "r-schema decomposition" is applied to the r-schemas in the cascade decomposition until further decomposition is "considered unnecessary". This whole process is illustrated in Fig. 7.11.

The application representation task consists of three sub-tasks. Section 7.5.1 describes the sub-task of constructing the context diagram. The context diagram is a succinct view of the environment of the whole application including the proposed system. Section 7.5.2 describes the sub-task of the differentiation of the context diagram. This sub-task constructs and prioritises a set of prime r-schemas. Section 7.5.3 describes the decomposition sub-task. Decomposition is repeatedly applied to a selected prime r-schema hence generating a cascade decomposition of that r-schema. The context diagram together with the prime r-schemas and their cascade decompositions together constitute the *application description*. The application representation task plays a prime role in the incremental design process [Karbach et al., 1990]. That task determines the iterative sequence of the design by the choice and prioritisation of the prime r-schemas.

7.5.1 Context diagram

The first sub-task in the application representation task is the construction of the context diagram [Rumbaugh et al., 1991]. A *context diagram* has an outer frame labelled "Application Boundary". Inside this outer frame there is an inner frame labelled "System Boundary". Inside the outer frame and outside the inner frame are the *players*. The players are the people or things that interact with the system. Inside the inner frame a single r-schema representing the system is shown. The context diagram is the starting point for the application representation sub-task and so it is the starting point for the whole unified design process [Tasker, 1989]. The behaviours and the components of the single r-schema in the context diagram are phrased at a high level. Those behaviours and components may be refined before the next task of r-schema decomposition. A constraint in the context diagram might be that the whole project must be completed within a certain time, or within a certain budget.

Suppose that the application is concerned with the implementation, as a knowledge-based system, of a nation's taxation act called the "Tax Act". Suppose that the overall objective is "To exploit knowledge-based technology in so far as it can efficiently provide advice to individuals, corporations, taxation specialists and law improvement staff in their dealings with the Tax Act." During initial discussions with the domain specialist, the following functions for the proposed system might be identified:

- to at least partially automate the business of determining how much an individual or corporation should pay in tax;
- to enable taxation specialists to browse the Tax Act in an intelligent manner, and
- to provide support for the law improvement process, including the ability to modify existing taxation parameters and to explore new forms of taxation.

The context diagram for this application might look like the diagram shown in Fig. 7.12.

In the single r-schema in the context diagram each behaviour quoted should have both its item request type and its item response type external to the system. Consider the first behaviour shown in Fig. 7.12. For that behaviour the item request type comes from an individual or corporation and the corresponding item response type is to be returned to that individual or corporation. The second behaviour quoted could contain the more specific behaviour "to accept new heuristics from Taxation Specialists to guide searches of the Tax Act". This particular specific behaviour comes from a Taxation Specialist who is a source external to the system, and the corresponding response generated might be the delivery of the message "heuristic accepted" to that Specialist.

The choice of components in the context diagram determines the structure of the resulting system. If the components are chosen to reflect natural divisions in an existing, manual or automated, system then the resulting system will also reflect these divisions. The choice of components for the single r-schema in the context diagram is a major decision in the system architecture [Ford & Bradshaw, 1993]. The rationale on which this decision is made should be explicit. One rationale could be to reflect the natural divisions in some existing system. Another rationale could be to attempt to construct a computationally efficient system. Yet another rationale could be to structure the system in such a way as to yield sub-systems that can be re-used in other applications [Barnes & Bollinger, 1991]. These three different rationales could lead to three different designs of the system.

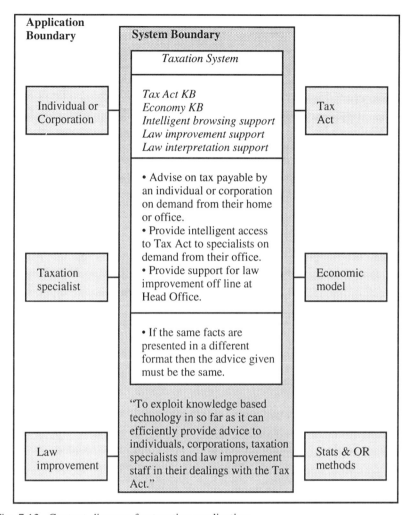

Fig. 7.12 Context diagram for taxation application

7.5.2 Differentiation

The second sub-task in the application representation task is differentiation. The
input to this sub-task is the context diagram. The output of this sub-task is a set
of one or more prioritised prime r-schemas. The behaviours of the r-schemas in
this set should together be able to perform completely the behaviours in the
context diagram [Yang, 1995]. The prime r-schemas should be independent in the
sense that the behaviours in each of them should not duplicate the behaviours in
the other prime r-schemas. Completeness and independence of the prime
r-schemas are not defined formally because requirements specification is an informal process.

Before constructing the prime r-schemas the behaviours and components in the single r-schema in the context diagram may need to be refined to ensure that they comply with the description of an r-schema as given in Sect. 7.4. The behaviours and components in the single r-schema in the context diagram may have been identified during informal discussions. They may not therefore completely satisfy the requirements of Sect. 7.4. The relationship between the behaviours and the components of this single r-schema may not satisfy the requirements of Sect. 7.4. Behaviours describe tasks that the system should be capable of performing. The components identify the sub-systems that can be used to perform these tasks. The behaviours and the components are interrelated. If a behaviour is complex then the choice of components may be inadequate. If the set of components for the single r-schema enables that r-schema's behaviours to be performed in more than one way then the choice of components is redundant. Once the relationship between the behaviours and the components of the single r-schema in the context diagram has been brought into line with the description given in Sect. 7.4 the differentiation procedure can commence.

Having constructed a set of prime r-schemas they are processed in the order of the priorities attached to those r-schemas. The construction of the prioritised prime r-schemas provides the basic mechanism to govern the incremental design process. The selection of the set of prime r-schemas determines the overall system architecture. The prime r-schemas should represent a breakdown of the design process that supports incremental design within the operational constraints placed on the whole design exercise. If the estimated cost of executing the design process for a particular prime r-schema exceeds the operational constraints then there are three alternative courses of action. First, the prime r-schemas can be re-constructed in such a way as to break down the prime r-schemas into a set of new prime r-schemas with lower design costs. Second, the decomposition procedure described in Sect. 7.5.3 can be applied to the prime r-schemas to generate a set of new prime r-schemas that can perform the behaviours of the original prime r-schemas. Third, the viability of the whole project may be reviewed.

7.5.3 Decomposition

The third sub-task in the application representation task is decomposition. The input to the decomposition sub-task is the prime r-schema of highest priority that has yet to be decomposed. The output of the decomposition sub-task is a cascade decomposition of that prime r-schema. The decomposition sub-task takes advantage of those parts of the application description that have already been developed during previous design iterations.

There is a procedure for r-schema decomposition. This procedure is technical and is described below. The general operation of the procedure is illustrated with an example. Consider the incomplete r-schema on the left of Fig. 7.13. The decomposition procedure adds in components to "support" that r-schema's behaviours. Possible components are shown in the r-schema on the right of Fig. 7.13. For each behaviour in the *tax adviser system* r-schema *either* one

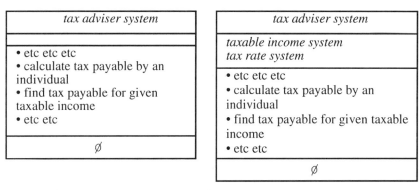

Fig. 7.13 Components added to the *tax adviser system*

component should be capable of completely performing that behaviour *or* one or more components should be capable of partially performing that behaviour. If a component is capable of completely performing a behaviour then that behaviour is transferred to that component. If one or more components are capable of partially performing a behaviour then a new component is created to represent that behaviour and that behaviour is transferred to it, the original behaviour is replaced by a rule that describes how the behaviour may be performed by the components. The result of the application of the decomposition procedure to the r-schema in Fig. 7.13 could be as shown in Fig. 7.14. In Fig. 7.14 the behaviour "find tax payable for a given taxable income" can be completely performed by the *tax rate system* component. That behaviour has been transferred to that component. The behaviour "calculate tax payable by an individual" can be performed partially by the *taxable income system* component and by the *tax rate system* component. That behaviour has been transferred to the new component *individual/tax-payable*. That behaviour has been replaced in the *tax adviser system* r-schema by the rule "the tax payable by an individual is the tax payable at a rate determined by that individual's taxable income". When all of the behaviours in the *tax adviser system* r-schema have been dealt with in this way the decomposition procedure is then applied to the new r-schemas that have been created.

The application of the decomposition procedure to a given r-schema, modifies that given r-schema and generates a set of new r-schemas. The product of the decomposition procedure is the modified r-schema and the set of new r-schemas. The material presented in Sect. 7.4 applies to the construction of these new r-schemas. The set of new r-schemas generated by r-schema decomposition should intuitively represent a set of building blocks in terms of which the behaviours of the given r-schema can be described. The decomposition procedure is applied repeatedly to the new r-schemas generated in turn until further decomposition is "considered unnecessary". What is meant by "considering the decomposition of an r-schema to be unnecessary" is described below.

When the decomposition procedure has been applied to all of the prime r-schemas, a framework of r-schemas has been developed that represents a decomposition of the behaviours in the single r-schema in the context diagram. This

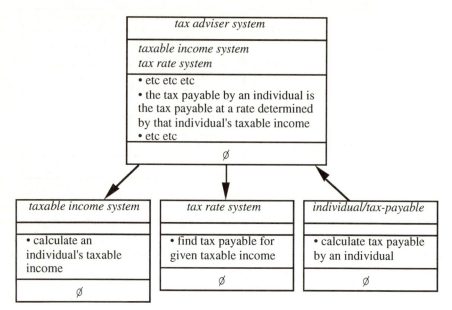

Fig. 7.14 Decomposed r-schema

framework determines the structure for the conceptual model during the following system analysis step. This framework determines the whole system architecture. The decomposition procedure is non-deterministic. There is considerable flexibility in the choice of r-schema components at each stage in the decomposition. The choice of r-schema components may effect the structure of the final solution. So the decomposition procedure should be performed with some idea of the structure of the solution in mind. This idea of the structure may develop as the decomposition proceeds. By "some idea of the structure of the solution" is meant some idea of *what* resources are required to provide the functionality described by the behaviours, but not necessarily an idea of *how* those resources might be employed. An understanding is required of what items are required to represent the information flowing into the system in the form of inputs, and an understanding is required of what items are required to represent the information flowing out of the system in the form of outputs. An understanding of the items that represent inputs and outputs prevents the decomposition from developing r-schemas that lie beyond the boundary of the system as represented by the context diagram.

Some idea is required of what items are required to represent the information flowing into the system in the form of updates. These items are *input items*. By convention the names of input items are underlined in the requirements model. The system transactions move through the framework of r-schemas as the decomposition procedure is applied. By convention the system transactions are labelled with a non-italicised label written within single quotes. The identification of the input items and the location of the system transactions is essential to determining the functional flow of the system.

The non-deterministic procedure for decomposing r-schemas is shown in Fig. 7.15. This procedure refers to three ideas that have yet to be discussed. The first idea is the idea of the decomposition of an r-schema being "considered unnecessary". The second idea is the idea of the expression of a behaviour being "sufficiently explicit" with respect to a set of components. The third idea is the idea of "a set of components reflecting a desired architectural design".

The idea of the decomposition of an r-schema being "considered unnecessary" is described. Decomposition of an r-schema is not *possible* when the r-schema represents a simple data item. The decomposition of information items can usually be performed intuitively. During requirements specification further decomposition is *considered unnecessary* when the r-schemas constructed appears to have only data items as components.

The idea of the expression of a behaviour being "sufficiently explicit" with respect to a set of components is described. The expression of r-schema behaviour can be rather vague. The structure of an r-schema is determined by the relationship between that r-schema's behaviours and that r-schema's components. The expression of r-schema behaviour should state how each behaviour can be effected using the available components. If the expression of an r-schema behaviour does not state how that behaviour can be effected using the available components then that behaviour is not *sufficiently explicit* and should be re-phrased so that the relationship between it and the r-schema's components is clear.

The idea of "a set of components reflecting a desired architectural design" is described. The decomposition procedure refers to the addition of components to the given r-schema to "reflect the desired architectural design". The choice of components completely determines the structure of the design that is "created" during the decomposition sub-task. If no components are introduced then one r-schema represents all of the knowledge in the application. If components are introduced then the knowledge will be divided between the r-schema and its components. The choice of components provides the ability to systematically develop the architecture of the design.

The procedure for the decomposition of r-schemas is shown in Fig. 7.15. The application of this procedure down to and including Step 4 to a four component r-schema, A, is shown in Fig. 7.16. In Fig. 7.16 there are four components that are capable of supporting the three behaviours in one way or another. The behaviour "b_2" of r-schema A is identified in Fig. 7.16. The behaviour b_2 is marked using the notation of Fig. 7.4. Consider Step 5, Step 6 and Step 7 of the procedure shown in Fig. 7.15. First, suppose that behaviour b_2 in Fig. 7.16 can be performed completely by the new r-schema C then the resulting decomposition is shown in Fig. 7.17. In that decomposition behaviour b_2 has been deleted from r-schema A and has been entered in r-schema C. Second, suppose that behaviour b_2 in Fig. 7.16 can be performed in part by each of b_4, b_5 and b_6 in r-schemas B, D and E respectively. Then a new component r-schema F is introduced. r-schema F has the single behaviour b_2. The behaviour b_2 in r-schema A is replaced with behaviour b_7 that contains a rule that references F and states how the behaviours b_4, b_5 and b_6 in r-schemas B, D and E can be employed to perform the behaviour b_2. The resulting decomposition is shown in Fig. 7.18.

When the procedure shown in Fig. 7.15 has been applied repeatedly to a prime r-schema the result is a tree structure that is referred to here as a "cascade decomposition". The end nodes of this tree should be r-schemas whose decomposition is

given an r-schema 's' that is not marked "processed" mark 's' "processed"
if 's' is equivalent to another r-schema that appears elsewhere in the application
      description **then** link 's' to that r-schema **and stop** [Step 1] **else if** the
      decomposition of 's' is considered unnecessary **then stop else if** 's' is
      an input item **then** mark 's' "input" **and stop** [Step 2] **else**
    add components to 's' that are disjoint with respect to the behaviours of 's'
      and that reflect the architectural design [Step 3]
    for each component, if any, of 's', **construct** a new component r-schema
      whose name is the same as that component **and construct** the
      mission for that new r-schema **and** add an arc from 's' to that new
      r-schema [Step 4]
    for each behaviour 'b' in 's' **if** the expression of 'b' is not sufficiently
      explicit with respect to the components of 's' **then** re-express 'b'
      so that the relevance of each component to 'b' is stated [Step 5]
    if there exists a component r-schema 'c' of 's' that can perform 'b'
      completely **then add** 'b' to 'c' **and delete** 'b' from 's' **else**
    if no single component r-schema of 's' can perform 'b' completely **then**
      identify a set of component r-schemas of 's' each of which can
        contribute to performing 'b' **and** mark each identified
        component r-schema with a "generalised" behaviour that
        describes its contribution to 'b'
      and if the generalised behaviours of the identified set of component
        r-schemas of 's' together with the other behaviours in 's' are
        not sufficient to perform 'b' collectively **then add** sufficient
        additional behaviours to 's'
      and add a new component 'c' to 's' **and create** a new component
        r-schema named 'c' whose behaviour is 'b' **and** add an arc from
        'c' to 's' **and** mark 'c' "processed"
        [Note. If 'b' can be interpreted as either a reference to, or a
        modification of, an item then name that item 'c'.]
      and replace 'b' in 's' with a new behaviour that states how the
        generalised behaviours of the identified components together
        with the other behaviours in 's' may achieve the performance of
        'b' in 'c' [Step 6]
    for each component r-schema, **mark** its components as 'empty' [Step 7]
    for each constraint in 's', **identify** those component r-schemas for which
      that constraint is relevant to at least one behaviour of those
      component r-schemas **then** restrict that constraint to the scope of
      those behaviours of those component r-schemas **and enter** these
      restrictions of that constraint in those component r-schemas **add**
      any additional constraints [Step 8]

Fig. 7.15 Procedure for decomposing r-schema

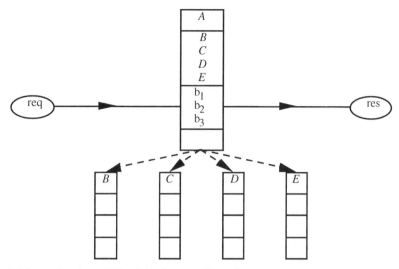

Fig. 7.16 Application of Fig. 7.15 down to [Step 4] only

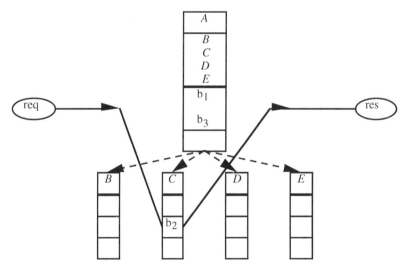

Fig. 7.17 An application of Fig. 7.15 to b_2 down to [Step 7] only

considered unnecessary. That is, they should either represent data items or information items. In a *complete* decomposition information items are represented by
nodes that are "one level up" from the nodes that represent data items. The
remaining nodes represent knowledge items [Turner, 1992]. The structure of the
tree brings an order to the gathered knowledge as it is developed. This structure
determines the basic shape of the whole design.

The procedure shown in Fig. 7.15 refers to r-schemas as being "marked". The
same r-schema can occur in a number of different places in a cascade decomposi-

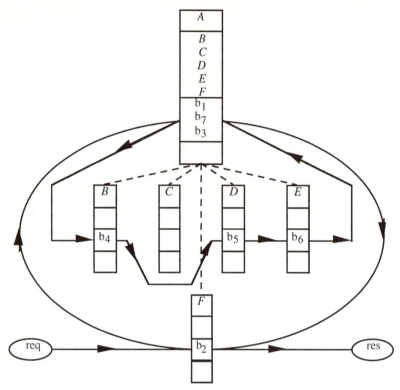

Fig. 7.18 Another application of Fig. 7.15 to b_2 down to [Step 7] only

tion. The device of "marking" r-schemas is designed to prevent the same r-schema being decomposed more than once when it appears more than once in the application description. The multiple occurrence of r-schemas in the application description is common. The identification of multiple occurrences of the same r-schema prevents unnecessary work.

The procedure shown in Fig. 7.15 requires one qualification. The procedure refers to "generalised" behaviour. Suppose in Fig. 7.18 that the item response type of r-schema B is a string of numbers each representing the speed of a passing car. Further suppose that r-schema D is concerned with the calculation of the statistical "standard deviation". Then the item request type to r-schema D "need not know" that the numbers being presented represent the speeds of passing cars. When specifying the item request type of r-schema D a *generalised behaviour* is specified. The item request type for r-schema D is "a finite string of numbers". There are no hard and fast rules for generalising behaviour. This process of generalisation is no more than the natural behaviour of program designers who attempt to build modules that are "reasonably general". So the "item response type" of one item is not necessarily the same as the "item request type" of an adjacent item and the description in Sect. 7.3 of r-schema behaviour is not redundant. In Fig. 7.18 the item response type of r-schema B is not necessarily the same as the item request type of r-schema D. The response type of r-schema B must be a "specialisation" of the corresponding request type of r-schema D.

Section 7.3 describes r-schema behaviour. In that description five features of the three aspects of behaviour are identified. These five features are the behaviour "perspectives". One of these five behaviour perspectives is *who* else is involved. During the decomposition procedure described above the *who* perspective of each behaviour must be identified *if the "who" refers to something or somebody external to the system*. The identification of who else is involved is invaluable when the functional aspects of the system are developed during the third step in the unified methodology, namely system function. In Fig. 7.18 if the item request "req" of behaviour 'b_7' is from a source external to the system then for this particular behaviour r-schema A receives a request from a source external to the system but r-schema D does not. The description of the behaviour b_7 should then identify the external source of this request.

The decomposition procedure described above consists of a combination of functional and structural decomposition. This is achieved by the focus moving alternately to and fro between the r-schema behaviour and r-schema components. This alternation between "what tasks should be performed" and "what is needed to perform each task" yields a blend of functional and structural decomposition.

7.6 Requirements identification

Requirements identification is the second of the two tasks in the requirements specification step. In an incremental design, part of the requirements model may have already been completed when requirements identification is performed [Lee & Foong, 1994]. Requirements identification is applied to the cascade decomposition developed from a selected prime r-schema. The inputs to the requirements identification task are the requirements model developed so far and the cascade decomposition developed from that selected prime r-schema. The output of the requirements identification task is a generation of the requirements model that includes that cascade decomposition. The cascade decomposition is developed during the first task of "application representation".

If the requirements identification task has been completed for all of the prime r-schemas then the requirements model is complete. The requirements model should be a fairly complete description of the tasks that the proposed system is required to perform. The requirements model should contain a specification of the components that are required to perform those tasks. The structure of the requirements model describes the overall architecture of the system [Bryd et al., 1992]. The requirements model identifies what has to be built. The requirements model does not specify the way in which the system is to be built. The requirements model does not specify the order in which the system is to be built.

The requirements model consists of the context diagram, a set of prime r-schemas and cascade decompositions of classified r-schemas derived from each prime r-schema. The selection of any particular r-schema from a requirements model together with the cascade decomposition derived from that particular r-schema identifies a complete sub-system.

The requirements identification task consists of the following sub-tasks:

* prime scoping;
* re-use;
* feasibility;
* classification, and
* volatility.

Each of these five sub-tasks is applied to the cascade decomposition that has been developed during the application representation task. The prime scoping sub-task attempts to confirm that the cascade decomposition can support the prime r-schema from which it has been developed. The re-use sub-task identifies the r-schema in the cascade decomposition that should be implemented by re-using an existing software component [Faget & Morel, 1993]. The feasibility sub-task identifies those r-schemas in the cascade decomposition that can not be implemented by re-using existing components and that are feasible to implement. This involves costing the system and may involve revising the scope of the system if necessary. The classification sub-task classifies those r-schemas in the cascade decomposition that are feasible to implement as "a knowledge-based system component", as "a conventionally programmed component" or in some other way. The volatility sub-task further annotates those r-schemas in the cascade decomposition that are classified "feasible to implement as a knowledge-based system component" with some measure of volatility. The *volatility* of an r-schema is a measure of expected rate of change of the knowledge represented by that r-schema. The product of these five sub-tasks is a classified cascade decomposition that is then included in the "requirements model". The final *requirements model* consists of the context diagram together with a classified cascade decomposition of r-schemas developed from each prime r-schema.

7.6.1 Prime scoping

This first sub-task is applied to the cascade decomposition developed from a selected prime r-schema. The prime scoping sub-tasks identifies those r-schemas in the cascade decomposition that are relevant to the prime r-schema from which that cascade decomposition is derived. Alternatively, it is concerned with the extraction of those r-schemas that are *irrelevant* to the scope of the system related to that prime r-schema.

The application representation task commenced with the construction of the context diagram as described in Sect. 7.5.1. The context diagram describes the scope of the system as it was initially conceived. The behaviours identified in the context diagram should give a high level description of the tasks that the proposed system should be capable of doing.

No matter how carefully the decomposition procedure described in Sect. 7.5.2 is applied to a prime r-schema, the resulting decomposition may be deficient in two ways. First, it may contain r-schemas that are irrelevant. Second, it may not contain r-schemas that are required. Of these two ways in which the decomposition may be deficient, the second is more common. The objective of this prime scoping sub-task then is to check to see that the cascade decomposition is not deficient in either of these two ways with respect to the prime r-schema from which that cascade decomposition is derived.

7.6.2 Re-use

The re-use sub-task identifies the r-schemas in the cascade decomposition that should be implemented by re-using an existing software component. The term "existing software components" does *not* refer to the existing r-schemas in the application description constructed so far. It refers to existing software components in some software library.

The prospect of re-using components of substantial size offers a potential cost saving that can effect the cost of a system as well as the time taken to construct it. Component re-use is not considered in detail here. If component re-use is to be taken seriously then the following should be established:

- a library of existing components is constructed and maintained;
- criteria are specified to determine what is, and what is not, an acceptable component in the library;
- criteria are specified to determine how those components that may be suitable to implement the component under consideration have been catalogued;
- a mechanism to locate suitable components, and
- a method for estimating the cost of using and maintaining an existing component from the library if it is to be employed as a component in the proposed system.

It only makes sense to re-use an existing component if it is cost effective to do so. The cost of re-using a component includes estimates of:

- the cost of locating possible components for re-use;
- the cost of selecting a useable component, if any;
- the cost of acquiring that component;
- the cost of rendering that component operational;
- the cost of integrating that component with the rest of the system, and
- the cost of maintaining that component.

Components for intelligent decision support systems tend to be costly to construct and costly to maintain. Any large organisation should consider the value in having a component library to enable components to be re-used.

7.6.3 Feasibility

The feasibility sub-task identifies those r-schemas in the cascade decomposition that can not be implemented by re-using existing components and that are feasible to implement. The consideration of cost takes place at the earliest stage at which it can be addressed accurately.

Estimating the cost of the system includes estimating the cost of the whole system with a view to deciding whether or not to build it. Estimating the cost of the system also includes estimating the cost of each significant component of the system with a view to deciding whether it is feasible to construct that component. The cost of a component includes the cost of *constructing* that component and the cost of *maintaining* that component. In the Taxation System example the determination of an individual's "professional deductions" may require access to current rulings by the Taxation Commissioner and so may be both complex and subject to continual change as new rulings are introduced. In this example, it may become apparent that it isn't worth while to implement the component relating to the determination of an individual's "professional deductions". It may be more cost effective to employ a human expert to provide such determinations for the system as required.

The cost of re-using re-useable components is considered in Sect. 7.6.2. Conversely, the cost of the proposed system should include an estimate of the opportunities for using the components of the proposed system in other systems. If components can be used more than once then the cost that those components contribute to the proposed system is reduced accordingly.

The scope of the system may be reduced at this stage in the design process. The system can be extended at a later stage when an initial system has proved its worth and effectiveness.

The product of this sub-task is a preliminary estimate of the cost of the major system components and the identification of those components of the system that it is proposed to implement.

7.6.4 Classification

This sub-task classifies those r-schemas in the cascade decomposition that are feasible to implement as "a knowledge-based system component", as "a conventionally programmed component" or in some other way.

This sub-task addresses the technical question of how each component should be treated during the remainder of the design process. It may be decided that a component should be implemented as a conventional database component, as a knowledge-based system component, as a conventionally programmed component or as a component that is to be implemented within a special purpose or high level language [King, 1990]. This decision is made on the basis of the inherent nature of the component and the software available.

7.6.5 Volatility

The volatility sub-task annotates those r-schemas in the cascade decomposition that are feasible to implement "as a knowledge-based system component" with a measure of volatility.

By this stage it has been decided which r-schemas in the cascade decomposition are to be implemented and how they will be implemented. When considering cost in Sect. 7.6.3, maintenance costs are mentioned. The volatility sub-task considers indirectly the issue of the extent to which development costs of each major component should be increased by normalising them. Normalisation reduces future maintenance costs. If components are not normalised then trust must be placed in the way that the system is designed and implemented so that the system isn't costly to maintain. Trust must also be placed in the skill of the maintenance staff to do their job efficiently.

Maintenance costs include both the cost of performing a maintenance operation and the cost resulting from the system being either inoperative or inaccurate while the maintenance task is being performed. In some applications there may be constraints on the time taken to effect maintenance tasks. In the Taxation System example it may be required to effect any changes in government legislation within one week. This constraint may have implications for the extent to which the knowledge base component in question is normalised.

This sub-task annotates r-schemas with a measure of volatility. This measure is used to determine the extent to which the representation of those r-schemas in the conceptual model should be normalised during the subsequent system analysis step. A decision to normalise the representation of an r-schema requires that the representations of all of its components should also be normalised. Normalisation can be an expensive process.

7.7 Summary

- The unified design methodology may be applied using a variety of different lifecycles including incremental design and sequential design.
- Item behaviour may be described by using a framework consisting of five aspects and three perspectives of behaviour.
- The requirements specification step consists of the two tasks of application representation and requirements identification.
- The application representation task consists of three sub-tasks. These three sub-tasks are the construction of the context diagram, differentiation and decomposition.
- The requirements identification task consists of five sub-tasks. These five sub-tasks are prime scoping, re-use, feasibility, classification and volatility.
- The product on the whole requirements specification step is the requirements model.
- The requirements model consists the context diagram together with of a cascade of classified r-schemas that has been constructed by applying the decomposition procedure to the single r-schema in the context diagram.
- The r-schemas in the requirements model are annotated to indicate re-use, the way in which they should be implemented, and their volatility.
- The classified set of r-schemas that comprises the requirements model is the starting point for the next step in the unified design process, namely system analysis.

8 Analysis

8.1 Introduction

This chapter describes the second step in a unified design methodology. This step is "system analysis". This unified methodology employs the unified representation for conceptual modelling developed in Chaps. 3 and 4. The system analysis step makes extensive use of the i-schema format for describing items (Sect. 5.2), and the o-schema format for describing objects (Sect. 5.5). The first step in the unified design methodology is requirements specification discussed in Chap. 7.

The principal product of the requirements specification step is the requirements model. In an incremental design each application of the requirements specification step generates new sections of the requirements model. The requirements model is a representation of the structure of the system to be built. Its structure is a cascade decomposition of classified r-schemas. The r-schemas in the requirements model are classified as to be processed:

- in some future generation of the system;
- in this generation of the system and implemented using a particular existing component;
- in this generation of the system and to be implemented in a specified manner, or
- in this generation of the system, to be implemented as a knowledge systems component to which an estimate of volatility is attached.

The system analysis step begins with the sections of the conceptual model constructed during previous generations of system analysis and with the particular section of the requirements model to be processed in this generation. The system analysis step generates a section of the conceptual model that corresponds to that particular section of the requirements model.

The items in the requirements model are represented in the r-schema notation. An r-schema represents a set of items. An r-schema contains details of *what* the

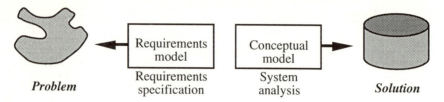

Fig. 8.1 Perspective of requirements specification and system analysis

items in that set should do but not of *how* they should do it. System analysis is concerned with *how* items should do what they are required to do. This shift in focus from the "what" to the "how" is a fundamental to the move from requirements specification to systems analysis. The requirements specification step is concerned with the description of the problem. The system analysis step develops a description of a solution to the problem. The perspective of requirements specification is towards the existing problem. The perspective of system analysis is towards the as yet non existent solution. This change of perspective is illustrated in Fig. 8.1. The conceptual model is developed from the requirements model. The conceptual model is more detailed than the requirements model and is one step closer to the complete design.

The approach taken to system analysis is in contrast with the approach taken to requirements specification. The approaches taken to these two steps are contrasted in Figs. 8.2 and 8.3. Despite the different characteristics of these two steps they are unified by the methodology in three distinct senses [Debenham, 1995]:

- *vertical unification* means that a single schema is used to represent the *data*, *information* and *knowledge* in each model.
- horizontal *model unification* means that the overall structure of one model acts as a detailed guide for the construction of the next model.
- horizontal *schema unification* means that the schemas used in one model translate naturally into the schemas used in the next model.

These three forms of unification for requirements specification and system analysis are illustrated in Fig. 8.4. Using the ideas introduced above, a *unified methodology* exhibits vertical unification. In addition the unified methodology achieves "horizontal unification" between each of the four design steps. A methodology exhibits *horizontal unification* if it exhibits both horizontal model unification and horizontal schema unification between each successive pair of design steps.

The system analysis step consists of four tasks:

- construction of the basis;
- construction of the conceptual view;
- construction of coupling map; and
- development of constraints.

The product of these four tasks is a section of the conceptual model described in Sect. 8.2. The four tasks are described in the following sections.

	Step	
	Requirements specification	System analysis
Produces	Requirements model	Conceptual model
Schema	r-schema	i-schema
Proceeds	Top-down	Bottom-up
Perspective	Problem	Solution
Builds	High level model quickly	Low level model thoroughly
Focus on	What	How

Fig. 8.2 Requirements specification and system analysis contrasted

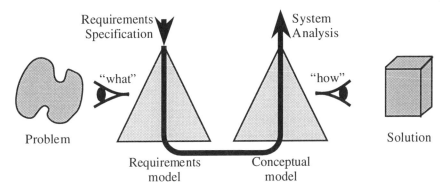

Fig. 8.3 Requirements specification and system analysis contrasted

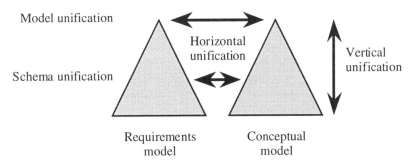

Fig. 8.4 Three forms of unification

8.2 Conceptual model

The conceptual model is the principal product of the system analysis step. Part of the conceptual model contains "coupling relationships". A *coupling relationship* joins two items if a modification to one of these items *could*, in general, require that the other item should be checked for correctness, and possibly modified, if the consistency of the conceptual model is to be preserved. The coupling relationships form a chaining structure. Modification leads to checking that may in turn lead to further modifications and hence to further checking and so on. Coupling relationships are discussed in detail in Sect. 8.5.

A *conceptual model* consists of:

- a conceptual view, and
- a c-coupling map.

The *conceptual view* is a collection of items. The *conceptual coupling map* or *c-coupling map* is a vertex labelled graph. For each item in the conceptual view there is a vertex in the c-coupling map labelled with that item's name. If an item in the conceptual view is not normal then its node in the c-coupling map is shown in an area labelled "not normalised". For those items in the conceptual view that are normal, an arc joins a pair of vertices in the c-coupling map if there is a coupling relationship between the normal items whose names are attached to those vertices. The set of items in the conceptual view may *either* be defined explicitly as items represented in either the λ-calculus or the i-schema notation *or* implicitly by representing each item as the result of the application of a sequence of object operators to a fundamental set of items called the "basis". These two ways of specifying the items in the conceptual view are identified by calling the resulting conceptual model either an "explicit conceptual model" or an "implicit conceptual model" respectively.

An *explicit conceptual model* is a conceptual model in which the items in the conceptual view are defined explicitly using either the λ-calculus notation or the i-schema notation.

An *implicit conceptual model* is a conceptual model in which the items in the conceptual view are defined implicitly as a sequence of object operators applied to a fundamental set of items called the "basis". The object operators are represented using either the λ-calculus notation or the o-schema notation. The items in the basis are represented using either the λ-calculus notation or the i-schema notation. The way the objects in the conceptual view are to be applied to the items in the basis is represented in a "conceptual diagram". In an implicit conceptual model the conceptual view consists of:

- a basis;
- an object library; and
- a conceptual diagram.

The basis, object library and conceptual diagram are described in detail below. In Chaps. 3, 4 and 6 it is argued that the use of a combination of objects and items permits a more natural analysis of maintainability than the use of items alone. From here the term *conceptual model* is taken to mean an implicit conceptual model.

A *basis* is a set of i-schemas that represents a minimal set of data items with the property that all of the items in the conceptual view can be constructed by applying the object operators in the object library to the items in the basis. Objects may be employed to represent sub-item relationships. A sub-item relationship between two data items is often called a *sub-type relationship* There are two different ways of choosing the basis. The *trivial basis* consists of only one i-schema that represents the universal data item U. A *non-trivial basis* consists of a set of i-schemas that does not include an i-schema that represents the universal data item U. The data items in an implicit conceptual model are either items in the basis or sub-types of items in the basis.

If the value sets of two data items contain some values that refer to the same real thing then one of these data items may be a sub-type of the other. Alternatively the value sets of the two items may "overlap" in some more subtle sense. In an application a particular real person may be both a "customer" and an "employee". Suppose that in the conceptual model of this application there is a data item *customer* whose value set contains the label "Miss Money". The label "Miss Money" refers to a particular real person. Further suppose that there is a data item *employee* whose value set contains the label "31678". The label "31678" also refers to the same particular real person. In this example a modification to the *employee* data item requires that the *customer* data item should be checked as well. In this example there should be a coupling relationship in the conceptual model between the two data items *employee* and *customer*.

The *object library* contains a representation of each object operator. The formal, λ-calculus notation for objects is complex. The informal o-schema notation described in Sect. 5.5 is comparatively simple. If there is any duplication among the objects in the object library then this complicates the coupling map. The detection of duplication between objects can be difficult.

The "conceptual diagram" shows how the o-schemas in the object library may be used to build the items in the conceptual view. The *conceptual diagram* is a vertex labelled graph in which each vertex either is labelled with the name of an item in the basis or is labelled with the name of an object operator from the object library together with an item name. If a vertex is labelled with an item name I and an object name O then arcs link that vertex to a set of vertices with the property that the application of the object O to the items at those vertices generates the item I. In the conceptual diagram item names are shown within rectangles and the object names are shown within parallelograms. If an object is used in the construction of more than one item then that object is represented more than once. In the conceptual diagram multiple representations of one object are linked by dotted lines. Suppose that in an application "parts and machines have a cost price, parts have a selling price, and the selling price of a part is the cost price marked up

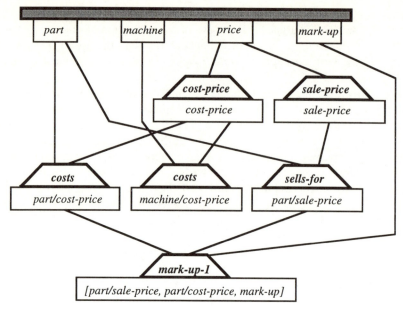

Fig. 8.5 Conceptual diagram for example application

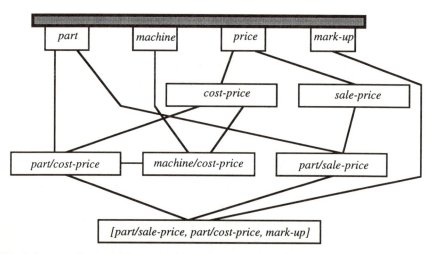

Fig. 8.6 c-coupling map for example application

by a universal mark-up factor". Then the conceptual diagram could be as shown in Fig. 8.5. The item *cost-price* is a sub-item of the item *price*.

The *coupling relationships* are introduced below. They are discussed again in Sect. 8.5. Coupling relationships are represented as arcs in the c-coupling map. These arcs provide a structure that supports maintenance. In Sect. 8.5 four different types of coupling relationship are identified. These four types are "component relationships", "equivalence relationships", "sub-item relationships" and "duplicate relationships". A *component relationship* joins two nodes in a c-coupling map if one is marked with an item that is a component of the other. An *equivalence relationship* joins two nodes in a c-coupling map if those nodes are marked with either items or objects that are weakly equivalent. A *sub-object relationship* joins two nodes in a c-coupling map if one node is marked with an object that is a sub-object of the object marked on the other node. If three nodes in a c-coupling map are marked with objects C, E and F where either object E or object F is non-tautological and:

$$C \simeq_w E \otimes_M F$$

where the join is monotonic then there are *duplicate relationships* between both the pair of nodes marked with C and E and the pair of nodes marked with C and F. If C is not normal and can be decomposed into two non-tautological objects E and F then there are duplicate relationships between the nodes marked with C and E and between the nodes marked with C and F. Consider the example whose conceptual diagram is shown in Fig. 8.5. The c-coupling map for this example is shown in Fig. 8.6 where there is a link between *part/cost-price* and *machine/cost-price*.

8.3 Basis

The first task in the system analysis step is to construct the basis. The construction of the basis principally involves the analysis of the fundamental data items. The construction of the basis task begins with the sections of the conceptual model constructed during previous generations of system analysis and with the particular section of the requirements model that is to be processed during this generation. The aim of this task is to produce the system "basis" that is described in Sect. 8.2. This task consists of five sub-tasks:

* identification of data items;
* construction of i-schema;
* removal of equivalences;
* identification of sub-types; and
* normalisation of the data.

The first sub-task is to examine the given sections of the requirements model and to identify the data items. The second sub-task is to construct an i-schema for each data item identified. The third sub-task is to identify and remove any equivalences between the i-schemas. The fourth sub-task is to identify any sub-type relationships between the i-schemas. The fifth sub-task is to normalise the data items as described in Chap. 6. The second and third of these sub-tasks may be performed together, "in tandem", and not sequentially, one after the other. The fourth sub-task may be dealt with together with the second and third. The outcome of the whole construction of the basis task is that section of the basis of the conceptual model derived from the particular section of the requirements model that is to be processed during this generation.

The basis is the foundation on which the whole conceptual model is built. The data items in the basis are used to build the information items, and in turn to build the knowledge items. Hence errors in the analysis of the data items will effect other items in the conceptual model. The system analysis step is a "bottom up" procedure. During system analysis the data items are considered first. Requirements specification is a "top down" procedure. The analysis of the data items is neither easy nor particularly fascinating.

The normalisation of knowledge is an inherently expensive process. Knowledge normalisation should only be applied to volatile sections of the conceptual model. There is little value in making a particular part of the model maintainable if there is not likely to be any need to maintain that part! The normalisation of data is not as expensive as the normalisation of information and knowledge. It is usually worth while to normalise the data items. Normalisation of the data *may* be omitted in small, stable systems for which maintenance is specifically not considered.

8.3.1 Data item identification

The first sub-task in the construction of the basis task is to examine the given section of the requirements model and to identify the data items. The requirements model consists of a cascade decomposition of r-schemas. This data item identification sub-task is not trivial for two reasons. First, the requirements model may be presented roughly, and, second, the requirements model may be large.

The requirements model may have been developed on a "white board" or on large sheets of paper over a period of time. The requirements model may be presented in a rough form. The requirements model may be incomplete and may contain inaccuracies. The decomposition of the requirements model may not have been carried out down to the data item level. In Sect. 7.5.2 it is suggested that the decomposition of an r-schema is unnecessary *during requirements specification* when the r-schema's components represented either data items or information items. The example in Fig. 8.7 illustrates the decomposition of an information item.

The requirements model may be large. Even a modest system may result in a requirements model containing several hundred r-schemas. In an incremental design, the given section of the requirements model may be large.

For a system of modest dimensions at least, the input to this sub-task is a large tree structure in which the terminal nodes should be r-schemas that either represent data items or whose components represent data items. If they do not then further decomposition of the terminal nodes is required.

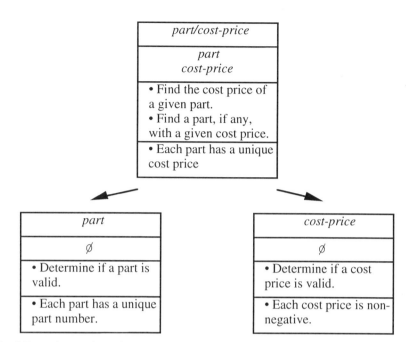

Fig. 8.7 r-schema view of an information item and its components

8.3.2 i-schema construction

The second of the five sub-tasks within the construction of the basis task is to construct an i-schema for each data item in the given section of the requirements model. This involves the specification of the item semantics and constraints. This second sub-task is usually performed at the same time as the first and third sub-task. In general an r-schema may represent a set of items. For data items, an r-schema usually represents a single item This sub-task involves the specification of the item semantics and constraints. For data items this is usually not difficult. An r-schema for a data item in the requirements model should describe what that data item is required to do. The i-schema's semantics describes *how* the data item does what it is required to do. Consider the example illustrated in Fig. 8.8. In this example, the r-schema's behaviour refers to the strictly functional activity of *given* a part number to *determine* whether the part number is valid. The i-schema's semantics is an expression that recognises valid part numbers. The i-schema semantics should be as general as possible and should not necessarily be concerned with representing the wisdom required to perform the particular tasks described in the corresponding r-schema's behaviour. The i-schema shown in Fig. 8.8 contains constraints that are not represented in the r-schema.

part
∅
• Determine if a part is valid.
Each part has a unique part number.

part
∅
(x)
is-a[x:part-number]
1 000<x<9 999
≤100

Fig. 8.8 An r-schema and corresponding i-schema

8.3.3 Removal of equivalences

The third of the five sub-tasks within the construction of the basis task is to identify and remove any data items that are "equivalent to" another data item. Weak
equivalence for two items A and B is defined in Sect. 3.7. Items A and B are
weakly equivalent, written $A \simeq_w B$, if there exists a permutation π such that:

$$(\forall x_1 x_2 ... x_n)[S_A(x_1, x_2, ..., x_n) \leftrightarrow S_B(\pi(x_1, x_2, ..., x_n))]$$

where the x_i are the n_i variables associated with the i'th component of A.

This sub-task is concerned with the identification and removal of weakly equivalent basis items. This sub-task is not trivial. The requirements model is a large
tree structure in which the terminal nodes should be annotated with r-schema representations of data items. As the requirements model is constructed using a top-
down approach a substantial amount of duplication can occur at the terminal
nodes. In a warehouse management system, the application may be substantially
concerned with the management of the "parts" that are stored in that warehouse. In
this example, a number of terminal r-schemas in the requirements model may
either be named *part* or may be named with a name that is equivalent to *part*. The
presence of two weakly equivalent data items means that a real data thing is represented twice as two data items with different names. The amount paid on an
insurance policy could be represented as an item *pay-out* and as another item
settlement. If duplications of this kind are undetected then they can cause the
conceptual model to be unnecessarily large and can cause havoc when that model is
used to direct the maintenance process. Unfortunately the detection of these duplications can be difficult.

    A non-deterministic procedure to perform the first, second and third sub-tasks
follows:

- The basis is as constructed in prior generations of system analysis, if none then set the basis to the 'empty set'.
- **If** all of the terminal nodes in the requirements model are marked "processed" **then stop otherwise** choose one of them.
- Given a chosen terminal node in the requirements model. **If** the r-schema on that terminal node represents a single data item **then** select it. **If** the r-schema on that terminal node does not represent a single data item **then** continually decompose that terminal node until the terminal nodes beneath it all represent single data items **and** select one of these terminal nodes.
- Given a selected terminal node whose r-schema represents a data item that has not yet been "processed". Construct a "new i-schema" for that node by choosing a unique item name A, set the item components to 'empty', introduce a dummy variable, construct the item's semantics and construct the item's constraints.
- **If** there is a node already in the basis that is marked with an i-schema B that is weakly equivalent to A **then** discard the new i-schema **and** add a link from the selected terminal node in the requirements model to the node in the basis that is marked with the i-schema B **and** mark the selected terminal node "processed".
- **If** the basis contains no node marked with an i-schema that is weakly equivalent to A **then** add a new node to the basis and mark that node with A **and** add a link from the selected terminal node in the requirements model to this new node in the basis that is marked with the i-schema A **and** mark the selected terminal node "processed".

This procedure searches amongst the already constructed i-schemas for an i-schema that is equivalent to the new i-schema. The identification of these weak equivalences is important. A variety of powerful tools are available to assist in the identification of weak equivalences. Data dictionary tools can be helpful in supporting this task. If two items are weakly equivalent then there is a high probability that they represent at least in part the same real thing, and so there is a possibility that the items are "equivalent". If two items appear to be weakly equivalent but are not equivalent then one may be a sub-type of the other.

In the above procedure, a new i-schema is constructed before attempting to find any weakly equivalent i-schemas. The reason for this is that each r-schema contains a description of an item's "behaviour". An item such as *part* could occur a large number of times in equivalent forms in the requirements model. Each occurrence of *part* could be with a different behaviour. The i-schema representation of each of these equivalent occurrences should be "similar" if not identical. When identifying whether two items are weakly equivalent it may be better to focus on *how* they do what they do rather than on *what* they might be asked to do.

The above procedure refers to the addition of "links" from a terminal node in the requirements model to a node in the basis. These links are represented by annotating each terminal node in the requirements model with the name of the corresponding i-schema attached to a node in the basis.

The third of the five sub-tasks within the construction of the basis task is to identify and remove any weak equivalences between the data items. This third sub-task is important because the existence of weakly equivalent data items within a conceptual model can cause that model to be unnecessarily large. Failure to remove the equivalence relationships between the data items can complicate the information items, and this, in turn, can complicate the knowledge items even more. There is a "multiplier effect" as the effect of poor data analysis passes up the hierarchy from information to knowledge and consequently spreads throughout the whole conceptual model.

Suppose that in the construction of the conceptual model a real data thing is represented as two data items A and A'. If the two data items A and A' are represented correctly then they are equivalent. They are also weakly equivalent. Any information item that contains the data item A as a component may also be duplicated as another weakly equivalent information item containing data item A'. Suppose that the data item A occurs as a component in the three information items P, Q and R. Further suppose that these three information items may be constructed by the application of the information object operators E, F and G as follows:

$$P = E(A, B)$$
$$Q = F(C, A)$$
$$R = G(A, D)$$

Then in addition to the three information items P, Q and R the three information items:

$$P' = E(A', B)$$
$$Q' = F(C, A')$$
$$R' = G(A', D)$$

may have also been identified in the conceptual model. If a single data thing is represented as two weakly equivalent data items then a complete representation of the information items contains a pair of information items for each information item that has that data item as a component. This duplication of the information items has a profound effect on the knowledge items.

If the gathered knowledge is complete then there will be a knowledge item that establishes a relationship between the two data items A and A':

$$H = I(A, A')$$

There will also be knowledge items that establish relationships between the three pairs of information items P, P', Q, Q', R and R':

$$J = M(P, P')$$
$$K = N(Q, Q')$$
$$L = O(R', R')$$

Further, knowledge items that have any of the six information items P, P', Q, Q', R and R' as components may give rise to yet further duplication. Suppose the knowledge item T_1 is identified:

$$T_1 = S_1(P, Q, R)$$

then any of the following seven knowledge items could also be identified:

$$T_2 = S_2(P', Q, R)$$
$$T_3 = S_3(P, Q', R)$$
$$T_4 = S_4(P, Q, R')$$
$$T_5 = S_5(P, Q', R')$$
$$T_6 = S_6(P', Q, R')$$
$$T_7 = S_7(P', Q', R)$$
$$T_8 = S_8(P', Q', R')$$

These seven knowledge items should all be weakly equivalent to the knowledge item T_1. If more than one of these eight knowledge items are introduced, then they, in turn, could give rise to duplication in any other items containing them as components, and so on, and so on.

The above discussion illustrates the chaos that can permeate the conceptual model as the result of a duplicate representation of a single data thing as two data items. This potential chaos has even more serious implications for the knowledge items than it does for the information items. Hence establishing the value of the principle "one real data thing in the application should be represented by one and only one data item".

8.3.4 Identification of sub-types

The fourth of the five sub-tasks within the construction of the basis task is to identify any sub-type relationships between the data items. Data dictionary tools can assist with this sub-task. Having identified the sub-type relationships these relationships should be represented using data object operators as described in Sect. 4.4. Sub-type relationships may be discovered whilst checking for equivalences during the third sub-task.

The definition of a sub-type is discussed in Sect. 3.3. Given two data items A and B, if π is permutation such that:

$$(\forall x_1 x_2 ... x_n)[S_A(x_1, x_2, ..., x_n) \leftarrow S_B(\pi(x_1, x_2, ..., x_n))]$$

then data item B is a *sub-type* of data item A. If data item B is a sub-type of data item A then at any time τ the (possibly permuted) value set of item B is a subset of the value set of item A. That is:

$$(\forall \tau) \, [\, \pi(\gamma^\tau(B)) \subset \gamma^\tau(A) \,]$$

In Sect. 4.4 data objects are employed to represent the sub-type relationships between data items. Consider the data item:

machine[λx•[is-a[x:machine-name]]•, λx•[x = AB ∨ x = CD]•,
   (Card ≥ 2)*machine*]

If 'lathes' are particular types of 'machine' then this relationship can be represented by introducing the data object:

lathe[λP:$\mathbf{D}^1$•λx•[$S_p(x)$ ∧ with-lathe(x)]••,

   λP:$\mathbf{X}^1$•λx•[$V_p(x)$ ∧ (name(x) → (x = AB))]••,

   λP:$\mathbf{X}^1$•[C_p ∧ (Card ≥ 1)$_{v\,(\mathbf{lathe},P)}$]•]

Then:

lathe(*machine*) =
   lathe[λx•[is-a[x:machine-name] ∧ with-lathe(x)]•,
      (λx•[x = AB]•)
      (Card ≥ 1)*lathe* ∧ (Card ≤ 2)*machine*]

In the conceptual model sub-type relationships between data items are represented by using data objects in this way.

There are two approaches to the identification of sub-type relationships. The first approach is to look at the semantics of the items and to investigate the possibility of a logical implication between the semantics expressions. The second approach is to look at the value sets of the items and to investigate common labels in their value sets.

8.3.5 Data normalisation

The last of the five sub-tasks within the construction of the basis task is to normalise the data items. Normalisation is described in Chap. 6. At the beginning of Sect. 8.3 it is suggested that this is the only sub-task in the construction of the basis task that *may* be omitted. The data normalisation sub-task should *only* be omitted when it is decided that the system will *never* require maintenance. It may be omitted for systems that will definitely be discarded if there is any change in circumstances. An example of such a system could be a demonstration prototype.

Consider the *"address"* item. Suppose that each address label includes a numeric postcode. Suppose that the numeric postcode may be determined by both the name of the town and the name of the state. An i-schema for this item is illustrated in Fig. 8.9. An address label has the form:

<street number> <street name>, <town name>, <state name> <postcode>

A typical label is shown in Fig. 8.10. As postcode is functionally dependent on both the name of the town and the name of the state then the information item:

town-name/state-name/postcode

is buried within the *address* data item. This data item should be normalised to obtain:

$$address = street\text{-}number\_street\text{-}name\_town\text{-}name\_state\text{-}name$$
$$\otimes_{\{town\text{-}name,\ state\text{-}name\}} town\text{-}name/state\text{-}name/postcode$$

If *street-number*, *street-name*, *town-name*, *state-name* and *postcode* had no other significance in the system, and if there is no functional relationship of the kind described above then there is nothing to be gained by further decomposing the *address* item into:

$$address = street\text{-}number \otimes_\emptyset street\text{-}name \otimes_\emptyset town\text{-}name$$
$$\otimes_\emptyset state\text{-}name \otimes_\emptyset postcode$$

There is nothing to be gained by decomposing a compound data items into a set of sub-items just for the sake of doing so. Such a decomposition increases the complexity of the conceptual model unnecessarily.

Consider the two items *employee* and *department* that have the two domains "employee-number" and "department-number" respectively. Suppose that the labels attached to employee-number are five digit integers where the first two digits of each integer are the number of the department in which that employee

address
$\emptyset$
(x)
is-a[x:address-label]
'x' is a non-null string
≥ 50

Fig. 8.9 i-schema for *address* item

246 Epping Highway, Lane Cove, NSW 2064

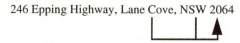

Fig. 8.10 A label in the value set of the *address* item

works. That is, employee number 12345 works in department number 12. In this example the item *employee* with domain employee-number is a compound data item and should be normalised:

$$employee = department \otimes_\emptyset index$$

The item *employee* should be replaced by the items *department* and *index*. The item *department* is buried within the item *employee*. Consider the item *machine* that has as its domain "machine-number". Suppose that the labels attached to machine-number are four digit integers where the first two digits are the number of the department in which that machine is situated. That is, machine number 2345 is situated in department number 23. In this example, the items *machine* and *employee* both have a common sub-item *department* and should be normalised.

The *address* example discussed above may appear to invalidate the methodology. In that example a data item is not normal because an information item is buried within it. But, the information items are not identified until the *next* task described in Sect. 8.4! This criticism is valid, but the analysis has to commence *somewhere*. When the semantics of a data item is identified and entered into an i-schema, it is worthwhile to ask whether "any label can be associated with the item's domain" and whether "a subset of each label has any significance elsewhere in the system". If the answer to either of these two questions is affirmative then the data item in question may require re-analysis later on.

This completes the data analysis step. The outcome of the data analysis step is the specification of a set of data items that may be normal. This set is the basis of the conceptual model.

8.4 Conceptual view

The second task in the system analysis step is the construction of the conceptual view. The *conceptual view* is a collection of items each of which represents a thing in the application. This task involves the identification of sub-type data items and the analysis of the information and knowledge items.

The principal product of the system analysis step is a conceptual model (Sect. 8.2) which consists of:

- a basis,
- an object library,

- a conceptual diagram, and
- a c-coupling map.

The basis is at least partially constructed during the first "construction of the basis" task. So when this the second task commences the following are available:

- the (partial) conceptual model constructed during previous generations, if any, of an incremental design;
- the requirements model that was developed during requirements specification and may well have been modified slightly during the construction of the basis; and
- a basis, that was at least partially constructed by the first task.

The prime objective of the construction of the conceptual view task is to produce:

- an object library, and
- a conceptual diagram.

The construction of the conceptual view task consists of eight sub-tasks:

- identification of the object operators for each non-basis item;
- construction of the object library;
- removal of equivalence relationships, and the construction of the conceptual diagram;
- refining object functionality;
- removal of labels;
- reduction of sub-items;
- decomposition of mixed type objects; and
- normalisation of the information.

The first sub-task is to identify both the object operators and the items that they generate in the requirements model. For each r-schema that represents a set of items, the second sub-task is to construct a set of o-schemas representing the objects that can generate that set of items. The third sub-task is to identify and remove equivalence relationships between the object operators in the object library, and between the items that those objects generate, and then to construct the conceptual diagram. The fourth sub-task is to refine the functional structure of objects. This is achieved by introducing sub-item relationships. The fifth sub-task is to remove any labels from the semantics and value constraints of the o-schemas. The sixth sub-task is to reduce sub-item relationships to sub-type relationships. The seventh sub-task is to decompose any o-schemas of mixed type. The last sub-task is to normalise the information items. The knowledge items are normalised during the following system function step. As in the previous construction of the basis task, the second and third sub-tasks may be performed together, "in tandem", and not sequentially, one after the other. The fourth of these sub-tasks may be dealt with in part together with the third sub-task. The fifth of these sub-tasks is a comment about good style, and should be applied as a matter of course. The outcome of the whole construction of the conceptual view task is a modified version of the requirements model, the object library and the conceptual diagram of the conceptual model.

8.4.1 Object identification

The first sub-task in the construction of the conceptual view task is to identify the object operators and the items that they generate for each item that is not in the basis. The items in the basis are identified during the previous construction of the basis task. The object operator identification sub-task is not trivial for three reasons. First, the requirements model may be presented roughly, second, the requirements model may be incomplete and inaccurate, and third, each node in the requirements model is annotated with an r-schema that may correspond to more than one i-schema. The decomposition of the requirements model may have generated some r-schemas that lead to complex object operators. If an r-schema on a node in the requirements model has a large number of components then the object operators that generates the corresponding set of items may be complex. If these object operators are complex then decompose that r-schema before proceeding. Further, the decomposition of the requirements model may well have failed to identify *all* components at every node. If such a failure occurs near the single node at the "top" of the requirements model then a large proportion of the requirements model may be missing.

Each node in the requirements model is annotated with an r-schema. An r-schema contains one or more behaviours and one or more components (Sect. 7.4). Given an r-schema, its components represent sub-systems that perform key sub-tasks of the tasks described in that r-schema's behaviours. So for any r-schema, each behaviour should be performable by employing the sub-systems named in its components *in a particular way*. The particular way in which an r-schema's behaviour can be performed by the sub-systems named is described in the conceptual model by an object operator.

Given a node in the requirements model, that node gives rise to a number of objects in the conceptual model. Each of these objects has as its arguments a set of items. Each item in this set corresponds to a component r-schema of the r-schema on that given node as long as that r-schema is complete. Consider the r-schema "*Individual Tax Advice*" in the portion of the requirements model shown in Fig. 8.11. This r-schema contains three different behaviours that are supported by five different components. Suppose that the first behaviour is represented by an object "*calculate individual tax*" whose arguments are {*Tax Act KB, Tax Profile Generator*}, the second behaviour is represented by an object "*Expected_Gross_Tax*" whose arguments are {*Tax Act KB, Population Data, Statistics Package*}, and the third behaviour is represented by an object "*Tax_Browser*" whose arguments are {*Tax Act KB, Hyperbook Constructor*}. When identifying the objects required to represent an r-schema, the r-schema's

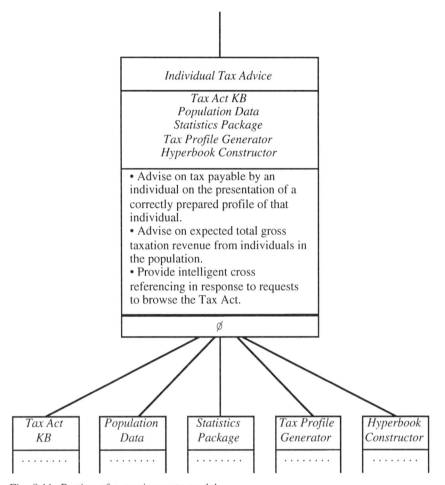

Fig. 8.11 Portion of a requirements model

components may not be sufficient to support those objects. If an r-schema's components are not sufficient then return to the requirements specification step and develop the requirements model further.

8.4.2 Object library construction

The second of the eight sub-tasks within the construction of the conceptual view task is to construct, for each r-schema on a node in the requirements model, the o-schemas of the set of objects that can generate the items described by that r-schema. The product of this sub-task is the object library. This sub-task involves the specification of the object semantics and constraints. This sub-task may be performed at the same time as the first and third sub-task. For items other than data items this sub-task may be complicated. It lies at the core of the shift in focus from "what" the items are required to do to "how" they do it. An r-schema's behaviours describe *what* the items have to do. An o-schema's semantics describes *how* the item does what it is required to do.

To illustrate the complexity of this sub-task consider the example in Fig. 8.12. In this example, the r-schema's behaviour refers to the strictly functional task of *given* a cost price to *calculate* a sale price. That o-schema's semantics contains considerably more wisdom than that required to perform this task. That o-schema's semantics contains sufficient wisdom to enable a cost price to be deduced from a sale price. The development of the o-schemas attempts to achieve this sort of generality. Each o-schema's semantics should be "reasonably general" and should not *necessarily* be restricted to representing the wisdom required to perform the particular tasks described by the r-schema's behaviour. The o-schema in Fig. 8.12 contains constraints that are not represented in the r-schema.

The o-schema format does not contain any indication of what the items that an o-schema might generate will be used for. The conceptual model is concerned with *how* things might be done. The unified methodology annotates the requirements model with "links" to the conceptual model. These links bring a statement about *what* it is expected to be able to do to the conceptual model.

8.4.3 Removal of equivalent objects

The third of the eight sub-tasks within the construction of the conceptual view task is to identify and remove any equivalence relationships between the objects in the object library, and to construct the conceptual diagram. An "equivalence relationship" in the c-coupling map is defined in Sect. 8.2. An *equivalence relationship* joins two nodes in a c-coupling map if those nodes are marked with either items or objects that are weakly equivalent. "Weak equivalence" for items is defined in Sect. 3.7, and for objects in Sect. 4.7. This sub-task is not trivial. During the construction of the basis, the requirements model is constructed top-down. A substantial amount of duplication may occur in the requirements model, particularly "towards the bottom" of that model. The existence of two equivalent objects may mean that two items are generated respectively by those two objects that could have been generated by one of those objects. In Sect. 8.3 it is noted that duplication of data items can cause the conceptual model to be unnecessarily large, and can cause havoc when the resulting design is used to support maintenance. The danger that equivalent object operators present to maintenance is as serious as the danger presented by the presence of equivalent data items in the basis. Detecting equivalent object operators is not easy. If two information objects have semantics:

$$\lambda P{:}\mathbf{X}^1 Q{:}\mathbf{X}^1 \bullet \lambda xy \bullet [S_P(x) \wedge S_Q(y) \wedge \text{costs}(x, y)] \bullet \bullet$$
$$\lambda P{:}\mathbf{X}^1 Q{:}\mathbf{X}^1 \bullet \lambda xy \bullet [S_P(x) \wedge S_Q(y) \wedge \text{has-price}(x, y)] \bullet \bullet$$

mark-up rule
part/sale-price
part/cost-price
mark-up
Given the cost price of a part to calculate the sale price of that part using a universal mark-up factor.
The sale price of a part is always greater than the cost price of that part.

"To represent the mark-up rule for parts."

mark-up-1		
X^2	X^2	X^1
(x, w)	(x, y)	(z)
$\to (w = z \times y)$		
$\to w > y$		
$\forall$	$\forall$	
--		O
O	--	
------------------	O	------------------

Fig. 8.12 An r-schema and corresponding o-schema

where 'costs' and 'has-price' mean the same thing then the weak equivalence of these two information objects could only be confirmed by reference to domain expertise.

A non-deterministic procedure to perform the first, second and third sub-tasks follows. This procedure is applied to the requirements model and the basis. The requirements model is modified with the addition of links during the construction of the basis. The terminal nodes in the requirements model give rise to the data items in the basis and should have already been marked "processed". The following procedure works systematically "up" the requirements model from the terminal nodes. The procedure continues to mark the nodes in the requirements model "processed" until no unmarked nodes remain. The outcome of the following procedure is a first draft of the conceptual diagram. The conceptual diagram shows how the object operators in the object library may be applied to the items in the basis and to the items already in the conceptual diagram to generate further items in the conceptual diagram. The description of the full procedure is technical. In outline the procedure is:

- In the requirements model choose a node whose r-schema is not complicated and whose components have already been processed.

- Construct objects that can support that r-schema's behaviours when applied to the set of items identified by the r-schema's components.
- For each object constructed check to see if an equivalent object has already been entered in the object library. If an equivalent object has already been entered in the object library then check on the conceptual diagram to see if any equivalent items have already been constructed.

The full procedure is:

- Take the conceptual diagram constructed in previous generations, if any. Construct the basis as described in Sect. 8.3. Take the object library constructed in previous generations, if any.
- **If** all of the nodes in the requirements model have been marked "processed" **then stop otherwise** choose a node with the property that all of its component nodes are already marked "processed". Suppose that those component nodes are linked to nodes on the conceptual diagram that are marked with the items named $\{X_1,...,X_n\}$.
- Given a chosen (non-terminal) node in the requirements model, determine the number of items, m say, that are required to represent the r-schema at that chosen node. For each such item, construct a rough version of the semantics of the object operator required to generate that item at this chosen node when applied to some subset of $\{X_1,...,X_n\}$. **If** the semantics of all of these items is not "complex" **then** select the chosen node **otherwise** decompose the chosen node and its r-schema and replace that node and its r-schema with that decomposition in the requirements model.
- Given a selected node in the requirements model whose r-schema's behaviours may be supported by a set of items that may be generated from the components $\{X_1,...,X_n\}$ by a set of object operators, where each of these object operators does not have "complex" semantics. Construct a set of "new o-schema" that can generate those items from the items $\{X_1,...,X_n\}$ by choosing a set of unique object names $\{B_1,...,B_m\}$, and for each of these objects by choosing the dummy tuple argument type pairs appropriately for its required subset of the items $\{X_1,...,X_n\}$, by constructing the object's semantics and by constructing the object's constraints. With each B_i associate a new item name A_i that is the name of the item that B_i generates when applied to its subset of the items $\{X_1,...,X_n\}$. Each object B_i's semantics and constraints should be as general as possible and should not *necessarily* be restricted to describing the behaviour specified in the r-schema on the selected node in the requirements model.
- As each new o-schema B_i is constructed, search the object library for an o-schema that is equivalent to B_i.
  - **If** an o-schema C, that is equivalent to B_i, is already in the object library **then** discard the new o-schema B_i **and** search the conceptual diagram for

a node marked with C, for each node marked with C on the conceptual diagram check to see if the item generated by object C at that node is equivalent to item A_i.

- **If** the item generated by object C at a node on the conceptual diagram is called D and is equivalent to item A_i **then** add a link from the selected node in the requirements model to this node marked with C and D on the conceptual diagram.
- **If** the conceptual diagram contains no node marked with C that generates an item that is equivalent to item A **then** to the conceptual diagram add a new node marked with object C, item A_i and add arcs from this node to the nodes marked with $\{X_1,...,X_n\}$ **and** add dotted arcs from this new node to the other nodes in the conceptual diagram that are marked with C **and** add a link from the selected node in the requirements model to this new node marked with C and A_i on the conceptual diagram.
- **If** the object library contains no o-schemas that are equivalent to B_i **then** add B_i to the object library **and** to the conceptual diagram add a new node marked with object B_i, item A_i **and** add arcs from this node to the nodes marked with $\{X_1,...,X_n\}$ **and** add a link from the selected node in the requirements model to this new node on the conceptual diagram.
- When all B_i have been dealt with mark the selected node in the requirements model "processed".

This procedure is elaborate. It focuses on the object operators rather than on the items that they generate for three reasons. First, objects are simpler to deal with than items. Second, it is easier to detect equivalence between objects than between items. Third, there are fewer object operators in the object library than there are items that they generate.

The above procedure depends on the availability of effective criteria to determine whether or not the semantics of an object is "complex". The notion of "complex" is subjective. The following example illustrates the intended meaning of "complex" semantics. Suppose that a portion of a requirements model is as shown in Fig. 8.13. In Fig. 8.13 node A has nine components. At least one of the object operators derived from the r-schema at node A may have complex semantics. If the complexity of the object operators derived from the r-schema at node A can be reduced by decomposing A as shown in Fig. 8.14 then the object operators derived from the r-schema in Fig. 8.14 should have simpler semantics than the object operators derived from the r-schema in Fig. 8.13. In the decomposition shown in Fig. 8.14 three new nodes have been added. Each node shown in Fig. 8.14 has at most four components.

The above procedure involves searching amongst the already constructed o-schemas and i-schemas for equivalent o-schemas and i-schemas. The correct identification of these equivalences is important. A variety of tools are available

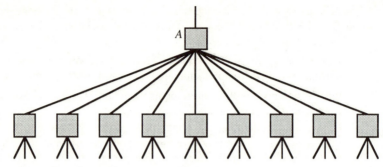

Fig. 8.13 Portion of a requirements model

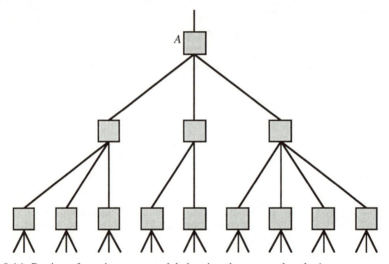

Fig. 8.14 Portion of requirements model showing decomposed node *A*

to assist with this search. "Equivalence" and "weak equivalence" are often related. If two items or objects are weakly equivalent then it is possible that they represent the same real thing. It is possible that weakly equivalent items or objects are equivalent. To check for equivalence, first check for weak equivalence, second if two items or objects are weakly equivalent then check to see if the items' or objects' constraints can be rephrased to make those items or objects equivalent.

In the above procedure, the new o-schemas are constructed before looking for equivalences. The r-schema contain descriptions of an items "behaviour". A knowledge object such as **mark-up-1** could be derived in a number of different ways from different r-schemas in the requirements model. Each of these different r-schemas could have different behaviours. In each derivation the o-schemas required to describe the wisdom to support these different behaviours should be "similar" if not identical. To identify whether two objects are equivalent set aside *what* the items that they generate might be asked to do and focus on *what* those two objects are.

The above procedure, and the procedure used in the construction of the basis, both refer to the addition of "links" from the nodes in the requirements model to the nodes in the conceptual diagram. As for the procedure used in the construction of the basis, these links are implemented by annotating the nodes in the requirements model with the names of the appropriate o-schema and i-schema pairs in the conceptual diagram. So the requirements model and the conceptual model are linked. The requirements model and the conceptual model each represents a different view of the system. The requirements model has a tree structure. The conceptual diagram does *not* have a tree structure. The procedure used for the construction of the basis and the procedure used for the construction of the conceptual diagram both modify the requirements model by adding links from the requirements model to the conceptual diagram. The conceptual diagram represents "how" the system does what it is asked to do. The structure of these links from the requirements model to the conceptual diagram imports "what" the items in the conceptual diagram are asked to do.

8.4.4 Refining object functionality

The fourth of the eight sub-tasks within the construction of the conceptual view task is to refine the functional structure of objects. This sub-task is achieved by introducing sub-item relationships. The notion of a sub-item is defined in Sect. 3.3. Given two items A and B, with semantics S_A and S_B respectively, where both items are expressed in terms of n variables, if π is permutation such that:

$$(\forall x_1 x_2 ... x_n)[S_A(x_1, x_2, ..., x_n) \leftarrow S_B(\pi(x_1, x_2, ..., x_n))]$$

then item B is a *sub-item* of item A. If a data item A is a sub-item of another data item B then item A is a *sub-type* of item B. The identification of sub-items contributes to the quality of the conceptual model. The sub-item structure can be complex. Sub-items may be introduced to refine the functional structure of objects.

The functional structure of an object is represented by its candidate constraints. The candidate constraints of an object are described in Sect. 4.3. A candidate constraint takes the form "Given an argument of that object, a set of other arguments are a candidate for that given argument". The given argument is the *subject argument* of the constraint and the set of candidates is the *candidate arguments* of the constraint. In the o-schema notation the subject is marked with an 'o', and the candidates are marked with a horizontal line. The general idea of the refining object functionality sub-task is to ensure that the functional structure of each object is as specific as possible. A general procedure to achieve this follows:

- identify a candidate constraint;
- introduce sub-items to ensure that the candidate arguments of that candidate constraint are all universal arguments (universal arguments are marked with an '∀' in the o-schema notation), and
- introduce a sub-item to ensure that the subject argument of that candidate constraint is a universal argument provided that the sub-item introduced is "meaningful and useful" in the application.

This procedure refers to "meaningful and useful" sub-items. The notion of "meaningful and useful" sub-items is discussed below.

Consider the o-schema *name-1* on the left of Fig. 8.15. This o-schema has a candidate constraint that requires that the labels in the value set of its "left hand" argument functionally determine the labels in the value set of its "right hand" argument. Its "left hand" argument is *not* the subject of a universal constraint. Not *all* members of the value set of the "left hand" argument are involved in this functional association. The second step in the above procedure introduces a sub-item to ensure that a universal constraint may be included as shown in the o-schema *name-2* on the right of Fig. 8.15. So for *name-2*, there is a genuine function from *all* of the members of the value set of the "left hand" argument to the value set of the "right hand" argument. If the object is an information object then in relational jargon this constraint ensures that a relation has a key. This idea can be applied to all objects.

Given an r-schema in the requirements model with the behaviour "To determine the employee who manages a given department". Suppose that the components of this r-schema are linked to the items *employee* and *department* in the conceptual diagram. The procedure first asks whether each department has at most one employee who manages it. Suppose that this is so then the procedure constructs the object *manages-1* that is shown in Fig. 8.16. The procedure then asks whether "All departments have a manager?". Suppose that they do. Then the procedure constructs *manages-2* that is also shown in Fig. 8.16. The procedure then asks whether "All employees manage departments". Suppose that this is not so. Then the procedure determines whether the subset of employees who manage departments is "meaningful and useful". Suppose that in this application these employees are known as "managers". Then the procedure replaces the *employee* component of the r-schema with *manager*, and links the r-schema's *manager*

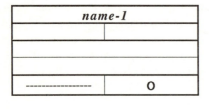

Fig. 8.15 Non-functional and functional o-schemas

manages-1	
X^1	X^1
(x)	(y)
'x' is manager of 'y'	
$\emptyset$	
O	-----------------

manages-2	
X^1	X^1
(x)	(y)
'x' is manager of 'y'	
$\emptyset$	
	$\forall$
O	-----------------

manages-3	
X^1	X^1
(x)	(y)
'x' is manager of 'y'	
$\emptyset$	
$\forall$	$\forall$
O	-----------------

manages-4	
X^1	X^1
(x)	(y)
'x' is manager of 'y'	
$\emptyset$	
$\forall$	$\forall$
O	-----------------
-----------------	O

Fig. 8.16 Four versions of the information object '*manages*'

component to an item *manager* in the conceptual diagram. The item *manager* is a sub-item of *employee*. Having done this the procedure constructs **manages-3** that is shown in Fig. 8.16. Finally the procedure asks whether "Each manager manages at most one department". If this is so then the procedure constructs **manages-4** that is also shown in Fig. 8.16. As the object set constraints of **manages-4** are complete the procedure terminates. The development from **manages-1** to **manages-4** is made possible by the introduction of a sub-item *manager* of the item *employee*.

Given an r-schema in the requirements model with the behaviour "To determine the address at which a given employee lives". Suppose that the components of this r-schema are linked to the items *employee* and *address* in the conceptual diagram. Suppose that the application of the procedure follows the same pattern as in the previous example until the procedure asks whether "All addresses have an employee living there". Suppose that they do not. The procedure then asks whether the set of "employee addresses" is "meaningful and useful" in the application. This is determined by the general context. Suppose that the notion of "employee addresses" is *not* "seen to be meaningful and useful" in the application. The procedure then terminates.

The examples considered above concern the refinement of an information object's functionality by introducing a sub-item. Knowledge objects too can be refined in this way. Given an r-schema in the requirements model with behaviour "Given an employee's position and the salary associated with that position, to determine the salary that that employee receives". Suppose that the components

salary-of-1		
X^2	X^2	X^2
(w, v)	(w, y)	(y, z)
$\rightarrow$ v = z		
v > 5 000 $\land$ v < 200 000		
O	--	

salary-of-2		
X^2	X^2	X^2
(w, v)	(w, y)	(y, z)
$\rightarrow$ v = z		
v > 5 000 $\land$ v < 200 000		
$\forall$	$\forall$	$\forall$
---		O
O	--	

Fig. 8.17 Two versions of the knowledge object '*salary-of*'

of this r-schema are linked to the items *employee/salary*, *employee/position* and *position/salary* in the conceptual diagram. Given the rule "if an employee's position is known and if the salary associated with that position is known also then that employee receives the salary associated with that employee's position" this rule could be represented as *salary-of-1* shown in Fig. 8.17. This example is not described in detail. The object *salary-of-2* in Fig. 8.17 represents a reasonable outcome of the application of the above procedure without the need to introduce any new sub-items. The *salary-of-2* object does *not* state that knowing the salary of an employee and the salary of each position determines the position of that employee because two different positions may attract the same salary.

This sub-task of refining object functionality has implications for the role of object operators. One way of regarding the basis and object library in the conceptual model is to think of the objects as general system building operators. That is, to think of the object library as containing a few general operators rather than a larger number of more specific operators. The approach described here derives operators that are representations of particular associations in the application.

8.4.5 Removal of labels

The fifth of the eight sub-tasks within the construction of the conceptual view task is to remove labels from the expression of the semantics of the objects identified. Labels belong to the value sets of items. Labels should not occur in the expression of either item or object semantics and value constraints. The removal of labels from the object semantics and value constraints is equivalent to the

mark-up-A	
X^2	X^2
(x, y)	(x, z)
→ y = 1.2 × z	
→ y > z	
∀	∀
O	-------------------
-------------------	O

mark-up
∅
z
is-a[z:mark-up-factor]
0<z<3
∅

Fig. 8.18 o-schema for '*mark-up-A*' and i-schema for '*mark-up*'

mark-up-B		
X^2	X^2	X^2
(y, v)	(y, 'car')	(y, z)
→ v = 1.4 × z		
→ v > z		
(y, v)	(y, 'truck')	(y, z)
→ v = 1.6 × z		
→ v > z		
(y, v)	(y, 'cycle')	(y, z)
→ v = 1.5 × z		
→ v > z		
∀	∀	∀
---		O
O	---	

Fig. 8.19 o-schema for knowledge object '*mark-up-B*'

programming practice of not using constants explicitly in programs unless absolutely necessary. An example of the acceptable use of a constant is the use in a semantics expression, or in a program, of the number '100' where the '100' represents "a hundred percent". There will always be one hundred percent. So this constant will never have to be modified.

For an example of the removal of a label from an object, consider the object **mark-up-A** in Fig. 8.18. In the conceptual diagram this object is applied to the two items *part/sale-price* and *part/cost-price*. The resulting item represents a crude mark-up rule in which all spare parts are marked up by 20%. The semantics of this object contains the label '1.2'. This object's semantics contains a label. The object **mark-up-A** should be replaced by the knowledge object **mark-up-1** shown in Fig. 8.12 and by the '*mark-up*' data item shown in Fig. 8.18. In this example a label from the value set of a data item is buried within the semantics of a knowledge object.

Another example involves labels from the value set of an information item being buried within the semantics of a knowledge object. Consider the object **mark-up-B** shown in Fig. 8.19. In the conceptual diagram this object is applied to the three items *vehicle/sale-price*, *vehicle/type* and *vehicle/cost-price*. The resulting item represents the mark up formula for three different types of vehicle namely 'car', 'truck' and 'cycle'. This object should be replaced by the knowledge object **mark-up-C** shown in Fig. 8.20 and the information object **rate-of** shown in Fig. 8.21. In the conceptual diagram the object **rate-of** is applied to the two items *type* and *mark-up-rate* and generates the *type/mark-up-rate* information item. The value set of this information item is shown in Fig. 8.22. In the conceptual diagram the object **mark-up-C** is applied to the four information

mark-up-C			
X^2	X^2	X^2	X^2
(w, v)	(w, y)	(w, x)	(y, z)
$\rightarrow$ v = x × z			
$\rightarrow$ v > x			
∀	∀	∀	∀
--------------------------------		O	-------------
O	--		

Fig. 8.20 o-schema for knowledge object '**mark-up-C**'

rate-of	
X^1	X^1
(x)	(y)
'x' has rate 'y'	
∅	
∀	
----------------	O

Fig. 8.21 o-schema for information object '**rate-of**'

type/mark-up-rate	
vehicle-type	rate-%
car	1.4
truck	1.6
cycle	1.5

Fig. 8.22 Value set of the *type/mark-up-rate* item

items *vehicle/sale-price, vehicle/type, vehicle/cost-price* and *type/mark-up*.

The removal of labels from the object semantics and value constraints is equivalent to the programming practice of not using constants in programs unless absolutely necessary. Consider the clause group to implement the semantics of an item derived by applying the object **mark-up-B** to the items *vehicle/sale-price*, *vehicle/type* and *vehicle/cost-price*:

vehicle/sale-price(x, y) ← vehicle/type(x, 'car'),
    vehicle/cost-price(x, z), y = z × 1.4
vehicle/sale-price(x, y) ← vehicle/type(x, 'truck'),
    vehicle/cost-price(x, z), y = z × 1.6
vehicle/sale-price(x, y) ← vehicle/type(x, 'cycle'),
    vehicle/cost-price(x, z), y = z × 1.5   [1]

The value set associated with the *"type/mark-up-rate"* item has been distributed throughout group [1]. This value set is shown in Fig. 8.22. A clause group to implement the semantics of the item derived by applying the object **mark-up-C** to the items *vehicle/sale-price, vehicle/type, vehicle/cost-price* and *type/mark-up-rate* is:

vehicle/sale-price(x, y) ← vehicle/type(x, w), vehicle/cost-price(x, z),
    type/mark-up-rate(w, v), y = z × v   [2]

Unlike group [1], group [2] is insulated against changes in the mark-up rate structure of the different types of vehicle.

8.4.6 Reduction of sub-items

The sixth of the eight sub-tasks within the construction of the conceptual view task is to reduce sub-item relationships to sub-type relationships. Consider the derivation of the item *car-part/cost-price* in Fig. 8.23. The left hand version is unacceptable if the object operator **car-cost** is a sub-object of the operator **costs**. There is nothing inherently wrong with sub-objects. If the object structure can be simplified at the expense of complicating the data item structure then the resulting model is easier to maintain. In Fig. 8.23 the right hand version is unacceptable because an object operator has been applied to an information item to generate another information item. The object operator **car-costs** has been applied to the item *part/cost-price*. There is nothing inherently wrong with operators that generate sub-information items. If sub-information operators can be reduced to sub-data operators then the resulting model is easier to maintain. Consider another derivation of the item *car-part/cost-price* in Fig. 8.24. If more than one type of derivation is permitted then this may lead to unnecessary duplication and may complicate the structure of the conceptual model.

This sub-task transfers "sub-item operators" down to the data items where they become sub-type operators. This method is iterative and moves each "sub-item

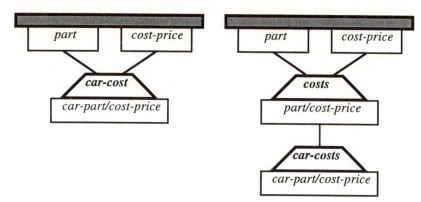

Fig. 8.23 Two derivations of the item *car-part/cost-price*

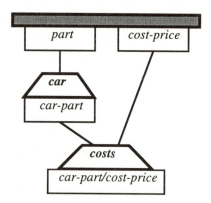

Fig. 8.24 Valid derivation of the item *car-part/cost-price*

operator" down towards the basis one step at a time. The left hand version in Fig. 8.25 establishes item *x* as a sub-item of item *d* using object *e*. The value set of item *x* is a sub-set of the value set of item *d*. Item *d* is derived using object *c*. The method constructs sub-items of items *a* and *b* to which object *c* may be applied to generate item *x*. The method introduces objects *f* and *j* that reduce the value sets of items *a* and *b* sufficiently so that object *c* can be applied to items *g* and *k* to generate item *x*. In the right hand version in Fig. 8.25 object *c* has moved one step further from the basis and the sub-item relationships have moved one step closer to the basis than the left hand version. This method is applied until all sub-item relationships are reduced to sub-type relationships. If items *a* and *b* are not data items then the method is applied again to reduce the sub-item relationships between items *g* and *a*, and between items *k* and *b*.

This sub-task removes all sub-item operators between information items and knowledge items from the conceptual model. Sub-item operators between information items and knowledge items may be represented as value constraints. In Fig. 8.25 item *x* is a sub-item of item *d* is a value constraint on item *x*. In

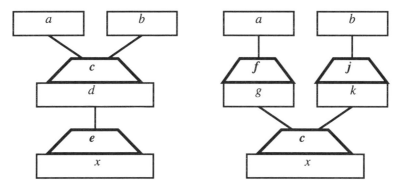

Fig. 8.25 Method for reducing sub-item relationships

Fig. 8.23 the item *car-part/cost-price* is a sub-item of the item *part/cost-price*. This fact is a value constraint on the item *car-part/cost-price*.

8.4.7 Mixed-type decomposition

The seventh of the eight sub-tasks within the construction of the conceptual view task is to decompose mixed type objects. The aim of this sub-task is to ensure that each object constructed is either a data object, or an information object or a knowledge object. An object is decomposed if its semantics contains more than one "type" of statement.

Mixed type decomposition is to a crude form of normalisation. In Sect. 8.5 it is shown that normalisation is an expensive process and should not necessarily be applied to the entire conceptual model. A component of the cost of normalising an object is the cost of determining whether that object is decomposable. Once it is known that an object is decomposable then it is comparatively inexpensive to decompose it. Determining whether an object is of mixed type is comparatively inexpensive.

An item, or object, is of *mixed type* if its semantics is a conjunction of two expressions of different type. An example of a mixed type object **mix** is shown in Fig. 8.26. The semantics of the object **mix** contains both implicit and explicit features. Considered by itself it is difficult to see *how* the **mix** object should be decomposed. But if the object **costs** had already been identified then the identification of the explicit part of **mix** is easier. It is difficult to see what is wrong with **mix** without knowing the items to which **mix** is to be applied on the conceptual diagram and the other objects associated with those items. The object **mix** is unacceptable.

Suppose that on the conceptual diagram the object **mix** is applied to the items *item/tax*, *item/type* and *cost/tax* and that the resulting item's semantics is implemented as the clause group:

$$\text{item/tax}(w, z) \leftarrow \text{item/type}(w, x), \text{type/cost}(x, y), \text{cost/tax}(y, z) \qquad [3]$$

	mix	
X^2	X^2	X^2
(w, v)	(w, x)	(y, z)
('x' costs 'y') → v = z		
∅		
∀	∀	∀
--		O
O	--	

Fig. 8.26   o-schema for mixed type object 'mix

	$tax\text{-}payable$		
X^2	X^2	X^2	X^2
(w, v)	(w, x)	(x, y)	(y, z)
→ v = z			
∅			
∀	∀	∀	∀
O	---		

Fig. 8.27   o-schema for knowledge object '$tax\text{-}payable$

This clause group represents the rule that "the tax payable on an item is determined by the cost of that item". The *mix* object should be discarded in favour of
the *tax-payable* object shown in Fig. 8.27.   In the conceptual diagram if the
tax-payable object is applied to the items *item/tax*, *item/type*, *type/cost* and
cost/tax then the semantics of the resulting item may also be implemented by
clause group [3] above.

The previous example illustrates that it is easy to *identify* an object of mixed
type, and that it may be difficult to *decompose* an object of mixed type unless the
object is considered in conjunction with both the items on the conceptual diagram
to which it is applied and any other objects that are associated with those items.

8.4.8 Information normalisation

The last of the eight sub-tasks within the construction of the conceptual view task
is to normalise the information objects.   The last sub-task in the previous
"construction of the basis" task is to normalise the data.   When the data and the
information have been normalised this leaves the knowledge to be normalised.
The normalisation of knowledge can be expensive. The normalisation of knowledge is considered during the system function step.   This ensures that the only
knowledge objects that are normalised are those required for the system. Although

the normalisation of knowledge is considered during the system function step, it is worth ensuring that each knowledge item is an association between all of its components in order to ensure that at least one candidate constraint includes all of the components.

Normalisation is considered in Chap. 6. The section of the requirements model that formed the starting point for the system analysis step contained annotations on the r-schemas to indicate their volatility. These annotations are passed to the o-schemas in the conceptual model. Volatile items and objects are considered as candidates for normalisation. The normalisation of information is not an expensive process. Information objects are annotated "to be normalised" whether they have been marked "volatile" or not. During this sub-task:

- normalise each information o-schema that is annotated "to be normalised" and annotate it "normalised", replace that o-schema in the object library with the normalised form, replace that object on the conceptual diagram with the normalised form and update the links from the requirements model to the conceptual model, and
- for each o-schema that is annotated "normalised", locate all o-schemas on items in the conceptual diagram to which that o-schema is applied and that are not annotated and annotate all of those o-schemas "to be normalised".

At the end of this sub-task the information objects in the conceptual model that implement the r-schemas in the requirements model that are annotated "to be normalised" have been normalised. During the normalisation process no structural changes take place to the requirements model.

8.5 c-coupling map

The fourth task in the system analysis step is the construction of the c-coupling map. The previous tasks in the system analysis step construct the conceptual view consisting of:

- the basis,
- the object library, and
- the conceptual diagram.

To complete the un-normalised conceptual model it remains to construct the:

- the c-coupling map represents the "coupling relationships", and
- the constraints.

This section describes the construction of the c-coupling map. Section 8.6 describes the construction of the constraints. Coupling relationships are discussed briefly in Sect. 8.2.

If the conceptual model is to support maintenance then it should include a mechanism for identifying those parts of that model that should be checked and possibly modified in response to a particular change in circumstance in the application. In the unified design methodology this mechanism is provided by establishing a "coupling relationship" between a pair of items in the conceptual model if modifying one of them could mean that the other has to be modified too [Filman, 1988]. A maintenance task is effected by first locating an item that needs to be modified in response to a particular change in circumstance in the application, second my modifying that item, and third by following the coupling relationships from that item to other items and so on.

Two items are *logically inconsistent* if there exists a permutation π and a non-trivial expression μ such that both:

$$(\forall x_1 x_2 ... x_n)[S_A(x_1,x_2,...,x_n) \rightarrow \mu(x_1,x_2,...,x_n)]$$
$$(\forall x_1 x_2 ... x_n)[S_B(x_1,x_2,...,x_n) \rightarrow \sim\mu(\pi(x_1,x_2,...,x_n))]$$

If a conceptual model contains two items that are logically inconsistent then that model is inconsistent. By following the coupling relationships in the c-coupling map during each maintenance task the introduction of logically inconsistent items can be prevented.

A "coupling relationship" joins two nodes in the c-coupling map if one node is marked with an item that if modified could, in general, require that the item on the other node should be checked for correctness so that the consistency of the conceptual model is preserved [Ginsberg & Williamson, 1993]. The *c-coupling map* is a vertex labelled graph. For each item in the conceptual view there is a vertex in the c-coupling map labelled with that item's name. If an item in the conceptual view has not been normalised then its node in the c-coupling map is shown in an area labelled "not normalised", and that node has no coupling relationships. For those items in the conceptual view that are normal an arc joins a pair of vertices in the c-coupling map if there is a coupling relationship between the items whose names are attached to those vertices. So an arc joins a pair of vertices if modification to one of the two items in general necessarily requires that the other item be checked for correctness so that the consistency of the conceptual model is preserved. Un-normalised items may have a large number of coupling relationships.

In Sect. 8.2 four kinds of coupling relationships are described. First, a "component relationship" is a coupling relationship between an item in a conceptual model and its component items in that model. Second, an "equivalence relationship" exists between two items if they are weakly equivalent. Third, a "sub-item relationship" exists between two items if one is a sub-item of the other. Fourth, a "duplicate relationship" exists between two items if their semantics expressions "overlap" in a sense that is described below. The coupling relationships in the c-coupling map are inherited by the functional and internal models.

The coupling relationships are implemented as "coupling links" in the physical model.

In the unified design methodology maintenance is directed by following the coupling relationships. The preservation of the maintainability of the design is concerned with the management of the coupling relationships. If all of the coupling relationships are known in a c-coupling map then the coupling relationships can form the basis for a procedure to direct the maintenance process. This procedure is:

- Suppose that in response to a change in circumstances an initial modification is made to a particular item in the conceptual model then flag that item "checked", and flag all other items that are joined by a coupling relationship to that item, "to be checked".
- For each item that is flagged "to be checked":
  if that item needs to be modified *then* modify it, flag that item "checked" and
  for all other items that are both:
  - not flagged "checked" and
  - have a coupling relationship with that item
  flag those items "to be checked".
  if that item does *not* need to be modified *then* flag that item "checked".

The efficiency of this procedure depends on the number of coupling relationships in the conceptual model. The efficiency of this procedure increases if the number of coupling relationships in the conceptual model are reduced. The reduction of the number of coupling relationships in the conceptual model is one goal in the construction of a "good" conceptual model

Four forms of coupling relationship are identified. Given object A:

$$A[\ E_A,\ F_A,\ G_A\ ]$$

with semantics:

$$E_A = \lambda Q_1 : X_1^{i_1} Q_2 : X_2^{i_2} ... Q_j : X_j^{i_j} \bullet \lambda y_1^1 ... y_{m_1}^1 ... y_{m_n}^n \bullet [S_{P_1}(y_1^1,...,y_{m_1}^1)$$
$$\wedge\ S_{P_2}(y_1^2,...,y_{m_2}^2)\ \wedge\ ....\ \wedge\ S_{P_n}(y_1^n,...,y_{m_n}^n)$$
$$\wedge\ J(y_1^1...y_{m_1}^1...y_{m_n}^n)]\bullet\bullet$$

A can be applied to the set of items $(I_1, I_2,..., I_j)$ to generate the item I:

$$I\ =\ A[\ E_A,\ F_A,\ G_A\ ](I_1, I_2,..., I_j)$$

with semantics:

$$S_I = \bullet \lambda y_1^1 ... y_{m_1}^1 ... y_{m_n}^n \bullet [S_{R_1}(y_1^1,...,y_{m_1}^1)$$
$$\wedge \ S_{R_2}(y_1^2,...,y_{m_2}^2) \wedge .... \wedge S_{R_n}(y_1^n,...,y_{m_n}^n) \wedge \ J(y_1^1...y_{m_1}^1...y_{m_n}^n)] \bullet$$

where:

for all $i = 1,..,n$ there exists k such that $1 \le k \le j$ and $R_i = I_k$.

If the semantics of item I should change then either the semantics of one of its components changes or the expression J changes. That is, if the semantics of item I should change then either the semantics of one of its components changes or the semantics of object A changes.

If the semantics of an item I that is not in the basis changes then this *may* mean that the semantics of one of its components has changed. Such an item's components may be in the basis. If the semantics of one of an item's components changes then this may mean that the item's semantics changes. So in general there should be a coupling relationship between each item I that is not in the basis and its components. There are three cases. First if I has more than one component then the coupling relationship between I and its components are *component links*. Second if I has only one component and A is the identity object then the coupling relationship between I and its single component is an *equivalence link*. Third if I has only one component and A is *not* the identity object then the coupling relationship between I and its single component is a *sub-item link*. In Sect. 8.4.6 sub-item links are reduced to *sub-type* links.

If the semantics of an item that is not in the basis changes then this may mean that the semantics of the object operator that generates that item has changed. If the semantics of the object that generates an item changes then this may mean that the item's semantics changes. So in general there should be a coupling relationship between an item $I = A(I_1, I_2,..., I_j)$ and the object A. This leads indirectly to links between two items if they have been constructed with the same object operator. There is a link between the items *part/cost-price* and *machine/cost-price* in Fig. 8.6.

An object A is decomposable into $A = \{O_1, O_2, ..,O_n\}$ if:

- O_i is not tautological for all i,
- $O = O_1 \otimes O_2 \otimes ... \otimes O_n$, where
- each composition is monotonic

If the semantics of a decomposable object A changes then this may mean that the semantics of at least one of the objects in its decomposition has changed. If the semantics of one of the objects in A's decomposition changes then this may mean that A's semantics changes. So in general there should be a coupling relationship between a decomposable object and the objects in its decomposition. Further any item constructed with a decomposable object A should be linked to any item constructed with an object in a decomposition of A. These links are *duplicate links*. If the conceptual model is normal there are no duplicate links in the c-coupling map.

Duplicate links are hard to detect. Suppose that objects *A* and *B* are decomposable as follows:

$$A \simeq_{w} E \otimes_{M} F$$
$$B \simeq_{w} E \otimes_{M} G$$

Then objects *A* and *B* should both be linked to object *E*. If the decompositions of *A* and *B* have not been identified then object *E* may not have been identified and the implicit link between objects *A* and *B* may not be identified.

The coupling relationships [Debenham, 1996a] identified above have one of the following forms:

- between nodes marked with equivalent items;
- between a node marked with an item that is a sub-item of the item marked on another node;
- between a node marked with an item and the nodes marked with that item's components;
- between a node marked with an item constructed by a decomposable object and nodes constructed with that objects decomposition;
- between a node marked with an item constructed by one object and nodes constructed with another object that is equivalent to the first object, and
- between a node marked with an item constructed by one object and nodes constructed with another object that is a sub-object of the first object.

In Sect. 8.4.6 sub-item relationships between non-data items are reduced to sub-type relationships between data items. So if:

- all equivalent items and objects have been removed by re-naming, and
- sub-item relationships between non-data items have been reduced to sub-type relationships between data items

then the following is a description of the coupling relationships identified:

- between a node marked with a data item that is a sub-type of the data item marked on another node, these are the *sub-type relationships*;
- between a node marked with an item and the nodes marked with that item's components, these are the *component relationships*;
- between two nodes constructed by the same object, these are *equivalence relationships*, and
- between a node marked with an item constructed by a decomposable object and nodes constructed with that objects decomposition, these are the *duplicate relationships*.

Further, if the objects employed to construct the conceptual model are normal then the coupling relationships identified are either sub-type relationships, component relationships or equivalence relationships. The sub-type relationships, component relationships and equivalence relationships cannot be removed from the conceptual model.

Four kinds of coupling relationship between two nodes in the c-coupling map have been examined. Each of these four kinds of coupling relationship indicates that the items at those nodes "have something in common". First, a *component relationship* joins two nodes that are marked respectively with an item and one of its component items. Component relationships are in a sense representations of the "grammatical structure" of the application. Second, an *equivalence relationship* joins two nodes that are marked with items or objects that are weakly equivalent. Third, a *sub-object relationship* joins two nodes if one is marked with an object that is a sub-object of the object marked on the other. Fourth, a *duplicate relationship* joins the node marked with the object C and the node marked with the non-tautological object E, and between the node marked with the object C and the node marked with the non-tautological object F if:

$$C \simeq_W E \otimes_M F$$

where this join is monotonic. These four kinds of relationship are examined in detail.

Section 6.2 describes the meaning of a "normal" set of items or objects. In an "ideal" conceptual model each "atomic" maintenance operation could be executed as a single modification to one part only of the model. This ideal is not attainable in the conceptual model described here. The component relationships at least must be followed during maintenance. This raises the question of which of the four kinds of coupling relationship identified above can be removed from the conceptual model. This question is considered during the detailed discussion of the four kinds of coupling relationship that follows.

A consistent conceptual model of a knowledge systems application is *completely normal* if that conceptual model has the property that a maintenance operation may be completely executed by tracing *only* the component relationships and the sub-item relationships in that model. The component relationships and the sub-item relationships are easy to identify. The equivalence relationships and duplicate relationships are not easy to identify. The equivalence relationships and the duplicate relationships may be removed from the conceptual model at a cost. Given a completely normal conceptual model and a particular maintenance task to be performed on it. Suppose that a particular item in the model has been identified that when modified it represents that given maintenance task. Then as the model is completely normal, the modification of that item, together with the modification of only those other items that are identified by following the component relationships and the sub-item relationships using the procedure stated above will ensure that the given maintenance task has been executed. A goal of this chapter is the construction of a conceptual model that can support the maintenance of volatile sections of that model.

8.5.1 Component relationships

The component relationships are representations of the grammatical structure of the application. They cannot be removed and play a necessary role guiding maintenance. The component relationships connect two nodes in a conceptual diagram and a c-coupling map that are marked respectively with an item and one of its component items. If an item named *item* in the conceptual model is defined by:

$$item = object(item_1, item_2, ..., item_n)$$

where $n > 1$ then there is a component relationship between the node marked with the item named *item* and the nodes marked with the items named $item_1$, $item_2, ..., item_n$.

Component relationships are coupling relationships. During the complete execution of a maintenance operation the component relationships *have* to be followed if the consistency of the conceptual model is to be preserved. Suppose that a retailing application is concerned with a department that sells spare parts. In this application each spare part is identified by a unique "spare-part-number". Suppose further that in the conceptual diagram there is a node marked with the "*part*" data item, a node marked with the "*part/cost-price*" information item and a node marked with the:

[part/cost-price, part/sale-price, mark-up]

knowledge item. This knowledge item represents a rule that may be used to calculate the selling price of spare parts on the basis of their cost price and a universal mark-up rate. Suppose that a new spare part is to be stocked. A new spare part number should be added, as a new label, to the value set of the "*part*" item. A tuple should be added to the value set of the "*part/cost-price*" item. The "*[part/cost-price, part/sale-price, mark-up]*" item should be modified if the rule represented by this knowledge item does not apply to this particular new spare part. So the syntactic structure of the model requires that this atomic modification is effected by checking, and possibly modifying, at least three items in the model. The component relationships define a path for the execution of this maintenance task. So the business of adding a new spare part to the system entails the addition of a label to the value set of a data item, the modification of the tuples in the value set of any information item in which that data item is a total component, the possible modification of the tuples in the value set of any information item in which that data item is not a total component, and the possible modification of other items in which that data item, or those information items, occur. The addition of a label to the value set of a data item may require further modifications

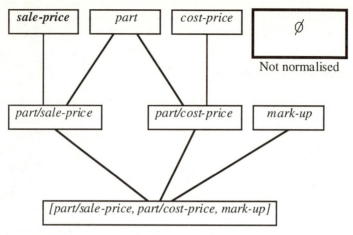

Fig. 8.28   c-coupling map

to other data, information and knowledge items if consistency is to be preserved. The component relationships referred to in this example are the only relationships in the c-coupling map shown in Fig. 8.28.

8.5.2 Equivalence relationships

The equivalence relationships link two nodes in a c-coupling map that are marked with items or objects that are weakly equivalent. The equivalence relationships can not be derived from the component relationships. Given an information item A, if $A \simeq_w B$ and if the components of B are weakly equivalent to, but not the same as, the components of A then there is no chain of component relationships joining A to B. An equivalence relationship indicates that a real thing has been represented as two weakly equivalent items. The rule that calculates the amount paid on an insurance policy could be represented both as a knowledge item *pay-out-rule* and as a knowledge item *dividend-rule*. If undetected, a duplication of this kind can cause havoc when a conceptual model is used to direct the mainte-nance process. This kind of duplication is discussed in Sect. 8.3.3 and in Sect. 8.4.3. Equivalence relationships are shown on the conceptual diagram and on the c-coupling map. An equivalence relationship between two nodes is shown as a double line linking those nodes.

8.5.3 Sub-item relationships

Section 3.3 defines the notion of one item being a "sub-item" of another item. Given two items A and B, where both items are expressed in terms of n variables, with semantics S_A and S_B respectively, if π is permutation such that:

$$(\forall x_1 x_2 ... x_n)[\ S_A(x_1, x_2, ..., x_n) \leftarrow S_B(\pi(x_1, x_2, ..., x_n))\ ]$$

then item *B* is a *sub-item* of item *A*. Sub-item relationships must be followed during maintenance. They are coupling relationships. In Sect. 8.4.6 it is shown that sub-item relationships can be reduced to sub-type relationships between data items. This reduction is not difficult to perform. It simplifies the structure of the c-coupling map. In Chap. 4 it is noted that the notion of a sub-item is a generalisation of the notion of a sub-type as used in traditional data analysis. Sub-types play a role in the unified methodology as described in Sect. 8.3.4. By convention, a sub-item relationship between two nodes is shown in the c-coupling map using an arrowed line linking those nodes. This arrow points *from* the node that is marked with the sub-item.

8.5.4 Duplicate relationships

Duplicate relationships link a node in a c-coupling map that are marked with the object *A* with a node marked with the non-tautological object *C*, and link the node marked with the object *A* with a node marked with the non-tautological object *D* if:

$$A \ \simeq_{\text{W}} \ D \otimes_{\text{M}} C$$

where this join is monotonic. If this weak equivalence holds then object *A* has objects *C* and *D* buried within it. Duplicate relationships must be followed during maintenance. They are coupling relationships. Duplicate relationships link two nodes in the c-coupling map that represent, to some degree, the same real thing. A duplicate relationship indicates that a real thing has been represented, at least in part, in more than one place. If there is duplicate relationship between two nodes marked with objects *A* and *B* then either *A* or *B* are non-normal. So if the objects in the conceptual model are all normal then there are no duplicate relationships in the c-coupling map. Duplicate relationships are shown on the c-coupling map by a line marked with a 'n' symbol.

If some of the items and objects in the conceptual model are not normal then a real thing may have been represented both as one item and be buried implicitly within another item. The normal forms for relations in traditional relational database technology attempt to identify if one relation is buried within another in this way. Traditional normalisation attempts to prevent duplications of this kind from occurring by breaking complex relations down into simpler forms.

The duplicate relationships are hard to identify. Having identified a duplicate relationship it is then comparatively easy to remove it. Further, the identification of the duplicate relationships is essential if maintenance tasks are to be performed completely and efficiently. The construction of a maintainable conceptual model is concerned first with the identification of the volatile sections of the model, second with the identification of the duplicate relationships in those sections and third with the removal of those duplicate relationships.

The normalisation of knowledge objects is more expensive than the normalisation of information and data objects. Consider the extent to which the whole

Data items	Information items	Knowledge items	Normalisation cost	Maintenance cost
Non-normal	Non-normal	Non-normal	Nil	Very high
Normal	Non-normal	Non-normal	Low	High
Normal	Normal	Non-normal	Medium	Medium
Normal	Normal	Normal	High	Low

Fig. 8.29   Indicative costs and benefits of normalisation

conceptual model should be normalised. Normalisation can be applied only to the volatile sections of the conceptual model. Indicative relative costs and benefits in normalising the three types of item are shown in Fig. 8.29. A "normalisation strategy" is given in Sect. 7.6.5.

Section 8.5 describes a procedure for directing maintenance based on the c-coupling map. There are four kinds of coupling relationship. That procedure pursues all coupling relationships from any knowledge, information or data item that requires modification. Even if the model has been normalised, and if the equivalence relationships have been removed, this procedure can be costly and can result in a substantial proportion of the conceptual model being checked for correctness during maintenance. Chapter 11 shows how "referential constraints" may be employed to prune this search considerably. Methods are given for the removal of the equivalence relationships and the duplicate relationships, and the reduction of sub-item relationships to sub-type relationships. Chapter 6 describes normalisation, which removes duplicate relationships from the c-coupling map. The component relationships and sub-type relationships cannot be removed from the c-coupling map.

The coupling relationships in the c-coupling map are inherited by the functional model, the internal model and the physical model. In the physical model some data items are associated with a set of real labels, some information items are associated with a set of real tuples and some knowledge items are associated with one or more clause groups. In Chap. 10 the coupling relationships in both the internal and the physical model are simplified once it is known which item's value sets are to be stored in the physical model.

Section 8.4.7 discussed the decomposition of items of mixed type. If this decomposition has been performed then all items are classified as data, information or knowledge. So if a fact is represented twice then the items that represent it are either classified in the same way (as data, information or knowledge) or they are classified differently. If duplications are caused by two items that are classified in the same way then they can be removed by normalisation, otherwise they may be prevented by a systematic analysis. Consider three different representations of the fact "the mark up rate for pencils is 35%". This fact could be represented by attaching the tuple ('pencil', '35%') to the value set of the information item "*part/mark-up-rate*". Then this fact is an information thing that is represented by an information item. The same fact could also be represented by including the clause:

part/sale-price('pencil', y) ← part/cost-price('pencil', z), y = z × 1.35

in the semantics of the knowledge item "*[part/sale-price, part/cost-price]*" and so the fact is a knowledge thing. The same fact could also be represented by attaching the label '35%' to the value set of the data item '*pencil-mark-up-rate*'. So the fact is a data thing that is represented by a data item. So one real fact can be correctly represented as either a data item, an information item or a knowledge item. If all three of these representations had found their way into the conceptual model and the mark-up rate for pencils should happen to change then all three representations should be modified to preserve consistency. Duplications caused by representations of facts that are classified differently can be avoided by applying an analysis method. If the fact in the above example had been represented as an information item then the design superstructure should prevent the explicit representation of "mark-up-rate" as data or knowledge.

8.6 Constraints

Items were introduced in Chap. 3 as a unified formalism for representing real things. The basic structure of items is independent of whether an item represents a data thing, an information thing or a knowledge thing. Items incorporate constraints. The way these item constraints are expressed is also independent of whether an item represents a data thing, an information thing or a knowledge thing. So items provide the basis for a unified approach to modelling knowledge-based systems, but they fail to provide an adequate basis for a complete analysis of maintenance. Chapter 4 introduced "objects" as operators on items. Objects provide an adequate basis for analysing maintenance. Complex items may be constructed by applying a sequence of object operators to simpler items. Both items and objects may be normalised. The *conceptual model* consists of a representation of each thing as an item. This representation consists of a basis of fundamental data items, an object library, a conceptual diagram and the c-coupling map. Both items and objects contain two classes of constraint. These two classes are the value constraints and the set constraints.

In the unified design methodology, constraints play two distinct roles:

• constraints are attached to the representation with the intention of preserving the integrity of that representation, and
• constraints are employed by the maintenance procedure with the intention of making that procedure more efficient.

Constraints that are attached to the representation with the intention of preserving the integrity of that representation are *pragmatic constraints*. Constraints that are employed by the maintenance procedure with the intention of making that procedure more efficient are *referential constraints*. Referential constraints are discussed in Chap. 11. Pragmatic constraints are discussed here.

Pragmatic constraints are constraints on the conceptual model. They are inherited by the internal model and by the physical model. Pragmatic constraints are of two distinct types:

- Constraints that are attached to each item and to each object in the conceptual model are the *individual constraints*:
  - the value constraints, and
  - the set constraints.
- Constraints that are attached to the conceptual model itself are the *model constraints*.

8.6.1 Individual constraints

Individual constraints are a part of each item and each object. They consist of:

- the value constraints, and
- the set constraints.

Chapter 3 contains examples of item constraints. Chapter 4 contains examples of object constraints. Those examples are all "static constraints". *Static constraints* are constraints on how something must be. In contrast to static constraints *dynamic constraints* are constraints on how something is permitted to change.

The static set constraints illustrated in Chaps. 3 and 4 are restricted to being cardinality constraints, universal constraints and candidate constraints. The permissible types of static constraint are determined by the chosen software platform. The types of static constraints illustrated in previous chapters are not representative of the constraints that are supported. Examples of other types of static item constraints include:

- the *entity type constraint* by which the labels in an item's value set are restricted to belong to a specific set of labels;
- the *lexical constraint* by which the character strings that makes up the labels in an item's value set are restricted, for example there may be a restriction on the number of characters that may occur in a label;
- the *tuple set constraint* by which the set of labels in an item's value set must be equal to, a subset of, or disjoint from, the set of labels in another item's value set;
- the *domain set constraint* by which the set of values in a nominated domain of the labels in an item's value set must be equal to, a subset of, or disjoint from, the set of values in a particular domain of the labels in another item's value set;

- the *domain cardinality constraint* by which the set of distinct values that may occur in a particular domain in the labels in an item's value set is restricted, for example the number of distinct values that may occur may be restricted;
- the *occurrence frequency constraint* by which for a particular domain in an item's value set if a value occurs in the labels of that domain then it must occur in that value set in a specified number of labels, and
- the *reflexive constraint*, *symmetric constraint* and *transitive constraint* on an item that hold if the value set is:

reflexive:	xRx	for all x
symmetric:	$xRy \rightarrow yRx$	for all x and y
transitive:	$xRy, yRz \rightarrow xRz$	for all x, y and z

likewise *irreflexive constraint*, *asymmetric constraint* and *intransitive constraint*.

Dynamic constraints are constraints on how something is permitted to change. "The mark-up rate may not change by more than 10% at a time" is an example of a dynamic constraint. No particular notation is adopted here for representing dynamic constraints. For example:

$$(\Delta \leq x\%)_A$$

could represent the constraint that "any value in the value set of item *A* cannot change by more than x%". Then the constraint in the above example could be:

$$(\Delta \leq 10\%)_{mark-up}$$

Objects may contain dynamic as well as static constraints.

8.6.2 Model constraints

Model constraints are constraints on the conceptual model. They are used in database technology. The rule "the selling price of parts is always greater than the cost price of parts" is an example of a chunk of knowledge that could be a constraint on the information in a database. The information in the database is constrained to be consistent with this particular chunk of knowledge. Such a constraint is a *knowledge model constraint*. They may be used for knowledge-based systems. For knowledge-based systems the inverse of this idea can be used. In knowledge-based systems a chunk of information can be used as a constraint on the knowledge in the conceptual model. Such a constraint is an *information model constraint*.

Consider the set of relations shown in Fig. 8.30. This set of relations shows possible sets of tuples that could form the value sets of items "*part/sale-price*", "*part/cost-price*" and "*part/mark-up*". These tuples are consistent with the knowledge represented in the knowledge item "*[part/sale-price, part/cost-price, part/mark-up]*" discussed in Chap. 3. An inference engine can be used to demon-

part/sale-price		part/cost-price		part/mark-up	
part-number	dollar-amount	part-number	dollar-amount	part-number	mark-up-factor
1234	1.44	1234	1.20	1234	1.2
2479	3.84	2479	2.56	2479	1.5
5312	0.90	5312	0.75	5312	1.2
2643	5.44	2643	3.40	2643	1.6

Fig. 8.30 A simple information model

strate automatically that these tuples are consistent with that knowledge item. An example of an information model constraint on the knowledge item *"[part/sale-price, part/cost-price, part/mark-up]"* is the requirement that this knowledge item must remain consistent with the particular information model shown in Fig. 8.30. This constraint could be implemented in the physical model as a constraint on three clause-groups that implement this item. Hand-coded, simple but non-trivial information models can provide powerful information model constraints. Information model constraints are simple, powerful and effective constraints on the knowledge in the conceptual model. They may be useful in applications where the knowledge is subject to a high rate of change and the information is comparatively stable.

Other types of model constraints include:

- the system must always be capable of performing a specified task, and
- the overall size of the system, measured in some suitable units, must be less than some specified bound.

8.7 Summary

- System analysis is the second step in the unified design methodology.
- The system analysis step takes the requirements model and constructs the conceptual model.
- The conceptual model consists of:
  - a conceptual view, and
  - a c-coupling map.
- The conceptual view consists of:
  - a basis,
  - an object library, and
  - a conceptual diagram.
- System analysis consists of four tasks:
  - construction of the basis,
  - construction of the conceptual view,
  - construction of c-coupling map, and
  - development of constraints.
- The c-coupling map contains:
  - equivalence relationships,
  - sub-item relationships,
  - component relationships, and
  - duplicate relationships.
- Equivalence relationships may be removed by renaming.
- Sub-item relationships may be reduced to sub-type relationships.
- The conceptual model may be normalised. This removes the duplicate relationships from the c-coupling map.
- Pragmatic constraints are attached to the representation with the intention of preserving the integrity of that representation.
- Referential constraints are a tool for increasing the efficiency of maintenance.
- The following is a taxonomy of constraints:
  - pragmatic constraints
    - individual constraints
      - value constraints
      - set constraints
    - model constraints
  - referential constraints

9 Function

9.1 Introduction

This chapter describes the third step in the unified design methodology. This step is "system function". The system function step uses the i-schema format for describing items, the o-schema format for describing objects, and the t-schema format for describing transactions. These formats are discussed in Sects. 5.2, 5.5 and 5.7 respectively. The first step in the unified design methodology is requirements specification discussed in Chap. 7. The second step in the unified design methodology is system analysis discussed in Chap. 8.

The system function step commences with the product of requirements specification and system analysis. The input to the system function step is a section of the requirements model and a corresponding section of the conceptual model. System function focuses on the functional requirements and derives a functional model that can support the required tasks and has, in some sense, the least complexity. In an incremental design each application of these two previous design steps generates new sections of the requirements model and corresponding sections of the conceptual model. The requirements model consists of a cascade decomposition of annotated r-schemas. These r-schemas are annotated as:

- to be processed in some future generation of the system;
- to be processed in this generation and implemented using a particular existing component;
- to be processed in this generation and to be implemented in a specified manner, that could include a knowledge systems component, or
- to be processed in this generation, to be implemented as a knowledge systems component that is to be normalised.

The conceptual model consists of:

- a conceptual view, and
- a c-coupling map.

Portions of the conceptual model may have been normalised and constraints may have been developed.

The system function step combines the *what* of the requirements model with the *how* of the conceptual model to produce a "functional model" [Yu & Mylopoulos, 1994]. The functional model supports the identified system transactions. The requirements model is expressed in terms of r-schemas and the conceptual model in terms of a combination of i-schemas and o-schemas. The requirements model is a representation of *what* the system should be able to do. The conceptual model is a representation of *how* the system does what it is required to do. The requirements model is linked to the conceptual model. The r-schemas in the requirements model are linked to the i-schemas in the conceptual model. These links enable the "what" and the "how" to be combined.

During the previous knowledge analysis step the conceptual model is constructed. The overall structure of the conceptual model is inherited by the functional model. The functional model describes how the working system behaves. A working system will require the contents of the value sets of at least some of the data items and at least some of the information items. If the contents of the value sets of at least some of the data and information items are available then the knowledge items can then be employed to deduce the value sets of the remaining data and information items. One by-product of the system function step is to give some items in the conceptual model pointers to value sets that enable the system to do all that it is required to do.

The system function step consists of the four tasks:

- analysis of transactions,
- construction of the functional view,
- construction of the f-coupling map, and
- refinement of the constraints.

The product of these four tasks is a section of the functional model. The functional model represents both the "what" and the "how" aspects of the system. The functional model is discussed in Sect. 9.2 The four tasks are described in Sects. 9.3–9.6. The first task is the analysis of the system transactions. This task represents the system query types and the system update types. The second task is the construction of the functional view. The functional view is derived from the conceptual view and from the system transactions. The functional view shows how the knowledge in the conceptual view may be used to perform the system transactions. The knowledge items in the functional view are functional and so they represent rules. The third task is the construction of the f-coupling map. The f-coupling map is derived from the c-coupling map in the conceptual model. The fourth task is the refinement of constraints. The constraints specified for the conceptual model are strengthened and refined for the functional model. In Sect. 9.7 the complexity of the system function step is analysed.

9.2 Functional model

The goal of the system function step is the construction of a "functional model" which is derived from the conceptual model and from the system transactions. The functional model has a similar structure to the conceptual model. The conceptual model has a "conceptual view", and the functional model has a "functional view". The conceptual model contains a c-coupling map, and the functional model contains an f-coupling map. One difference between the conceptual model and the functional model is that the knowledge items in the conceptual model represent knowledge and the knowledge items in the functional model represent rules [Debenham, 1997c].

The *functional model* consists of:

- a functional view, and
- an f-coupling map.

The *functional view* contains a collection of items that is capable of delivering the required functionality of the system. The functional view contains a "transaction library" that describes of what the system is required to do. The *f-coupling map* is a vertex labelled graph. For each item in the functional view there is a vertex in the f-coupling map labelled with that item's name. If an item in the functional view has not been normalised then its node in the f-coupling map is shown in an area labelled "not normalised". For those items in the functional view that are normal, an arc joins a pair of vertices in the f-coupling map if there is a coupling relationship between the items whose names are attached to those vertices. The set of items in the functional view may *either* be defined explicitly as items using the λ-calculus or the i-schema notation *or* implicitly by representing each item as the result of the application of a sequence of object operators to a fundamental set of data items called the "basis". An *explicit functional model* is a functional model in which the items in the functional view are defined explicitly using either the λ-calculus notation or the i-schema notation to represent each item. An *implicit functional model* is a functional model in which the items in the functional view are defined implicitly as a sequence of object operators applied to a fundamental set of items called the "basis".

During the system function step the normalisation process is applied for the last time. This final application of normalisation is described in Sect. 9.4.4. Once normalisation has been finally applied the object structure has little value. Items are convenient program specifications. The implicit functional model is used until normalisation is complete. After normalisation is complete the explicit functional model is used. The way in which the o-schemas in the functional view are applied to the i-schemas in the basis is represented in a "functional diagram". In an implicit functional model the functional view consists of:

- a basis;
- an object library;
- a functional diagram;
- a flow diagram, and
- a transaction library.

The basis, object library and functional diagram are a subset of respectively the basis, the object library and the functional diagram in the conceptual model. The flow diagram is described in Sect. 9.4.3 [Aamodt, 1990] and the transaction library in Sect. 9.3.

9.3 Analysis of transactions

The analysis of transactions is the first task in the system function step. The inputs to the system function step are the requirements model and the conceptual model as developed for those prime r-schemas that have been processed so far in an incremental design, as well as the functional model developed during previous iterations if any. All transactions should be identified on the requirements model. The names of the transactions are written in non-italicised script between single quotation marks.

An implemented knowledge-based system receives requests delivers responses. A "transaction" is initiated externally to the system, is activated by the delivery of a transaction request to the system, causes the system to do something and may involve the delivery of a response to a person, agent or system external to the given system [Bonarini & Maniezzo, 1991]. This whole exercise of request, activity and response is a *transaction*. A transaction request may be to retrieve something or a transaction request may be to modify some part of the system.

Section 7.3 describes item behaviour. A system transaction is a behaviour of the single item that represents the whole system. So transactions inherit the three aspects of behaviour. The three aspects of behaviour are illustrated in Fig. 9.1. A transaction response could be the "answer" to a query such as "find the salary of employee called X". The transaction response contains a flag 'OK' that is returned as 'true' if the transaction is completed successfully and 'false' if the transaction is completed unsuccessfully. In response to the request "find the salary of employee called X" if the salary of the employee called X is returned in the response then the flag 'OK' is set to 'true'. If no employee called X could be found then the flag 'OK' is set to 'false'.

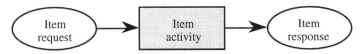

Fig. 9.1 Aspects of behaviour

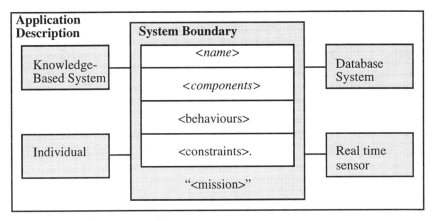

Fig. 9.2 Schema for a context diagram

The implemented system interacts with the players shown in the context diagram. The context diagram is discussed in Sect. 7.5.1. These interactions are all transactions. These players may include individuals, other knowledge-based systems, knowledge bases, conventional database systems [Adams, 1992] and real time sensors. The term "knowledge bases" is used here in a different sense to "knowledge-based systems". A *knowledge base* is a representation and implementation of knowledge alone. A knowledge base does not posses the supporting data and information component. The general wisdom contained in the Taxation Act, in so far as it determines how much an individual should pay in tax, could be a represented and implemented as a knowledge base. The schema for a context diagram showing four different types of players is shown in Fig. 9.2. Figure 9.2 shows that that system interacts with individuals, knowledge-based systems, real time sensors and databases.

Consider a request by a system for a player in the context diagram to provide some information. The significance of such a request is determined by the location of the value set of the item to which that information belongs. If the value set of the *part/cost-price* item is stored internally within the system then a request to a player to provide the cost of a part is a system update. If the value set of the *part/cost-price* item is stored externally in that player's files then a request to that individual to provide the cost of a part is a reference to the value set of the *part/cost-price* item. An update is a modification to the value set of a real item, no matter where that value set is stored.

The analysis of the transactions is the first task in the system function step. The system function step begins with both the requirements model, that focuses on *what* the system is required to do, and the conceptual model, that focuses on *how* the system can do what the system is required to do [Despres & Rosenthal-Sabroux, 1992]. The links from the requirements model to the conceptual model identify those parts of the conceptual model that support the various behaviours described in the requirements model.

There are two different types of transaction. Some transactions have the property that when their response has been fully delivered, the system to which that transaction was presented is unchanged. The transaction that requests the salary of employee called X may not change the system in any way. If a transaction leaves the system to which it is presented unchanged then it is an *examination*. Some transactions may change the system to which they are presented. If a transaction changes the system to which it is applied then it is an *alteration*. The transaction "change the salary of Managers to $80 000 per annum" may modify the system to which it is presented. This transaction could result in a modification to the value set of the *job/sal* item. The transaction "change the salary of Managers to $80 000 per annum" is an alteration. The transaction "the way in which department managers is determined is...." may cause substantial change to the system. This transaction may cause substantial changes to the conceptual model. So some alterations can be readily accommodated within an existing conceptual model and some alterations require substantial modification to the conceptual model. If an examination results in an activity that refers to:

- existing system constraints;
- a particular item's semantics or constraints, or
- a particular item's value set

then that examination is a *query*. If an examination is not a query then it is an *interrogation*. An interrogation may result in an activity that changes the design.

There are two different types of query. A *value query* is an examination that results in an activity that refers to a particular item's value set. A value query may be serviced solely from the values in the value set of an item. A *model query* is a query that is not a value query. A model query can not be answered on the basis of the contents of the value set of a particular item.

The form of permissible model queries is determined by the software chosen to implement the knowledge-based system. So model queries are not considered here. Model queries are part of any knowledge-based system. The description of a model query includes the description of that model query's behaviour. The framework presented in Sect. 7.3 is used to describe model query behaviour.

If an alteration results in an activity that:

- adds a new system constraint;
- modifies a particular item's semantics or constraints, or
- modifies a particular item's value set

then that alteration is an *update*. If an alteration is not an update then it is a *revision*. A revision may result in substantial changes to the design. There are two different types of update. A *value update* is an update that results in an activity that modifies a particular item's value set. A value update may be serviced solely by modifying the values in the value set of an item. A *model update* is an update that is not a value update. A model update does not necessarily change the contents of the value set of any item.

During the analysis of transactions task each transaction is represented and then linked to a set of items in the conceptual model that can effect that transaction. The items in the conceptual model to which transactions are linked are also in the functional model. There are two sub-tasks that are performed during the analysis of transactions task. These two sub-tasks are performed for each transaction. These sub-tasks are:

- construct a t-schema, and
- link that t-schema to a set of items in the conceptual model.

The link between each t-schema and a set of items in the conceptual model is expressed as a logic program. When that logic program is executed it implements the transaction described by the t-schema. When these two sub-tasks have been completed for each transaction the set of t-schemas and the corresponding program links constitutes the *transaction library*.

9.3.1 t-schema construction

Section 7.3 gives a framework for describing item behaviour. This framework is applied to the description of item behaviour during the requirements specification step. During requirements specification this framework is not rigorously applied. Only those aspects of behaviour that are considered to be important are recorded.

All non-trivial transactions cause something to happen. Not all transactions will change the system to which they are applied. The five perspectives described in Sect. 7.3, namely "what", "why", "who", "when" and "where", are used to describe the three aspects of a transaction. These three aspects are:

- the presentation of the transaction request;
- the activity caused by the presentation of the transaction request, and
- the delivery of the transaction response.

As with the description of item behaviour during requirements specification, only those features of a transaction's behaviour are included that appear to be important. It may be decided to specify that a certain transaction should only be accepted from a particular individual, or that a transaction will be presented to the system at a particular location and the value of that transaction should be delivered to another location. It may be decided to specify that the entire value set of an item should be replaced with the contents of the part/cost-price relation in the "Inventory

Database". If a transaction's behaviour is to add, delete, or replace a tuple, or set of tuples, with another tuple or set of tuples then the description of that transaction's behaviour includes a pointer to where those tuples can be found. Transaction behaviour is described using t-schemas. t-schemas are described in Sect. 5.7.

A transaction is presented for a reason. The *transaction trigger* is the event that takes place in the application that creates the reason for presenting the transaction. The cost price of a real spare part might change, this change could trigger a transaction. The system might request the current date. The system has triggered this transaction.

The t-schema construction sub-task constructs a t-schema for each transaction shown in the requirements model. The general format for a t-schema is shown in Fig. 9.3. The t-schema "name" is the name of the transaction as shown in the requirements model. The t-schema specification is the description in natural language of what the transaction is to achieve. The *request player* is the name of the person, agent or system that initiates the transaction request. There may be more than one "request player". The *system* is the name of the system that

name		
specification		
request player	*system*	response player
request name	sys_req	
	sys_resp	response name
instruction		

Fig. 9.3 t-schema format

find_sale-price		
find the sale price for a given part		
Sales Clerk	*price system*	Sales Clerk
part number	pt_no	
	(s_pri, ok)	(sale price, ok)
find_sale-price(pt_no, s_pri, ok)		

Fig. 9.4 Sample t-schema

update_cost-prices			
update the cost prices for each spare part			
Accounts Clerk	*system*	Accounts Clerk	manager
cost file	cost_f		
	date, ok	ok	'update at' date ok
up_cost(cost_f, date, ok)			

Fig. 9.5 Sample t-schema

receives the request, that performs the resulting activity and that delivers the response. The *response player* is the name of the person, agent or system that receives the response from the system. There may be more than one "response player". The *request names* are the names that the request player gives to any variables or constants in a request. The "sys_req" shown in Fig. 9.3 is the corresponding name that the system gives to any variables or constants in a request. The "sys_resp" shown in Fig. 9.3 is the name that the system gives to any variables or constants in the response. The *response names* are the names that the response player gives to any variables or constants in the response. The *instruction* is the name of the procedure, together with appropriate variable and constant arguments, that performs the transaction. A sample t-schema is given in Fig. 9.4. A more complex t-schema is shown in Fig. 9.5.

9.3.2 Transaction linkage

A transaction causes an activity. The transaction linkage construction sub-task is concerned with the construction of a program that implements that activity to achieve the goal of the transaction. The conceptual model may contain an item *part/sale-price* whose value set contains the sale price for each part. Suppose that there is a transaction specified in the requirements model 'find_sale-price' that is to find the sale price for any given part. The t-schema for this transaction could be as shown in Fig. 9.4. The instruction line of that t-schema is:

find_sale-price(pt_no, s_pri, ok)

the program associated with this instruction could be:

find_sale-price(pt_no, s_pri, ok) ←
    FIND(pt_no, s_pri)IN(*part/sale-price*)RES(ok)

The sub-task to link each t-schema to a set of items in the conceptual model is performed for each t-schema by:

- locating the t-schema's behaviour in the requirements model;
- using the requirements model to identify a set of items that can support the t-schema's behaviour, and
- constructing a program that performs the t-schema's behaviour with reference to the t-schema's instruction and the identified items.

The choice of programming language in which the program is constructed is not important. Logic programming is used here. Logic programming is discussed in Chap. 1.

9.4 Functional view

The second task in the system function step is to construct the functional view which is a subset of the conceptual view that supports the behaviours required of the system. The behaviours the system is required to be able to perform are identified during requirements specification and are represented as r-schema behaviours in the requirements model. These r-schemas are linked to items in the conceptual view. These r-schemas are associated with t-schemas constructed during the previous task.

The construction of the functional view task is concerned with extracting those items from the conceptual view that can support the transactions. There are two aspects to this task. First, to perform this task it is necessary to know the *input items*, which are a set of items that can represent naturally the information flowing into the system. Second, there may be more than one functional view, this aspect is considered in Sect. 9.7.

When the construction of the functional view task commences the following are available:

- the functional model constructed during previous iterations if any;
- the requirements model (constructed during this iteration and during previous iterations);
- the conceptual model (constructed during this iteration and during previous iterations), and
- the transaction library (constructed during the previous analysis of transactions task).

The transactions in the transaction library are linked to a set of one or more items in the conceptual model. The product of the construction of the functional view task is:

- a basis,
- an object library,
- a functional diagram,
- a flow diagram, and
- a transaction library.

as introduced in Sect. 9.2.

The links from the r-schemas in the requirements model to sets of items in the conceptual model identify sufficient items in the conceptual model to perform the behaviours identified during requirements specification. The items and objects selected in this way appear in the functional model. A functional model follows the paths of deduction that are identified during requirements specification. This selection is a "natural" one in that it should follow the way in which the behaviours are described in the requirements model. The functional model may be

mark-up-1		
X^2	X^2	X^1
(x, v)	(x, y)	(z)
$\rightarrow$ v = z × y		
$\rightarrow$ v > y		
$\forall$	$\forall$	
---		O
O	---	
-------------------	O	-------------------

Fig. 9.6 o-schema for knowledge object '*mark-up-1*'

redundant. Requirements specification determines the structure of the knowledge represented in the conceptual model. Requirements specification is task-oriented, which may mean that a subset of that knowledge could support the transactions, and may be, in some sense, a "better" subset.

Two operations turn a conceptual view to which representations of the transactions have been added into a functional view. First decide which items are going to be of use. Second decide which of the possible functional flows within those items are required to service the transactions. Consider the object *mark-up-1* shown in Fig. 9.6. This object can be used to generate a number of different items. Suppose that this object is applied to the items *part/selling-price*, *part/cost-price* and *mark-up* to obtain the knowledge item *[part/selling-price, part/cost-price, mark-up]*. This knowledge item can be used to perform a number of different operations. It can be used to deduce the selling price of parts from their cost price and from the mark-up rate. So to decide whether the object *mark-up-1* in the conceptual view is going to be in the functional view, decide *whether* it generates an item that may be used to support a transaction and if so *how* that item supports that transaction.

The construction of the functional view task consists of the following subtasks:

- identification of transaction items,
- identification of supporting input items,
- selection of intermediate items, and
- knowledge normalisation.

These sub-tasks together construct the functional view task. Each of them is now described in turn.

9.4.1 Identification of transaction items

The previous task in the system function step constructs the transaction library. The transaction library contains a t-schema for each transaction. Each t-schema contains a program that can perform a transaction by employing knowledge in the conceptual model. The identification of transaction items sub-task is concerned with the identification of those items in the conceptual model that are used by these programs to perform the transactions. These items are *transaction items*. This sub-task is not difficult to perform. This sub-task identifies the items in the conceptual model that are included in the functional model.

9.4.2 Identification of input items

During requirements specification the input items are identified. During system analysis the input items in the requirements model are represented in the conceptual model. During the previous sub-task the transaction items are identified. The "identification of supporting input items" sub-task identifies sufficient input items in the conceptual model to enable the knowledge in the conceptual model to support the transactions in the transaction library.

There may be some flexibility in the choice of supporting input items. This flexibility is considered in detail in Sect. 9.7, where the complexity of the system function problem is considered and algorithms for deriving a set of supporting input items are given. As far as the present discussion is concerned it is assumed that a set of supporting input items can be identified informally. The set of input items identified during this sub-task only has to be "sufficient". It doesn't matter if too many input items are identified during this sub-task.

9.4.3 Intermediate item selection

The previous two sub-tasks in the construction of the functional view task identify the transaction items and identify a sufficient set of supporting input items in the conceptual model. To complete the functional view items are selected from the conceptual model that enable the transaction items to be derived from the input items. The comments made in the previous section concerning the complexity of the previous sub-task apply equally to this sub-task. The selection of these items is guided by the structure of the requirements model. The structure of the requirements model represents the way in which the transactions should be performed. This means that the functional model shares this representation of the way in which the transactions should be performed. Having selected sufficient items from the conceptual model to enable the transaction items to be derived from the input items, a particular functional flow is identified within each knowledge item selected.

The conceptual diagram provides a summary of the structure of the conceptual view. The functional diagram provides a summary of the structure of the func-

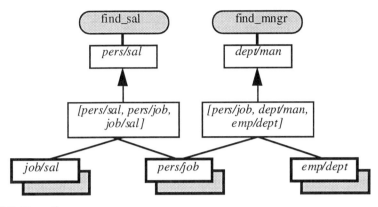

Fig. 9.7 Flow diagram

tional view. The *functional diagram* is the same as the conceptual diagram with the exception that only the selected items are shown. In addition to the functional diagram there is a "flow diagram". The *flow diagram* shows:

- the input items that are shown as "relief" nodes;
- the selected items that are shown using a functional "arrow" notation; and
- the t-schema for each transaction, which are shown as shaded, oval nodes and are linked to their respective transaction items

A flow diagram is shown in Fig. 9.7. A functional diagram for the same example is shown in Fig. 9.8. That flow diagram shows the particular functional flows within each knowledge item that have been chosen to perform the transactions. The flow diagram represents rules. The functional diagram represents knowledge.

9.4.4 Knowledge normalisation

The last of the four sub-tasks within the construction of the functional view task is to normalise the knowledge items selected during the previous intermediate item selection sub-task. The final sub-task in the construction of the basis task is to normalise the data. The final sub-task during the construction of the conceptual view task is to normalise the information. When the data and the information have been normalised this leaves the knowledge to be normalised. The normalisation of knowledge can be expensive. It is noted in Chap. 8 that the normalisation of knowledge need not be considered until the system function step. There is no *requirement* for the normalisation of knowledge to be deferred until the system function step. If the knowledge has not been normalised by this step then this is when normalisation is considered.

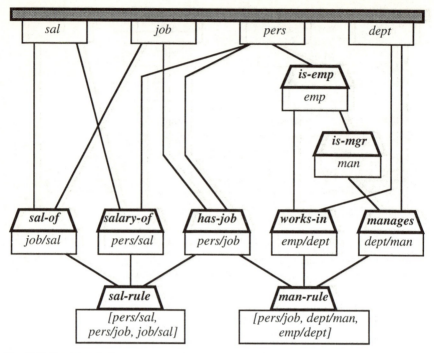

Fig. 9.8 Functional diagram

Normalisation is described in detail in Chap. 6. The requirements model contains annotations on its r-schemas to indicate whether or not they, together with their component r-schemas, should be normalised. These annotations are passed to the i-schemas and the o-schemas in the conceptual model. Those annotations are passed in turn to the i-schemas and the o-schemas in the functional model. The normalisation of data and information is typically not expensive.

The knowledge normalisation sub-task is:

- to normalise each knowledge o-schema that is annotated "to be normalised", replace that o-schema in the object library with the normalised form, annotate it "normalised", replace that object on the functional diagram with the normalised form and update the links from the requirements model to the conceptual model and to the functional model;
- for each o-schema that is annotated "normalised", locate all o-schemas on items in the functional diagram to which that o-schema is applied and that are not annotated and annotate all of those o-schemas "to be normalised".

At the end of this sub-task the knowledge objects in the functional model that are annotated "to be normalised" are normalised. During the knowledge normalisation sub-task no structural changes take place in the requirements model.

9.5 f-coupling map

Both the conceptual model and the functional model have a "coupling map". A *coupling relationship* exists between two items if a modification to one of these items *could*, in general, require that the other item should be checked for correctness, and possibly modified, if the consistency of the conceptual model is to be preserved. As for the c-coupling map, the *f-coupling map* is a vertex labelled graph. For each item in the functional view there is a vertex in the f-coupling map labelled with that item's name. If an item in the functional view has not been normalised then its node in the f-coupling map is shown in an area labelled "not normalised". For those items in the functional view that are normal, an arc joins a pair of vertices in the f-coupling map if there is a coupling relationship between the items whose names are attached to those vertices.

The main difference between the c-coupling map and the f-coupling map is that the latter should be simpler than the former. It should be simpler for two reasons. First, there are fewer items in the functional model than in the conceptual model. Second, the knowledge items in the functional model represent rules, and the knowledge items in the conceptual model represent knowledge.

For the example considered in the previous section all of the items are normal. For that example the structure of the f-coupling map is derived from the functional diagram that is shown in Fig. 9.8. The f-coupling map for that example is shown in Fig. 9.9.

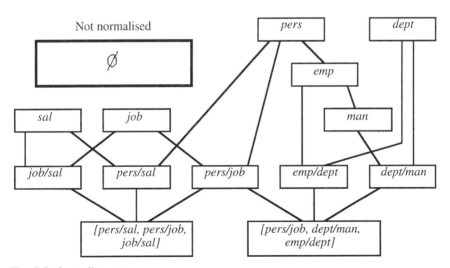

Fig. 9.9 f-coupling map

9.6 Constraints

Section 8.6.1 discusses individual constraints. Individual constraints are the value constraints and the set constraints within each item and object. Individual constraints are part of the conceptual model. When constructing the functional model review the extent to which further constraints should be introduced to protect the functional aspects of the system. Section 8.6.2 discusses model constraints. Information model constraints and knowledge model constraints are part of the functional model.

During the system function step the input items are identified. The contents of the value sets of the input items in a sense "drives" the whole system. The value sets of the input items may change with each update transaction. The integrity of the contents of the value sets of the input items is vital to the correct operation of the system. So a set of *input item constraints* is designed whose job is to preserve the integrity of the value sets of the input items. The input item constraints ensure that the value sets of any information items derived using the knowledge in the functional view are correct. An input item constraint may take the form of a knowledge model constraint.

During the system function step those knowledge items are selected from the conceptual model that are required to support the operation of the system. The integrity of this selected knowledge is vital for the correct operation of the system. The integrity of this selected knowledge is protected with *system constraints* whose job is to preserve the integrity of that knowledge. A set of system constraints can take the form of an information model constraint.

During the system function step revision operations are considered. Revision operations in general entail modifications to the requirements, conceptual and functional models. There is a variety of possible revision operations so it is not possible to prescribe how they should be constrained. *Maintenance constraints* are be introduced whose job is to preserve the integrity of the conceptual model as a result of the execution of specific types of revision operation. Maintenance constraints are designed by considering what should remain unchanged when a revision operation has been completed. The consideration of what should remain unchanged is called focussing on the invariants of the operation. Suppose that in a retail example spare parts are marked up using some formula on their cost price to obtain their selling price. A maintenance constraint is a statement that should always be satisfied no matter how this calculation is performed. The constraint that the selling price should never be more than five times the cost price could be included.

The refinement of constraints task consists of:
- the design of constraints for the set of input items, these constraints may be knowledge model constraints;
- the design of constraints for the knowledge items on the flow diagram, these constraints may be information model constraints, and
- the design of any other system constraints.

The constraints designed during this task, and the refinement of constraints task executed during the following system layout step, should together constitute a powerful mechanism for protecting the overall integrity of the system.

9.7 System function problem

Suppose that the input items and the transaction items have been identified in the conceptual diagram. The problem of constructing the flow diagram can be decomposed as:

- the problem of selecting a set of items in the conceptual diagram, and
- for each item selected, the problem of identifying a particular "functional flow" (as defined by the candidate constraints)

so that the selected items, and identified functional flows, support the system transactions on the input items. Such a selection of items is a "selection". The system function problem is "to choose the selection of least complexity". A flow diagram is a solution to the system function problem. The complexity of the system function problem is investigated. Complexity measures for selections are described. Algorithms that generate a reasonably good solution to the system function problem are given.

If a set of knowledge items enables the value sets of a set of data and information items X to be deduced from the value sets of a set of data and information items Y then that set of knowledge items is said to *support* X on Y. A *selection* is a set of knowledge items that supports the transaction items on the input items. A selection enables the value sets of the query items to be deduced from the value sets of the input items and enables the updates to be effected. A *circuit* is a sequence of items $\{ A^1 ,..., A^{n+1} \}$ where, for each pair (A^i , A^{i+1}) for $i = 1,...,n$, there is an item with a candidate constraint that has A^i as the head of that candidate constraint and has A^{i+1} in the body of that candidate constraint, $A^1 = A^{n+1}$, and $n > 1$. The flow diagram does not contain a circuit because the represented knowledge contains a specific "direction" determined by the transactions.

The *complexity of a selection* is the sum of the complexities of the items in that selection. Measures of the complexity of items are described later. For the time being it is assumed that an item cannot have negative complexity. This additive definition of complexity of items in a selection is reasonable. It is reasonable because any least complex selection contains at most one item with any specified item as its head component. Head components are defined by the candidate constraints. The *system function problem* is to find the selection of least complexity. In Sect. 9.7.1 this problem is shown to be "NP-complete". The system function problem remains "NP-complete" even if the functional flows in the conceptual diagram do not contain a circuit.

A solution to the system function problem is a selection of least complexity. This solution is represented as the *flow diagram*. This flow diagram shows each item in that selection and the particular flow that each item is required to support. The transaction items are shown in the flow diagram as oval nodes labelled with the transaction name. An example of a flow diagram is shown in Fig. 9.7.

The complexity of the system analysis step tends to vary as the number of items in the system. The complexities of the system function step and the system layout step increase exponentially with the size of the problem. In the small worked example given in Chap. 12, the system function and the system layout steps appear comparatively trivial. These steps are *not* trivial for larger problems. For small problems with ten or so knowledge items, finding an optimal manual solution can be unfeasible. The worked example considered in Chap. 12 contains six knowledge items.

9.7.1 Problem complexity

Complexity measures are intended to given meaning to the statement that "one functional model is a better solution to the system function problem than another". The "system function problem" is the problem of selecting the "best" flow diagram. The theoretical complexity of this problem is investigated in this section. Two algorithms are described that give reasonably good solutions to the system function problem in polynomial time.

The problem of selecting the "least complex" sub-set of the conceptual model to perform the tasks specified on the requirements model may not appear intuitively to be complex. The conceptual model may contain sufficient wisdom to enable a given task to be performed in a number of different ways. So one conceptual model can give rise to a large number of functional models all of which satisfy the system requirements. The system function problem is, in theory, complex. The task oriented manner in which the application description is constructed tends to lead to a "reasonably good" functional model.

This section contains algorithms and techniques that give rise to extensive calculations. In practice these calculations are not performed by hand.

The system function problem is NP-complete. The demonstration of this result is principally of theoretical interest. The proof demonstrates that the system function problem remains NP-complete if this problem is restricted to circuitless sets of items with non-recursive semantics.

Theorem
The system function problem is NP-complete.

Proof
The proof is by reduction to the "Optimum solution to AND/OR graphs" problem, [Sahni, 1974].

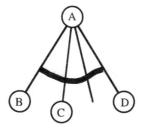

Fig. 9.10 AND construct

An AND/OR graph can be transformed into a set of items so that the problem of finding the optimum solution to the AND/OR graph is transformed into a restriction of the system function problem.

Given an AND/OR graph, proceed as follows:

Step 1.
Each AND construct, with n arcs, is replaced by an item with n components. The AND construct shown in Fig. 9.10 becomes an item *[A, B, C,..., D]* with set constraint:

Can(A, {B, C, .., D})

and the complexity of this item is the sum of the weights of the arcs flowing from the AND node "A".

Step 2.
Each OR constructs, with n arcs, is replaced with n items. The OR construct shown in Fig. 9.11 becomes n items *[A, B]*, *[A, C]*,.., *[A, D]* with set constraints:

Can(A, {B})
Can(A, {C})
. . . .
Can(A, {D})

and the complexities of these n items are the weights of the corresponding arcs flowing from the OR node "A".

The semantics of the individual items constructed in Step 1 and Step 2 are required to functionally determine the component A in terms of the other components. Subject to this requirement the semantics can have any form. The set of items constructed by Step 1 and Step 2 does not contain a circuit.

The (unique) item that is not in the body of a candidate constraint in any other item is the (single) query item. The set of items that are not the subject of a candidate constraint are the set of input items. So an optimal solution to the given AND/OR graph transforms to a solution of the system function problem for this set of items. ❏

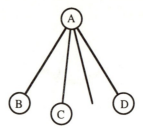

Fig. 9.11 OR construct

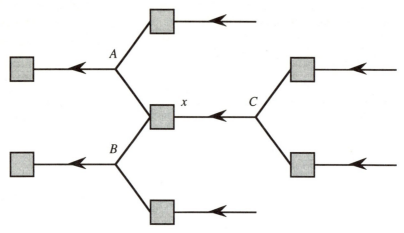

Fig. 9.12 Symptoms of a problem requiring "look ahead"

This proof shows that the system function problem remains NP-complete for circuitless sets of items with arbitrarily simple semantics. The difficulty with the system function problem is that in a structure of the kind shown in Fig. 9.12 if *C* is chosen to support *A* then it can also be used to support *B* at no extra cost. These are classic symptoms of a problem that requires "look ahead" and admits only an exponential solution.

A component that is the head of a candidate constraint in one item and is also in the body of candidate constraints in two or more other items is a *critical item*. The nodes corresponding to critical items, that are the "foot" of more that one tree, are *critical nodes*. Node x, in Fig. 9.12, is a critical node.

9.7.2 Complexity measures

Measures of complexity of items are measures of the complexity of the *representation* of items. They are not intended to be "functional measures of complexity". *Functional measures of complexity* are measures of the complexity in *using* an item. So notions such as the relative frequency of presentation of transactions are not considered here. The complexity measures are used to choose the least complex functional representation. This choice should remain a "good" choice as demands on the system change. The complexity measures noted below are crude. The objective here is to define simple, meaningful measures that are effective in identifying the least complex items.

Complexity measures are given for both the explicit and the implicit functional model. For the explicit functional model three complexity measures for the items are:

- The *trivial measure*, by which the complexity of any item is unity.
- The *domain measure*, by which the complexity of any item is its number of components.
- The *relation measure*, by which the complexity of any item is an estimate of the time to retrieve a tuple from that item's value set if it is stored as a relation.

These measures make no attempt to measure the complexity of an items semantics.

Complexity measures are given for the implicit functional model. Two complexity measures are given for the basis data items, and one complexity measure is given for non-basis items. The two complexity measures for the basis data items are the trivial measure and the relation measure as defined above. The complexity measure for a non-basis item is the sum of the complexities of that item's components.

9.7.3 Sub-optimal item selection

Section 9.7.1 shows that the system function problem is NP-complete. The solution to the system function problem is the selection with least complexity. In Sect. 9.7 the complexity of a selection is defined to be the sum of the complexities of the items in that selection. So each item in a selection contributes its own complexity to this sum once no matter how many times it is used as a component by the other items in that selection.

An alternative notion of complexity is introduced. Consider the *combined diagram* consisting of the dependency diagrams of all rules that can be derived from the items in the conceptual model so that each item name occurs on one node only. On the combined diagram, for any particular item in a selection there is a finite number of paths from its head node to the query nodes in the combined diagram. This finite number is the *item weight* of that item. The *tree complexity* of a selection of items is the sum, over all the items in that selection, of the products of the item complexities and the corresponding item weights. The problem of finding the selection with least tree complexity is not the system function problem. It is the *tree cover problem* that may be solved in polynomial time. In a combined diagram, if Q is the set of identified query nodes and U is the set of

ALGORITHM A.

1.   Construct the *combined diagram* consisting of the dependency diagrams of all rules that can be extracted from the items in the conceptual model so that each item name occurs on one node only in that diagram

2.   In the combined diagram, mark all dependency diagrams "not chosen". Mark the set of input nodes U "active" and "visited", and mark all other nodes "passive" and "unvisited", and mark the set of nodes U with zero cost.

3.   **while** there are nodes in Q marked "unvisited"

do for all items with "active" body components and "unvisited" head components, calculate the sum of the item cost and all its body component costs, mark the item with the least such sum as being "chosen", mark the head component of that item with this sum, mark the head component of that item "active" and "visited", mark each body component of that item "passive" as long as that body component is not also a body component in another item whose head component is marked "unvisited".

endwhile

4.   T[Q , U] is the set of items marked "chosen". The tree complexity of this selection, comp(T[Q , U]), is the sum of the costs marked on the set of query nodes Q.

Fig. 9.13   Algorithm A

identified input nodes, then the selection that is the solution to the tree cover problem is denoted by T[Q , U].

Algorithm A in Fig. 9.13 finds T[Q , U]. In that algorithm all nodes are marked either "active" or "passive", and either "visited" or "unvisited". All items are marked either "chosen" or "not chosen". This algorithm systematically marks each node x with a *least support cost*, this cost is the tree complexity of the selection T[{x} , U].

The correctness of Algorithm A in Fig. 9.13 follows from the observation that *if* the active nodes are marked with their least support cost, *then* the cost marked on the head component of the item chosen in step 3 of the algorithm must be the least support cost for that component item. If it is possible to support the set Q on the set U then the algorithm will terminate with each node in Q marked "visited". Algorithm A systematically "builds across" from the input items towards the query items. Algorithm A does not attempt to "look ahead" to identify any critical nodes that might offer a cost saving.

The complexity of Algorithm A depends on the amount of inter connectivity in the combined diagram. If a combined diagram has the property that each (critical) node is a body component in at most k items, for some fixed constant k, then the time complexity for Algorithm A is a linear function of the number of items in that combined diagram. In general, the time complexity is a quadratic function of the number of items in the combined diagram.

Algorithm B finds reasonably intelligent solutions to the system function problem in polynomial time. Algorithm B starts with the solution to the tree cover problem. Then it adds critical nodes to that solution, in the order of the cost

ALGORITHM B.

1. Construct the *combined diagram* consisting of the dependency diagrams of all rules that can be extracted from the items in the conceptual model so that each item name occurs on one node only in that diagram

2. In the combined diagram initialise X to be the set, Q, of query nodes. Let U be the set of update nodes.

3. **while** there is a critical node, c, in the combined diagram, for which the expression

comp(T[X , U]) - comp(T[X , U ∪ {c}]) - comp(T[{c} , U]) is positive

   do choose the critical node, c, for which the above expression is greatest
and find all nodes on direct paths from c to X in the calculation of
T[X , U ∪ {c}] **and** add these nodes to the set X
   endwhile

4. The solution is T[X , U] when step 3 terminates. The set X contains the incorporated critical nodes.

Fig. 9.14 Algorithm B

savings that they offer individually, provided that this cost saving is positive. Algorithm B is shown in Fig. 9.14. That algorithm is phrased in terms of Algorithm A shown in Fig. 9.13.

Algorithm B, shown in Fig. 9.14, implements the method described above because if the expression given in step 3 is positive then at least two paths must go from {c} to the set X in the graph T[X , U ∪ {c}].

In Algorithm B, if c lies on T[X , U] then the expression quoted in step 3 is always positive. The value of this expression is a multiple of comp(T[{c} , U]). So if all critical nodes lie on T[Q , U] then no new nodes are added and the critical nodes are all incorporated into the set X, one at a time, starting with those "nearest to" the query nodes. If, at any stage, a critical node c is added that does not lie on T[X , U] then the result of applying one iteration of step 3 in Algorithm B changes the set X by adding node c and all nodes on all paths from c to U to the set X.

The complexity of Algorithm B depends on the proportion of nodes in the combined diagram that are critical. If the proportion of nodes in the combined diagram that are critical is bounded by a quadratic function of the number of trees in the combined diagram, n, then the time complexity of Algorithm B is bounded by a cubic or quartic function of n, depending on the bound for the solution to the tree cover problem given in Algorithm A shown in Fig. 9.13. If, in any iteration in Algorithm B, the critical node chosen in step 3 is already in the tree T[X , U] then the amount of computation for that particular iteration is reduced.

9.8 Summary

- System function is the third step in the unified design methodology.
- The system function step takes the requirements model and the conceptual model and constructs the functional model.
- The functional model consists of:
  - a functional view, and
  - an f-coupling map.
- The functional view consists of:
  - a basis,
  - an object library,
  - a functional diagram,
  - a flow diagram, and
  - a transaction library.
- System function consists of four tasks:
  - analysis of transactions,
  - construction of the functional view,
  - construction of the f-coupling map, and
  - refinement of the constraints.
- The system function problem is NP-complete.
- Algorithms based on complexity measures may be used to find reasonably good solutions to the system function problem in polynomial time.

10 Layout

10.1 Introduction

This chapter describes the fourth step in the unified design methodology. This step is "system layout". The system layout step uses the i-schema format for describing items discussed in Sect. 5.2. The first step in the unified design methodology is requirements specification discussed in Chap. 7. The second step in the unified design methodology is system analysis discussed in Chap. 8. The third step in the unified design methodology is system function discussed in Chap. 9.

In an incremental design these three previous design steps generate new sections of the requirements model, the conceptual model and the functional model. The requirements model is expressed in terms of r-schemas. The conceptual model is expressed in terms of a combination of i-schemas and o-schemas. The functional model is expressed in terms of i-schemas, o-schemas and t-schemas. The requirements model is a representation of *what* the system should be able to do. The conceptual model is a representation of *how* the system does what it is required to do. The functional model is a representation of how the system performs the system transactions. The requirements model is linked to the conceptual model. The r-schemas in the requirements model are linked to the i-schemas in the conceptual model. These links enable the "what" and the "how" to be combined when the functional model is generated.

The system layout step takes the functional model and the operational requirements and develops the internal model which is a complete system specification. In addition to the information in the functional model, the internal model specifies those items that should be stored in the physical model so that the operational requirements are satisfied and that performance is optimised. The system layout step also refines the system constraints.

The product of the system layout step is the internal model. This model inherits both the "what" and the "how" aspects of the system from the functional model. The internal model contains implementation details so that the imple-

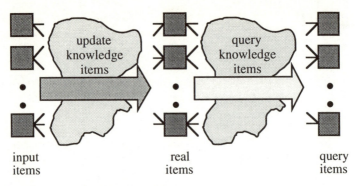

input
items

real
items

query
items

Fig. 10.1 Structure of the internal model

mented system should satisfy the operational requirements and should optimise performance.

Updates can only be made to value sets that are stored. Queries are serviced by direct or indirect reference to value sets that are stored. When a system is implemented the contents of the value sets of some information and data items are available *without* the use of any knowledge items, and the contents of the value sets of the remaining information and data items may be *deduced* using knowledge items from the value sets of other information and data items. If the value set of an information or data item is stored then that item is a *real item*. If the value set of an information or data item is not stored but can be deduced from the value sets of other information and data items that are stored then that item is a *virtual item*. The real items may well be distinct from the input items. The value sets of input items should be retained to support updates and to enable the system to be restarted in case of failure. The internal model contains a set of *update knowledge items* that support the value update transactions by calculating the real items from the input items, and another set of *query knowledge items* that support the value query transactions by calculating the query items from the real items. The structure of the internal model is shown in Fig. 10.1.

The system layout step consists of four tasks:

- analysis of operational requirements,
- construction of the internal view,
- construction of the i-coupling map, and
- refinement of the constraints.

The product of these four tasks is a section of the internal model. The internal model is described in Sect. 10.2, and the four tasks in Sects. 10.3–10.6 respectively. The first task is the analysis of the operational requirements. The operational requirements include operational requirements for the system query types, the system update types and the system integrity checks. The second task is the construction of the internal view. The internal view is derived from the functional view. The internal view contains details of those items that are real and those

items that are virtual. The third task is the construction of the i-coupling map.
The i-coupling map is derived from the f-coupling map. The fourth task is the
refinement of the constraints specified for the functional model. Those constraints
are refined for the internal model.

The "system layout problem" is introduced in Sect. 10.7. It is the problem of
deciding which of the items shown on the flow diagram should be real and which
should be virtual. The complexity of the system layout problem is investigated in
Sect. 10.7.2. The system layout problem could have been called the "*storage
layout problem*". Cost measures for storage layouts are introduced. These cost
measures are used to determine whether one solution to the system layout problem
is "better than" another. An algorithm that finds reasonably good solutions to the
system layout problem in a reasonable time is discussed in Sect. 10.7.3.

As with the system function problem considered in the previous chapter, the
system layout problem is complex. The complexity of the system layout problem is established in Sect. 10.7 which is of theoretical interest. Sub-optimal
algorithms may be used to derive acceptable solutions to the system layout problem. This chapter contains algorithms and techniques that give rise to extensive
calculations. These calculations are illustrated in worked examples. For non-
trivial applications these calculations are not performed by hand.

10.2 Internal model

The goal of the system layout step is the construction of an "internal model". The
internal model is derived from the functional model. The internal model has a
similar structure to the functional model. The functional model has a "functional
view". The internal model has an "internal view". The internal model contains an
i-coupling map that is described in Sect. 10.5. The *internal model* consists of:

- an internal view, and
- an i-coupling map.

The *internal view* is similar to the explicit functional view, and contains a
"storage diagram". It does not contain a "flow diagram". The storage diagram
shows for each item whether that item is real or virtual in the physical model.
The functional view consists of a library of items that together are capable of
delivering the required functionality of the system together with a "transaction
library" that contains a description of what the system is required to do. As for
both the c-coupling and f-coupling maps, the *i-coupling map* is a vertex labelled
graph. For each item in the internal view there is a vertex in the i-coupling map
labelled with that item's name. If an item in the internal view has not been
normalised then its node in the i-coupling map is shown in an area labelled "not
normalised". For those items in the internal view that are normal, an arc joins a

pair of vertices in the i-coupling map if there is a coupling relationship between the items whose names are attached to those vertices.

As for the conceptual model and functional model, the internal view may be specified implicitly or explicitly. During the system function step the normalisation process is applied for the last time (see Sect. 9.4.4). Once normalisation has been finally applied there is nothing to be gained in retaining the object structure. Items provide convenient program specifications. So the explicit internal model is used. An *explicit internal model* is an internal model in which the items in the internal view are defined explicitly. The λ-calculus notation or the i-schema notation are used to represent each item. The *explicit internal view* consists of:

- an item library,
- an internal diagram,
- a storage diagram,
- a transaction library, and
- operational requirements.

The item library consists of those items in the functional model. The internal diagram is an explicit version of the functional diagram. The storage diagram is discussed in Sect. 10.4. The transaction library is as in the functional model together with the operational requirements for each transaction. Operational requirements are discussed in Sect. 10.3.

10.3 Operational requirements

The operational requirements for a knowledge-based system include the operation of the transactions identified during requirements specification and analysed during system function. Operational requirements also include the operation of the integrity checks identified during requirements specification, system analysis and system function. The *operational requirements* are:

- The maximum permissible response time for each transaction. This gives a limit to the amount of computation and the amount of reference to storage for each transaction.
- The maximum permissible run time for each system integrity check. This gives a limit to the amount of computation and the amount of reference to storage for each integrity check type.
- An estimation of the expected frequency of presentation of each transaction and integrity check. This provides a foundation for the notion of an "optimal" solution to the knowledge-based systems design problem.
- The amount of available storage. This gives a limit to the total amount of stored data and information.

- Some measure of the "flexibility" of the storage layout. The notion *flexibility* is a measure of the likelihood of the storage layout to be able to cope with additional transactions without modification. If the query items are stored then the system is as inflexible as it could be. If the input items are stored then the system is as flexible as it could be. Placing a value on increased flexibility of the storage layout establishes a preference for the real items to be "close" to the input items.
- Some measure of the cost of maintaining the consistency of the real items. Placing a value on keeping this cost low establishes a preference for low "redundancy" in the storage layout.

An *admissible layout* is a storage layout that satisfies the operational requirements [Domingue et al., 1993]. A particular set of operational requirements may mean that there is no admissible layout. There is no admissible layout if the maximum allowed response times for all query and update types permitted one relation reference only, except in the trivial case when all query items are input items, and all query types use the key of the corresponding query relation. The system layout problem is to determine the admissible layout that is the "optimal" solution.

The analysis of operational requirements task consists of:

- the analysis of the operational requirements for each transaction in the transaction library, and
- the analysis of the operational requirements for each integrity check.

This task is the first task in the system layout step.

10.4 Internal view

The second task in the system layout step is to construct the internal view. The internal view contains the items in the functional view. Each item in the internal view, with the exception of the input items, is classified as "real" or "virtual". The value set of a real item is stored in the physical model. The value set of a virtual item is *not* stored in the physical model. The classification of items as either "real" or "virtual" should satisfy the operational requirements. The operational requirements are discussed in Sect. 10.3. The value sets of the input items are always stored. They may be stored on some form of backing store. The value sets of input items may be required at any time to restart the system in the event of a system failure.

When the construction of the internal view task begins the following are available:

- the internal model (constructed during previous iterations if any);
- the functional model (constructed during this iteration and during previous iterations if any);
- the operational requirements (analysed during the previous analysis of operational requirements task).

The system layout task derives the internal model. The internal model satisfies the operational requirements and optimises performance. The internal view consists of:

- an item library;
- an internal diagram;
- a storage diagram;
- a transaction library, and
- operational requirements.

The *item library* contains the items, represented implicitly, that are in the functional view. The *internal diagram* contains the items, but not the objects, that are in the functional diagram. The *storage diagram* has the same structure as the flow diagram and, in addition, the nodes are shown as representing either "input", "real" or "virtual" items. On the storage diagram:

- virtual items are shown as rectangles drawn with broken lines;
- input items that are not real items are shown as rectangular relief nodes;

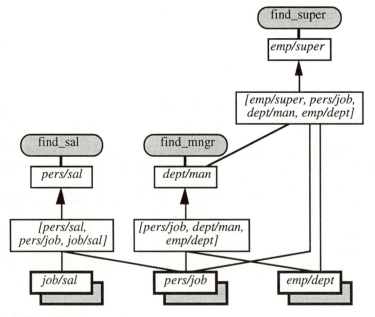

Fig. 10.2 Flow diagram

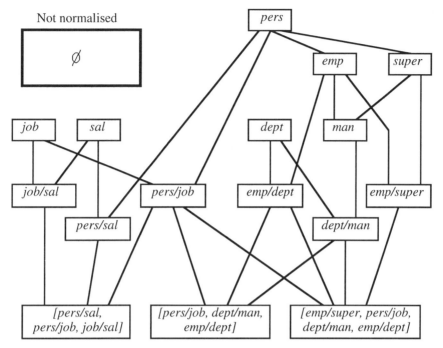

Fig. 10.3 f-coupling map

- real items that are not input items are shown as diamond-shaped relief nodes, and
- items that are both real and input items are shown as hexagonal-shaped relief nodes.

The *transaction library* is inherited from the functional view. In the internal model each transaction is linked to its operational requirements. The operational requirements are analysed in Sect. 10.3.

The structure of the functional model is shown on a flow diagram. An example of a flow diagram is shown in Fig. 10.2. The corresponding f-coupling map is shown in Fig. 10.3. There are no objects shown in Fig. 10.3.

During the construction of the internal view task items classified as "input items", "real items" or "virtual items" so that the operational requirements are satisfied and that the system performance is optimal. This is the "system layout problem" that is discussed in Sect. 10.7. A reasonably good solution to the system layout problem may be derived by hand. In Sect. 10.7 the system layout problem is shown to be inherently complex. Algorithmic solutions to the system layout problem have exponential time bounds and may only be applied to small applications. The material in Sect. 10.7 is of theoretical interest.

In the flow diagram shown in Fig. 10.2 if the input items are the only real information items then the resulting storage diagram is as shown in Fig. 10.4.

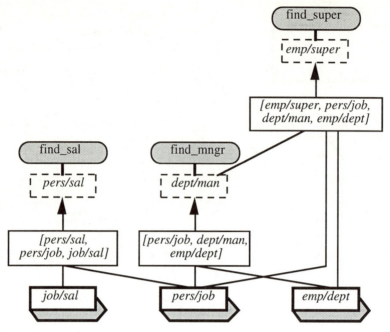

Fig. 10.4 Storage diagram

The storage diagram in Fig. 10.4 contains three virtual information items and three items that are both input and real items.

10.5 i-coupling map

As for the conceptual model and functional model, the *i-coupling map* in the internal model is a vertex labelled graph. For each item in the internal view there is a vertex in the i-coupling map labelled with that item's name. If an item in the internal view has not been normalised then its node in the i-coupling map is shown in an area labelled "not normalised". For those items in the internal view that are normal, an arc joins a pair of vertices in the i-coupling map if there is a coupling relationship between the items whose names are attached to those vertices.

The main difference between the f-coupling map in the functional model and the i-coupling map in the internal model is that the i-coupling map distinguishes between the input items, the real items and the virtual items. In the *i-coupling map* only real items are shown in boxes with non-broken lines. In the i-coupling map arcs between boxes with broken lines are shown as broken arcs. The i-coupling map that corresponds to the storage diagram shown in Fig. 10.4 is shown in Fig. 10.5. The i-coupling map is used to guide initial attempts to

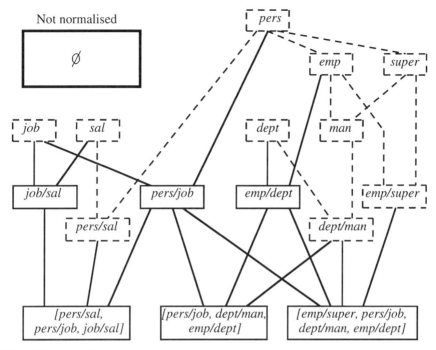

Fig. 10.5 i-coupling map

maintain a system. When the extent of a revision task has been determined, that revision task is reflected in all of the models that are to be retained as part of the system design. All of the models, from the requirements model to the internal model, should be retained as part of the system design.

10.6 Constraints

The system analysis step is described in Chap. 8. During system analysis the individual item and object constraints are constructed. During system analysis model constraints are constructed. During the system function step constraints for the input items are constructed. During the system layout step the constraints are finalised. During the system layout step further constraints are constructed to protect the integrity of the system [Debenham, 1994]. Section 8.6.2 introduces information model constraints and knowledge model constraints. Information model constraints and knowledge model constraints are used during the system layout step.

During the system layout step the real items are identified. The contents of the value sets of the real items may change with each update transaction. The integrity of the contents of the value sets of the real items is vital to the operation of the system. A set of *real item constraints* preserves the integrity of the value sets of the real items. A real item constraint can be a knowledge model constraint.

During the system layout step the knowledge items in the functional model are partitioned into two disjoint sets. These two sets are the update knowledge items and the query knowledge items as shown in Fig. 10.1. The integrity of these two sets of selected knowledge items is vital to the operation of the system. The integrity of these two sets of knowledge items are protected with the update knowledge constraints and the query knowledge constraints respectively. The role of these two sets of constraints is to preserve the integrity of the update knowledge items and the query knowledge items. An update knowledge constraint and a query knowledge constraint can be an information model constraint. That is a set of system constraints can consist of a set of relations and tuples with which these two sets of knowledge items are required to be consistent.

The refinement of constraints task consists of:

- The design of constraints for the set of real items. These constraints may be knowledge model constraints.
- The design of constraints for the update knowledge items and the query knowledge items. These constraints may be information model constraints.
- The design of any other system constraints.

The constraints designed during this task, together with the constraints designed during the refinement of constraints task in the system function step, aim to be a powerful mechanism for protecting the integrity of the system.

10.7 System layout problem

The previous design step is system function. The product of system function is the functional model. The functional model contains a set of items that can support the system transactions. The flow diagram is a useful presentation of this set. The *system layout problem* is:

- to decide which of the items shown on the functional diagram should be stored so that
- the operational requirements are satisfied and
- the overall system performance is "optimal".

When a system is implemented, the value sets of some items are stored and the contents of their value sets are *retrieved* when required. Those items are the *real items*. A set of real items is referred to collectively as a *storage layout*. The value sets of some items are *not* stored and the contents of their value sets are *calculated* when required. Those items are the *virtual items*. Satisfaction of the system operational requirements helps to determine those items that are real and those items that are virtual. The second task in the system layout step is to decide whether each item on the functional diagram should be real or virtual.

The input items are not necessarily real items. A history of modifications to the input items should be retained to enable the system to be restarted in event of a failure. Input items whose value sets are retained for archival, or system back-up purposes are *not* real items.

The definition of the system layout problem given above refers to "optimal" system performance. The *system performance* of a storage layout is:

$$\sum_{q\in Q} \tau\,(q) \times f(q)\; +\; \sum_{u\in U} \tau\,(u) \times f(u)\; +\; \sum_{i\in I} \tau\,(i) \times f(i)$$

where Q is the set of query types, U is the set of update types and I is the set of integrity checks. τ is a "cost function", where $\tau(x)$ is the "cost of servicing the transaction x". f is the "expected frequency function", where $f(x)$ is the "expected frequency of presentation of the transaction x".

For each query type q, update type u and integrity check i, let T(q), T(u) and T(i) respectively denote the maximum permissible cost of response for that transaction. For each item r, let $\gamma\,(r)$ denote the cost of storing the value set of r. Let C denote the total cost of the available storage.

The system layout problem
Given a functional diagram, given T(q), T(u) and T(i) for each $q\in Q$, $u\in U$ and $i\in I$, and given C, to choose a set of items R to be the real such that:

$(\forall q\in Q)\; \tau\,(q) \leq T(q)$
$(\forall u\in U)\; \tau\,(u) \leq T(u)$
$(\forall i\in I)\; \tau\,(i) \leq T(i)$

$$\sum_{r\in R} \gamma\,(r) \leq C$$

are satisfied and:

$$\sum_{q\in Q} \tau\,(q) \times f(q)\; +\; \sum_{u\in U} \tau\,(u) \times f(u)\; +\; \sum_{i\in I} \tau\,(i) \times f(i)$$

is minimised [Debenham & Devedžić, 1996].

A knowledge item in the storage diagram is either a query knowledge item or an update knowledge item. Query knowledge items are used to service the query transactions. Update knowledge items are used to service the update transactions. The knowledge items that have been identified during requirements specification

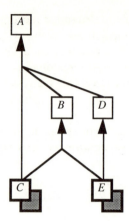

Fig. 10.6 Flow diagram

but are not shown on the storage diagram either become integrity checks or reside in a reservoir of spare knowledge. So knowledge items are classified as being *query knowledge items, input knowledge items, integrity check knowledge items* or *dormant knowledge items* respectively. These four sets of knowledge items are disjoint. Part of the system layout problem is the problem of classifying the knowledge items.

A solution to the system layout problem should incorporate the following:

• a method for determining those items that are to be real so that the performance of the system satisfies the operational requirements, and
• a method for designing an effective integrity checking strategy, so that
• the overall system performance is optimal.

In addition, the following is a desirable feature of a solution to the system layout problem:

• a method for automatically rearranging the layout in response to changing demands.

This final feature is addressed by the algorithms in Sect. 10.7.3.

10.7.1 Calculation of minimal storage

The notation for the flow diagram constructed during system function is described in Sect. 9.4.3. A flow diagram is shown in Fig. 10.6.

In a connected flow diagram:

• The nodes that represent query items are *query nodes*. The set of query nodes includes all nodes that have no out-going arcs.

- The nodes that represent input items are *input nodes*. The set of input nodes is the set of all nodes that have no in-coming arcs.

The notion of "support" is introduced in Sect. 9.7. The knowledge items in the flow diagram support the query nodes on the input nodes. In the flow diagram shown in Fig. 10.6 A is a query node, and E and C are the only input nodes. In a flow diagram, a node X is said to *depend* on node Y if there is a path *from Y to X* in that flow diagram. In the flow diagram shown in Fig. 10.6, D depends on E, B depends on E and C, and A depends on all the other nodes in that diagram.

Consider a set of items that has been derived by system function, and that has been summarised on a flow diagram. There are a number of different ways in which this set of items could be implemented. Three possible alternatives are:

- The value sets of all of the data and information items are stored so that the storage costs and update costs are high.
- The value sets of all of the data and information query items are stored so that the update costs are high.
- The value sets of all of the data and information input items are stored so that the query costs are high.

The input items need not be real. The value sets of the input items need not necessarily be stored in the high speed memory. The value sets of all input items should be retained in some sort of archive. All that matters is:

- the value sets of the real items should be derivable from the value sets of the input items, and
- the value sets of all of the query items should be derivable from the value sets of the real items.

The set of real items divides the storage diagram into two portions. A *storage layout* is a subset of the set of nodes in a storage diagram such that if the storage layout is removed from the storage diagram, then the resulting diagram consists of two connected, possibly empty, components with one component containing no query nodes and the other component containing no input nodes. In a storage diagram the storage layout supports the set of query nodes. In a storage diagram the set of input nodes supports the storage layout. The storage layout is the set of real items in the storage diagram. In the flow diagram shown in Fig. 10.6, four different storage layouts show that A is supported by the four sets $\{B, C, D\}$, $\{D, E, C\}$, $\{E, B, C\}$ and $\{C, E\}$. These four sets are identified by the four different lines shown on the diagram in Fig. 10.7.

An *irredundant storage layout* is a storage layout with the property that if one node is removed from that storage layout, then the resulting set ceases to be a storage layout. An irredundant storage layout can be visualised as a minimal set of nodes that divides the storage diagram into two portions. An "irredundant storage layout" is a "storage layout". In Fig. 10.7 two of the storage layouts shown

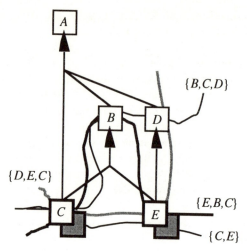

Fig. 10.7 Four different storage layouts

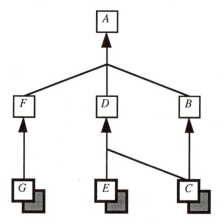

Fig. 10.8 Flow diagram

are irredundant storage layouts. They are $\{B, C, D\}$ and $\{C, E\}$. In the storage layout $\{B, C, D\}$ the contents of the value set of E cannot be recovered from $\{B, C, D\}$ unless additional knowledge is available. In this example, if the value set of E is subsequently required then it should be stored in some sort of archive.

A storage layout, selected from a flow diagram, is a *division* if it contains no two nodes that depend on each other. If a selection is a "division" then that selection ceases to be a storage layout if any node is removed from that selection. All divisions are irredundant storage layouts. There is a difference between an irredundant storage layout and a division. In the flow diagram shown in Fig. 10.8 the storage layout $\{C, D, F\}$ is an irredundant storage layout because if any one of these three nodes are removed then it ceases to be a storage layout. But

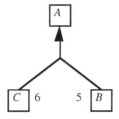

Fig. 10.9 Flow diagram with costs

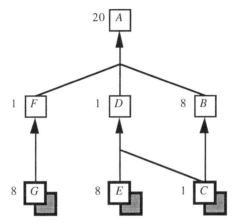

Fig. 10.10 Flow diagram

{ C, D, F } is *not* a division because D depends on C. The storage layout
{ B, D, F } *is* a division.

A division may be visualised informally as a storage layout chosen by cutting
the flow diagram in half where the cut goes "from left to right without straying
unduly up or down". There may appear to be little value in storage layouts that
are not divisions. A single node can be used in different ways by different transactions. Non-division storage layouts can be of value. Divisions are significant
because if a storage layout contains one node that depends on another, then any
updates to the second node should be reflected in updates to the first. When
updates are being performed on-line, divisions should require less elaborate file
locking than storage layouts that are not divisions.

Costs are introduced to the storage diagram. These costs are intended to represent the cost of storing each item. These costs are written beside the node that
represents that item. If the cost of storing item B is 5 and the cost of storing item
C is 6, then this is denoted as shown on the diagram in Fig. 10.9.

A storage layout is a *minimal storage layout* if that storage layout is the least
cost set of nodes that supports the query nodes in the storage diagram. Minimal
storage layouts are irredundant storage layouts but they are not necessarily
divisions. Consider the flow diagram that is shown in Fig. 10.10. In that
diagram the minimal storage layout is the set { C, D, F }. That storage layout

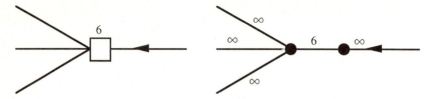

Fig. 10.11 The node on the left is replaced by the structure on the right

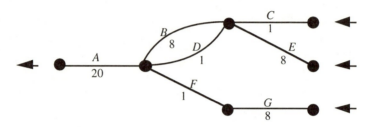

Fig. 10.12 Division-dual diagram

is irredundant but is not a division. The calculation of both the division with least cost and the minimal storage layout is considered below.

Problem 1
To calculate the division with least cost.

This problem can be solved by applying the (polynomial time) minimum-cut algorithm to a modified version of the flow diagram. This modification is performed in two steps. First, mark all arcs on the flow diagram with "infinite" cost, and replace each node with a "pseudo-arc" marked with that node's cost. The node shown on the left of Fig. 10.11 is replaced by the structure shown on the right. In the second step, all arcs marked with infinite cost are "collapsed" to a node. The resulting diagram is the *division-dual diagram*. The solution to Problem 1 may be found by applying the minimum-cut algorithm to the division dual diagram. When the minimum-cut has been calculated, the pseudo-arcs that lie on the minimum-cut correspond to the nodes in the division with least cost. See any good book on algorithmic graph theory, for a description of the minimum-cut algorithm [Even, 1979].

Consider the flow diagram shown in Fig. 10.10. For that diagram the division-dual diagram is shown in Fig. 10.12. By applying the minimum-cut algorithm to the diagram shown in Fig. 10.12 the division of least cost is { C, E, F } or { B, D, F } with a total cost of 10. An arc in the division-dual diagram corresponds to a node in the original flow diagram, and vice versa.

Problem 2
To calculate the irredundant storage layout with least cost. The irredundant storage layout with least cost is the minimal storage layout.

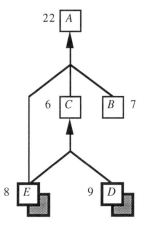

Fig. 10.13 Flow diagram

This problem can be solved by applying the (polynomial time) minimum-cut algorithm to a modified version of the flow diagram that is similar to the division dual diagram considered in the solution to Problem 1. The modification for Problem 2 is performed in three steps. First, all of the "thick" arcs in the flow diagram are "collapsed" to a point and then the remaining "thin" arcs are marked with "infinite cost". Second, replace each node with a "pseudo-polygon" as follows:

- A node that is connected to one or two other nodes is replaced by a pseudo-arc as in the solution to Problem 1. This pseudo-arc is marked with the node cost.
- A node that is connected to n other nodes, where n > 2, is replaced by an n-sided pseudo-polygon with one corner of the polygon connected to the arc that is connected to each of the n nodes. The sides of the polygon are marked with the original node cost divided by two.

In the third step, all arcs marked with infinite cost are "collapsed" to a node. The resulting diagram is the *dual diagram*. The solution to Problem 2 may be found by applying the minimum-cut algorithm to this dual diagram. When the minimum-cut has been calculated, the pseudo-polygons that lie on the cut correspond to the nodes in the minimal storage layout.

The flow diagram shown in Fig. 10.13 is replaced by the dual diagram shown in Fig. 10.14. By applying the minimum-cut algorithm to the dual diagram shown in Fig. 10.14 the minimal storage layout is { B, C, E } with a cost of 21.

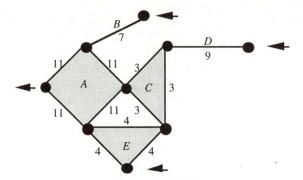

Fig. 10.14 Dual diagram

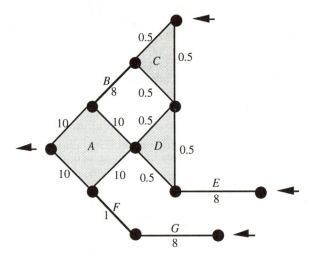

Fig. 10.15 Dual diagram

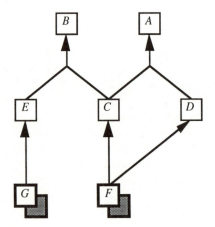

Fig. 10.16 Flow diagram

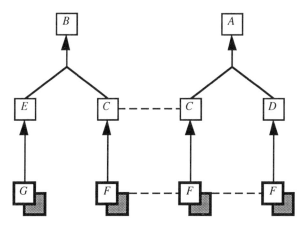

Fig. 10.17 Separated diagram

Consider the flow diagram shown in Fig. 10.10. Its dual diagram is shown in Fig. 10.15. By applying the minimum-cut algorithm to the dual diagram shown in Fig. 10.15 the minimal storage layout is { C, D, F } with a total cost of 3.

The operational requirements may prevent a division from being a storage layout. The operational requirements may require that the storage layout be non-minimal.

A notation is described that can be used to design redundant storage layouts. This notation is a "tree" version of the flow diagram. Given a set of items represented on a flow diagram, the *separated-diagram* is constructed by drawing a tree that supports each query node on the input nodes. Where possible occurrences of the same node label on branches of different trees are drawn beside each other. These different occurrences of the same label are joined by undirected dotted arcs. Given the flow diagram shown in Fig. 10.16 the separated diagram is as shown in Fig. 10.17. The arcs in the flow diagram correspond to equivalence classes of arcs in the separated-diagram identified by the dotted lines. Costs can be marked on the separated diagram. The minimal storage layout for each query node is then considered separately, and a strategy devised for deducing an overall, possibly redundant, storage layout.

10.7.2 Problem complexity

The operational constraints and optimally criterion in the system layout problem together comprise a complex set of conflicting constraints. The problem of determining an optimal, minimal storage layout is difficult even when gross simplifications are made to those constraints. The problem of determining an admissible layout, never mind an optimal solution, to the system layout problem is hard.

Theorem
The system layout problem is NP-complete.

Proof
A restriction of the system layout problem is equivalent to the "Minimum-Cut Into Bounded Sets" problem that is known to be NP-complete [Garey & Johnson, 1979] [Garey, Johnson and Stockmeyer, 1979].

First, assume that there is only one query item, q, one input item, u, and no integrity checks. Then the system layout problem is as follows. Given a flow diagram, given constants T(q), T(u) and C, choose a set of items R to be the real items such that:

$$\tau(q) \leq T(q)$$
$$\tau(u) \leq T(u)$$

$$\sum_{r \in R} \gamma(r) \leq C$$

are satisfied, and:

$$(\tau(q) \times f(q)) + (\tau(u) \times f(u))$$

is minimised.

Second, adopt the following trivial measure for τ, this measure defines $\tau(q)$ to be the number of items involved in servicing the transaction q. $\tau(q)$ is the number of items required to support q on R. In addition, further restrict the problem to the special case when T(q) = T(u) = T. Then the system layout problem is "Given a flow diagram, given constants T and C, to choose a set of items R to be the real items such that:

The number of items needed to support q on R is less than or equal to T.
The number of items needed to support R on u is less than or equal to T.

$$\sum_{r \in R} \gamma(r) \leq C$$

are satisfied, and:

$$(\tau(q) \times f(q)) + (\tau(u) \times f(u))$$

is minimised". This restriction of the system layout problem may be interpreted in terms of the division dual diagram representation discussed in the previous section.

Third, the expression to be minimised is ignored. That is, only the constraints are considered. On the division dual diagram, data and information items are denoted by arcs and knowledge items are denoted by nodes. The system layout problem as restricted so far reads "Given a division dual diagram, constants T and C, to choose a partition of the nodes on that diagram into two disjoint sets V_1 and V_2 such that the single query node q is connected to a node in V_1 and the single input node u is connected to a node in V_2 such that:

$$|V_1| \leq T$$
$$|V_2| \leq T$$

$$\sum_{r \in R} \gamma \ (r) \leq C$$

where |V| means "the number of elements in the set V", and R is the set of arcs with one node in V_1 and the other in V_2."

This final restriction of the system layout problem is the "Minimum-Cut into Bounded Sets" problem. This completes the proof. ❑

The proof of the above result demonstrates that the problem of finding an *admissible layout* for the system layout problem is NP-complete. Never mind the problem of finding an *optimal* admissible layout.

Corollary
Given a flow diagram, the problem of finding an admissible layout, that is not necessarily optimal, to the system layout problem is NP-complete.

The "Minimum-Cut into Bounded Sets" problem remains NP-complete even if $\gamma(r) = 1 \ \ (\forall r \in R)$, and if $T = |V| \div 2$. The following restriction of the system layout problem is also NP-complete. Given a dual diagram and constant C, choose a partition of the nodes in the diagram into two disjoint sets V_1 and V_2 such that the single query node q is connected to a node in V_1 and the single input node u is connected to a node in V_2 such that:

$$|V_1| = |V| \div 2$$
$$|V_2| = |V| \div 2$$
$$|R| \leq C$$

In the special case when $T = |V|$ the problem of finding an admissible, but not necessarily optimal, solution to the system layout problem reduces to satisfying the single constraint:

$$\sum_{r\in R} \gamma\,(r) \le C$$

This reduction of the system layout problem can be solved in polynomial time by the minimum-cut algorithm.

The proof of the above result employs the restriction that there is only one query node and only one input node. As this restriction is NP-complete, the general case, with any number of query and input nodes, is NP-complete. This restriction also leads to another form of the system layout problem. The system layout problem refers to a "given flow diagram", on this flow diagram connect all query nodes to a single "dummy query node" q'. Likewise, connect all input nodes to another, single "dummy input node" u'. In this version of the problem, suppose that the cost function, $\kappa\,(q)$, is the number of items involved in servicing q in the *separated diagram*. Likewise, $\kappa\,(u)$ is the number of items involved in servicing u in the *separated diagram*. Then the constraints for this problem read:

$$\kappa(q') = \sum_{q\in Q} \kappa\,(q) \le T(q')$$
$$\kappa(u') = \sum_{u\in U} \kappa\,(u) \le T(u')$$

$$\sum_{r\in R} \gamma\,(r) \le C$$

Dividing by suitable constants, and introducing T' and T":

$$\frac{1}{|Q|} \times \kappa(q') = \frac{1}{|Q|} \times \sum_{q\in Q} \kappa\,(q) \le T' = \frac{1}{|Q|} \times T(q')$$
$$\frac{1}{|U|} \times \kappa(u') = \frac{1}{|U|} \times \sum_{u\in U} \kappa\,(u) \le T" = \frac{1}{|U|} \times T(u')$$

$$\sum_{r\in R} \gamma\,(r) \le C$$

So the following variation of the system layout problem is also NP-complete "Given a functional diagram, constants T', T" and C, choose a set of items R to be the real items such that:

The mean cost of servicing the query types is less than or equal to T'.
The mean cost of servicing the update types is less than or equal to T".

$$\sum_{r\in R} \gamma\,(r) \le C$$

are satisfied and:

$$\sum_{q\in Q} \kappa\ (q) \times f(q)\ +\sum_{u\in U} \kappa\ (u) \times f(u)$$

is minimal." As before, the problem of finding an admissible, but not necessarily optimal, solution to this problem is NP-complete.

10.7.3 Sub-optimal storage layout

In Sect. 10.7.2 the system layout problem is shown to be NP-complete. This does not mean that all classes of sub-problems of the system layout problem are necessarily NP-complete. The costs on the arcs in either the separated diagram or the flow diagram may be related to each other. This observation, and others like it, may lead to some simplification.

Any method for solving the system layout problem is either based on a (polynomial time) soluble sub-problem, or on a sub-optimal (polynomial time) method. A sub-optimal algorithm is given for calculating the (hopefully) minimal storage layout that satisfies the operational requirements. This algorithm performs well when the application has a loose set of operational requirements. If the application has tight operational requirements then the algorithm may not find a solution. In the statement of the algorithm, integrity checks are ignored.

The algorithm begins with the unconstrained minimal storage layout as calculated in Sect. 10.7.1. This minimal storage layout is then "modified" to form other storage layouts that are all irredundant. It is assumed that these modifications remain within the available storage constraint. The algorithm makes no reference to the satisfaction of the total storage constraint. There are three reasons for this. First, the availability of storage is seldom a problem. Second, the update constraints impose an implicit constraint on the amount of storage used. If a large number of items are real, then the update operations are necessarily slow. Third, the algorithm produces an irredundant storage layout and this should ensure that storage costs are "low".

In the statement of the following algorithm, the following notation is used. If, in a functional diagram, S is an irredundant storage layout and n is a node not in S, then $S \uparrow \{n\}$ denotes the set of nodes obtained by adding n to S and removing from S any nodes that, as a result of n being added, prevent $S \cup \{n\}$ from being irredundant.

Algorithm
Find the minimal storage layout by using the method given in Sect. 10.7.1 on the dual diagram. If there is more than one minimal storage layout, then choose the storage layout that violates fewest operational requirements. A storage layout consists of a set of items. On the dual diagram a storage layout is represented by a

set of arcs. On the flow diagram the minimal storage layout is represented as a "cut". Then:

begin(constraints)

        let the storage layout S **be** the minimal storage layout as described above

    while   there are query nodes that have unsatisfied operational requirements

    do   **let** P^Q **be** the nodes in S on which query nodes with unsatisfied operational requirements depend

           let P^{GB} **be** the set of knowledge items with at least one body node in P^Q

           let P^H **be** $\{\, n : n \notin S$ and n is the head node of a knowledge item in $P^{GB} \,\}$

           if there is a node n in P^H such that $S \uparrow \{n\}$ satisfies a presently unsatisfied query constraint **then let** N **be** n **else let** N **be** the node with the property that the storage layout $S \uparrow \{N\}$ has the lowest query cost of all the storage layouts
$$\{\, S \uparrow \{n\} : n \in P^H \,\}$$

           let S **be** $S \uparrow \{N\}$

    endwhile

(At this stage S is an irredundant storage layout that satisfies the operational requirements for all query items.)

    while   there are input nodes with unsatisfied operational requirements

    do   **let** P^U **be** the nodes in S that depend on one or more input nodes that have unsatisfied operational requirements

           let P^{GH} **be** the set of knowledge items with head node in P^U

           let P^B **be** $\{\, n : n \notin S,\ n$ is a body node of a knowledge item in P^{GH} and $S \uparrow \{n\}$ violates no query constraints $\}$

           if $P^B = \emptyset$ **then halt** ("unsuccessful") **else**

           if there is a node n in P^B such that $S \uparrow \{n\}$ satisfies a presently unsatisfied update constraint **then let** N **be** n **else let** N **be** the node with the property that the storage layout $S \uparrow \{N\}$ has the lowest update cost of all the storage layouts
$$\{\, S \uparrow \{n\} : n \in P^B \,\}$$

           let S **be** $S \uparrow \{N\}$

    endwhile

end

(At this stage S is an irredundant storage layout that satisfies all the transaction operational requirements but may not give rise to optimal system performance.)

begin(optimise)

      let P^{GH} **be** the set of knowledge items with head node in S

      let P^B **be** { $n : n \notin S$, n is a body node of a knowledge item in P^{GH} and $S \uparrow \{n\}$ violates no transaction operational requirements }

      let P^{GB} **be** the set of knowledge items with at least one body node in S

      let P^H **be** { $n : n \notin S$, n is the head node of a knowledge item in P^{GB} and $S \uparrow \{n\}$ violates no transaction operational requirements }

      if $P^B \cup P^H = \emptyset$ **then halt**("successful") **else**

      let P^O **be** { $n : n \in P^B \cup P^H$ such that the system performance of $S \uparrow \{n\}$ is lower than the system performance of S }

      if $P^O = \emptyset$ **then halt** ("successful") **else**

      let N **be** the node in P^O with the property that the storage layout $S \uparrow \{N\}$ has the lowest system performance of all the storage layouts { $S \uparrow \{n\} : n \in P^O$ }

      let S **be** $S \uparrow \{N\}$

      repeat(optimise)

end

If this algorithm halts signalling "successful", then it halts in polynomial time.

10.8 Summary

- System layout is the fourth and final step in the unified design methodology.
- The system layout step takes the functional model and the operational requirements and constructs the internal model.
- The internal model is a complete specification of the knowledge-based system that may be used as a programming specification.
- The internal model consists of:
  - an internal view, and
  - an i-coupling map.
- The internal view consists of:
  - an item library,
  - an internal diagram,
  - a storage diagram,
  - a transaction library, and
  - operational requirements.
- System layout consist of four tasks:
  - analysis of transactions,
  - construction of the functional view,
  - construction of the f-coupling map, and
  - refinement of the constraints.
- The system layout problem is NP-complete.
- A sub-optimal algorithm for the system layout problem operates in polynomial time when the application is not heavily constrained.
- The problem of finding the division of least cost may be solved in polynomial time.
- The problem of finding the minimal storage layout may be solved in polynomial time.

11 Maintenance

11.1 Introduction

This chapter describes the maintenance of knowledge-based systems. The unified design methodology has four steps The first step is requirements specification discussed in Chap. 7. The second step is system analysis discussed in Chap. 8. The third step is system function discussed in Chap. 9. The fourth step is system layout discussed in Chap. 10.

This chapter is concerned with maintenance. The unified design methodology is intended for team work. If it is used by a team, then some of those management issues are particularly significant. This chapter considers those management issues.

The chapter begins with a summary of the unified design methodology in Sect. 11.2. Set constraints are discussed in Sect. 11.3. Section 11.4 describes the approach to system maintenance. The significance of normalisation is discussed in Sect. 11.5. Section 11.6 discusses various types of constraints. Management issues are discussed in Sect. 11.7.

11.2 Methodology summary

The overall structure of the methodology is discussed in Chap. 7. The methodology structure diagram is reproduced in Fig. 11.1. The steps, tasks and sub-tasks of the unified methodology are:
- requirements specification
  - application representation
    - construction of the context diagram
    - differentiation of the context diagram
    - decomposition

- requirements identification
  - prime scoping
  - re-use
  - feasibility
  - classification
  - volatility
- system analysis
  - construction of the basis
    - identification of data items
    - construction of i-schema
    - removal of equivalences
    - identification of sub-types
    - normalisation of the data
  - construction of the conceptual view
    - identification of object operators for each non-basis item
    - construction of the object library
    - removal of equivalence relationships, and construction of the conceptual diagram
    - refining object functionality
    - removal of labels
    - reduction of sub-items
    - decomposition of mixed type objects
    - normalisation of the information
  - construction of c-coupling map
  - development of constraints
    - individual constraints
    - model constraints
- system function
  - analysis of transactions
    - construct a t-schema
    - link that t-schema to a set of items in the conceptual model
  - construction of the functional view
    - identification of transaction items
    - identification of supporting input items
    - selection of intermediate items
    - knowledge normalisation
  - construction of the f-coupling map
  - refinement of the constraints
- system layout
  - analysis of operational requirements
    - the analysis of the operational requirements for each transaction in the transaction library
    - the analysis of the operational requirements for each integrity check
  - construction of the internal view
  - construction of the i-coupling map

- refinement of the constraints

The deliverables for each step are:

- requirements specification step
  - requirements model
- system analysis step
  - conceptual model
- system function step
  - functional model
- system layout step
  - internal model

Section 7.2 discusses the suitability of the incremental design life cycle to knowledge-based systems. Chapter 7 describes the prime r-schemas as the governing mechanism for incremental design. There is substantial flexibility in the way in which an incremental design may be performed. In Chap. 7 it is suggested that the four design steps should each be completed for successive prime r-schema in an incremental design. There is no need to follow this suggestion. In an incremental design there is no need to complete the whole design process for each prime r-schema. For each prime r-schema it may be decided to perform the design process as far as the conceptual model. Then, when the whole conceptual model is complete, to perform the system function step and the system layout step. *Incremental design* as a system *life cycle* is used here in this looser sense.

The deliverables of the four design steps are the four models. These four models are interlinked. The requirements model, the conceptual model, the functional model and the internal model taken together are the *design* for the system. Once the physical model is complete, the extent to which the design is preserved during maintenance is a management decision. The design divides the knowledge

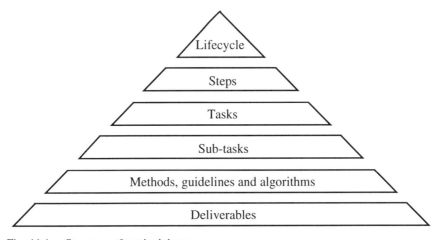

Fig. 11.1   Structure of methodology

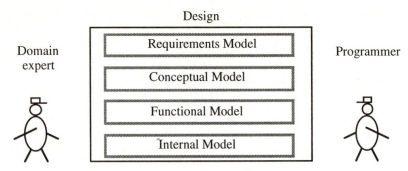

Fig. 11.2 Domain expert, design and programmer

engineering process into two distinct parts. See Fig. 11.2. The first part is the construction of the design. The second part uses the design to construct the physical model.

A uniform approach is used for modelling. This approach is based on items and objects. No matter how modelling is performed, information is built out of data, and knowledge is built out of data and information. The representation of the data determines the vocabulary in terms of which the information must be represented, and the representation of the information and data together determine the vocabulary in terms of which the knowledge must be represented. The data and information items should be sufficient to provide the vocabulary to represent the whole system.

A step in the construction of the unified design is the normalisation of knowledge, as well as the normalisation of the information and data. Knowledge normalisation is difficult. Information normalisation is comparatively easy. The potential cost of maintaining knowledge can be high. If an application is designed for maintenance then the knowledge should be normalised. If the knowledge source is expensive to access then normalisation is expensive.

11.3 Set constraints

The correct identification of set constraints is relevant to both design and maintenance. Knowledge items represent explicit functional associations between information and/or data items. The particular functional associations represented in an item are specified by that item's set constraints. The set constraints specify the different functional ways in which an item can contribute to the functional model [Wald, 1988]. If any valid set constraints are omitted for an item then that item may be prevented from playing a role in the final system. If an item is prevented from playing a role in the final system then this may lead to an unnecessarily complex system and to unnecessarily complex maintenance. The more that valid set constraints are identified the greater the likelihood that that design will be able to accommodate new transactions without the need for extending the design. The more that valid set constraints are identified the easier that design should be to maintain.

The importance of identifying set constraints is illustrated. Consider an item that has three components and that potentially has three set constraints. If raw facts are presented in a form that does not imply any particular functional dependency then some functional dependencies may be overlooked. The fact "the selling price for a part is the purchase price multiplied by the mark-up rate" contains no particular functional dependency. This fact could be interpreted as:

if a part's buying price is known **and** a part's mark-up rate is known, **then** the part's selling price is the buying price multiplied by the mark-up rate.

It is also possible that:

if a part's selling price is known **and** a part's mark-up rate is known, **then** the part's buying price is the selling price divided by the mark-up rate.
if a part's selling price is known **and** a part's buying price is known, **then** the mark-up rate is the quotient of the selling price and the buying price.

are both valid interpretations of this fact. Each of these three if-then forms is logically independent of the other two. If all three of these interpretations are valid, then they should all be represented. The if-then interpretations are identified by the set constraints. An i-schema for an item that represents the example above and shows all three set constraints is shown in Fig. 11.3.

A practical problem occurs in the correct identification of set constraints when the raw fact appears to contain only one "obvious" set constraint. This problem can occur if a causal connection is interpreted as a logical implication. The raw fact "worn piston rings produce blue smoke in the exhaust" could appear to be in the functional form:

if the piston rings are worn, **then** the exhaust contains blue smoke.

[part/sale-price, part/cost-price, part/mark-up]		
part/sale-price	part/cost-price	part/mark-up
(x, w)	(x, y)	(x, z)
→ (w = z × y)		
→ w > y		
∀	∀	
--		O
O	--	
-------------------------	O	-------------------------

Fig. 11.3 i-schema for *[part/sale-price, part/cost-price, part/mark-up]*

If this functional interpretation is the only if-then interpretation represented then a diagnostic rule that deduces the probability of a car's piston rings being worn, given that the exhaust contains blue smoke, may have been lost. Such a rule might be:

if the exhaust contains blue smoke, **then with probability 0.6** [the piston rings are worn]

The relationships between these two functional forms can be expressed using Bayes' theorem. These two functional forms are logically independent of each other.

A practical problem occurs when a raw fact appears to establish an "obvious" "answer". That is, the raw fact seems to establish an answer to a question that seems "bound to reflect the deductive flow of the system". This identified answer may then be the subject of the only set constraint identified. Given the raw fact "the selling price for a part is the purchase price multiplied by the mark-up rate". This fact may imply that:

if a part's selling price is known **and** a part's mark-up rate is known, **then** the part's buying price is the selling price divided by the mark-up rate.

is valid. But this if-then interpretation could be thought of as "useless".

The business of constructing all valid set constraints does not necessarily amount to "permuting" each item's components as in the "buying price versus selling price" example considered above. In the Case Study reported in Chap. 12, the item *[emp/super, pers/job, dept/man, emp/dept]* is identified. The i-schema for this item is shown in Fig. 11.4. In this item {*emp/super*} is a candidate for *pers/job* and { *dept/man, emp/dept* } is a candidate for *emp/super*. There is no symmetry in the set constraints in this item.

[emp/super, pers/job, dept/man, emp/dept]			
emp/super	*pers/job*	*dept/man*	*emp/dept*
(x, w)	(x, 'worker')	(x, z)	(z, y)
$\rightarrow$ (w = y)			
$\emptyset$			
(x, w)	(x, 'manager') (y, 'general manager')	($\perp$, $\perp$)	($\perp$, $\perp$)
$\rightarrow$ (w = y)			
$\emptyset$			
$\forall$		$\forall$	
------------------	O		
O		--	

Fig. 11.4 i-schema for *[emp/super, pers/job, dept/man, emp/dept]*

If all if-then interpretations of a raw fact are gathered then they may be normalised leading to an improved representation of that fact. The different if-then interpretations of a raw fact are not independent of each other. In Chap. 12 the normalisation of the *[emp/super, pers/job, dept/man, emp/dept]* knowledge item shown in Fig. 11.4 is considered. In the normalisation of that item one of the if-then interpretations is employed to normalise another, then the if-then interpretation created by normalisation becomes a candidate for normalising yet another. It is worth representing all valid set constraints whether they are to become part of the functional model or not. The business of representing all valid set constraints is part of the model building process and contributes to the normalisation process. The different if-then interpretations of a raw fact may be used to normalise each other.

11.4 Strategy for maintenance

Knowledge-based systems are well suited to an incremental design life cycle. The modular nature of knowledge enables knowledge-based system to be "grown" by first building an operational sub-system and then "grafting" other sub-systems onto that sub-system until the system is complete. For an incremental design the point at which "design" ceases and "maintenance" begins may be ill-defined. For any system, at some stage "design" as such ceases and "maintenance" begins. The time at which this occurs does not matter.

When the maintenance phase has begun, sooner or later the system design and the physical model may require modification [Compton et al., 1991]. The system design consists of:

- the requirements model;
- the conceptual model;
- the functional model, and
- the internal model.

The internal model is a specification for the physical model. Much of the design may not have been implemented. A transaction that is not part of the design is a *maintenance operation*. The physical model consists of:

- implementations of the value sets of real items, possibly in a relational database management system;
- implementations of the value sets of any input items that are not real items, possibly in a relational database management system;
- implementations of the semantics of some knowledge items, possibly in a knowledge base management system;

- implementations of the transaction linkage programs for each transaction, possibly in a programming language, and
- implementations of the various item and system constraints, possibly in a programming language.

A maintenance operation in general requires that both the design and the physical model should be modified. Only input items and real items have value sets that are *stored*. If the value set of an item is not stored then it may be possible to derive the members of that value set from value sets that are stored. Derived value sets may not be modified. Derived value sets can be used to check for correctness and consistency.

Chapter 9 discusses the distinction between transactions that are alterations and transactions that are examinations. Alterations are transactions that change the system to which they are applied. Examinations do not change the system.

11.4.1 Alterations

An alteration may be of one of the following five different types of modification to:

- the value set of an input item;
- the semantics of an item;
- the program of a transaction linkage;
- the constraints of an item, or
- to the conceptual model constraints.

These five types of alteration may present varying degrees of difficulty to effect. When an alteration is presented the first task is to identify the type of that alteration. The second task is to implement the alteration in the design. The coupling maps may be used to identify those parts of the design that require modification for any given alteration. The third task is implement the alteration in the physical model. A specification for the alterations required to the physical model is provided by the alterations made to the items, value sets, transactions and constraints in the design.

Chapter 9 describes two classes of alteration. These two classes are "updates" and "revisions". If an alteration results in an activity that:

- adds a new system constraint,
- modifies a particular item's semantics or constraints, or
- modifies a particular item's value set

then that alteration is an *update*. An alteration that is not an update then is a *revision*. In general, a revision may result substantial changes to design.

There are two different types of update. A *value update* is an update that results in an activity that modifies a particular item's value set. A value update may be serviced solely by modifying the values in the value set of an item. A *model update* is an update that is not a value update. A model update does not necessarily change the contents of the value set of any item. The execution of value updates and model updates during maintenance are similar. The semantics of an item is a recognising function for that item's value set. If the semantics of an item is modified then this may mean that the value set of that item should change. Consider the item *[part/sale-price, part/cost-price, mark-up]* whose semantics is:

$$\lambda x_1 x_2 x_1 y_2 z \bullet [\ (\ S_{part/sale\text{-}price}(x_1, x_2)$$
$$\wedge \ S_{part/cost\text{-}price}(y_1 = x_1, y_2) \wedge S_{mark\text{-}up}(z) \ )$$
$$\rightarrow (x_2 = z \times y_2) \ ] \bullet$$

if this expression is modified to:

$$\lambda x_1 x_2 x_1 y_2 z \bullet [\ (\ S_{part/sale\text{-}price}(x_1, x_2)$$
$$\wedge \ S_{part/cost\text{-}price}(y_1 = x_1, y_2) \wedge S_{mark\text{-}up}(z) \ )$$
$$\rightarrow (x_2 = z \times y_2 + 10) \ ] \bullet$$

then the value set of that item should change. If the semantics expression is modified to:

$$\lambda x_1 x_2 x_1 y_2 z \bullet [\ (\ S_{part/sale\text{-}price}(x_1, x_2)$$
$$\wedge \ S_{part/cost\text{-}price}(y_1 = x_1, y_2) \wedge S_{mark\text{-}up}(z) \ )$$
$$\rightarrow ((x_2 = z \times y_2) \wedge \text{sells-for}(x_1, x_2)) \ ] \bullet$$

then the value set of that item may not change. If the contents of the value set of an item changes then the semantics of that item must change. The semantics expression should contain an explicit reference to time. Time may be omitted. If the semantics expression is interpreted as an expression "that is currently valid" then there appears to be no need for time. The semantics of the *part/cost-price* item is:

$$\lambda xy \bullet [\ \text{costs}(x\text{:part-number}, y\text{:dollar-amount}) \ ] \bullet$$

the 'costs' predicate could have been defined as "costs(x,y) means x costs y at time τ". The semantics of this item could have been represented as:

$$\lambda xy \bullet [\ \text{costs}_\tau(x\text{:part-number}, y\text{:dollar-amount}) \ ] \bullet$$

If the cost price of parts changes and the value set of this item is stored then the semantics of this item should be modified as well. If the 'costs' predicate is defined as "costs(x,y) means x costs y at the present time" then this definition may be dangerous.

An update may be naturally associated with an item whose value set is not stored. If a system delivers an incorrect response then this may result in the correct response being presented as an update to a query item. That update could be naturally associated with a query item. The storage diagram shows the deductive flow in the internal model. The storage diagram shows how the internal model should be implemented. If a system delivers and incorrect response then the storage diagram may be used to diagnose where the system has failed. In a retail application suppose that the selling price of things is represented by the item *thing/sale-price*. Suppose that the value set of this item is deduced from the value sets of the *thing/cost-price* item and the *mark-up* item. Suppose that "pencils sell for 95¢" and that the system calculates the selling price as 85¢. Then this incorrect response can not be directly absorbed into the design because the value set for the *thing/sale-price* item is not stored in the physical model. The storage diagram may be used to identify the part of the design that is incorrect.

If an update is naturally associated with an item whose value set is stored then the semantics and value set of that item may be modified. That modification should not present any difficulty provided that the update satisfies the item and system constraints. Having modified the item with which the update is naturally associated the coupling map is used to determine a chain of further modifications to other items to ensure that the update is completely represented in the design [Van Zuylen, 1993]. The general method for dealing with updates follows.

If the update α:

- can be performed completely by an existing system transaction then:
    - use this existing transaction to perform α, and finish.
- can be represented as a new system constraint then:
    - modify the existing constraints if necessary to ensure consistency and add α as a system constraint and finish.
- can be represented naturally as a modification to the semantics or value set of a particular item β in the conceptual diagram then:
    - generalise the update α to a new transaction γ such that γ can be represented completely as a modification to the semantics of β then:
    - follow the relationships from β in the i-coupling map to identify other items whose semantics will also have to be modified by γ:
    - add γ to the transaction library, perform α using γ, and finish.
- can be represented completely as a modification to a particular item β's constraints then:
    - modify β's constraints and
    - follow the relationships from β in the i-coupling map to ensure that the update is completely executed and finish.
    when the above is complete:
    - mark any items, transactions or constraints that have been modified with the modifications performed on them, and use the marked design as a specification of the maintenance required on the physical model.

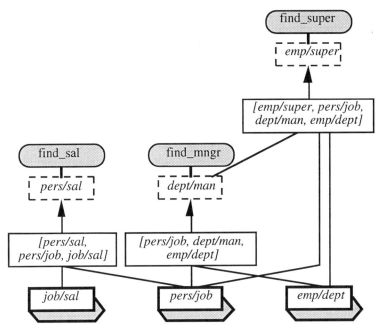

Fig. 11.5   Storage diagram

Revisions may entail substantial modifications to the design. It is not possible to decide whether a presented alteration is an update or a revision without reference to the storage diagram. The alteration "pencils sell for 95¢" is an update if there is both a transaction that can represent this fact and an input item whose value set can readily accommodate this fact without violating any constraints. If there is no such transaction and corresponding input item then this alteration is a revision.

The storage diagram and the i-coupling map play a role in directing alterations.

The storage diagram is used to identify those items that require modification when the system behaves incorrectly. The storage diagram may be used to retrace the deductive flow from any virtual item to locate a set of knowledge items or real items that, if modified, could effect the given maintenance operation. Given the storage diagram shown in Fig. 11.5. Suppose that "XYZ is the supervisor of PQR". If this fact is at variance with the supervisor derived using the transaction "find_super" then the storage diagram can be used to systematically determine where the design requires modification so that the system performs correctly.

The i-coupling map may be used to direct the maintenance procedure. Begin at the item with which the transaction is naturally associated and work from there through the i-coupling map. The i-coupling map may be visualised in an "unwrapped" form as a tree with the item with which the transaction is naturally associated shown at the root. A tree representation of the first two levels of an i-coupling map with the root node "*dept*" is shown in Fig. 11.6. In this example,

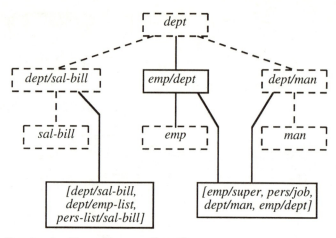

Fig. 11.6 Two levels of i-coupling map from *dept*

if a modification to the item *dept* is performed then the correctness of the first level items *dept/sal-bill*, *emp/dept* and *dept/man* are investigated. If none these three items require modification then the process halts. If one or more of these items does require modification then the coupling relationships from those first-level items that have been modified are followed and so on.

11.4.2 Examinations

Examinations are of five different types:

- reference to the value set of an input item;
- reference to the semantics of an item;
- reference to the program of a transaction linkage;
- reference to the constraints of an item, or
- reference to the conceptual model constraints.

These five types present varying degrees of difficulty to effect. When an examination is presented the first task to be performed is to identify the type of that examination.

Chapter 9 describes two classes of examination. These two classes are "queries" and "interrogations". If an examination results in an activity that refers to:

- existing system constraints;
- a particular item's semantics or constraints, or
- a particular item's value set

then that examination is a *query*. If an examination is not a query then it is an *interrogation*. No general method is given here for dealing with interrogations. There are two different types of query. A *value query* is an examination that results in an activity that refers to a particular item's value set. A value query may be serviced solely from the values in the value set of an item. A *model query* is a query that is not a value query. A model query can not be answered on the basis of the contents of the value set of a particular item.

If a value query is naturally associated with a real item then it may be executed by reference to the value set of that item. Executing such a value query should not present any difficulty. If a value query is naturally associated with a virtual item then its execution is more complicated. Model queries may be executed by reference to the semantics or constraints of an item. The general method for dealing with queries follows. If the query α:

- can be performed completely by an existing system transaction then:
  - use this existing transaction to perform α, and finish.
- can be deduced from the existing system constraints then:
  - deduce α from the existing system constraints and finish.
- can be performed completely by reference to the value set of a particular item β in the conceptual diagram then:
  - generalise the query α to a new transaction γ such that γ can be performed completely by reference to the value set of β and:
  - add γ to the transaction library, revise the design, if necessary add β to the storage diagram, perform α using γ, and finish.
- can be performed completely by reference to a particular item β's semantics or constraints then:
  - use β's semantics or constraints to perform α, and finish.

Interrogations may entail a substantial navigation of the design. It is not possible to decide whether a presented transaction is an query or an interrogation without reference to the storage diagram. The command "retrieve the selling price of pencils" is a query if there is a transaction that can represent this fact and an item whose value set contains the answers that can satisfy this command. If there is no such transaction and no such item then the command is an interrogation.

The conceptual diagram is the starting point in the design for investigating the implementation of an examination.

11.5 Significance of normalisation

Normalisation is a procedure that removes the duplicate relationships from the coupling map. During the system analysis step the data items and the information items may be normalised. During the knowledge engineering step the knowledge items may be normalised. There may be a substantial cost involved in normalising the knowledge items, so the procedure is not necessarily applied.

The basis consists of a set of data items. These data items are the foundation of the conceptual model. If the basis is not normal then maintenance operations on the conceptual model may prove to be costly. If the basis is not normal then the coupling map collapses to the trivial coupling map in which every item is joined to every other item. If raw data is gathered with care then it may not be normal. The identification of two different data items that mean the same thing may appear to be a trivial mistake. If the design is being conducted by a team then the identification of two different data items that mean the same thing does occur. Suppose that in an insurance company application two items in the basis are "*benefit*" and "*payout*". Suppose that the two items "*benefit*" and "*payout*" mean the same thing. Then the information item "*policy/benefit*" has a coupling relationship to the information item "*policy/payout*", and any knowledge item that has the item "*policy/benefit*" as a component has a coupling relationship to a similar knowledge item that has the item "*policy/payout*" as a component. So an unnecessary equivalence relationship in the basis causes a proliferation of coupling relationships at the information level and at the knowledge level.

If there are unnecessary coupling relationships in the basis then there are also such relationships between the information items and knowledge items in the coupling map. This means that the conceptual model is unnecessarily hard to maintain. The presence of unnecessary coupling relationships between the information items leads to such relationships between the knowledge items. The presence of unnecessary coupling relationships in the knowledge items effects the ease with which the conceptual model can be maintained. The data items are the easiest to normalise and the knowledge items are the hardest to normalise. Subjective general observations on the costs and benefits of normalisation are summarised in Fig. 11.7. These observations lead to the practical consideration of how much of the design to normalise. The extent to which the design is normalised substantially depends on the frequency and type of maintenance operations that are to be performed. If the knowledge items are stable then it may well be advisable to avoid the cost of normalising them.

It is difficult to demonstrate that a conceptual model is normal and that it contains no duplicate relationships. It is realistic to assume that a conceptual model may not be normal no matter how carefully it has been derived. So it is also realistic to assume that if maintenance tasks follow the procedure described in the previous section then they may not be fully executed.

Data items	Information items	Knowledge items	Normalisation cost	Maintenance cost
Non-normal	Non-normal	Non-normal	Nil	Very high
Normal	Non-normal	Non-normal	Low	High
Normal	Normal	Non-normal	Medium	Medium
Normal	Normal	Normal	High	Low

Fig. 11.7 The costs and benefits of normalisation

11.6 System constraints

The *system constraints* are constructed during the system analysis, system function and system layout steps. Section 8.6.2 describes model constraints. Section 9.6 describes the refinement of system constraints task within the system function step. Section 10.6 describes the further refinement of system constraints task within the system layout step.

During the system function step the refinement of constraints task consists of:

- the design of constraints for the set of input items, these constraints may be knowledge model constraints;
- the design of constraints for the knowledge items on the flow diagram, these constraints may be information model constraints, and
- the design of any other system constraints.

During the system layout step the refinement of constraints task consists of:

- the design of constraints for the set of real items, these constraints may be knowledge model constraints;
- the design of constraints for the update knowledge items and the query knowledge items, these two sets of constraints may be information model constraints, and
- the design of any other system constraints.

The constraints designed during these two tasks should together constitute a powerful mechanism for protecting the overall integrity of the system [Qian, 1988].

The practical importance of system constraints and integrity checks to the maintenance of information systems is well understood. As far as system maintenance is concerned, a difference between information systems and knowledge-based systems is that a knowledge-based system is designed to receive modifications and updates to the knowledge represented in it on a regular basis [Gottinger & Weimann, 1992]. In addition to the conventional constraints and integrity checks for the data and information, constraints and integrity checks for knowledge are required. Constraints for individual knowledge items are discussed in Chaps. 3–4. Constraints for knowledge items aim to preserve the integrity of those individual knowledge items [Holtzman, 1989]. In addition, system constraints are included. Constraints for knowledge play two roles. First, constraints are a safety alarm that sounds when unexpected transactions are presented. Second, constraints are a specification of the bounds within which modifications may be made without destabilising the system. Both of these roles are considered when the system constraints for knowledge-based systems are designed.

Once the system layout step has been performed and the whole design process is complete, there is a supply of knowledge items in the conceptual model that have not been selected for the internal model. This spare knowledge may be useful for the system integrity checks. An example of such an integrity check is the use of spare knowledge to calculate values for the value set of an input item from the value sets of the real items. These calculations may be carried out automatically in much the same way that information model constraints are applied. By applying these integrity checks during periods of low system usage, a powerful array of checks can be applied for a low additional cost [Sage, 1991].

The coupling relationships define a search space that direct the execution of maintenance operations. By blindly following every coupling relationship in this space a substantial proportion of the design may be checked during the execution of each maintenance operation. Normalisation may be employed to remove the duplicate relationships. If the duplicate relationships have been removed then the only coupling relationships that remain are the equivalence relationships, the sub-item relationships and the component relationships. Sub-item relationships may be reduced to sub-type relationships. "Referential" constraints may be employed to prune this search space.

The maintenance procedure is guided by the coupling map. This procedure is activated by the modification of an item. An item's semantics recognises the members of its value set. If an item's value set is modified then that item's semantics has been modified. The value set of the *part/cost-price* item may be stored in a relation R. The predicate "$costs_\tau(x,y)$" occurs in the semantics of this item. This predicate means that "x costs y at time τ". If a tuple is added, modified or deleted in the relation R then all of the coupling relationships from the item *part/cost-price* should be investigated. So a simple maintenance task on the contents of a relation can generate a significant maintenance exercise. *Referential constraints* may be applied to isolate the effect of simple maintenance tasks such as this.

Consider the item *[part/sale-price, part/cost-price, mark-up]* that is the only knowledge item in the conceptual model. Suppose that the internal model states that the value set of the *mark-up* data item and the value set of the *part/cost-price* information item should both be stored. There are three distinct if-then interpretations of this single knowledge item. The interpretation that derives the value set of the *part/sale-price* information item is required. The constraint that "the value set of the information item *part/cost-price* is *fixed in* the knowledge item *[part/sale-price, part/cost-price, mark-up]*" is a referential constraint. This constraint means that if the tuples in the relation part/cost-price are modified without violating the *part/cost-price* item constraints then it is not necessary to follow the component link to the item *[part/sale-price, part/cost-price, mark-up]*. That is "the validity of the knowledge item *[part/sale-price, part/cost-price, mark-up]* is invariant of the contents of the value set of its component information item *part/cost-price*". This referential constraint is a static constraint on the item *[part/sale-price, part/cost-price, mark-up]*. This constraint states that this knowledge item must apply to any tuple that satisfies the item constraints of the information item *part/cost-price*. This constraint prunes the component relationship *from* the information item *part/cost-price to* the knowledge item *[part/sale-price, part/cost-price, mark-up]* as long as the value set of item *part/cost-price* is modified and the item constraints of the *part/cost-price* item are not violated.

The referential constraint above prunes a component relationship *from* an information item *to* a knowledge item. Component relationships *from* knowledge items *to* their constituent data or information items can be pruned in a similar way. The constraint that "the value set of the knowledge item *[part/sale-price, part/cost-price, mark-up]*" is *fixed on* the information item *part/cost-price*" is a referential constraint. This referential constraint means that if the item *[part/sale-price, part/cost-price, mark-up]* is modified then it is not necessary to follow the component link to the tuples of the value set of the item *part/cost-price*. That is "the validity of the value set of the information item *part/cost-price* is invariant of the item *[part/sale-price, part/cost-price, mark-up]*". This referential constraint is a static constraint on the information item *part//cost-price*. This constraint prunes the component relationship *from* the knowledge item *[part/sale-price, part/cost-price, mark-up] to* the information item *part/cost-price* as long as the clauses that implement the knowledge item *[part/sale-price, part/cost-price, mark-up]* are modified without violating the constraints of that knowledge item.

Referential constraints are constraints that state that a particular component relationship need not be followed during the complete execution of a maintenance operation.

11.7 Management of maintenance

There is considerable flexibility in the way in which an incremental design may be managed. There is considerable flexibility in the way in which maintenance is managed [Rasch & Tosi, 1992]. The knowledge engineering process generates four interlinked models. This leads to the question of how much of the design should be retained and maintained after the initial design process is complete. Choices include:

• discard the entire design and maintain the physical model;
• retain the internal model only, and
• retain the entire design.

If any or all of the design is retained then every maintenance operation should be represented in the design [Chen, Y., 1989]. If a design becomes inconsistent with the physical model then the value of that design to maintenance is diminished [Turban, 1993].

The business of maintenance is related to the structure of the unified design methodology. The first two steps in the unified design process are "requirements

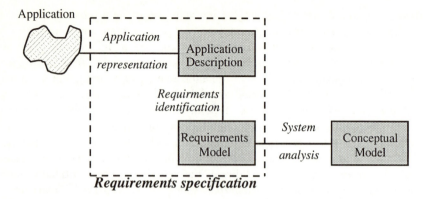

Fig. 11.8 Requirements specification and system analysis

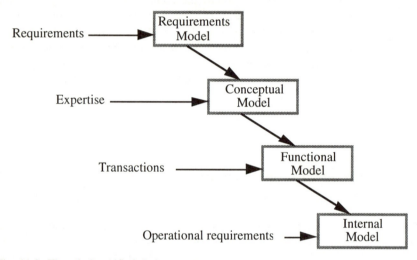

Fig. 11.9 The whole unified design process

specification" and "system analysis". The relationship between these two steps is shown in Fig. 11.8.

The first step of the unified design process focuses on requirements and generates the requirements model. The second step focuses on the expertise and generates the conceptual model. The third step focuses on the transactions and generates the functional model. The fourth step focuses on the operational requirements and generates the internal model. The whole unified design process is represented for a sequential life cycle model in Fig. 11.9.

When the transactions are analysed during the system function step this may lead to a "partial revisit" to the requirements specification step. A "partial revisit" means that such subsequent requirements specification should be consistent with the conceptual model derived to that point. If the possibility of such partial revisits are ignored that this leads to a hierarchy for maintenance operations. In this hierarchy changes to the operational requirements may be accommodated by revisiting the system layout step only. Changes to the transactions may be accommodated by revisiting the system function step provided that the conceptual model is rich enough to represent these changes. Changes to the expertise may be accommodated by revisiting the system analysis step provided that the structure of the conceptual model is rich enough to represent these changes. Changes to the requirements may be accommodated by revisiting the requirements specification step and the modifications are then be passed through the whole unified design.

The construction of the requirements model is the point at which non-trivial modifications are fed into the design. The conceptual model is the first step in the design that is formal. If the design is to be used to direct the maintenance process then the correctness of the conceptual model should be preserved. Any maintenance operation consists of five steps:

1. The statements in the requirements model that are no longer valid, if any, are identified.
2. Those statements that are no longer valid are removed from the requirements model and representations of these statements are removed from the conceptual model, functional model and internal model.
3. Any new statements are added to the requirements model.
4. System analysis, including normalisation, is performed to generate a new conceptual model, functional model and internal model.
5. The resulting modifications to the internal model are a specification of the modifications required to the physical model.

Changes to the operational requirements are common. Typical changes to the operational requirements are changes to the frequency of presentation of the transactions, and changes to the maximum permissible response time for a transaction. Small changes to the operational requirements may occur daily. Criteria may be specified that identify when sufficient changes to the operational requirements have been observed to justify revisiting the system layout step. If the system layout algorithms are embedded in the system then this should result in the knowledge base "automatically reorganising" itself so that its general performance is improved.

Changes to the transactions are common. Typical changes to the transactions are the identification of new transactions or the modification of existing transactions. Dealing with a change in the transactions may mean that the requirements specification step is performed. If a new transaction can be expressed in terms of the items identified in the conceptual model, then it is not necessary to revisit the requirements specification step. Otherwise it is necessary to revisit the requirements specification step.

The unified design methodology is intended for use by a design team. Sections 11.2, 11.3 and 11.5 describe features of the methodology that require management if the methodology is to be used by a team. The unified methodology can be employed to build "large" systems. A crude measure of the *size of a design* is the number of items in the flow diagram for that design. As a rough rule, a design is "large" if it contains at least a few hundred items. A design can be "large" in two different ways. First, a design can contain substantial "depth" of knowledge. Second, a design can contain substantial "breadth" of knowledge. Three measures of the *depth* of a design are the "maximum", "minimum" and "mean" depth. The *depth* of an item is the length of the longest path from that item to the update items in the flow diagram. In the flow diagram shown in Fig. 11.10, item A has depth 3. The *maximum depth, minimum depth* and *mean depth* of a design are defined respectively to be the maximum, minimum and mean, over all query transactions, of the depth of the query items. The maximum depth in the flow diagram shown in Fig. 11.10 is 3, the minimum depth is 2 and the mean depth is 2.6.

Three measures of the *breadth* of a design are as follows. The *maximum breadth, minimum breadth* and *mean breadth* of a design are defined respectively to be the maximum, minimum and mean, over all divisions on the flow diagram, of the number of items in those divisions. The maximum breadth in the example shown in Fig. 11.10 is 5, the minimum breadth is 4, and the mean breadth is 4.8.

If a design has substantial breadth or substantial depth then it is large. In large applications the conceptual model becomes too large for it to be understood easily. In a large design it becomes difficult to relate modifications in the application to the conceptual model. One way of dealing with a design that is too large is to decompose it into a number of smaller sub-systems. This process is called *partitioning* a design.

There are two ways to partition a design. First, all the expertise can be gathered, analysed and normalised then, using some algorithm, the flow diagram can be broken up into workable chunks in such a way as to minimise the number of relationships between its chunks. This method may lead to a partition that does not reflect the natural divisions in the application. The second approach is to establish the partitions to reflect the natural divisions in the application. One type of natural division is determined by the source of the knowledge. If knowledge is being

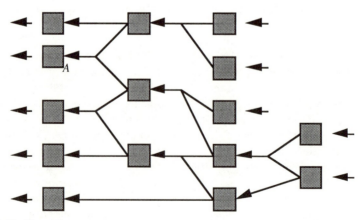

Fig. 11.10 Flow diagram

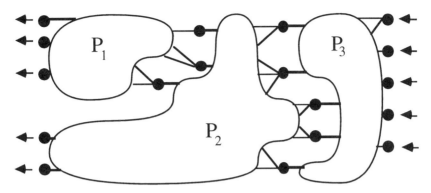

Fig. 11.11 Design in three partitions

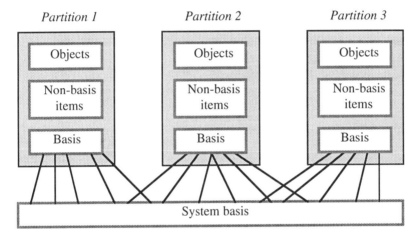

Fig. 11.12 The system basis

drawn from four experts who interact in the natural course of their business then the design can be partitioned into four components that interact in the same way as those experts. No matter how the design has been partitioned, when this has been done the query items in one partition may be the input items in another partition [Goh et al., 1994]. Consider the diagram shown in Fig. 11.11. Modifications performed on a partition are local to that partition if they do not affect the semantics of the query and input items in that partition.

Each partition is modelled separately. Each partition has its own data, information and knowledge items. This may seem like lunacy as it appears advocate the replication of many of the data and information items within the different partitions. A physical model derived from separate partitions is a synthesis of the partitioned knowledge. One way to achieve this synthesis is to construct a "system basis" [Zhang & Bell, 1991]. The *system basis* contains entries for every basis data item in each partition and records the relationships between those basis data items. A system basis is shown in Fig. 11.12. Having related the data items in each partition to the system basis, the business of identifying other items that are common to more than one partition is made easier [Blair, 1994b].

11.8 Summary

- Set constraints are a representation of the valid functional dependencies in items.
- Updates and queries may be executed by following a procedure based on the internal model.
- Normalisation may be applied to reduce maintenance costs.
- System constraints may be applied to the entire design.
- Referential constraints prune component relationships.
- The structure of the four models in a design may be used to accommodate different types of maintenance operation.
- Large systems may be partitioned.
- Modifications performed on a partition are local to that partition if they do not affect the semantics of the query and input items in that partition.
- Partitions may be unified using a system basis.

12 Case study

12.1 Introduction

The case study is set within a small organisation. There is one Managing Director and several employees. The employees each work in one of five departments. At present there are several databases on the organisation's computer. The problem is to design a "personnel management system". In this system the general intention is "to advise the Personnel Manager on staff structure and salaries". Further, suppose this required advice should be derived from the information in the "organisation chart" database and the "salary file" database that are already in existence. At present the "organisation chart" and "salary file" databases are maintained by the Accounts Clerk who is responsible for keeping them up to date. Suppose that the system should only accept queries from the Personnel Manager and should only accept updates from the Accounts Clerk.

The description in this chapter of the application of the unified methodology to this case study is intended to illustrate the use of the methodology. This description shows in detail how the methodology is applied to a simple problem. As a result the description is long and laborious. The amount of design material generated in practice is considerably less than the amount of material presented here. In the working that follows "deliberate mistakes" have not been included. The method is robust in the sense that mistakes made during any step can be corrected during a subsequent step. Subsequent corrections do increase the overall cost of the design. So it may be worthwhile to "double check" each step before proceeding to the next. Alternative designs are considered at various stages in the process. These alternatives substantially increase the length of the description.

12.2 Requirements specification (1)

The requirements specification step is applied to the case study. This step begins with the application representation task that in turn begins with the construction of the context diagram sub-task.

12.2.1 Context diagram

A decision made when constructing the context diagram is the *scope* of a system, which is extent of the problem that the system addresses. If the existing organisation chart and salary file is left as they are then the system will refer to them as required, but if the organisation chart and the salary file are considered to be part of the system then they will be incorporated into the design.

For the time being suppose that the existing organisation chart and salary file should be left as they are and should be considered to be external to the system. The actions of the Accounts Clerk in keeping the organisation chart and salary file up to date would then have nothing to do with the system as such. Then the only thing that the system has to do is to advise the Personnel Manager on staff structure and salaries. Suppose that it is decided to reflect the structure of the existing system by identifying two components. The first component is the component *organisation chart sub-system* that extracts facts from the existing organisation chart database, and the second component is the *salary file sub-system* that extracts facts from the salary file database. The context diagram could then be as shown in Fig. 12.1. By making this decision the scope of a system has been defined so that it does not have to accommodate regular updates to the two fundamental databases, namely the organisation chart database and the salary file database. That is, by restricting the scope the update problem has been substantially avoided. As a result, the system specified in Fig. 12.1 is rather uninteresting.

Alternatively suppose that it is decided that the existing organisation chart

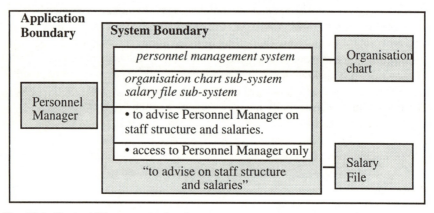

Fig. 12.1 Context Diagram: version 1

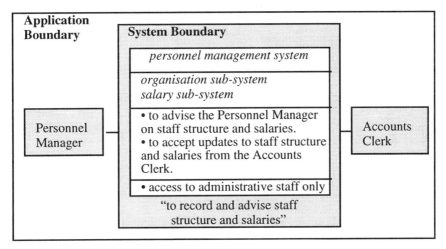

Fig. 12.2 Context Diagram: version 2

database and salary file database should be incorporated into the proposed system. The actions of the Accounts Clerk in keeping the organisation chart database and salary file database up to date become behaviours of the proposed system. Then the system has to do two different things. First it is to advise the Personnel Manager on staff structure and salaries. Second it is to accommodate the updates presented by the Accounts Clerk. Suppose that it is decided to reflect the structure of the existing system by identifying two components. The first component is the component *organisation sub-system* that contains the existing organisation chart database, maintains it and extracts facts from it. The second component is the *salary sub-system* that contains the salary file database, maintains it and extracts facts from it. Both the Personnel Manager and the Accounts Clerk use both of these components. The context diagram could then be as shown in Fig. 12.2: from here on it is assumed that the scope of the system is as shown.

12.2.2 Differentiation

The context diagram shown in Fig. 12.2 shows two players who interact with the system: the Personnel Manager and the Accounts Clerk. If the methodology is applied sequentially and if the requirements of both of these players are examined then this would generate a complex requirements model. It is decided to apply the methodology incrementally.

The differentiation sub-task is concerned with the addition of prioritised prime r-schemas to the context diagram. These prioritised prime r-schemas should be both independent and complete in the sense described in Sect. 7.5.2. The first issue addressed is the criteria on which the prime r-schemas are to be prioritised.

Suppose that the prime r-schemas are prioritised on the basis of how much influence they have on the general "structure" of the system. Suppose that the requirements of the Personnel Manager has a greater influence on the structure of

the system than the requirements of the Accounts Clerk. Prioritise the importance
of the two players identified in the context diagram in terms of their influence on
the structure of the system. The Accounts Clerk is concerned with maintaining
the validity of the tuples in two simple databases. There are two prime r-schemas.
The first, with highest priority, represents the Personnel Manager's requirements.
The second, with lowest priority, represents the Accounts Clerk's requirements.

First consider the prime r-schema that represents the Personnel Manager's
requirements. Suppose the system should be designed to enable the Personnel
Manager to:

- find the supervisor of any given employee;
- find the list of employees supervised by a given person;
- find the manager of any given department;
- find the salary of any given person, and
- find the salary bill for any given department.

The five behaviours noted above all happen to be queries. They lead naturally to
the specification of five behaviours for the single prime r-schema shown in
Fig. 12.3. In the next section this single r-schema is decomposed.

The context diagram is as shown in Fig. 12.2. The prime r-schema for the
Personnel Manager's requirements is shown in Fig. 12.3. The r-schema shown in
Fig. 12.3 makes no reference to the requirements of the Accounts Clerk. From
the context diagram extract the second prime r-schema for the Accounts Clerk's
requirements. Suppose that the Accounts Clerk's requirements are:

personnel management system
organisation sub-system   *salary sub-system*
For the Personnel Manager to: • find the supervisor of any given employee 'find_super'   • find the list of employees supervised by a given person 'find_supervised-list'   • find the manager of any given department 'find_mngr'   • find the salary of any given person 'find_sal'   • find the salary bill for any given department 'find_sal-bill'
• access to Personnel Manager only

"to advise Personnel Manager on staff
structure and salaries"

Fig. 12.3 Prime r-schema for Personnel Manager's requirements

- to create a new organisation in which there are three types of job with associated salaries, no departments and one person who is the Managing Director;
- to modify the salary of a given job;
- to modify the department of a given employee;
- to add a new employee to an existing organisation;
- to delete an existing employee from an existing organisation;
- to add a new department to an existing organisation;
- to delete an existing department from an existing organisation, and
- to delete an existing organisation.

The eight behaviours noted above all happen to be updates. They lead naturally to the specification of eight behaviours for the single prime r-schema shown in Fig. 12.4.

The result of applying the differentiation sub-task to the context diagram shown in Fig. 12.2 is the two prime r-schemas shown in Figs. 12.3–12.4. The two behaviours on the context diagram shown in Fig. 12.2 are independent. As each of the prime r-schemas addresses completely one of those behaviours the two prime r-schemas are both independent and complete. Of these two r-schemas the r-schema in Fig. 12.3 has the higher priority and is processed first. The prime r-schema shown in Fig. 12.4 is set aside and will be processed in Sect. 12.5.

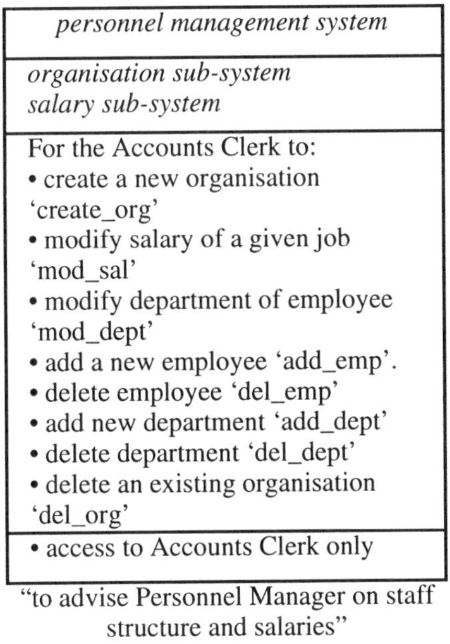

personnel management system
organisation sub-system *salary sub-system*
For the Accounts Clerk to: • create a new organisation 'create_org' • modify salary of a given job 'mod_sal' • modify department of employee 'mod_dept' • add a new employee 'add_emp'. • delete employee 'del_emp' • add new department 'add_dept' • delete department 'del_dept' • delete an existing organisation 'del_org'
• access to Accounts Clerk only

"to advise Personnel Manager on staff
structure and salaries"

Fig. 12.4 Prime r-schema for Account Clerk's requirements

12.2.3 Decomposition

Apply the procedure described in Sect. 7.5.3, and shown in Fig. 7.15, to the decomposition of the prime r-schema shown in Fig. 12.3. This prime r-schema has two components *organisation sub-system* and *salary sub-system*. This leads to the identification of two new r-schemas, and their mission statements as shown in Fig. 12.5. Examine the five behaviours of the single r-schema in Fig. 12.3 and explore how these five behaviours can be broken down into behaviours for the two new r-schemas.

1) "find the supervisor of any given employee". Suppose that in the existing system the answer to this query is deduced from the information in the organisation chart database. So the first behaviour can be entirely resolved within the *organisation sub-system*, and it is moved down to that sub-system.
2) "find the list of employees supervised by a given person". Suppose that in the existing system the answer to this query can be deduced from the information in the organisation chart database. So the second behaviour can be resolved entirely within the *organisation sub-system*, and it is moved down to that sub-system.
3) "find the manager of any given department". Suppose that in the existing system the answer to this query is extracted directly from the organisation chart database that contains the manager of each department. So the third behaviour can be resolved entirely within the *organisation sub-system*, and it is moved down to that sub-system.
4) "find the salary of any given person". Suppose that in the existing system the answer to this query is deduced from the information in both the organisation chart database and the salary file database using the rule:

"The salary of a person is the salary associated with the job that that person has".

The fourth behaviour is achieved in the existing system by extracting the job that a person has from the organisation chart database and the salary for each job from the salary file database. So add the behaviour "find the job of any given person" to the *organisation sub-system*, and add the behaviour "find the salary for any given job" to the *salary sub-system*. Introduce a new component for the *personnel management system*. This component is named *pers/sal*, and it has the behaviour "find the salary of any given person". Replace the fourth behaviour with a behaviour that states how the behaviour of *pers/sal* may be performed by the two behaviours "find the job of any given person" and "find the salary for any given job". So the fourth behaviour is replaced by "the salary of a person *pers/sal* is the salary associated with the job that that person has".

5) "find the salary bill for any given department". Suppose that in the existing system the answer to this query is deduced from the information in both the organisation chart database and the salary file database using the rule:

"The salary bill of a department is the total salary bill associated with the list of jobs associated with that department".

The fifth behaviour is achieved in the existing system by using the organisation chart database to find the list of jobs for all persons in the given department and then using the salary file database to find the salary bill for this list of jobs. So add the behaviour "find the list of jobs for all persons in a given department" to the *organisation sub-system*, and add the behaviour "find the salary bill for a given list of jobs" to the *salary sub-system*. Introduce a new component for the *personnel management system*. This component is named *dept/sal-bill*, and it has the behaviour "find the salary bill for any given department". Replace the fifth behaviour with a behaviour that states how the behaviour of *dept/sal-bill* may be performed by the two behaviours "find the list of jobs for all persons in a given department" and "find the salary bill for a given list of jobs". So the fifth behaviour is replaced by "the salary bill of a department *dept/sal-bill* is the salary bill associated with the list of jobs of all persons in that department".

This completes the application of the procedure in Fig. 7.15 to the single r-schema in Fig. 12.3. The resulting diagram is shown in Fig. 12.5. In line with recommended practice during requirements specification, the full r-schemas for the components *pers/sal* and *dept/sal-bill* have not been given because they appear to represent information items. The *personnel management system* r-schema has been dealt with. It remains to process the *organisation sub-system* r-schema and the *salary sub-system* r-schema. The *organisation sub-system* is chosen first.

Consider the *organisation sub-system* r-schema in Fig. 12.5 and decompose it. This r-schema has five behaviours. In the existing system, the organisation chart database contains details of "the job for each person" and "the department in which each employee works". Two new components *job sub-system* and *location sub-system* could have been introduced to reflect the structure of the organisation chart database, but due to the trivial nature of these two sub-systems decomposition of the *organisation sub-system* is commenced with no components specified.

1) "find the supervisor of any given employee". Suppose that in the existing system the answer to this query is deduced using the rule:

"Workers are supervised by the managers of the departments in which they work and departmental managers are supervised by the general manager".

The first behaviour is achieved in the existing system by finding the employee's job and then, for workers, the supervisor is the manager of the department in which that employee works, for department managers, the supervisor is the general manager. Introduce a new component to the *organisation sub-system*. This component is named *emp/super*, and it has the behaviour "find the supervisor of a given employee". Add the behaviours "find the job of a person", "find the department of any employee" and "find the manager of a department" to the *organisation sub-system* r-schema but the first and the third of these are already there. Replace the first behaviour with a behaviour that states how the behaviour of *emp/super* may be achieved by the three behaviours "find the job of any person", "find the department of any employee" and "find the manager of any department". So the first behaviour is replaced by "the supervisor of an employee *emp/super* is for workers the manager of the department in which they work, and for departmental managers the general manager".

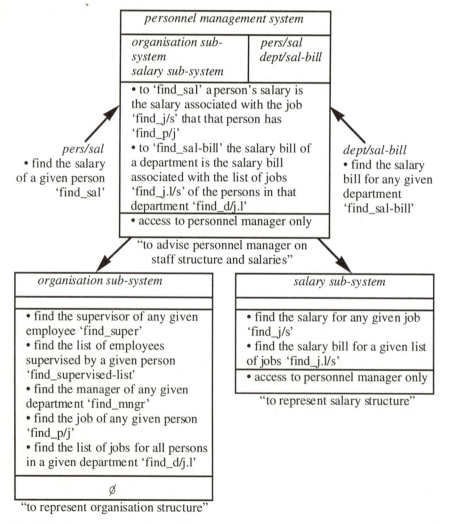

Fig. 12.5 Requirements model for first prime r-schema: first iteration

2) "find the list of employees supervised by a given person". Suppose that in the existing system the answer to this query is deduced by finding the supervisor of each person and inverting this list. Introduce a new component to the *organisation sub-system*. This component is named *super/emp-list*, and it has the behaviour "find the list of employees supervised by a given person". Then identify the existing component *emp/super* that can contribute to this behaviour. Replace the second behaviour with a behaviour that states how the behaviour of *super/emp-list* may be achieved by the behaviour "find the super-visor of a given employee". So the second behaviour is replaced by "the list of employees supervised by a given person *super/emp-list* is deduced by inverting the list containing the supervisor of each employee *emp/super*".

3) "find the manager of any given department". Suppose that in the existing system the answer to this query is available directly from the organisation chart database that contains the manager of each department. Introduce a new component to the *organisation sub-system*. This component is named *dept/man*, and it has the behaviour "find the manager of a given department". Suppose that this behaviour can be performed completely by the component *dept/man*, and that *dept/man* is an input item. Delete the third behaviour from the *organisation sub-system* and add it to the component *dept/man*.

4) "find the job of any given person". Suppose that in the existing system the answer to this query is available directly from the organisation chart database that contains the job of each person. Introduce a new component to the *organisation sub-system*. This component is named *pers/job*, and it has the behaviour "find the job of a given person". Suppose that this behaviour can be performed completely by the component *pers/job*, and that *pers/job* is an input item. Delete the fourth behaviour from the *organisation sub-system* and add it to the component *pers/job*.

5) "find the list of jobs for all persons in a given department". Suppose that in the existing system the answer to this query is deduced using the rule:

"The list of jobs associated with a department is the list of jobs of the list of all employees working in that department"

The fifth behaviour is achieved in the existing system by finding the list of employees who work in the given department and then constructing the list of jobs for those employees. Introduce a new component to the *organisation sub-system*. This component is named *dept/job-list*, and it has the behaviour "find the list of jobs for all persons in a given department". Add the behaviours "find the list of employees who work in a given department" and "find the list of jobs for a given list of persons" to the *organisation sub-system* r-schema. Replace the fifth behaviour with a behaviour that states how the behaviour of *dept/job-list* may be achieved by the two behaviours "find the list of employees who work in a given department" and "find the list of jobs for a given list of persons". The fifth behaviour is replaced by "the list of jobs associated with a department *dept/job-list* is constructed by finding the list of all employees working in that department and then finding the list of jobs for that list of employees".

This completes the decomposition of the five behaviours. This decomposition introduces three new behaviours for the *organisation sub-system*. These three new behaviours are:

* "find the department of any employee";
* "find the list of employees who work in a given department", and
* "find the list of jobs for a given list of persons".

To complete the decomposition of the *organisation sub-system* decompose these three behaviours. The partly completed decomposition is shown in Fig. 12.6. Continue the decomposition of the *organisation sub-system* with the decomposition of these three new behaviours.

1) "find the department of any employee". Suppose that in the existing system the answer to this query is available directly from the organisation chart

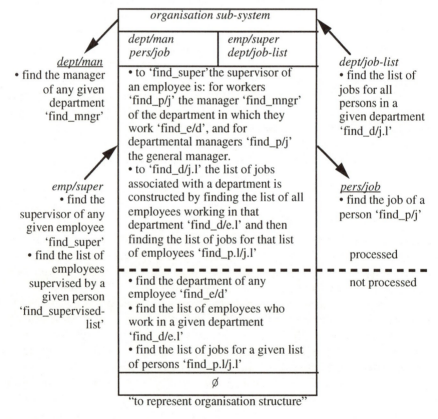

Fig. 12.6 Partly completed decomposition of *organisation sub-system*

database that contains the department for each employee. Introduce a new component to the *organisation sub-system*. This component is named *emp/dept*, and it has the behaviour "find the department of a given employee". Suppose that this behaviour can be performed completely by the component *emp/dept*, and that *emp/dept* is an input item. Delete the first new behaviour from the *organisation sub-system* and add it to the component *emp/dept*.

2) "find the list of employees who work in a given department". Suppose that in the existing system the answer to this query is deduced by finding the depart-

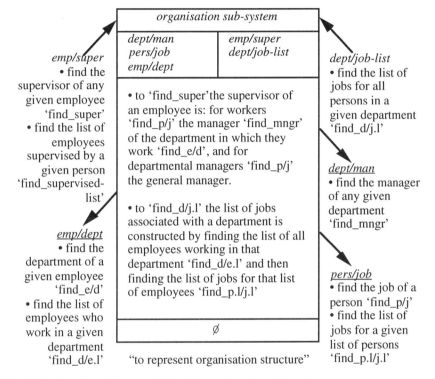

Fig. 12.7 Completed decomposition of *organisation sub-system*

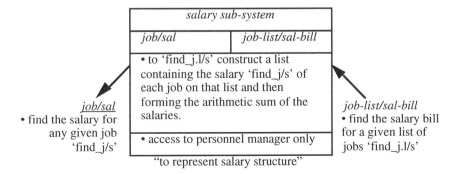

Fig. 12.8 Completed decomposition of *salary sub-system*

ment of each employee and then by inverting this list. Introduce a new component to the *organisation sub-system*. This component is named *dept/emp-list*, and it has the behaviour "find the list of employees who work in a given department". Identify the existing component *emp/dept* that can contribute to this behaviour. Replace the second new behaviour with a behaviour that states how the behaviour of *dept/emp-list* may be achieved by the behaviour "find the department of a given employee". The second new behaviour is replaced by "the list of employees who work in a given department *dept/emp-list* is deduced by inverting the list containing the department of each employee *emp/dept*".

3) "find the list of jobs for a given list of persons". Suppose that in the existing system the answer to this query is deduced using the rule:

"The list of jobs of a list of persons is a list containing the job of each person on the list".

The third new behaviour is achieved in the existing system by finding the list of persons and then by constructing the list of jobs for each person on that list. Introduce a new component to the *organisation sub-system*. This component is named *pers-list/job-list*, and it has the behaviour "find the list of jobs for a given list of persons". Identify the existing component *pers/job* that can contribute to this behaviour. Replace the third new behaviour with a behaviour that states how the behaviour of *pers-list/job-list* may be achieved by the behaviour "find the job of a given person". The third new behaviour is replaced by "the list of jobs of a list of persons *pers-list/job-list* is deduced by constructing a list containing the job of each person on the list using *emp/job*".

This completes the decomposition of the *organisation sub-system*. The final version is shown in Fig. 12.7. Consider the *salary sub-system*. This sub-system contains two behaviours:

1) "find the salary for any given job". Suppose that in the existing system the answer to this query is available directly in the salary file that contains the salary for each job. Introduce a new component to the *salary sub-system*. This component is named *job/sal*, and it has the behaviour "find the salary for a given job". Suppose that this behaviour may be performed completely by the component *job/sal*, and that *job/sal* is an input item. Delete the first behaviour from the *salary sub-system* and add it to the component *job/sal*.

2) "find the salary bill for any given list of jobs". Suppose that in the existing system the answer to this query is deduced using the rule:

"The total salary bill associated with a list of jobs is the arithmetic sum the of the salaries associated with each job in the list".

The second behaviour is achieved in the existing system by taking a list of jobs and then constructing the list of salaries for each job on that list and then forming the arithmetic sum of that list of salaries. Introduce a new component to the *salary sub-system*. This component is named *job-list/sal-bill*, and it has the behaviour "find the salary bill for any given list of jobs". Identify the existing component *job/sal* that can contribute to this behaviour. Replace the second behaviour with a behaviour that states how the behaviour of *job-list/sal-bill* may be achieved by the behaviour "find the job of a given person". The third new behaviour is replaced by "the total salary bill associated with a list of jobs *job-list/sal-bill* is deduced by constructing a list containing the salary of each job on that list using *job/sal* and then forming the arithmetic sum of the salaries".

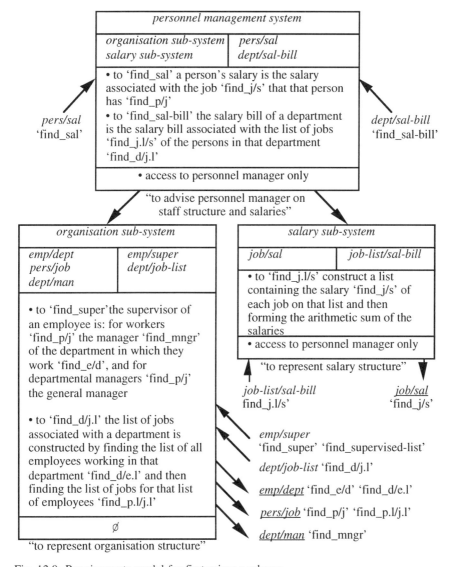

Fig. 12.9 Requirements model for first prime r-schema

pers/sal
pers
sal
• find the salary of any given person 'find_sal'.
• access to Personnel Manager only

dept/sal-bill
dept
sal-bill
• find the salary bill of any given department 'find_sal-bill'.
• access to Personnel Manager only

job-list/sal-bill
job-list
sal-bill
• find the salary for any given list of jobs 'find_j.l/s'.
• access to Personnel Manager only

job/sal
job
sal
• find the salary for any given job 'find_j/s'.
• access to Personnel Manager only

dept/man
dept
man
• find the manager of any given department 'find_mngr'.
∅

pers/job
pers
job
• find the job of any given person 'find_p/j'.
∅

emp/dept
emp
dept
• find the department of any given employee 'find_e/d'.
∅

dept/job-list
dept
job-list
• find the list of jobs of employees in given department 'find_d/j.l'.
∅

super/emp-list
super
emp-list
• find the list of employees supervised by a given person 'find_supervised-list'.
∅

emp/super
emp
super
• find the supervisor of any given employee 'find_super'.
∅

dept/emp-list
dept
emp-list
• find the list of employees in a given department 'find_d/e.l'.
∅

pers-list/job-list
pers-list
job-list
• find list of jobs for a given list of persons 'find_p.l/j.l'.
∅

Fig. 12.10 Information r-schema

This completes the decomposition of the *salary sub-system* r-schema. The decomposition is shown in Fig. 12.8. The decompositions performed have been performed down the identification of r-schemas that represent information items. In line with the criterion in Sect. 7.5.2 further decomposition is considered unnecessary. This completes the decomposition of the single r-schema shown in the Fig. 12.3 into fifteen new r-schemas. For convenience the decomposition of the *personnel management system* r-schema is shown in Fig. 12.9 where the behaviours of the information r-schemas have been omitted due to lack of space. For completeness the information r-schemas are shown in full in Fig. 12.10.

The prime r-schema with highest priority in Fig. 12.3 has been decomposed initially into three new r-schemas, and then into further r-schemas until no further decomposition is considered necessary. This decomposition generates fifteen r-schemas. The twelve information r-schemas are *pers/sal, dept/sal-bill, dept/man, pers/job, emp/dept, dept/job-list, dept/emp-list, super/emp-list, emp/super, pers-list/job-list, job-list/sal-bill* and *job/sal*. They are shown in Fig. 12.10. During system analysis, these twelve r-schemas are further decomposed to yield eight non-decomposable r-schemas that represent data items. These eight non-decomposable r-schemas are named *emp, super, pers, job, dept, man, sal* and *sal-bill*. This completes the decomposition process and completes the requirements specification step for the prime r-schema with highest priority in this example.

12.2.4 Requirements identification

The second task in requirements specification is the "requirements identification" task. This task contains five sub-tasks.

- *Prime scoping* is concerned with identifying those r-schemas in the cascade decomposition that are relevant to the prime r-schemas from which the cascade decomposition is derived. As this example is small the application representation task has been completed accurately and all of the r-schemas are required.
- *Re-use* is concerned with the identification of the r-schemas in the cascade decomposition that should be implemented by re-using an existing software component. In this example the organisation chart database contains the relations 'person/job' and 'employee/department' and that the salary file database contains the relation 'job/salary'. These three relations can be re-used to implement the items *pers/job, emp/dept* and *job/sal* respectively. Suppose that no further re-use is possible.
- *Feasibility* is concerned with the identification of r-schemas in the cascade decomposition that can not be implemented by re-using existing components and that are feasible to implement. All of the r-schemas that can not be implemented by re-using existing components are feasible to implement.
- *Classification* is concerned with the classification of those r-schemas in the cascade decomposition that are feasible to implement "as a knowledge-based system component", "as a conventionally programmed component" or in some

other way. All of the r-schemas are classified as knowledge-based systems components.

- *Volatility* is concerned with the further classification of those r-schemas in the cascade decomposition that are feasible to implement "as a knowledge-based system component" as either "volatile" or "non-volatile" on the basis of whether or not the expense of normalisation is warranted to reduce the subsequent maintenance cost of those r-schemas. The whole system is classified as volatile.

This completes both the requirements identification task and the whole requirements specification step for the prime r-schema with highest priority.

12.3 Analysis (1)

The next step is system analysis. The input to the system analysis step is the requirements model. An incremental design with two steps has been used. For the prime r-schema with highest priority the requirements model is as shown in Fig. 12.9.

The first task in the system analysis step is the construction of the basis. First decompose the r-schemas in the requirements model, as shown in Fig. 12.9, until non-decomposable r-schemas are constructed. As is noted in Sect. 12.2, there are twelve binary information r-schemas that give rise to twenty four data items when decomposed. Many of the non-decomposable r-schemas obtained in this way may have different names. They may have been constructed by different people. A major task at this stage of the analysis is to identify which of the non-decomposable r-schemas obtained are equivalent. In this small exercise this task is trivialised by naming the non-decomposable r-schemas correctly in the first place. They are *emp, super, pers, job, dept, man, sal* and *sal-bill*. Focus on the identifi-

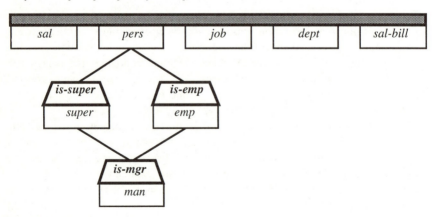

Fig. 12.11 Data items showing sub-types

cation of a normal set of data items. Detect any equivalence relationships and sub-type relationships between data items. Suppose that the resulting eight data items and their sub-type structure is as shown in Fig. 12.11. The i-schemas for the five basis items are shown in Fig. 12.12 and the three o-schemas to derive the three sub-type items are shown in Fig. 12.13.

The next task in the system analysis step is the construction of the conceptual view. The first two sub-tasks in this task are object identification and object library construction. These are "bottom up" tasks that build up from the basis that has already been identified and is shown in Fig. 12.11. Having identified the data items using the terminal nodes of the requirements model, work back up one layer of the requirements model and identify the information items. This next layer of the requirements model is shown in Fig. 12.10. Using this layer identify twelve information items. A conceptual diagram containing the eight data and the twelve information items only is shown in Fig. 12.14. The ten information object operators to generate the twelve information items are shown in Figs. 12.15–12.16. The twelve information items in the conceptual diagram inherit the behaviours from the corresponding r-schemas in the requirements model. These twelve behaviours are shown in Fig. 12.17.

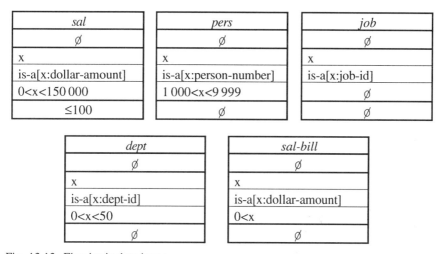

sal	pers	job
$\emptyset$	$\emptyset$	$\emptyset$
x	x	x
is-a[x:dollar-amount]	is-a[x:person-number]	is-a[x:job-id]
0<x<150 000	1 000<x<9 999	$\emptyset$
≤100	$\emptyset$	$\emptyset$

dept	sal-bill
$\emptyset$	$\emptyset$
x	x
is-a[x:dept-id]	is-a[x:dollar-amount]
0<x<50	0<x
$\emptyset$	$\emptyset$

Fig. 12.12 Five basis data items

is-super	is-mgr	ie-emp
X^1	X^1	X^1
(x)	(x)	(x)
'x' is a supervisor-no.	'x' is a manager-no.	'x' is an employee-no.
1 000<x<9 999	1 000<x<9 999	1 000<x<9 999
≤100	$\emptyset$	$\emptyset$

Fig. 12.13 Three sub-type data objects

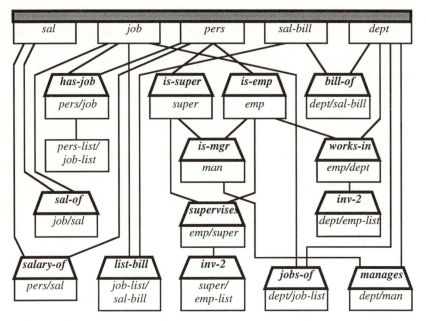

Fig. 12.14 Conceptual diagram: data and information items only

Having identified the twelve information items using those r-schemas in the requirements model that are one level up from the terminal nodes as shown in Fig. 12.10, the next step is to identify the knowledge items. The portion of the requirements model that has not yet been examined contains the three r-schemas shown in Fig. 12.9. The *personal management system* r-schema is at the top of the decomposition and it should be examined last. Select the *salary sub-system* r-schema. This r-schema is shown in Fig. 12.8 which contains one behaviour:

"the total salary bill associated with a list of jobs *job-list/sal-bill* is deduced by constructing a list containing the salary of each job on that list using *job/sal* and then forming the arithmetic sum of the salaries."

The wisdom expressed in this statement establishes an association between the information items *job-list/sal-bill* and *job/sal*. The salary sub-system r-schema gives rise to one knowledge item named *[job-list/sal-bill, job/sal]*. Name the object operator that generates this item **sum-sal**. The item *[job-list/sal-bill, job/sal]* and the object **sum-sal** are shown on the conceptual diagram in Fig. 12.18. The object **sum-sal** is shown in Fig. 12.19.

Select the *organisation sub-system* r-schema. This r-schema contains five behaviours. The first behaviour is:

"the supervisor of an employee *emp/super* is for workers the manager of the department in which they work, and for departmental managers the general manager"

The wisdom expressed in this statement establishes an association between the information items *emp/super, pers/job, emp/dept* and *dept/man*. This behaviour gives rise to a knowledge item named *[emp/super, pers/job, emp/dept, dept/man]*. Name the object operator that generates this item **sup-rule**. The item *[emp/super, pers/job, emp/dept, dept/man]* and the object **sup-rule** are shown on the conceptual diagram in Fig. 12.18. The object **sup-rule** is shown in Fig. 12.19. The second behaviour in the *organisation sub-system* is:

"the list of employees supervised by a given person *super/emp-list* is deduced by inverting the list containing the supervisor of each employee *emp/super*"

The wisdom expressed in this statement establishes an association between the information items *super/emp-list*, and *emp/super*. This behaviour gives rise to a knowledge item named *[super/emp-list, emp/super]*. *super/emp-list* is the inverse of *emp/super*. The object operator that generates this item is **inv-2**. The item *super/emp-list* and the object **inv-2** are shown on Fig. 12.14. The object **inv-2** is shown in Fig. 12.16. The third behaviour in the *organisation sub-system* is:

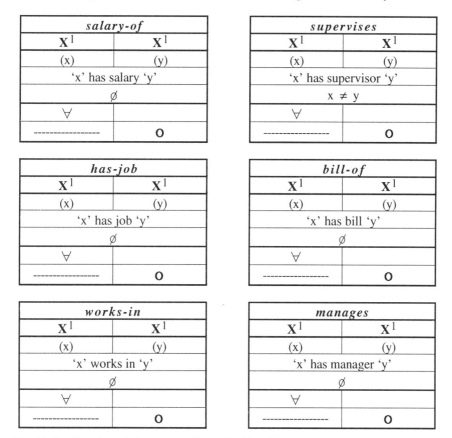

Fig. 12.15 Six of ten information objects in object library

sal-of	
X^1	X^1
(x)	(y)
'x' attracts salary of 'y'	
$\emptyset$	
$\forall$	
-----------------	O

inv-2
X^2
(x, y)
invert on second argument
$\emptyset$
$\forall$
-----------------   O

list-bill	
X^1	X^1
(x)	(y)
job list 'x' has salary bill of 'y'	
$\emptyset$	
-----------------	O

jobs-of	
X^1	X^1
(x)	(y)
dept 'x' has list of jobs 'y'	
$\emptyset$	
$\forall$	
-----------------	O

Fig. 12.16   Four of ten information objects in object library

"the list of jobs associated with a department *dept/job-list* is constructed by finding the list of all employees working in that department and then finding the list of jobs for that list of employees"

The wisdom expressed in this statement establishes an association between the information items *dept/job-list, pers-list/job-list* and *dept/emp-list*. This behaviour gives rise to an item named *[dept/job-list, pers-list/job-list, dept/emp-list]*. Name the object operator that generates this item **dep-job**. The item *[dept/job-list, pers-list/job-list, dept/emp-list]* and the object **dep-job** are shown on the conceptual diagram in Fig. 12.18. The object **dep-job** is shown in Fig. 12.20. The fourth behaviour in the *organisation sub-system* is:

"the list of employees who work in a given department *dept/emp-list* is deduced by inverting the list containing the department of each employee *emp/dept*"

The wisdom expressed in this statement establishes an association between the information items *dept/emp-list* and *emp/dept*. This behaviour gives rise to a knowledge item named *[dept/emp-list, emp/dept]*. *dept/emp-list* is the inverse of *emp/dept*. The object operator that generates this item is **inv-2**. The item *dept/emp-list* and the object **inv-2** are shown on Fig. 12.14. The object **inv-2** is shown in Fig. 12.16. The fifth behaviour in the *organisation sub-system* is:

"the list of jobs of a list of persons *pers-list/job-list* is deduced by constructing a list containing the job of each person on the list using *pers/job*"

The wisdom expressed in this statement establishes an association between the information items *pers-list/job-list* and *pers/job*. This behaviour gives rise to an item named *[pers-list/job-list, pers/job]*. Name the object operator that generates this item **list-job**. The item *[pers-list/job-list, pers/job]* and the object **list-job** are shown on the conceptual diagram in Fig. 12.18. The object **list-job** is shown in Fig. 12.20.

Finally select the *personnel management system* r-schema. This r-schema contains two behaviours. The first behaviour in the *personnel management system* is:

"the salary of a person *pers/sal* is the salary associated with the job that that person has"

The wisdom expressed in this statement establishes an association between the information items *pers/sal*, *pers/job* and *job/sal*. This behaviour gives rise to an item named *[pers/sal, pers/job, job/sal]*. Name the object operator that generates this item **sal-rule**. The item *[pers/sal, pers/job, job/sal]* and the object **sal-rule** are shown on the conceptual diagram in Fig. 12.18. The object **sal-rule** is shown in Fig. 12.19. The second behaviour in the *personnel management system* is:

"the salary bill of a department *dept/sal-bill* is the salary bill associated with the list of jobs of the persons in that department"

The wisdom expressed in this statement establishes an association between the information items *dept/sal-bill*, *dept/job-list* and *job-list/sal-bill*. This behaviour

Item	Behaviour
pers/sal	• find the salary of any given person 'find_sal'
dept/sal-bill	• find the salary bill of any given department 'find_sal-bill'
job-list/sal-bill	• find the salary bill for any given list of jobs
job/sal	• find the salary for any given job
dept/man	• find the manager of any given department 'find_mngr'
pers/job	• find the job of any given person
emp/dept	• find the department of any given employee
dept/job-list	• find the list of jobs of all employees in a given department
super/emp-list	• find the list of employees supervised by a given person 'find_supervised-list'
emp/super	• find the supervisor of any given employee 'find_super'
pers-list/job-list	• find list of jobs for a given list of persons
dept/emp-list	• find the list of employees in a given department

Fig. 12.17 Behaviours of the twelve information items

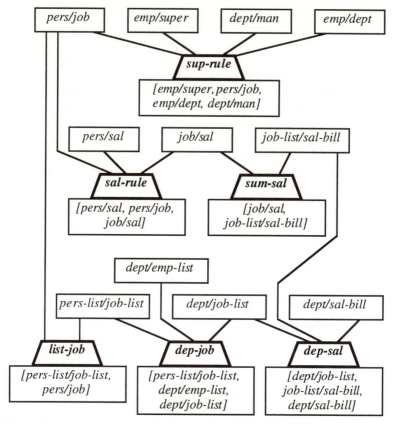

Fig. 12.18 Conceptual diagram: knowledge and associated items only

gives rise to an item named *[dept/sal-bill, dept/job-list, job-list/sal-bill]*. Name the object operator that generates this item **dep-sal**. The item *[dept/sal-bill, dept/job-list, job-list/sal-bill]* and the object **dep-sal** are shown on the conceptual diagram in Fig. 12.18. The object **dep-sal** is shown in Fig. 12.20.

This completes the first two sub-tasks in the construction of the conceptual view task. The following five sub-tasks are removal of equivalent objects, refining object functionality, removal of labels, reduction of sub-items and mixed type decomposition. In this example none of these five sub-tasks leads to any change in the conceptual view.

The final sub-task in the construction of the conceptual view task is to consider the normalisation of the conceptual model. Normalisation is discussed in Sect. 11.5. One choice is to normalise the knowledge in the conceptual model, a less expensive choice is to normalise the knowledge in the functional model. For the sake of illustration both options are considered here. Before considering normalisation first check that no item component may be derived from a sub-set of the other item components.

Investigate the conceptual diagram in Fig. 12.18 to ensure that no item component may be derived from a sub-set of the other item components. Suppose that the item *dept/man* may be derived from the items *pers/job* and *emp/dept*. This derivation may be achieved by the rule:

sup-rule			
X^2	X^2	X^2	X^2
(x, w)	(x, 'worker')	(x, z)	(z, y)
$\rightarrow$ (w = y)			
$\emptyset$			
(x, w)	(x, 'manager') (y, 'general manager')	($\perp$, $\perp$)	($\perp$, $\perp$)
$\rightarrow$ (w = y)			
$\emptyset$			
$\forall$		$\forall$	
------------------	O		
O		--	

sum-sal	
(LX, R)	(X, R)
('$\emptyset$', 0)	($\perp$, $\perp$)
$\emptyset$	
$\emptyset$	
(x.y, z) (y, w)	(x, u)
$\rightarrow$ (z = w + u))	
$\emptyset$	
O	-----------------------------

sal-rule		
X^2	X^2	X^2
(x, w)	(x, y)	(y, z)
$\rightarrow$ (w = z)		
$\emptyset$		
O	--	
--		O

Fig. 12.19 Knowledge objects: part 1

list-job		
LX^2		**X**^{2}
('ø', 'ø')		($\perp$, $\perp$)
	ø	
	ø	
(w.y, x.z) (y, z)		(w, x)
	ø	
	ø	
O		--------------------------------

dep-job		
(X, LX)	**(X, LX)**	**LX**^{2}
(x, z)	(x, y)	(y, z)
	ø	
	ø	
O	---	

dep-sal		
(X, R)	**(X, LX)**	**(LX, R)**
(x, z)	(x, y)	(y, z)
	ø	
	ø	
O	---	

Fig. 12.20 Knowledge objects: part 2

"the manager of a department *dept/man* is the employee who works in that department and whose job is that of 'manager'"

This statement should have been identified as a behaviour in the *organisation subsystem* and the requirements model should be modified. This modification replaces a real component with a virtual component. The wisdom expressed in this statement establishes an association between the information items *dept/man*, *pers/job* and *emp/dept*. This statement leads to an addition to the object **sup-rule**. Look for other ways in which an item component may be derived from a sub-set of other item components. Suppose that the item *emp/dept* may be derived from the items *emp/super* and *dept/man* by the rule:

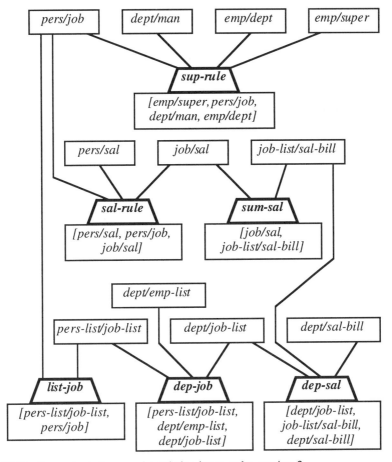

Fig. 12.21   Conceptual diagram: knowledge items only: version 2

"an employee works in a department *emp/dept* if *either* that employee is manager of that department *or* that employee is supervised by the manager of that department"

This statement should have been identified as a behaviour in the *organisation sub-system* but the requirements model should *not* be modified. Such a modification cannot be accommodated by replacing a real component with a virtual component. The wisdom expressed in this statement establishes an association between the information items *dept/man*, *emp/super* and *emp/dept*. This statement leads to a second addition to the object *sup-rule*. Notice how the process of normalisation has requires that the requirements specification step should be re-visited. As no item component may be derived from a sub-set of the other item components the conceptual diagram is as shown in Fig. 12.21.

Suppose that the conceptual model is to be normalised. The current version of the conceptual diagram is shown in Fig. 12.21. The visual structure of the conceptual diagram shown in Fig. 12.21 is useful in achieving this. The structure identified by the object *sal-rule* and the structure identified by the four objects *list-job*, *dep-job*, *dep-sal* and *sum-sal* both "hang from" the two information items *pers/job* and *job/sal*. So find out whether the wisdom expressed within the *sal-rule* structure is contained within the other. It is contained within the other and the conceptual diagram simplifies to the version shown in Fig. 12.22. The second behaviour in the *personnel management system* should be re-expressed as:

"the salary bill of a department *dept/sal-bill* is the total salary bill for the list of employees who work in that department"

The wisdom expressed in this statement establishes an association between the information items *dept/emp-list*, *pers-list/sal-bill* and *dept/sal-bill*. This behaviour gives rise to an item named *[dept/emp-list, pers-list/sal-bill, dept/sal-bill]*. Name the object operator that generates this item *sal-dep*. The item *[dept/emp-list, pers-list/sal-bill, dept/sal-bill]* and the object *sal-dep* are shown on the conceptual diagram in Fig. 12.22. The object *sal-dep* is shown in Fig. 12.26.

Consider why this simpler version was not identified in the first place. The simpler version employs the information item *pers-list/sal-bill*. This item was not identified in the initial analysis because it belongs to neither the *organisation sub-system* nor the *salary sub-system*. The two chosen components shown in the context diagram have prevented the identification of this information item.

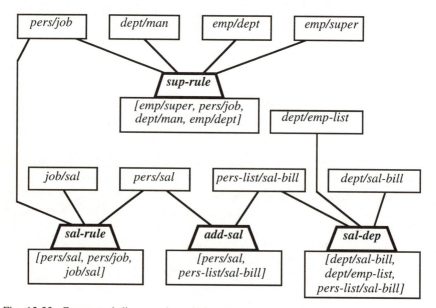

Fig. 12.22 Conceptual diagram: knowledge items only: version 3

Having added the statement above to the *personnel management system*, in line with the decomposition procedure, also add the behaviour "• find the salary bill for a given list of persons.". Following the decomposition procedure, this behaviour is passed to the *pers-list/sal-bill* r-schema and is replaced by:

"the total salary bill associated with a list of persons *pers-list/sal-bill* is deduced by constructing a list containing the salary of each person on that list using *pers/sal* and then forming the arithmetic sum of the salaries."

The wisdom expressed in this statement establishes an association between the information items *pers-list/sal-bill* and *pers/sal*. This behaviour gives rise to an item named *[pers-list/sal-bill, pers/sal]*. Name the object operator that generates this item ***add-sal***. The item *[pers-list/sal-bill, pers/sal]* and the object ***add-sal*** are shown on the conceptual diagram in Fig. 12.22. The object ***add-sal*** is shown in Fig. 12.25.

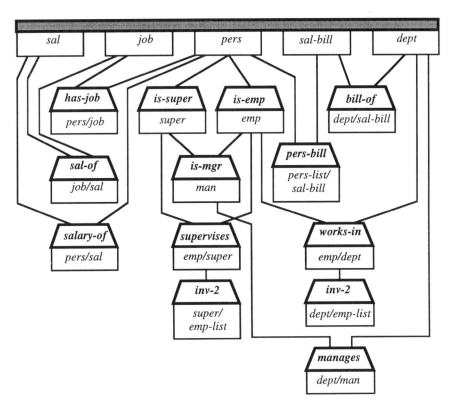

Fig. 12.23 Conceptual diagram: data and information items only: version 3

salary-of	
X^1	X^1
(x)	(y)
'x' has salary 'y'	
∅	
∀	
----------------	O

supervises	
X^1	X^1
(x)	(y)
'x' has supervisor 'y'	
x ≠ y	
∀	
----------------	O

has-job	
X^1	X^1
(x)	(y)
'x' has job 'y'	
∅	
∀	
----------------	O

bill-of	
X^1	X^1
(x)	(y)
'x' has bill 'y'	
∅	
∀	
----------------	O

works-in	
X^1	X^1
(x)	(y)
'x' works in 'y'	
∅	
∀	
----------------	O

manages	
X^1	X^1
(x)	(y)
'x' has manager 'y'	
∅	
∀	
----------------	O

sal-of	
X^1	X^1
(x)	(y)
'x' attracts salary of 'y'	
∅	
∀	
----------------	O

inv-2
X^2
(x, y)
invert on second argument
∅
∀
---------------- O

pers-bill	
LX^1	R^1
(x)	(y)
list of persons 'x' has salary bill of 'y'	
∅	
----------------	O

Fig. 12.24 Nine information objects in object library

sup-rule			
$\mathbf{X}^2$	$\mathbf{X}^2$	$\mathbf{X}^2$	$\mathbf{X}^2$
(x, w)	(x, 'worker')	(x, z)	(z, y)
$\to (w = y)$			
$\emptyset$			
(x, w)	(x, 'manager') (y, 'general manager')	$(\perp, \perp)$	$(\perp, \perp)$
$\to (w = y)$			
$\emptyset$			
$\forall$		$\forall$	
-----------------	O		
O		---------------------------------------	

add-sal	
(LX, R)	**(X, R)**
('$\emptyset$', 0)	$(\perp, \perp)$
$\emptyset$	
$\emptyset$	
(y.u, v) (u, x)	(y, z)
$\to (v = x + z))$	
$\emptyset$	
O	---------------------------

Fig. 12.25 Two of four knowledge objects

The normalised conceptual diagram is as shown in Figs. 12.22–12.23. The basis is as in the original version shown in Fig. 12.11. The nine information objects are as shown in Fig. 12.24. The four knowledge objects are as shown in Figs. 12.25–12.26. The behaviour of the items in the conceptual model are inherited from the requirements model. The requirements model has been modified during system analysis. The current version of the requirements model is shown in Fig. 12.27. Once the conceptual model has been normalised objects cease to have any immediate value. The normalised explicit conceptual diagram is shown in Fig. 12.28. The "what" and the "how" are combined during the next section to generate the functional model. The wisdom represented in the conceptual model is *capable* of doing considerably more than it is initially *required* to do.

The next task in the system analysis step is the construction of the c-coupling map. As the model has been normalised and the only "sub-" relationships are sub-item relationships between data items the only coupling relationships are the components relationships that are shown on the conceptual diagram in Fig. 12.28. The c-coupling map is as shown in Fig. 12.29.

To complete the system analysis step the final task is the design of the constraints. Individual constraints have been defined in the items and objects defined above. In this example no model constraints are defined.

12.4 Function (1)

The next step is system function. The input to the system function step is the requirements model and the conceptual model. This example uses an incremental design with two steps. From the prime r-schema with highest priority the requirements model is as shown in Fig. 12.27, and the conceptual diagram for the corresponding conceptual model is as shown in Figs. 12.22–12.23.

The first task in the system function step is the analysis of transactions. During this task represent each transaction and then link each transaction to the items in the conceptual model. The first sub-task is to construct a t-schema for each transaction. The five transactions discussed during the requirements specification step for the first prime r-schema are:

- find the supervisor of any given employee.
- find the list of employees supervised by a given person.
- find the manager of any given department.
- find the salary of any given person.
- find the salary bill for any given department.

sal-rule		
X^2	X^2	X^2
(x, w)	(x, y)	(y, z)
$\to$ (w = z)		
$\emptyset$		
O	------------------------------	
------------------------------		O

sal-dep		
X^2	(X, LX)	(LX, X)
(x, w)	(x, y)	(y, z)
$\to$ (w = z)		
$\emptyset$		
O	------------------------------	

Fig. 12.26 Two of four knowledge objects

The t-schemas for these five transactions are shown in Fig. 12.30.

The second sub-task in the analysis of transactions task is to link the t-schemas to a set of items in the conceptual model. To achieve this for each t-schema:

- locate the t-schema's behaviour in the requirements model;
- use the requirements model to identify a set of items that can support the t-schema's behaviour, and
- construct a program that performs the t-schema's behaviour with reference to the t-schema's instruction and the identified items.

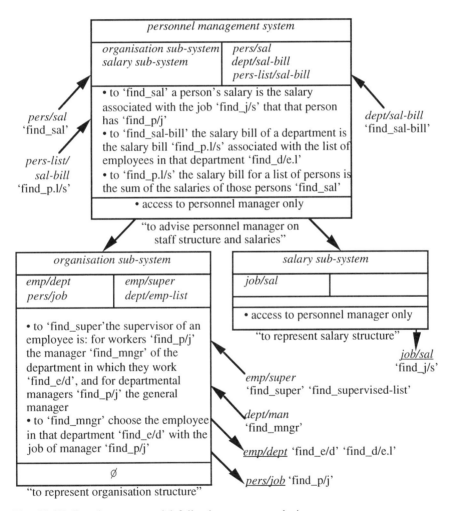

Fig. 12.27 Requirements model following system analysis

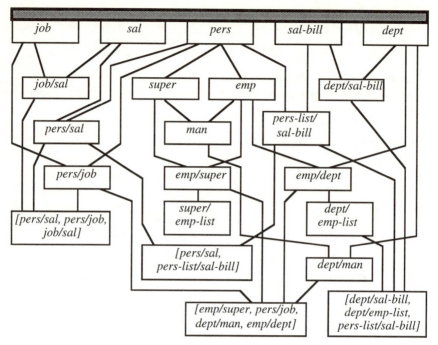

Fig. 12.28 Normalised explicit conceptual diagram

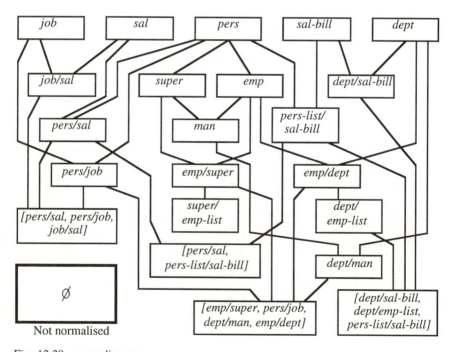

Fig. 12.29 c-coupling map

find_super		
find the supervisor of an employee		
Personnel Manager	*personnel management system*	Personnel Manager
employee number	<emp_no.>	
	(super, OK)	(supervisor, OK)
find_super(<emp_no.>, super, OK)		

find_supervised-list		
find the list of employees supervised by a given person		
Personnel Manager	*personnel management system*	Personnel Manager
person number	<pers_no.>	
	(emp-list, OK)	(employee list, OK)
find_supervised-list(<pers_no.>, emp-list, OK)		

find_mngr		
find the manager of any given department		
Personnel Manager	*personnel management system*	Personnel Manager
department name	<dept_name>	
	(pers_no., OK)	(person, OK)
find_mngr(<dept_name>, pers_no., OK)		

find_sal		
find the salary of any given person		
Personnel Manager	*personnel management system*	Personnel Manager
person number	<pers_no.>	
	(sal, OK)	(salary, OK)
find_sal(<pers_no.>, sal, OK)		

find_sal-bill		
find the salary bill for a given department		
Personnel Manager	*personnel management system*	Personnel Manager
department name	<dept_name>	
	(sal-bill, OK)	(salary bill, OK)
find_sal-bill(<dept_name>, sal-bill, OK)		

Fig. 12.30 t-schema for first prime r-schema

Using Fig. 12.27 locate the five behaviours and identify the items that can support those behaviours. The result of this operation is shown in Fig. 12.31. The behaviours of the five t-schemas shown in Fig. 12.30 may be satisfied directly using the value sets of the five items *emp/super, super/emp-list, dept/man, pers/sal* and *dept/sal-bill*. These five items are in the conceptual model as shown in Fig. 12.28. To complete this sub-task it remains to construct the programs. The logic programs to link these five t-schemas to the items in the conceptual model are:

find_super(<emp_no.>, super, OK) ←
    FIND(<emp_no.>, super)IN(*emp/super*)RES(OK)

find_supervised-list(<pers_no.>, emp-list, OK) ←
    FIND(<pers_no.>, emp-list)IN(*super/emp-list*)RES(OK)

find_mngr(<dept_name>, pers_no., OK) ←
    FIND(<dept_name>, pers_no.)IN(*dept/man*)RES(OK)

find_sal(<pers_no.>, sal, OK) ←
    FIND(<pers_no.>, sal)IN(*pers/sal*)RES(OK)

find_sal-bill(<dept_name>, sal-bill, OK) ←
    FIND(<dept_name>, sal-bill)IN(*dept/sal-bill*)RES(OK)

The construction of these five logic programs completes the analysis of transactions task for the first prime r-schema.

Figure 12.31 shows the items that support transactions directly. For completeness Fig. 12.32 shows the behaviours of the remaining information and knowledge items in the conceptual model as shown in Fig. 12.28.

The second task in the system function step is the construction of the functional view. During the initial requirements specification the following items were identified as input items *dept/man, pers/job, emp/dept* and *job/sal*. During system analysis it was discovered that the item *dept/man* could be derived from the items *pers/job* and *emp/dept*. Proceed on the basis that there are three input items namely *pers/job, emp/dept* and *job/sal*.

In Sect. 12.3 considers two options. The first option is the partly normalised conceptual model whose conceptual diagram is shown in Fig. 12.21. The second option is the completely normalised conceptual model whose conceptual diagram is as shown in Fig. 12.22. Consider the construction of the functional view commencing from both of these models as starting points. Both lead to the same result.

Consider the simplest case. Start from the completely normalised conceptual model whose conceptual diagram is as shown in Fig. 12.22. The resulting flow diagram is shown in Fig. 12.33. This flow diagram shows the three input items, the five transaction and sufficient intermediate items. It satisfies the functional requirements noted above.

Item	Behaviour
emp/super	• find the supervisor of any given employee 'find_super' • find the list of employees supervised by a given person 'find_supervised-list'
dept/man	• find the manager of any given department 'find_mngr'
pers/sal	• find the salary of any given person 'find_sal'
dept/sal-bill	• find the salary bill of any given department 'find_sal-bill'

Fig. 12.31 Information items that support a transaction directly

Information items that do not support a transaction directly

Item	Behaviour
pers/job	• find the job of any given person 'find_p/j'
job/sal	• find the salary for any given job 'find_j/s'
pers-list/sal-bill	• find the salary bill for any given list of persons 'find_p.l/s'
emp/dept	• find the department of any given employee 'find_e/d' • find the list of employees in any given department 'find_d/e.l'

Knowledge items

Item	Behaviour
[emp/super, pers/job, dept/man, emp/dept]	• to 'find_super' the supervisor of an employee is for workers 'find_p/j' the manager 'find_mngr' of the department in which they work 'find_e/d', and for departmental managers 'find_p/j' the general manager • to 'find_mngr' choose the employee in that department 'find_e/d' with the job of manager 'find_p/j'
[pers/sal, pers/job, job/sal]	• to 'find_sal' a person's salary is the salary associated with the job 'find_j/s' that that person has 'find_p/j'
[pers/sal, pers-list/sal-bill]	• to 'find_p.l/s' the salary bill for a list of persons is the sum of the salaries of those persons 'find_sal'
[dept/sal-bill, dept/emp-list, pers-list/sal-bill]	• to 'find_sal-bill' the salary bill of a department is the salary bill 'find_p.l/s' associated with the list of employees in that department 'find_d/e.l'

Fig. 12.32 Behaviours of remaining information and knowledge items

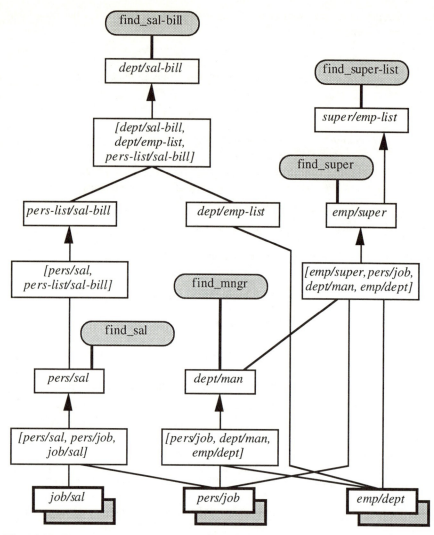

Fig. 12.33 Flow diagram for normalised functional model

Start from the partly normalised conceptual model whose conceptual diagram is as shown in Fig. 12.21. The resulting flow diagram is shown in Fig. 12.34. This flow diagram satisfies the functional requirements noted above. The potential for normalisation can be noted by the structure of the flow diagram. Consider the two sub-structures shown in Fig. 12.35. Inspection of these sub-structures leads to normalisation and the sub-structures shown in Fig. 12.36.

No matter how it may have been derived, consider the normalised functional model whose flow diagram as shown in Fig. 12.33.

The third task in the system function step is the construction of the f-coupling map. In this example the f-coupling map is the same as the c-coupling map shown in Fig. 12.29.

The final task in the system function step is the refinement of constraints. Particularly the development of constraints for the input items. As the first prime r-schema contained no update transactions it is sensible to defer the consideration of constraints for the input items until the updates have been analysed. This is done during the analysis of the second prime r-schema.

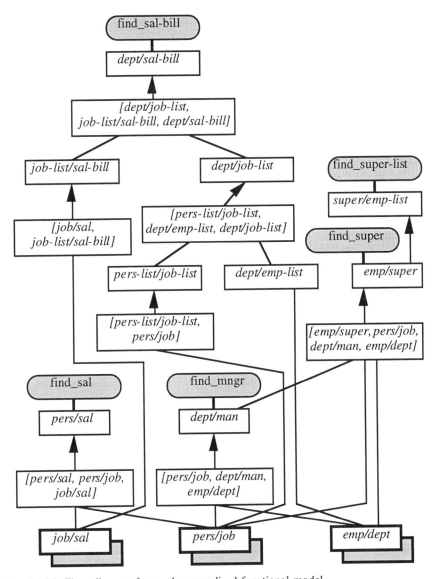

Fig. 12.34 Flow diagram for partly normalised functional model

Before proceeding to the system layout step return to the beginning of the whole design process and complete requirements specification and system analysis for the second prime r-schema. It might appear that another major analytical exercise is about to commence. If the first prime r-schema is well chosen then this subsequent analysis of the second prime r-schema should dovetail neatly into the work already performed.

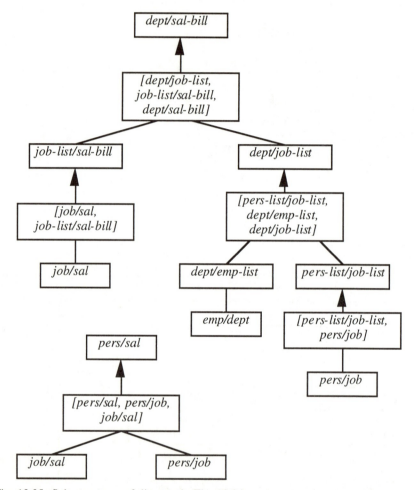

Fig. 12.35 Sub-structures of diagram in Fig. 12.34

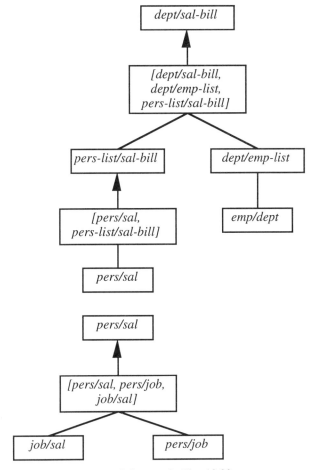

Fig. 12.36 Normal sub-structures of diagram in Fig. 12.33

12.5 Second prime r-schema

The first three design steps, namely requirements specification, system analysis, and system function have been completed for the first prime r-schema that represents the Personnel Manager's requirements. A normalised functional model has been derived from the first prime r-schema. In the incremental design consider the second prime r-schema that represents the Accounts Clerk's requirements.

12.5.1 Requirements specification (2)

The context diagram is as shown in Fig. 12.2. The prime r-schema for the Personnel Manager's requirements that was extracted from the context diagram is as shown in Fig. 12.3. The prime r-schema shown in Fig. 12.3 makes no reference to the requirements of the Accounts Clerk. The prime r-schema for the Accounts Clerk's requirements was shown in Fig. 12.4. For convenience this prime r-schema is shown again in Fig. 12.37.

Apply the decomposition procedure to the prime r-schema shown in Fig. 12.37.

- the first behaviour is "to create a new organisation in which there are three types of job with associated salaries, no departments and one person who is the Managing Director". Suppose that in the existing system this is achieved by

personnel management system
organisation sub-system *salary sub-system*
For the Accounts Clerk to: • create a new organisation 'create_org' • modify salary of a given job 'mod_sal' • modify department of employee 'mod_dept' • add a new employee 'add_emp'. • delete employee 'del_emp' • add new department 'add_dept' • delete department 'del_dept' • delete an existing organisation 'del_org'
• access to Accounts Clerk only

"to advise Personnel Manager on staff
structure and salaries"

Fig. 12.37 Prime r-schema for Account Clerk's requirements

creating a new organisation chart database that contains no departments and with one person who holds the job of Managing Director, a new salary file database containing three job categories and their respective salaries. The first behaviour can be achieved by actions in the *organisation sub-system* and the *salary sub-system* and the rule "to create a new organisation initialise the *organisation sub-system* and initialise the *salary sub-system*".

- the second behaviour is "to modify the salary of a given job". Suppose that in the existing system this is achieved by a modification to the salary file database. This behaviour can be achieved entirely within the *salary sub-system*, and it is moved down to that sub-system.
- the third behaviour is "to modify the department of a given employee". Suppose that in the existing system this is achieved by a modification to the organisation chart database. This behaviour can be achieved entirely within the *organisation sub-system*, and it is moved down to that sub-system.
- the fourth behaviour is "to add a new employee to an existing organisation".

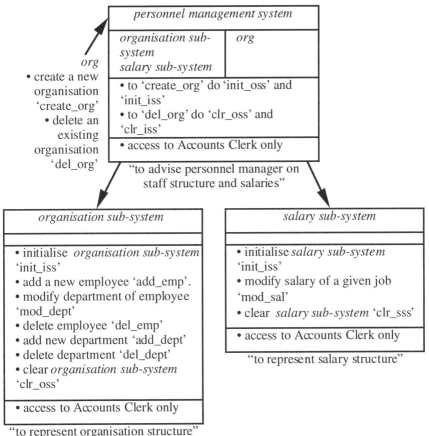

Fig. 12.38 Requirements model for second prime r-schema: first iteration

Suppose that in the existing system this is achieved by doing two things in the organisation chart database. First, the employee is recorded as having a certain job. Second, the employee is allocated to a department. This is subject to the constraint that there is a one to one correspondence between each Department and a particular employee with the job of Manager. This behaviour can be achieved entirely within the *organisation sub-system*, and it is moved down to that sub-system.

- the fifth behaviour is "to delete an existing employee from an existing organisation". Suppose that in the existing system this is achieved by doing two things in the organisation chart database. First, the employee is deleted from the file that contains that employee's job. Second, the employee is deleted from the file that contains that employee's department. This is also subject to the constraint that there is a one to one correspondence between each Department and a particular employee with the job of Manager. This behaviour can be achieved entirely within the *organisation sub-system*, and it is moved down to that sub-system.

- the sixth behaviour is "to add a new department to an existing organisation". Suppose that in the existing system this is achieved by doing two things in the organisation chart database. First, an employee who has the job Worker is given the job Manager. Second, that employee is represented as belonging to the new department. This is also subject to the constraint that there is a one to one correspondence between each Department and a particular employee with the job of Manager. This behaviour can be achieved entirely within the *organisation sub-system*, and it is moved down to that sub-system.

- the seventh behaviour is "to delete an existing department from an existing organisation". Suppose that in the existing system this is achieved by doing three things in the organisation chart database. First, the employee who works in that Department and has the job Manager is given the job Worker. Second, all employees who work in that department are reallocated to another department. This is also subject to the constraint that there is a one to one correspondence between each Department and a particular employee with the job of Manager. This behaviour can be achieved entirely within the *organisation sub-system*, and it is moved down to that sub-system.

- the eighth behaviour is "to delete an existing organisation". Suppose that in the existing system this is achieved by deleting the contents of the organisation chart database that contains the job of each person and the department of each employee, and deleting the contents of the salary file database that contains the three job categories and their respective salaries. The first behaviour can be achieved by actions in the *organisation sub-system* and the *salary sub-system* and the rule "to delete an existing organisation clear the *organisation sub-system* and clear the *salary sub-system*".

This completes the application of the procedure in Fig. 7.15 to the single r-schema in Fig. 12.37. The resulting diagram is shown in Fig. 12.38. The *personnel management system* r-schema has been dealt with. It remains to process the *organisation sub-system* r-schema and the *salary sub-system* r-schema. Deal with the *organisation sub-system* first.

Consider the *organisation sub-system* r-schema in Fig. 12.38 and decompose it. This r-schema has seven behaviours. In line with the analysis of the *organisation sub-system* performed for the first prime r-schema, no components for the *organisation sub-system* are introduced before performing the decomposition. During the analysis of the first prime r-schema the two components *emp/dept* and *pers/job* were identified for the *organisation sub-system* as re-useable real components. Without going into unnecessary detail, the seven behaviours in the *organisation sub-system* may be replaced by:

"to initialise the *organisation sub-system* first the *organisation sub-system* and second add the name of the Managing Director in γ(*pers/job*)"

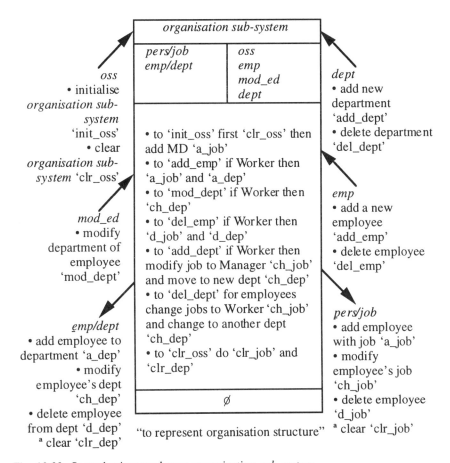

Fig. 12.39 Second prime r-schema: *organisation sub-system*

"to clear the *organisation sub-system* first clear γ(*pers/job*), second clear γ(*emp/dept*)"

"given an employee and a department, to add an employee to that department first add the name of the employee to γ(*pers/job*) with the job 'Worker' and second add the name of the employee to γ(*emp/dept*) with the name of that employee's department"

"given an employee and a department, to modify the department of that employee first confirm that the employee is a 'Worker' in γ(*pers/job*) and then modify γ(*emp/dept*) with the name of that employee's new department"

"given an employee, to delete that employee delete the employee from γ(*pers/job*) as a 'Worker' and from γ(*emp/dept*)"

"given an employee and a department, to add a new department with that employee as manager first replace the employee's job of 'Worker' with 'Manager' in γ(*pers/job*) and second replace the employee's department in γ(*emp/dept*)"

"given two departments deptA and deptB, to delete deptA first confirm that no employee allocated to deptA in γ(*emp/dept*) is a 'Worker' in γ(*pers/job*), second find manager of deptA in γ(*dept/man*), and third replace the manager's job 'Manager' with 'Worker' in γ(*pers/job*) and fourth replace the former manager's department with deptB in γ(*emp/dept*)"

These seven behaviours may be effected by modifying the value sets of the items *emp/dept* and *pers/job*. This completes the decomposition of the seven behaviours in the *organisation sub-system*. The decomposition is shown in Fig. 12.39.

Consider the *salary sub-system* r-schema in Fig. 12.38 and decompose it. This sub-system has three behaviours. In line with the analysis of the *salary sub-*

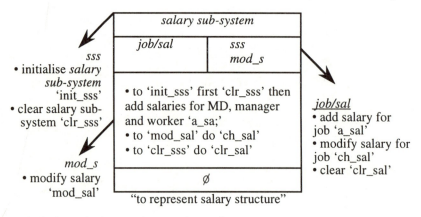

Fig. 12.40 Second prime r-schema: *salary sub-system*

system performed for the first prime r-schema, no components are introduced for the *salary sub-system* before performing the decomposition. During the analysis of the first prime r-schema the single component *job/sal* was identified for the *salary sub-system* as a re-useable real component. Without going into unnecessary detail, the three behaviours may be replaced by:

"to initialise the *salary sub-system* first clear the *salary sub-system*, second add to γ (*job/sal*) tuples for Managing Director, Manager and Worker"

"to clear the *salary sub-system* clear γ (*job/sal*)"

"to modify the salary of a given job replace the salary of that job with a new salary in γ (*job/sal*)"

These three behaviours may be effected by modifying the value set of the item *job/sal*. This completes the decomposition of the three behaviours in the *salary sub-system*. The decomposition is shown in Fig. 12.40.

The requirements model for the eight behaviours of the second prime r-schema is represented in Figs. 12.38–12.40. Consider the system analysis step for the second prime r-schema.

12.5.2 Analysis (2)

In Sect. 12.2 the prime r-schemas are selected on the basis of how much influence they have on the general "structure" of the system. If the first prime r-schema has been well chosen then the application of system analysis to the second prime r-schema should be an extension of the conceptual model developed during the analysis of the second prime r-schema. The requirements model for the second prime r-schema refers to the items *job/sal*, *pers/job* and *emp/dept* that are in both the existing conceptual diagram and the existing functional model. These three items are the three chosen input items in the existing functional model. The requirements model for the second prime r-schema also contains eight transaction types mod_sal, add_emp, mod_dept, del_emp, add_dep, del_dep, create_org and del_org. These eight transaction types may all be effected as modifications to the value sets of the input items *job/sal*, *pers/job* and *emp/dept*. So the existing conceptual model can accommodate the behaviours of the second prime r-schema.

12.5.3 Function (2)

Consider the system function step for the second prime r-schema. The first task in the system function step is the analysis of transactions. During this task represent each transaction and then link each transaction to the items in the conceptual model. The first sub-task is to construct a t-schema for each transaction. The

eight transactions discussed during the requirements specification step for the
second prime r-schema are:

- to create a new organisation in which there are three types of job with associated salaries, no departments and one person who is the Managing Director;
- to modify the salary of a given job;
- to modify the department of a given employee;
- to add a new employee to an existing organisation;
- to delete an existing employee from an existing organisation;
- to add a new department to an existing organisation;
- to delete an existing department from an existing organisation, and
- to delete an existing organisation.

The t-schemas for these eight transactions are shown in Figs. 12.41–12.42.

The second sub-task in the analysis of transactions task is to link the t-schemas
to a set of items in the conceptual model. To achieve this for each t-schema:

- locate the t-schema's behaviour in the requirements model;
- use the requirements model to identify a set of items that can support the
  t-schema's behaviour, and
- construct a program that performs the t-schema's behaviour with reference to
  the t-schema's instruction and the identified items.

The behaviours of the eight t-schemas shown in Figs. 12.41–12.42 may be
satisfied directly using the value sets of the four items *job/sal*, *pers/job*, *emp/dept*
and *dept/man*. These four items are in the conceptual model as shown in
Fig. 12.28. To complete this sub-task it remains to construct the programs. The
logic programs to link these eight t-schemas to the items in the conceptual model
are:

create_org(w, x, y, z, ok) ← init_oss(w, ok1),
    init_sss(x, y, z, ok2),
    ∧(ok1.ok2, ok)

init_oss(w, ok) ← clr_oss(ok1),
    ADD(w, 'MD')TO(*pers/job*)RES(ok2),
    ∧(ok1.ok2, ok)

init_sss(x, y, z, ok) ← clr_sss(ok1),
    ADD('MD', x)TO(*job/sal*)RES(ok2),
    ADD('Manager', y)TO(*job/sal*)RES(ok3),
    ADD('Worker', z)TO(*job/sal*)RES(ok4),
    ∧(ok1.ok2.ok3.ok4, ok)

create_org		
create a new organisation		
Accounts Clerk	*personnel management system*	Accounts Clerk
(employee_number, MD_salary, Manager_salary, Worker_salary)	(<emp>, <sal_MD>, <sal_M>, <sal_W>)	
	(OK)	(OK)
create_org(<emp>, <sal_MD>, <sal_M>, <sal_W>, OK)		

mod_sal		
change a salary rate		
Accounts Clerk	*personnel management system*	Accounts Clerk
(job description, salary)	(<job>, <sal>)	
	(OK)	(OK)
mod_sal(<job>, <sal>, OK)		

mod_dept		
move an employee to a new department		
Accounts Clerk	*personnel management system*	Accounts Clerk
(employee_number, department_number)	(<emp>, <dept>)	
	(OK)	(OK)
mod_ed(<emp>, <dept>, OK)		

add_emp		
add a new employee		
Accounts Clerk	*personnel management system*	Accounts Clerk
(employee_number, department_name)	(<emp_no.>, <dept>)	
	(OK)	(OK)
add_emp(<emp_no.>, <dept>, OK)		

Fig. 12.41 t-schema for second prime r-schema: part 1

del_emp		
delete an existing employee		
Accounts Clerk	*personnel management system*	Accounts Clerk
employee number	<emp_no.>	
	(OK)	(OK)
del_emp(<emp_no.>, OK)		

add_dept		
create a new department		
Accounts Clerk	*personnel management system*	Accounts Clerk
(department_name, employee_number)	(<dept>, <emp>)	
	(OK)	(OK)
add_dept(<dept>, <emp>, OK)		

del_dept		
delete an existing department		
Accounts Clerk	*personnel management system*	Accounts Clerk
(department_name, department_name)	(<dept_1>, <dept_2>)	
	(OK)	(OK)
del_dept(<dept_1>, <dept_2>, OK)		

del_org		
delete an existing organisation		
Accounts Clerk	*personnel management system*	Accounts Clerk
∅	∅	
	(OK)	(OK)
del_org(OK)		

Fig. 12.42 t-schema for second prime r-schema: part 2

clr_oss(ok) ← CLEAR (*pers/job*) RES(ok1),
  CLEAR (*emp/dept*) RES(ok2),
  ∧(ok1.ok2, ok)

clr_sss(ok) ← CLEAR (*job/sal*) RES(OK)

mod_sal(x, y, ok) ← REPLACE(x, z)WITH(x, y)IN(*job/sal*)RES(OK)

mod_dept(x, y, ok) ← FIND(x, 'Worker')IN (*pers/job*) RES(ok1),
  REPLACE(x, z)WITH(x, y)IN(*emp/dept*)RES(ok2),
  ∧(ok1.ok2, ok)

add_emp(x, y, ok) ← ADD('x, 'Worker')TO(*pers/job*)RES(ok1),
  ADD(x, y)TO(*emp/dept*)RES(ok2), ∧(ok1.ok2, ok)

del_emp(x, ok) ← DELETE('x, 'Worker')FROM(*pers/job*)RES(ok1),
  DELETE(x, y)FROM(*emp/dept*)RES(ok2),
  ∧(ok1.ok2, ok)

add_dept(x, y, ok) ← REPLACE(y, 'Worker')
        WITH(y, 'Manager')IN(*pers/job*) RES(ok1),
  REPLACE(y, z)WITH(y, x)IN(*emp/dept*)RES(ok2),
  ∧(ok1.ok2, ok)

del_dept(x, y, ok) ← FIND(z, x)IN (*emp/dept*) RES(ok1),
  FIND(z, 'Worker')IN (*pers/job*) RES(ok2),
  ∧(ok1.~ok2, ok3),
  FIND(x, w)IN (*dept/man*) RES(ok4),
  REPLACE(w, 'Manager')WITH(w, 'Worker')IN(*pers/job*) RES(ok5),
  REPLACE(w, x)WITH(w, y)IN(*emp/dept*) RES(ok6),
  ∧(ok3.ok4.ok5.ok6, ok)

del_org(ok) ← clr_oss(ok1),
  clr_sss(ok2)
  ∧(ok1.ok2, ok)

The construction of these twelve logic programs completes the analysis of transactions task for the second prime r-schema.

The second task in the system function step is the construction of the functional view. There are three input items namely *pers/job*, *emp/dept* and *job/sal*. The resulting flow diagram as shown in Fig. 12.43. This flow diagram shows the three input items and four transaction items. It shows the twelve transactions and it satisfies the functional requirements noted above.

The third task in the system function step is the construction of the f-coupling map. In this example the f-coupling map is the same as the c-coupling map shown in Fig. 12.29.

The final task in the system function step is the refinement of constraints. Particularly the development of constraints for the input items. This completes the functional model. The design of constraints, that was deferred during the analysis of the first prime r-schema, is considered here. The objective is to introduce constraints that protect the integrity of the input items. Two possible constraints are:

- every employee in *emp/dept* is also in *pers/job*, and
- every job in *pers/job* is also in *job/sal*.

There are many other possible constraints. These constraints may be knowledge model constraints. That is, they take the form of a set of rules with which the value sets of the input items should remain consistent.

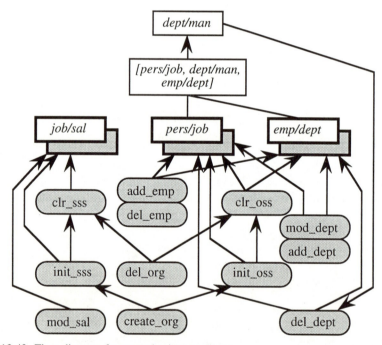

Fig. 12.43 Flow diagram for second prime r-schema

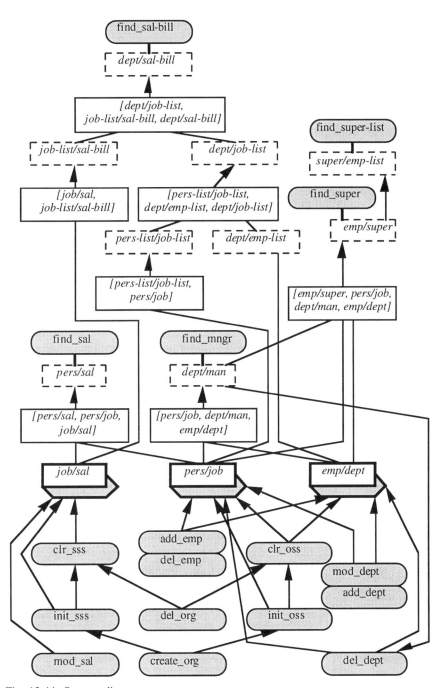

Fig. 12.44 Storage diagram

12.6 Layout

The final step in the design is system layout. In the particular form of iterative design that has been adopted for this example, system layout has been deferred until the system function step has been completed for all of the prime r-schemas.

The first task in the system layout step is the analysis of operational requirements. Suppose that:

- the maximum permissible response time, and
- the expected frequency of presentation

are given for each of the thirteen transactions identified for the two prime r-schemas. In this small example operational requirements are not considered.

The second task in the system layout step is the construction of the internal view. The items in the item library are those shown on Fig. 12.28. The internal diagram is the same diagram as that shown in Fig. 12.28. To derive the storage diagram determine those items that will be stored in the physical model. Suppose that, in the absence of any operational requirements, the input items and the knowledge items are real, and all other information items are virtual. The storage diagram is shown in Fig. 12.44. The transaction library contains the transactions together with their respective operational requirements. As there are no opera-

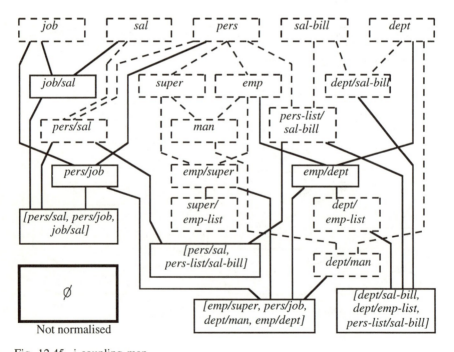

Fig. 12.45 i-coupling map

tional requirements in this example the transaction library consists of the thirteen t-schemas shown in Fig. 12.30 and Figs. 12.41–12.42.

The third task in the system layout step is the construction of the i-coupling map. This is derived from the c-coupling map as shown in Fig. 12.29. The

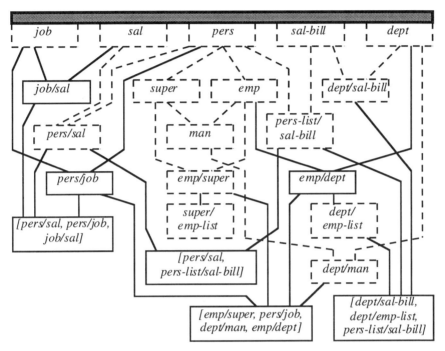

Fig. 12.46 Internal Diagram

Value set of:	Deduced by:	Deduced from value sets of:	Value sets stored in the relations:
emp/super	[emp/super, pers/job, emp/dept]	pers/job emp/dept	person/job employee/department
super/emp-list	inv-2	emp/super	
dept/man	[pers/job, dept/man, emp/dept]	pers/job emp/dept	person/job employee/department
pers/sal	[pers/sal, pers/job, job/sal]	pers/job job/sal	person/job job/salary
pers-list/sal-bill	[pers/sal, pers-list/sal-bill]	pers/sal	
dept/emp-list	inv-2	emp/dept	employee/department
dept/sal-bill	[dept/sal-bill, dept/emp-list, pers-list/sal-bill]	pers-list/sal-bill dept/emp-list	

Fig. 12.47 The deductive flow

f-coupling map is shown in Fig. 12.45.   The internal diagram is shown in Fig. 12.46.

The three input items, namely *job/sal*, *pers/job* and *emp/dept* are those whose value sets are to be stored. The value sets of all other items are to be deduced. This choice of system layout then leads to a deductive flow as summarised in Fig. 12.47.

12.7 Maintenance

The eight maintenance problems that follow are intended to illustrate the design procedure described in Sect. 11.3.

The procedure makes use of the various models that form part of the design. When maintenance tasks are carried out they are carried out completely. That is, if the procedure described in Sect. 11.3 is employed then the resulting system is consistent. The value of normalisation to the maintenance process is hidden by the simplicity of the maintenance procedure. If the conceptual model had not been normalised then the maintenance problems considered below would have been far more complex to execute completely.

Maintenance Problem 1
"The Hardware Department is to be re-named the Home Supplies Department."
1. Can not be performed by an existing transaction. Generalise this task to the transaction "Re-name a department". This is an update task associated with the item *dept*.
2. The transaction "Re-name a department" can be performed completely by modifying the value set of the *dept* item. The item *dept* is in the conceptual diagram, but is not in the storage diagram. Investigate the implementation of this transaction as a modification to the value sets of the input items. The second level extract of the i-coupling map from *dept* is shown in Fig. 12.48. This extract helps to guide this investigation. On the coupling map *dept* is linked to three items of which only one is real, namely *emp/dept*, also none of the second level items require modification as a result of this transaction. If a department is re-named then this may be effected by re-naming that department in the real *emp/dept* item. This new transaction can be introduced without modifying the conceptual model it is shown in Fig. 12.49. The logic program that links the t-schema in Fig. 12.49 to the items in the conceptual model is:

rename_dept(x, y, ok) ← REPLACE(w, x)
        WITH(w, y)IN(*emp/dept*) RES(ok)

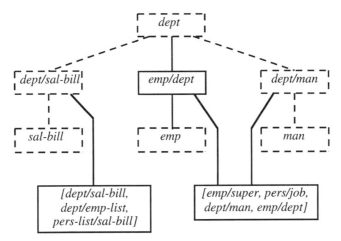

Fig. 12.48 Two levels of i-coupling map from *dept*

rename_dept		
change the name of a department		
Accounts Clerk	*personnel management system*	Accounts Clerk
(old name, new name)	(old_n, new_n)	
	(old_n, new_n, OK)	(OK)
rename_dept(old_n, new_n, OK)		

Fig. 12.49 t-schema for transaction to re-name a department

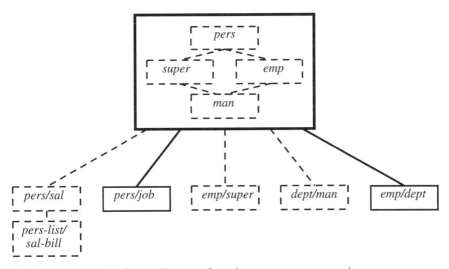

Fig. 12.50 One level of i-coupling map from {*pers, super, emp, man*}

Maintenance Problem 2

"Mr Grumpy is to be moved to the Home Supplies Department."

1. This is an update task associated with the item *emp/dept*. This task can be performed by the existing transaction "mod_dept".

Maintenance Problem 3

"Mr Boss, the General Manager, has retired. The new General Manager is Mr Head."

1. This can not be performed by an existing transaction. Generalise this task to the transaction "Re-name a person". This is an update task associated with the item *pers*.

2. The transaction "Re-name a person" is naturally associated with the *pers* item. This transaction can be performed completely by modifying the value set of the *pers* item. The item *pers* is in the conceptual diagram, but is not in the storage diagram. Investigate the implementation of this transaction as a modification to the value sets of the input items. The first level extract of the i-coupling map from *pers* is shown in Fig. 12.50, and the second level is shown in Fig. 12.51. These extracts help to guide this investigation. On the coupling map *pers* and its sub-items are linked to seven items of which only two are real, namely *pers/job* and *emp/dept*. Also, none of the second level items require modification as a result of this transaction. If a person is re-named then this may be effected by re-naming that person in the real *pers/job* and *emp/dept* items. This new transaction can be introduced without modifying the conceptual model it is shown in

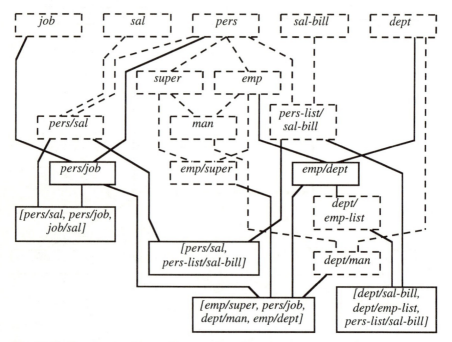

Fig. 12.51 Two levels of i-coupling map from {*pers, super, emp, man*}

rename_emp		
change the name of an employee		
Accounts Clerk	*personnel management system*	Accounts Clerk
(old name, new name)	(old_n, new_n)	
	(old_n, new_n, OK)	(OK)
rename_emp(old_n, new_n, OK)		

Fig. 12.52 t-schema for transaction to re-name an employee

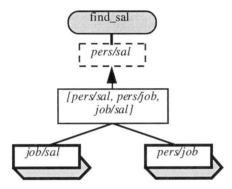

Fig. 12.53 Extract of storage diagram

Fig. 12.52. The logic program that links the t-schema in Fig. 12.52 to the items in the conceptual model is:

rename_emp(x, y, ok) ← REPLACE(x, z)
      WITH(y, z)IN(*emp/dept*) RES(ok1),
  REPLACE(x, w)WITH(y, w)IN(*pers/job*) RES(ok2),
  ∧(ok1.ok2, ok)

Maintenance Problem 4
"Ms Bossy receives a salary of $80 000."
1. This is an update statement that is naturally associated with the item *pers/sal*. This statement is inconsistent with the value set of *pers/sal*. According to the existing transaction 'find_sal' Ms Bossy receives a salary of $60 000.
2. Examine the relevant parts of the storage diagram to locate the source of this inconsistency. An extract of the storage diagram is shown in Fig. 12.53 By considering the extract of the storage diagram shown in Fig. 12.53, this inconsistency is caused by one of three real items. Either the value set of *job/sal* or the value set of *pers/job* or the semantics of *[pers/sal, pers/job, job/sal]* is in error. Suppose that the error is that 'Ms Bossy' is incorrectly represented in *pers/job* as a 'Worker'. There is no existing transaction to resolve this inconsistency. This inconsistency could be resolved by the update task "to change the job of a person". This update task can be processed in a similar way to Maintenance Problem 3.

Maintenance Problem 5

"To find the list of employees working in any given department".
1. This can not be performed by an existing transaction. This is a value query that is naturally associated with the item *dept/emp-list*.
2. The transaction "To find the list of employees working in any given department" can be performed completely by reference to the value set of the item *dept/emp-list*. The item *dept/emp-list* is a virtual item in the storage diagram. This transaction can be introduced without modifying the conceptual model. It is shown in Fig. 12.54. The logic program to link the t-schema in Fig. 12.54 to the items in the conceptual model is:
find_emp-list(x, y, ok) ← FIND(x, y)IN(*dept/emp-list*) RES(ok)

Maintenance Problem 6

"There should be one more tuple in the value set of the item *pers/job* than in the value set of the item *emp/dept*."
1. This is a new system constraint. It can be dealt with without difficulty.

Maintenance Problem 7

"Every employee should have another employee as an understudy."
1. This is a statement. This statement would be an update statement if there had been an item *per/understudy* in the conceptual diagram. If the normality of the system is to be preserved then the inclusion of this statement requires a complete re-design. So this statement is a revision.

Maintenance Problem 8

"Persons are now to be paid a wage that consists of a pay that is determined by their job (as previously for salary) plus a loading that is calculated at $100 per annum for every year the person has worked for Egs P/L. The query type "To calculate the total salary for any given department" becomes "To calculate the total wage for any given department"."
1. This is a combination of a statement and a task. Neither are updates as the new concepts of "wage" and "loading" have to be introduced. So despite the fact that the statement might appear to be naturally associated with the item *[pers/sal, pers/job, job/sal]* a complete redesign is required. This statement is a revision.

find_emp-list		
change the name of a department		
Personnel Manager	*personnel management system*	Personnel Manager
(dept name)	(dept)	
	(e_list, OK)	(emp_list, OK)
find_emp-list(dept, e_list, OK)		

Fig. 12.54 t-schema for transaction to find list of employees

References

Aakvik, G., Aamodt, A., Nordbo, I. (1991) A knowledge representation framework supporting knowledge modelling. Proceedings of the Fifth European Knowledge Acquisition for Knowledge-based Systems Workshop, Crieff, Scotland, May 1991

Aamodt, A. (1990) A computational model of knowledge-intensive problem solving and learning. In: B. Wielinga, J. Boose, B. Gaines, G. Schreiber, M. Van Someren (eds.) Current trends in knowledge acquisition. Amsterdam, IOS Press, pp. 1—20

Adams, D.A. (1992) Perceived usefulness, ease of use, and usage of information technology: a replication. MIS Quarterly 16(2), 227—241

Addis, T.R. (1985) Designing knowledge-based systems. London, Kogan-Page

Barnes, B. H., Bollinger, T.B. (1991) Making reuse cost-effective. IEEE Software 8(1), 19—24

Benchimol, G., Levine, P., Pomerol, J.C. (1987) Developing expert systems for business. London, North Oxford Academic Publishers

Blair, A. (1994a) Methods of integrating knowledge-based and database systems. Proceedings of the Fifth Australasian Database Conference, Christchurch, New Zealand, January 1994, pp. 274—291. Singapore, Global Publications Services

Blair, A. (1994b) Inter-connection of software components in intelligent decision support systems. Australian Computer Journal 26(1), 11—19

Blair, A. (1994c) A design methodology for knowledge-based decision support systems. Proceedings of the Second International Conference on Expert Systems for Development, Bangkok, Thailand, March 1994, pp. 18—23. IEEE Computer Society Press

Blair, A., Debenham, J.K., Edwards, J. (1994) Requirements analysis for intelligent decision support systems. Proceedings of the Australian and New Zealand Conference on Intelligent Information Systems, Brisbane, Australia, November 1994, pp. 482—486. IEEE Computer Society Press

Blair, A., Debenham, J.K., Edwards, J. (1995) A comparative study of formal methodologies for designing IDSSs. Proceedings of the Eighth Australian Joint Conference on Artificial Intelligence, Canberra, Australia, November 1995, pp. 403—410. Singapore, World Scientific

Blum, B.I. (1994) A taxonomy of software development methods. Communications of the ACM 37(11), 82—94

Bonarini, A., Maniezzo, V. (1991) Integrating expert systems and decision support systems: principles and practice. Knowledge-Based Systems 4(3), 172—176

Bowen, K.A., Kowalski, R. (1982) Amalgamating language and metalanguage in logic programming. In: K.L. Clark, S.A. Tarnlund (eds.) Logic programming, pp. 153––172. London, Academic Press

Brightman, H.J., Harris, S.E. (1994) An exploratory study of DSS design and use. In: P. Gray (ed.) Decision support and executive information systems, pp. 134—144. Englewood Cliffs, NJ, Prentice Hall

Brodie, M.L., Mylopoulos J., Schmidt, J. (1984) On conceptual modelling. New York, Springer-Verlag

Bryd, T.A., Cossick, K.L., Zmud, R.W. (1992) A synthesis of research on requirements analysis and knowledge acquisition techniques. MIS Quarterly 16(1), 117—138

Buckner, G., Shah, V. (1991) Intelligent decision support systems. Journal of Computer Information Systems 31(2), 61—66

Campbell, L., Halpin, T. (1994) Abstraction techniques for conceptual schemas. Proceedings of the Fifth Australasian Database Conference, Christchurch, New Zealand, January 1994, pp. 374—388. Singapore, Global Publications Services

Chakravarthy, U.S., Minker, J., Tran, D. (1982) Interfacing predicate-logic languages and relational data bases. Proceedings of the First International Logic Programming Conference, Faculte des Sciences de Luminy, Marseille, France. September 1982, pp. 91—98 Marseille, ADDP-GIA

Chang, C-L., Lee, R.C-T. (1973) Symbolic logic and mechanical theorem proving. New York, Academic Press

Chen, P.P. (1976) The entity-relationship model — towards a unified view of data. ACM Transactions on Databases Systems 1(1), 9—36

Chen, Y. (1989) Organisational strategies for decision support and expert systems. Journal of Information Science Principles and Practice 15, 27—34

Clark, K.L. (1978) Negation as failure. In: H. Gallaire, J. Minker (eds.) Logic and data bases, pp. 293—322. New York, Plenum Press

Clark, K.L., Mccabe, F.G. (1982) PROLOG: a language for implementing expert systems. In: Hayes, J., Michie, D. (eds.) Machine Intelligence 10, pp. 455—476. Chichester, UK, Ellis Horwood

Clark, K.L., Mccabe, F.G., Gregory, S. (1982) IC-PROLOG language features. In: K.L. Clark, S.A. Tarnlund, (eds.) Logic programming, pp. 253—266. London, Academic Press

Clocksin, W.F., Mellish, C.S. (1994) Programming in PROLOG. Berlin, Springer-Verlag, 4th edn. 1994

Compton, P., Srinivasan, A., Edwards, G., Malor R., Lazarus, L. (1991) Knowledge base maintenance without a knowledge engineer. In: J. Liebowitz (ed.) Proceedings Expert Systems World Congress. New York, Pergamon Press

Covington, M.A., Nute, D., Vellino, A. (1997) Prolog programming in depth. Englewood Cliffs, NJ, Prentice Hall

Dahl, V. (1982) On database systems development through logic. ACM Transactions on Database Systems 7(1), 102—123

Dalal, N.P., Yadav, S.B. (1992) The design of a knowledge-based decision support system to support the information analyst in determining requirements. Decision Sciences 23(6), 1373—1384

Date, C.J. (1995) An introduction to database systems. 6th edn. Reading, MA, Addison-Wesley

Davis, A.M. (1993) Software requirements: objects, functions, and states. Englewood Cliffs, NJ, Prentice Hall

Debenham, J.K. (1989) Knowledge systems design. Sydney, Prentice Hall

Debenham, J.K. (1993a) Decomposition of four component items. Proceedings of the Fourth International Conference on Database and Expert Systems Applications, Prague, September 1993, LNCS vol. 720   Springer-Verlag, pp. 457—460. Berlin, Springer-Verlag

Debenham, J.K. (1993b) Normalising knowledge objects. Proceedings of the Second International Conference on Information and Knowledge Management, Washington, November, 1993, pp. 335—343

Debenham, J.K. (1994) Managing knowledge base integrity. Proceedings of the British Computer Society Expert Systems Conference pp. 235-244. Cambridge, UK, Cambridge University Press

Debenham, J.K. (1995) A unified approach to requirements specification and system analysis in the design of knowledge-based systems. Proceedings of the Seventh International Conference on Software Engineering and Knowledge Engineering, Washington DC, June 1995, pp. 144—146

Debenham, J.K. (1996a) Characterising maintenance links. Proceedings of the Third World Congress on Expert Systems, Seoul, February 1996, pp. 665—672

Debenham, J.K. (1996b) Knowledge simplification. Proceedings of the Ninth International Symposium on Methodologies for Intelligent Systems, (Zakopane, Poland, June 1996, LNCS vol. 1079 Springer-Verlag, pp. 305—314

Debenham, J.K. (1996c) Removing redundancy from a knowledge model. Proceedings of the Eighth International Conference on Software Engineering, Lake Tahoe, CA, June 1996, pp. 45—50

Debenham, J.K. (1997a) Requirements specification for knowledge-based systems. Proceedings of the Tenth International Conference on Industrial and Engineering Applications of Artificial Intelligence and Expert Systems, Atlanta, GA, June 1997, pp. 553—562

Debenham, J.K. (1997b) An analysis of database rules. Proceedings of the International Database Engineering and Applications Symposium, Montreal, August 1997, pp. 553—562

Debenham, J.K. (1997c) Constructing the functional model. Proceedings of the Eighth International Conference on Database and Expert Systems Applications, Toulouse, September 1997, LNCS vol. 1308 Springer-Verlag, pp. 553—562

Debenham, J.K., Devedžić, V., (1996) Designing knowledge-based systems for optimal performance. Proceedings of the Seventh International Conference on Database and Expert Systems Applications, Zurich, Switzerland, September 1996, pp. 728—737

Despres, S., Rosenthal-Sabroux, C. (1992) Designing decision support systems and expert systems with a better end use. European Journal of Operations Research 61(1-2), 145—153

Domingue, J., Motta, E., Watt, S. (1993) The emerging VITAL workbench. Proceedings of the Seventh European Knowledge Acquisition Workshop, LNCS vol. 723 Berlin, Springer-Verlag, pp. 320—339

Durkin, J. (1994) Expert systems design and development. Englewood Cliffs, NJ, Prentice Hall

Even, S. (1979) Graph algorithms. Potomac, MD, Computer Science Press

Faget, J., Morel, J.-M. (1993) The REBOOT environment. Proceedings of the Second International Workshop on Software Reusability, Lucca, Italy, March 1993

Fensel, D. (1995) The knowledge acquisition and representation language KARL. Boston, Kluwer

Fensel, D., Poeck, K. (1994) A comparison of two approaches to model-based knowledge acquisition. Proceedings of the KADS Meeting, St. Augustin, Germany, March 1994, pp. 24—25

Fensel, D., Van Harmelen, F. (1994) A comparison of languages which operationalize and formalise KADS models of expertise. Knowledge Engineering Review 9(2), 105—146

Filman, R.E. (1988) Reasoning with worlds and truth maintenance in a knowledge-based programming environment. Communications of the ACM 31(4), 382—401

Ford, K., Bradshaw, J. (eds.) (1993) Knowledge acquisition as modelling. New York, John Wiley and Sons

Gaines, B.R. (1987) Foundations of knowledge engineering. In: M.A. Bramer (ed.) Research and Development in Expert Systems III. Cambridge UK, Cambridge University Press

Garey, M.R., Johnson, D.S. (1979) Computers and intractability. San Francisco, CA, W.H. Freeman and Co.

Garey, M.R., Johnson, D.S., Stockmeyer, L. (1976) Some simplified NP-complete graph problems. Theoretical Computer Science 1(3), 237—267

Ginsberg, A., Williamson, K. (1993) Inconsistency and redundancy checking for quasi-first-order-logic knowledge bases. International Journal of Expert Systems 6(3), 321—340

Goh, C.H., Madnick, S.E., Siegel, M.D. (1994) Context interchange: overcoming the challenges of large-scale interoperable database systems in a dynamic environment. Proceedings of the Third International Conference on Information and Knowledge Management, Gaithersburg, MD, November 1994, pp. 337—346

Gonzalez, A.J., Dankel, D.D. (1993) The engineering of knowledge-based systems. Englewood Cliffs, NJ, Prentice Hall

Gottinger, H.W., Weimann, P. (1992) Intelligent decision support systems. Journal of Decision Support Systems 8(4), 317—332

Gottinger, H.W., Weimann, H.P. (1995) Intelligent inference systems based on influence diagrams. Decision Support Systems 15, 27—43

Goul, M., Tonge, F. (1987) Project IPMA: an application of decision support system design principles to building expert-based systems. Decision Sciences 18, 448—467

Green, C.C. (1969) Theorem-proving by resolution as a basis for question-answering systems. In: B. Meltzer, D. Michie (eds.) Machine Intelligence 4, pp. 183—208. Edinburgh University Press

Griech, B., Pomerol, J.C. (1994) Design and implementation of a knowledge-based decision support system for estimating software development work-effort. Journal of Systems Integration 4, 171—184

Gries, D. (1981) The science of programming. New York, Springer-Verlag

Harris-Jones, C., Barret, T., Walker, T., Moores, T., Edwards, J. (1992) A methods model for the integration of KBS and conventional information technology. Proceedings of the Twelfth British Computer Society Expert Systems Conference pp. 25—43. Cambridge, UK, Cambridge University Press

Henderson-Sellers, B. (1992) A book of object-oriented knowledge. Sydney, Prentice Hall

Henderson-Sellers, B., Edwards, J. (1994) Book two of object-oriented knowledge: the working object. Sydney, Prentice Hall

Hogger, C. (1984) Introduction to logic programming. New York, Academic Press

Holtzman, S. (1989) Intelligent decision systems. New York, Addison-Wesley

Ioannidis, Y.E., Wong, E. (1988) Transforming nonlinear recursion to linear recursion. Proceedings of the Second International Conference on Expert Database Systems, George Mason University

Jullien, C., Shadbolt, N., Wielinga, B. (eds.) (1992) ACKnowledge project final report. ACK-CSI-WM-DL-007, Cap Gemini Innovation, Paris, France

Karbach, W. Linster, M., Voss, A. (1990) Models, methods, roles and tasks: many labels — one idea? Knowledge Acquisition 2(4), 279—300

Karunananda, A.S., Nwana, H.S., Brereton, P. (1994) Towards a domain analysis approach utilising metaphors for knowledge acquisition. Technical Report TR94-10, Univ. of Keele

Kent, W. (1983) A simple guide to five normal forms in relational database theory. Communications of the ACM 26(2), 120—125

King, D. (1990) Intelligent decision support: strategies for integrating decision support, database management, and expert system technologies. Expert Systems with Applications 1, 23—38

Klein, M., Methlie, L.B. (1995) Knowledge-based decision support systems with applications in business. 2nd edn. New York, John Wiley and Sons

Kowalski, R.A. (1979a) Algorithm = Logic + Control. Communications of the ACM 22(7), 424—436

Kowalski, R.A. (1979b) Logic for problem solving. London, North-Holland

Kowalski, R.A. (1982) Logic as a computer language. In: K.L. Clark, S.A. Tarnlund (eds.) Logic programming, pp. 3—18. London, Academic Press

Kowalski, R.A. (1991) Logic programming in artificial intelligence. Proceedings of the International Joint Conference on Artificial Intelligence, Sydney, Australia, August 1991, pp. 596—603

Le Roux, B. (1994) The CommonKADS and VITAL approaches: convergence and difference. Proceedings of the 4th KADS User Meeting, Germany

Lee, J. (1993) A task-based methodology for specifying expert systems. IEEE Expert 8(1), pp. 8—15

Lee, M.R., Compton, P. (1995) From heuristic knowledge to causal explanations. Proceedings of the Eighth Australian Joint Conference on Artificial Intelligence (AI'95), November 1995, Canberra, Australia, pp. 83—90. Singapore, World Scientific

Lee, M.R., Foong, K. (1994) A knowledge acquisition framework for an intelligent decision-support system. Proceedings of the Australian and New Zealand Conference on Intelligent Information Systems, Brisbane, Australia, November 1994. IEEE Computer Society Press

Lloyd, J.W. (1987) Foundations of logic programming. 2nd edn. Berlin, Springer-Verlag

Luger, G.F., Stubblefield, W.A. (1989) Artificial intelligence and the design of expert systems. Redwood City, CA, Benjamin Cummings

Martin, N. (1988) Software engineering of expert systems. Reading, MA, Addison-Wesley

Martins, J.P., Reinfrank, M. (eds.) (1991) Truth maintenance systems. Proceedings ECAI-90 Workshop, Stockholm, Sweden. LNCS vol. 515 Berlin, Springer-Verlag

Miles, M.B., Huberman, A.M. (1997)   Qualitative Data Analysis: An Expanded Sourcebook. 2nd edn. New York, Sage Publications

Mili, H., Mili, F., Mili, A. (1995)   Reusing software: issues and research directions. IEEE Transactions on Software Engineering 21(6), 528—562

Minker, J. (1988)   Perspectives in deductive databases. Journal of Logic Programming 5(1), 33—60

Mittra, S.S. (1998)   Structured techniques of system analysis, design, and implementation. New York, John Wiley and Sons

Napheys, B., Herkimer, D. (1988)   A look at loosely-coupled Prolog/database systems. Proceedings of the Second International Conference on Expert Database Systems, George Mason University, pp 107—116

Nijssen, G.M., Halpin, T.A. (1989)   Conceptual schema and relational data base design. Sydney, Prentice Hall

Nwana, H.S., Paton, R.C., Bench-Capon, T.J.M., Shave, M.J.R. (1991)   Facilitating the development of knowledge based systems: a critical review of acquisition tools and techniques. AICOM 4(2—3), 60—73

Puppe, F. (1993)   Systematic introduction to expert systems. Knowledge representations and problem-solving methods. Berlin, Springer-Verlag

Qian, X. (1988)   Distribution design of integrity constraints. Proceedings of the Second International Conference on Expert Database Systems, George Mason University, pp. 75—84

Rasch, R.H., Tosi, H.L. (1992)   Factors affecting software developers performance: an integrated approach. MIS Quarterly 16(3), 395—413

Reddy, M.P., Siegel, M., Gupta, A. (1993)   Towards an active schema integration architecture for heterogeneous database systems. Proceedings of the Third International Workshop on Software Engineering, pp. 178-183. IEEE Computer Society Press

Robinson, J.A. (1965)   A machine-oriented logic based on the resolution principle. Journal of the ACM 12, 23—41

Rumbaugh, J., Blaha, W., Premerlani, W., Eddy, F., Lorensen, W. (1991)   Object-oriented modelling and design. New York, Prentice Hall

Russell, S., Norvig, P. (1995)   Artificial intelligence: a modern approach. Englewood Cliffs, NJ, Prentice Hall

Sage, A. (1991)   Decision support systems engineering. New York, John Wiley and Sons

Sahni, S. (1974)   Computationally related problems. SIAM Computing 3(4), 262—279

Samson, D., Wirth, A. (1991)   Knowledge acquisition for intelligent decision systems. Journal of Decision Support Systems 7, 263—272

Schefe, P. (1982)   Some fundamental issues in knowledge representation. Proceedings of the Sixth German Workshop on Artificial Intelligence, Bad Honnef, pp. 42—62

Schmidt, J.W., Brodie, M.L. (1982)   Relational data base systems: analysis and comparison. Berlin, Springer-Verlag

Schreiber, G., Breuker, J., Biedeweg, B., Wielinga, B. (1993)   KADS — a principled approach to knowledge-based system development. New York, Academic Press

Sharp, H. (1994)   Knowledge acquisition or requirements analysis? Proceedings of the Second International Conference on Expert Systems for Development, Bangkok, Thailand, March 1994, pp. 63—68. IEEE Computer Society Press

Shaw, M.J. (1993) Machine learning methods for intelligent decision support: an introduction. Decision Support Systems 10(2), 79—83

Sølvberg, I., Nordbo, I., Vestli, M., Amble, T., Aakvik, G., Eggen, J., Aamodt, A. (1988) METAKREK — methodology and tool-kit for knowledge acquisition. ELAB-RUNIT Report STF14 A88046, SINTEF, Trondheim

Stonier, T. (1986) What is information? In: M.A. Bramer (ed.) Research and development in expert systems III. Proceedings of the Sixth British Computer Society Expert Systems Conference pp. 217—230. Cambridge, UK, Cambridge University Press

Stonier, T. (1990) Information and the internal structure of the universe. London, Springer-Verlag

Stonier, T. (1992) Beyond information: The natural history of intelligence. London, Springer-Verlag

Stonier, T. (1997) Information and meaning. An evolutionary perspective. London, Springer-Verlag

Tansley, D.S.W., Hayball, C.C. (1993) Knowledge-based systems analysis and design: a KADS developer's handbook. London, Prentice Hall

Tasker, D. (1989) Fourth generation data: a guide to data analysis for new and old systems. Sydney, Prentice Hall

Tsichritzis, D.C., Lochovsky, F.H. (1982) Data models. New York, Prentice Hall

Turban, E. (1993) Decision support and expert systems: management support systems. 3rd edn. New York, Macmillan

Turban, E., Watkins, P.R. (1988) Applied expert systems. Amsterdam, Elsevier Science

Turner, J. (1992) A comparison of the process of knowledge elicitation with that of information requirements determination. In: W.W. Cotterman, J.A. Senn (eds.) Challenges and strategies for research in systems development, pp. 415—430. New York, John Wiley and Sons

Van de Velde, W. (1993) Issues in knowledge level modelling. In: J.-M. David, J.-P. Krivine, R. Simmons (eds.) Second generation expert systems. Berlin, Springer-Verlag

Van Emden, M.H. (1977) Programming with resolution logic. In: E.W. Elcock, D. Michie (eds.) Machine Intelligence 8, pp. 266—299. Chichester, UK, Ellis Horwood

Van Harmelen, F., Balder, J. (1992) ML2: a formal language for KADS models of expertise. Knowledge Acquisition 4(1), 127—161

Van Weelderen, J.A., Sol, H.G. (1993) MEDESS: a methodology for designing expert support systems. Interfaces 23(3), 51—61

Van Zuylen, H. (ed.) (1993) The REDO compendium: reverse engineering for software maintenance. New York, John Wiley and Sons

Vanthiehen, J., Aerts, A., Mues, C. (1996) An illustration of verification and validation in the modelling phase of knowledge based systems. Proceedings of the Third World Congress on Expert Systems. February 1996, pp. 1024—1031. New York, Cognizant Communication Corporation

Verheijen, G.M.A., Van Bekkum, J. (1982), NIAM: an information analysis method. In: T.W. Olle, A.A. Verrijn-Stuart, (eds.) Information systems design methodologies: a comparative review. 643—646. IFIP, North-Holland

Wald, J.A. (1988) Implementing constraints in a knowledge-base. Proceedings of the Second International Conference on Expert Database Systems, George Mason University, pp. 53—62. Redwood City, Benjamin Cummings.

Walker, A. (1987) Knowledge systems and Prolog. Reading, MA, Addison-Wesley

Waterman, D.A. (1985) A guide to expert systems. Reading, MA, Addison-Wesley

Widom, J., Finkelstein, S.J. (1990) Set-oriented rules in relational database systems. IBM Research Report RJ 6880, IBM Almaden Research Center

Wirfs-Brock, R., Wilkerson, B., Wiener, L. (1990) Designing object-oriented software. Englewood Cliffs, NJ, Prentice Hall

Yang, H. (1995) Information/knowledge acquisition methods for decision support systems and expert systems. Information Processing and Management 31(1), 47—58

Yourdon, E. (1989) Modern Structured Analysis. Englewood Cliffs, NJ, Prentice Hall

Yu, E.S.K., Mylopoulos, J. (1994) Understanding 'why' in software process modelling, analysis and design. Proceedings of the Sixteenth International Conference on Software Engineering, pp. 159—168. IEEE Computer Society Press

Zeleznikow, J. (1995) Building intelligent legal decision support systems. Proceedings of the First Australian Workshop on IDSSs — Eighth Australian Joint Conference on Artificial Intelligence (AI'95), Canberra, Australia, November 1995, pp. 12—24

Zhang, C., Bell, D.A. (1991) HECODES: a framework for HEterogeneous COoperative Distributed Expert Systems. Data and Knowledge Engineering 6, 251—273

Zhang, C., Debenham, J.K., Lukose, D. (eds.) (1994) Artificial intelligence: sowing the seeds for the future. Singapore, World Scientific

Zhang, D., Nguyen, D. (1994) A tool for knowledge based verification. IEEE Transactions on Knowledge and Data Engineering 6(6), 983—989

Subject index

Springer Series
Artificial Intelligence

N. J. Nilsson: Principles of Artificial Intelligence. XV, 476 pages, 139 figs., 1982

J. H. Siekmann, G. Wrightson (Eds.): Automation of Reasoning 2. Classical Papers on Computational Logic 1967–1970. XXII, 638 pages, 1983

R. S. Michalski, J. G. Carbonell, T. M. Mitchell (Eds.): Machine Learning. An Artificial Intelligence Approach. XI, 572 pages, 1984

J. W. Lloyd: Foundations of Logic Programming. Second, extended edition. XII, 212 pages, 1987

N. Cercone, G. McCalla (Eds.): The Knowledge Frontier. Essays in the Representation of Knowledge. XXXV, 512 pages, 93 figs., 1987

G. Rayna: REDUCE. Software for Algebraic Computation. IX, 329 pages, 1987

L. Kanal, V. Kumar (Eds.): Search in Artificial Intelligence. X, 482 pages, 67 figs., 1988

H. Abramson, V. Dahl: Logic Grammars. XIV, 234 pages, 40 figs., 1989

P. Besnard: An Introduction to Default Logic. XI, 201 pages, 1989

A. Kobsa, W. Wahlster (Eds.): User Models in Dialog Systems. XI, 471 pages, 113 figs., 1989

Y. Peng, J. A. Reggia: Abductive Inference Models for Diagnostic Problem-Solving. XII, 284 pages, 25 figs., 1990

A. Bundy (Ed.): Catalogue of Artificial Intelligence Techniques. Fourth revised edition. XVI, 141 pages, 1997 (first three editions published in the series)

R. Kruse, E. Schwecke, J. Heinsohn: Uncertainty and Vagueness in Knowledge Based Systems. Numerical Methods. XI, 491 pages, 59 figs., 1991

Z. Michalewicz: Genetic Algorithms + Data Structures = Evolution Programs. Third, revised and extended edition. XX, 387 pages, 68 figs., 1996 (first edition published in the series)

V. W. Marek, M. Truszczyński: Nonmonotonic Logic. Context-Dependent Reasoning. XIII, 417 pages, 14 figs., 1993

V. S. Subrahmanian, S. Jajodia (Eds.): Multimedia Database Systems. XVI, 323 pages, 104 figs., 1996

Q. Yang: Intelligent Planning. XXII, 252 pages, 76 figs., 1997

J. Debenham: Knowledge Engineering. Unifying Knowledge Base and Database Design. XIV, 465 pages, 288 figs., 1998

Printing: Saladruck, Berlin
Binding: Buchbinderei Lüderitz & Bauer, Berlin